PUBLIC LIBRARY

J. Edgar Hoover

To Ralph de Toledano
With every good wish
J. Edgar Hoover
10·18·57

J. Edgar Hoover

The Man in His Time

Ralph de Toledano

ARLINGTON HOUSE   *New Rochelle, N.Y.*

BOOKS BY RALPH DE TOLEDANO:
Frontiers of Jazz (*an anthology*)
Seeds of Treason
Spies, Dupes & Diplomats
Day of Reckoning (*a novel*)
Nixon (*a biography*)
Lament for a Generation
The Greatest Plot in History
The Winning Side
R.F.K.—*The Man Who Would Be President*
America, I-Love-You
One Man Alone—Richard Nixon
Claude Kirk, Man & Myth (*with Philip V. Brennan Jr.*)
Little Cesar—*The Chavez Story*
J. Edgar Hoover

Library of Congress Catalog Card Number 72-91217

ISBN 0-87000-188-4

MANUFACTURED IN THE UNITED STATES OF AMERICA

Contents

Introduction

IT IS HARD FOR ME TO REMEMBER WHEN OR WHERE I FIRST MET JOHN
Edgar Hoover. From the very first days that the Federal Bureau
of Investigation became my beat as an editor and correspondent for *Newsweek,* I felt that I had known him. My contacts
with the Bureau, at the time of that first meeting, had covered
a span of many years. FBI agents had sought me out in the early
forties when I was an editor of the *New Leader* and its special-
ist on Communist and fascist subversion. I had spent many
hours talking to other agents in succeeding years. At first hand,
I had gotten an idea of the Bureau's *esprit de corps* during the
Hiss case as we watched the two trials unfold in a New York
Federal court.

There was much I learned from them which to this day I
would not repeat since it was elicited on an off-the record basis,

the product of mutual trust and mutual respect. But more than information and insight derived from this association. The idea of the FBI agent as a particular type, punched out by a cookie cutter in an image designed by Hoover—starched and pressed and lacking all individuality—disappeared very rapidly as I saw the agents at work, tired and rumpled but ready to put in that extra effort, those extra hours, after a more-than-full day. These were very dedicated, very human men who put their work above themselves.

But more impressive, to a young newspaperman who saw the measure of his calling in a cynical disbelief of hero worship, was the very genuine admiration they felt for their Director. I had been around government long enough to expect the automatic backbiting and rejection which characterizes the attitude of those who work in the many administrative units of the American bureaucracy. With no attempt at selling me a point of view, the agents I knew conveyed to me their deep understanding that however demanding Hoover might be, however strict a disciplinarian, he was not interested in self-aggrandizement, not wedded to domination. His only concern was in the success of the Bureau—and this they shared with him. When I got to know Louis B. Nichols, then de facto second-in-command, I realized that this attitude toward Hoover reached up to the highest echelons of the Bureau. I also realized that what the personnel of the Bureau felt was not sycophancy, as critics of the FBI were already saying, but a gut feeling. Nichols was a very superior human being, with very superior talents which could have taken him to place and fortune. But he remained in the FBI because he believed in the organization and he believed in Hoover.

The unimportant sometimes sticks in the mind more faithfully than the significant. When J. Edgar Hoover's name is mentioned, I think less in terms of the bulldog law enforcement officer than of a relaxed man I chatted with at Andrews Air Force Base in Virginia on the day that Nikita Khrushchev, the proletarian tsar of all the Russias, made his single visit to

Washington. Waiting to meet him was Dwight David Eisenhower, President of all the United States. But when the huge and ungainly Soviet plane, a turbo-prop, taxied to the apron where dignitaries and press were gathered, it moved in from left instead of the right—no political commentary. Hoover was there presumably as an important government official, though in reality his purpose was to see that security arrangements were properly handled. He laughed quietly, as many did, to see the President scooting under the body of the plane so that he could greet a descending Khrushchev. But Hoover was far more interested in the possibilities of trouble as confusion reigned than in the humor of a spectacle in which American officials forgot their dignity in order to preserve protocol. As always, he was the watchdog.

By that time, I knew more than most newspapermen about the workings of the FBI and the psyche of John Edgar Hoover. I could be detached about his alleged vagaries. But over the years and repeatedly, I was literally shocked by the misrepresentations and the exaggerations of those who wrote about him. In book after book and article after article dealing with the symbiotic Hoover-FBI relationship, a false picture of the man and his role in law enforcement emerged. He was painted as all hero or all villain. Oddly enough, ecstatic praise and unmitigated criticism crossed ideological lines. Among those turning thumbs down, there were outstanding pairs such as Senators Kenneth McKellar and George W. Norris, the *New York Daily News* and the *New Republic,* Drew Pearson and Westbrook Pegler. Among the defenders, Morris Ernst and Roger Baldwin, pillars of the American Civil Liberties Union, vied with the American Legion in praise.

Films, radio, and latterly, television were usually favorable to the FBI—and by extension to Hoover—but they focused on the cops-and-robbers or sleuths-versus-spies aspect of the Bureau's work. And they touched hardly at all on the organizational genius which had welded the FBI, or the ramifications of his work. On the other hand, the books which caught public attention—or at least that segment of the public which is dominated by those who write about books—were caustic and sometimes deliberately inaccurate in their attacks on Hoover and the FBI.

Among these, the most destructive was Max Lowenthal's *The Federal Bureau of Investigation,* copies of which were sent free to thousands of opinion makers, including members of Congress. It was Lowenthal, a friend of Harry S. Truman, who had conditioned the President's mind against Hoover. The book, with eighty pages of notes and with a massive bibliography, had all the trappings of scholarship—but its method was shabbily and calculatedly deceptive—leading Harry and Bonaro Overstreet in their book, *The FBI In Our Open Society,* to state that Lowenthal ". . . invites us to assume a trustworthy correspondence between what the text conveys and what is to be found in his (sources) . . . There are more—very many more—discrepancies between what the text implies and what the sources reveal than any reasonable margin for error could accommodate." Checking Lowenthal's truncated quotations against the full texts, which he listed as his source materials, shows that the Overstreets were too kind. For example, Lowenthal quotes from a Senate report read into the *Congressional Record* on February 11, 1909 to "prove" that Congress did not want a bureau of investigation within the Justice Department. In context, the very words quoted were an argument *for* such an investigative arm.*

In the debate over the creation of an investigatory arm for the Justice Department, Representative Walter I. Smith said on the floor of the House, "I think we ought all to be able to agree that some detective force is necessary to the enforcement of the criminal laws; and that, on the other hand, in a free country,

---

*Lowenthal quoted the report as stating: "It has never been the intention of any Congress to build up a spy system of that character." The following sentence was omitted: "The Department of Justice, to which ultimately all prosecutions of violations of Federal law must be referred, should have secret service agents to enable that department to properly conduct such prosecutions." A further reading of the report shows that what was objected to in the sentence quoted by Lowenthal was an enlargement of the Treasury Department's already established Secret Service.

no general system of spying upon and espionage of the people, such as has prevailed in Russia, in France under the Empire, and at one time in Ireland, should be allowed to grow up." And he added that he was "wholly at a loss to know why the Attorney General has not full power to organize a detective force under the numerous appropriations now at his disposal." Lowenthal quoted only the portion in italics—as evidence of Smith's opposition to an FBI!

The Lowenthal method is of interest because it was picked up by other writers to plague Hoover and the FBI. For instance, Lowenthal described the work of the early Bureau as "mere odds and ends" whereas the source he cites, the testimony of Attorney General Charles J. Bonaparte, made it very plain that in the antitrust field *alone* investigators were at work on cases involving Standard Oil, the "Tobacco Trust," the "Powder Trust," "against the Union Pacific and the Central Pacific, against the Harriman system generally," and against the anthracite coal interests in Pennsylvania—"seven or eight large cases" and "a certain number of small ones." Not inhibited by facts, Lowenthal asserted that passage of the Mann Act, outlawing the transportation for immoral purposes of women over state lines, gave the Bureau its "first big push toward an important place in the detective world." Seeking headlines and conscious that an assignment of this kind could be "one of the most spectacular tasks in police history," the Bureau presumably preempted it—a false observation since the Bureau was required by law to take it.*

---

*Later writers took up the implication that the Bureau devoted most of its energies to prosecuting hapless men who transported their women friends across state lines for a slap and a tickle. But a report of the Attorney General for the year the Mann Act was passed, and for subsequent years, shows that special attention was given to "the investigation of violations of the national banking laws, antitrust laws, peonage laws, bucket shop laws, and laws relating to fraudulent bankruptcies, the impersonation of government officials with intent to defraud, thefts, murders, and other offenses committed on government reservations or with respect to government property"—with only a passing mention among minor matters of the Mann Act. All studies by legal experts show that the Bureau pursued Mann Act violations with great moderation and usually where they involved organized prostitution.

• 11 •

Perhaps the most sordid of Lowenthal's charges against Hoover involved the arrest of Communists and others who had recruited men for combat in the Spanish Civil War—an "incident" which raised serious questions as to whether he had indoctrinated his "lawyer-detectives in the true meaning of the Constitution and the Bill of Rights ... Attorney General Jackson sent an investigator of his own to inquire into the facts; the latter reported that FBI agents had engaged in conduct that might constitute a violation of the Constitution." This was, of course, a complete fabrication. For the findings, as the Overstreets reported, "completely exonerated the Bureau's agents of having used brutal or illegal methods of arrest and questioning and of having denied the prisoners prompt access to counsel." Jackson, in point of fact, wrote a letter to Senator George W. Norris supporting Hoover, who had been following Justice Department orders, and noted that "since Mr. Hoover became head of the Bureau not one case has been reversed by an appellate court because of 'third degree' or other improper treatment of defendants."

The Overstreets could write that "In his role as lawyer, Lowenthal would doubtless agree that a show of bias disqualifies a witness. By this standard he would have to move that his own book be stricken from the record ... Its persuasiveness comes from its seeming to be scrupulously documented. Its fatal weakness is that the documentation cannot stand scrutiny."

But some of those who carried on Lowenthal's work not only failed to scrutinize Lowenthal's sources but rewrote him and added their own myths to the record. Foremost among these is Fred J. Cook, a newspaperman who has battened on stirring up liberal fears of imminent fascism in the United States. Cook, fired by the *New York World-Telegram* for resorting to fiction in what purported to be "investigative reporting," is the author of *The FBI Nobody Knows,* a title which lends itself to ironic interpretation. He brought to the book the same inattention to fact that made his account of Alger Hiss's trial and conviction notable. He is also a forgetful writer, for having said that the

Bureau was "created in secrecy, by Executive Order, in defiance of the will of Congress," he quotes at length from what he acknowledges is Lowenthal's account of the lengthy debates in Congress which preceded that presumably secret act of creation. His devotion to accuracy is further demonstrated when he asserts that the Lowenthal treatment of the FBI "was not factually discredited in any respect"—a curious statement from a reporter who worked on a newspaper which devoted columns to a painstaking analysis of the book's errors, falsifications, and distortions in an article by Frederick Woltman, a Pulitzer Prize winner.

Cook made use of all the exposed and discredited partial quotations of the Lowenthal book, adding his own touch simply by increasing the adjectival decibel-level. His star witness against Hoover and the FBI, however, is one Jack Levine, an agent who left the Bureau in "protest," tried to return, failed, and then when he had no chance at reemployment showed his principled disgust at what he would subsequently describe as a bureaucratic cloaca by writing Hoover a letter expressing loyalty and praise. Cook made much of Levine's "disclosures" of Hoover's vengefulness and of the professional ostracism which befell those who tangled with the Director. He made no attempt to square this with a bland statement by Levine that, once out of the FBI, he was offered a job with the Criminal Division of the Justice Department.

There were some humorous aspects of Levine's story, as told to Cook, to a New York radio station, and to all who would listen. For Cook took with dead seriousness Levine's "revelation" that he had wanted "to discuss some aspects—some very confidential aspects—of the FBI's penetration of the Communist Party with people over at the White House." He was concerned that the White House did not know how well the FBI had penetrated the "top levels of the Communist Party"—a fact so much part of the public consciousness that it had entered the national humor. But, sure enough, when Levine spoke to a staff member of the National Security Council, his worst fears were confirmed. No one knew—which shows how carelessly they had read the accounts of the Smith Act trial at which a series of FBI informants broke cover to testify about their infiltration of the party.

When the slender reed that was Levine bent badly under the weight of the evidence, Cook fell back on the old chestnut that veteran liberal senators, deeply concerned over Hoover's depredations, refused to talk because they were "afraid"—more a commentary on their courage and their principles than on J. Edgar Hoover. But the critics had another ex-agent to project on their screens—William J. Turner, a ten-year veteran of the Bureau who was fired, appealed the discharge all the way to the Supreme Court, but got no satisfaction for his efforts. Ten years later, Turner wrote *Hoover's FBI,* made up in large part of articles he had produced for *Saga,* for the New Leftist *Ramparts,* for the far-left *Nation,* and for *Playboy.* It purported to be an "insider's" view of the FBI, but on examination it was a rewrite of Lowenthal, Cook, newspaper clips, unattributed attacks, and unconfirmed rumors. It deprecated the FBI's interest in such "amateurish capers" as bank robberies, kidnappings, and car thefts, and Hoover's "obsession" with the national security. Turner's reliability as a commentator on police matters comes through clearly in two magazine pieces he wrote. In one he wrote of the assassination of President Kennedy that his "investigation" showed that Lee Harvey Oswald was the killer, "that he killed on his own," and that there was "no plot by left-wingers, right-wingers, or the crime syndicate." In another he applauded New Orleans District Attorney James Garrison for attributing the crime to "rabid anti-Castro Cubans in league with elements of the paramilitary right," with the "Federal Establishment" deeply involved.

All of this is of importance today only as background for my decision to write this book. Until the publication of Don Whitehead's *The FBI Story,* no serious account of the Bureau's work and history had been attempted or accomplished. But the Whitehead book, though an excellent traversal of the record, is predominantly concerned with the FBI. The story of John Edgar Hoover, who by main force and dedication built the Bureau and made it into the leading investigative agency in the world, had never been told. This is what appealed to me. It must be explained here, however, that Hoover, for all of his publicity-seeking reputation, did not want the book written and so told me. This closed certain doors to me and made it unwise to try the knobs of others.

But in a very real sense, this was more an advantage than a disadvantage. Hoover could have saved me considerable time by making available the library of newspaper clippings and magazine articles on the work of the Bureau and on himself, all on file at FBI headquarters in Washington. But by working closely to the subject of a biography, a writer can lose his independence and his objectivity. Unconsciously, he begins to filter what he sees through the personality of the person he is writing about, becoming an advocate. Since I had covered the Bureau for many years, developing some excellent contacts there, I did not need that reinforcement of my knowledge and understanding of the Hoover personality which a series of interviews might have supplied. I was fortunate in having folders of notes which corroborated or contradicted the public record and which, when coupled to what I like to think is a good reporter's memory, filled in gaps and added material not available to one entering a virgin field. Let me add that in a half-dozen instances, the FBI made available to me certain public papers which I once had in my files but which were inadvertently mislaid. This was its only help.

If I have any regrets, it is that this account of Hoover's life is not twice its present length. To make a complete historical record, certain episodes should have been amplified, others eliminated for space should have been included. But there are limits to a reader's and an editor's patience. Nothing was left out, in my judgment, which would have modified the picture of Hoover that emerges from these pages. Hoover was a strong and unique man—and one whose entire life was devoted to making the Bureau great and defending it from its enemies. An exhaustive compilation of anecdotes, either approving or opprobrious, would not have changed the picture. For, in the essence, Hoover painted his own portrait, warts and all. It was my job as a writer simply to put a frame around it.

J. Edgar Hoover

I.

The Man in His Time

ON FEBRUARY 22, 1929, THE *CONGRESSIONAL RECORD* DUTIFULLY RE-
ported, the Honorable Mr. Blanton, Democrat of Texas, rose to
address the House of Representatives. His remarks were long
and rambling, full of quotations from Mr. Justice Brandeis and
replete with condemnation of the Washington police force and
its mistreatment of "three Chinamen" in a now forgotten case.
But before launching into these matters, the congressman took
time to offer comments only tangentially apposite to his plaint.

"Mr. Chairman," he said, "I want to commend the present
Bureau of Investigation in the Department of Justice, presided
over at this time by Mr. J. Edgar Hoover. I have been very much
impressed with the high character of the splendid work they
are doing.

"There was a poor, unfortunate woman, you remember, who

was afraid to stay in Washington. Just as soon as she learned that she could find safety in the protection of the Department of Justice agents, she voluntarily got on the train in Chicago and came to Washington. She has been protected here by these agents. They arranged for her to come in here through the depot last night and there was a bunch of reporters and photographers waiting there for her. They brought her in here and took her to a hotel without one of these people knowing anything about it."

This was the first mention, fifty-seven months after he had been appointed to head what became known in 1935 as the Federal Bureau of Investigation, of John Edgar Hoover in the *Congressional Record*. It would be another four years before his name would arise significantly in congressional discussion, other than in the deliberations of House and Senate committees considering appropriations for the Justice Department and its investigative arm. In this second instance, it was Representative John McCormack, in later years to become the Speaker of the House, who deviated from a debate on the budget to offer his opinions of Hoover and the Bureau at some length.

"I wish to express briefly an opinion which I entertain with reference to the activities and efforts of this particular bureau," McCormack interposed.

During my period of service in the House, I have heard other departments or branches severely criticized, but on this occasion I am going to say a kind word for an activity of the Executive Branch of the Government. The Bureau of Investigation is at least one bureau in the Federal Government toward which the least breath of scandal has never been directed. Its personnel are men who are conscientiously and fearlessly carrying out the serious duties that are imposed upon them by law . . . This bureau is a credit to the Federal Government.
    It is under the leadership of a brilliant young man whom I greatly admire and whom I respect. Undoubtedly the high character of service rendered by those in the service of that bureau is the result of the type of leadership which they enjoy. That young man down there whom I have observed, Mr. J. Edgar Hoover, Director of the Bureau of Investigation, I consider one of the finest public officials in the service of the Federal Government. I take this opportunity to make these few

remarks . . . to let Mr. Hoover and those who are working under him to know that the Members of the national House of Representatives have watched their activities and are proud of the wonderful work they are doing, and we sincerely hope and trust that they will continue to render in the future the same high character of service they have rendered in the past.

To this, several members of the House added their amens in what would become ritual in succeeding years. These early references to Hoover, interestingly, were made long before he had mastered the arcane mysteries of public relations, long before he had become a household word as a nemesis of bank robbers, Nazis, Communists, and Ku Klux Klanners. He was not "Mr. FBI" then, nor the idol of millions of Americans. When Representative McCormack uncoiled his long frame from a House chair to speak the praises of J. Edgar Hoover, he was not bowing to his constituents or playing to the galleries.

In time, J. Edgar Hoover's every public utterance would be reproduced in the *Congressional Record*—sometimes read into its newsprint pages three or four times by members of House or Senate vying to surpass each other in adulation. No one has made a line count, but it is safe to say that Hoover took up more space in that wonderful diary of Congress than any other American of his contemporaneity. That this was so is one of the great paradoxes of Hoover's times, for he was neither a winning nor a warm character in his public presence. Even as a young man, there was something granitic about him, and the cauldron of Washington gossip bubbled over throughout his lifetime with stories of the manner in which he held the world at arm's length.

Yet he commanded the respect of friend and foe alike for a period measured in generations rather than the normal political span. It was not surprising in the Fifties that a fashionable civil liberties lawyer like Morris Ernst, who shuttled between defending the FBI and endorsing its most bitter enemies, should have joined the congregation. Of more significance was the testimonial of a former agent, Norman Ollestad, whose penny-dreadful memoirs of his years in the FBI included every unpleasant cliché and unsubstantiated rumor about J. Edgar Hoover available. For wrung out of Ollestad in that bilious account was a statement of Hoover's impact—his charisma, to resort to an abused word—even on those who hated him. Describing his one brief meeting with the Director, Ollestad observed:

Today I can honestly agree with the men who say you never truly know a man until you have worked for him; who say that a man can be kind to his wife and children and to his animals—but to his employees, *ruthless*. For this was true. Working for Hoover as a special agent of the FBI, I found him on many occasions to be inordinately cruel and intellectually dishonest. But his greatness is unmistakable. The history of America has been shaped by the Director.

This, coming from a minor cog in the FBI machine who never truly understood the importance of the Hoover contribution to law enforcement is remarkable enough. But other tributes can be found in the endless number of stories, friendly and antagonistic, told about Hoover. The fast patter of that 1960s television program, "That Was The Week That Was," memorialized Washington's attitude toward Hoover when it quipped: "President Johnson has declared that he does not intend to replace J. Edgar Hoover. However, J. Edgar Hoover has not disclosed whether he intends to replace President Johnson."

For some of Hoover's more sensitive supporters, this was *lèse majesté*. But Hoover was not offended—far from it—and the less touchy saw it as a flattering reflection of a state of affairs which few would gainsay—that J. Edgar Hoover was less subject to political pressure than the President of the United States. Having served under eight presidents, he knew—as he had known when the tally was shorter—that the lunges of the mighty would fail to shake him with his true constituency, the United States Congress and the American people.

He had, from the very start, a counter-constituency. It was made up for the most part of the media and the academy, including a few national legislators who felt that that their ox had been gored by FBI investigation—and they put together a vast literature of fact and fiction about him. But neither the scholarly tomes nor the popular studies succeeded in making more than a temporary dent in Hoover's prestige. The portrait of Hoover weaving webs of intrigue in the Federal Establishment failed to match the probative evidence. The men who were presumably the targets of his cloak and his dagger usually ended up as cordial to laudatory in their comments, as the writings and memoirs of Harold Ickes and Harry Hopkins, two liberal heroes, would later attest.

But what made the putative attacks unconvincing was not merely the paucity of facts on which they were based. They were directed as much against Hoover, the man—his tastes, predilections, and style—as they were against what he was presumed to have done. This snobbish displeasure did not impress the Hoover constituency. In fact, the reverse was true. Hoover's speeches, and the articles which appeared in such Middle American publications as the *Reader's Digest,* celebrated all the traditional virtues—patriotism, hard work, integrity, loyalty, devotion to home and family—in terms both platitudinous and unsophisticated. But though this convinced Hoover's critics that he was hypocritical, and that insincerity was the measure of the man, they were a true expression of himself and his character, and one which found widespread acceptance.

Even his detractors confessed themselves frequently disconcerted and disarmed by the way he tended to pop up on the side of their angels, as when he opposed President Roosevelt and Earl Warren in that black mark on the American shield, the internment of West Coast Japanese-Americans after Pearl Harbor. Those who bothered to study the record discovered to their chagrin that Hoover's rules for agents making arrests long anteceded those safeguards for the rights of the accused which the Supreme Court wrote into legal precedent. Though it was an article of faith in certain quarters that Hoover had little interest in illegal acts against Negroes in the South, that had been one of his first areas of concern and activity in the Twenties—long before it became an item of fashionable conversation.

Critics were therefore left to flounder among contradictions, to lament both his hypo- and hyper-efficiency. He was criticized for running the Bureau at his whim and for bowing to political pressure, for refusing to cooperate with attorneys general and for cooperating too much with presidents, for denying that the Mafia existed and for putting too many taps on the telephones of the *Mafiosi*. The attackers were plagued further by the poor and repetitive reporting of their spokesmen, whose passionate denunciations all too often left them hugging an intellectual nudity on the floor of the House or in the columns of the press. Sinister actions, on careful scrutiny, turned out to be dexterous operations with a frequency which discounted Hoover's occasional falls from grace. The myths ranged from the sublimely vicious—a metropolitan newspaper dropped its well-publicized researches into the ugly rumor that Hoover was a homosexual with the delicate hint that it had been subjected to FBI blackmail—to the viciously ridiculous—a journalistic invasion of Hoover's garbage pail.

Through all of this, Edgar Hoover went about his FBI work, dedicated to a degree that some in Washington saw as Freudian in its intensity—a man of average height whose stockiness gave the impression of shortness, his bulldog features accentuated by a broken nose sustained in boyhood on a baseball field, aging slowly yet remarkably escaping the more obvious incursions of age, to the end precise and short in his manner, still demanding of those who worked for him standards of dress and comportment that he imposed on himself, a rigid disciplinarian perpetually rejecting the slovenly waste that inheres in governmental bureaucracies. A resurgence of criticism in a troubled and uncivil time made him in his seventies overdefensive and undertactful, overprotective of his FBI, more prone to respond to attacks which might better have been left unanswered, less accurate in the counteroffensive, more certain that his way was the right and only way, less cautious and more argumentative in his dealing with a press establishment which, in the Biblical phrase, "knew not Joseph," jealously and zealously guarding his prerogatives and protecting his flanks.

His routine had remained supremely the same over the years. He was up betimes for a breakfast of orange juice, bacon (most of it captured by his cairn terriers), and black coffee. He would leave his trim and comfortable Georgian house, overlooking the rambling acres of Rock Creek Park in a Washington neighborhood midway between the fashionable and the middle-class, early enough to be at work before 9 a.m. His custom-built Cadillac, so heavily armored that it required a truck engine (license number a noncommittal collection of digits), had already picked up Clyde A. Tolson, nominally his second-in-command but in truth no more than an alter ego, when it pulled up at his door. In good weather, he would leave the car at a distance from the Justice Department building on 9th Street and Pennsylvania, walking the remaining distance. He did not like to share a crowded elevator, and his staff sedulously made sure that others did not venture in. Striding into his office, he would greet Sam Noisette, a Negro special agent who had been his receptionist for many years, greet Helen Gandy, a secretary who matched his tenure in government, and walk into his private quarters. The room is large, but neither so large nor so impressive as the Attorney General's regal office. On his government-issue desk, the morning's mail would be laid out for him.

The morning entrance was ritual and meant much to Hoover. His office was a symbol and a memorial to his years and achievements as Director of the FBI. At his behest, an outer room was a small museum of the gangbuster days, with memorabilia of the Dillinger case and other FBI exploits. Two American flags flanked the door to his sanctum, with the seal of the department overhead. On the walls of the room, there were landscapes of mountains and deserts, all representational paintings, and a portrait of Harlan Fiske Stone, the Attorney

General who appointed Hoover. A sixty-pound mounted sailfish commemorated the forty-five-minute battle in 1936 at which Hoover landed it. On a cabinet stood a bust of Dante.

Hoover's desk was usually bare of papers in the morning, unless he had left work behind the previous night. Then, those who cleaned and dusted made sure that nothing was disturbed. An intercom, a telephone, and a direct line to the White House were his contacts with the outside world. But that was enough for him to control an organization that reached across a continent and put him in touch with the field offices and the Special Agents in Charge who ran them. In this quiet and unostentatious office, its dignity in its simplicity, much of the nation's internal security resided, and Hoover was well aware of this. He was also proud that it symbolized the rise of law enforcement from grubby police stations to its eminence in what he archaically called "the Seat of Government." To interviewers he would say, "One achievement has made me happiest, that we have made law enforcement an honorable profession."

From that point on, the day would slip into what had become routine—if routine it could be called. At 10:30 a.m., he conferred with his top assistants—a ten-man team—on current cases, questions of internal policy, the administration of the Bureau, complaints which had reached him, the thousand-and-one matters which concern an important government agency. The team included Associate Director Tolson, the administrative assistants to the Director, the assistant directors, and the division chiefs. The nature of these "executive conferences" differed according to the personnel. In the Bureau's best days, it was a free-wheeling meeting at which points of view were frankly, sometimes forcefully, projected. They truly reflected Hoover's assertion about the FBI. "This isn't a one-man show," he told Don Whitehead, an Associated Press reporter, on the thirtieth anniversary of his tenure. "I tell my people constantly that one man can't build the reputation of the FBI—but one man can pull it down."

At that time, one member of the conference could say, "There are no holds barred in our meetings. We thrash out policies and procedures within the framework of our responsibilities. Each decision is arrived at by a vote. If there is a split vote, we must give the arguments on both sides to the Director for his final decision. The Director wants the best opinions even if they run counter to his own. Once a decision is made, we close ranks and carry out the job." And to this Hoover would add, "I don't want yes-men." In the final years, this changed, as men less tuned to the FBI's wave-length, fearful of Hoover's growing irascibility, said what they thought he wanted to hear. But there was always one constant. Hoover hated "griping and grapevine gossiping." "I tell my people to take their gripes to someone who can do something about it—or to bring them to me. There's nothing as bad as bellyaching behind the barn door," he said.

The "executive conference" over, Hoover would be on the phone to his Special Agents in Charge. There might be calls from the Attorney General, from senators and congressmen, from state and local officials in need of counsel or help on a crime problem. Reports and efficiency ratings would pile up on his desk. Answering the constant demand for articles and speeches, frequently from people of importance, was a chore, but Hoover handled it himself. And, after the resignation of Louis Nichols, perhaps the best man to serve as second man in the Bureau, there were his almost daily telephone calls to the Director in which he gave unpaid, unpublicized and valuable advice.

Hoover lunched every day with Tolson. For many years, they would eat only at Harvey's, a Washington landmark on Connecticut Avenue distinguished neither for its food nor its decor. Here again there was a ritual. The two men were always seated at the same table next to the cashier's cage, their backs to the wall. The waiter removed the other two chairs and rolled a serving cart to the table side, a barrier against autograph hunters. Hoover, who continually struggled to keep himself within the weight limits he had set for all FBI personnel, usually had the same lunch—grapefruit, cottage cheese, and black coffee.

Lunch was always his time for a break—for relaxation—and he barred shop talk. There was always some gentle joking with the waiters, none of it particularly inspired. Hoover and Tolson thought it amusing to order something that was not on the menu or to accuse their favorite waiter of shooting dice in the kitchen. There was always a small argument as to who would pick up the check. People lunched at Harvey's to see Hoover, but when one of them pushed his way around the serving cart to talk to him, Hoover turned gruff. "It always irritates me to have people come up and say, 'You don't know me, do you?' " Hoover once said. "I answer them, 'If you were ever in Alcatraz, I know you. We have a record on you.' "

Back at the office, he would pick up where he had left off in the morning—"taking the blood pressure of the Bureau," he called it. He might prepare testimony for a congressional committee, painstakingly mark up a draft of a speech written for him by an aide or an article about him submitted for his corrections. Assistant directors or division chiefs would be summoned individually to discuss specific problems. And as always, there was the continuing strict watch on Bureau personnel, leading to some complaints that he was a martinet. These he brushed aside, arguing the necessity. In 1971, he told *Nation's Business:*

A law enforcement agency is only as good as the support it receives from the public . . . Only demonstrated performance produces the respect and cooperation necessary to achieve results FBI responsibilities demand—and which the public has every right to expect. This attention to a goal of excellence requires its sacrifices. It means long, often grueling, hours of work on the part of our special agents . . . Some of my critics have charged me with being a harsh and autocratic administrator, but they fail to recognize the trust that must be generated from the proper discharge of FBI responsibilities. This fact leaves little room for error. An enforcement agency, by the very nature of its duties, is an easy and natural target for criticism.*

*It was disturbing to some agents that J. Edgar Hoover made it a part of that responsibility to know what they were doing at all times and to take them to task for the slightest deviation from the rigorous standards he imposed. Wil-

When the horses were running, Hoover went to the races, accompanied by Tolson and by friends who shared his enjoyment of the sport. There were some who saw this as a flaw in his character and a bad example to other law men. His defense was good-natured: "They call me strait-laced and then criticize the two-dollar bets I make at the track. But I love to watch the horses run. It's great relaxation. What's better than to get out in the fresh air for a few hours and become absorbed in something besides your work." But a friend remarked, "If he were as bad at catching criminals as he is at picking horses, the country would be in a hell of a shape. There was a time when he went twenty-three races without a win." Hoover himself would joke about his inability to pick winners. When the association of former agents presented him with a statuette of a stallion, he said wryly, "It's the first I've ever owned, though I've supported many of them."

In season, he would also be seen at the ball park watching the Washington Senators lose. Friends from Capitol Hill would sometimes accompany him, and when Richard Nixon was Vice President, the two were frequently seen together rooting for their team. "Nixon was a good man to have along," Hoover would recall. "He knew all the players by name and everything about them—batting, fielding, everything." In the chill of autumn, Hoover watched football on television.

Hoover would leave his office relatively late by Washington standards—at 6:30 p.m. or seven—and often later. Not until he left would FBI headquarters activity grind to a halt in a general exodus of Bureau officialdom which had been awaiting his departure. He returned to his admittedly spoiled cairn terriers

liam Turner, a former agent, objected to this strenuously in commentary that ran through his books and articles about the Bureau. It is ironic that Turner, who also belabored Hoover for betraying his responsibilities by allegedly being careless about facts and for misusing his power, should have chastised him for appearing "on national television [to] posthumously assassinate the character of former State Department official Harry Dexter White . . . The evidence against White was gossamer." The evidence against White was encyclopedic —and he had been an Assistant Secretary of the *Treasury*, not a State Department official.

and to a house which he had made into a showplace of his life. There, amid his antique jade and his bronzes, the many cases displaying his awards and the slight touch of luxury he never had as a boy or in the home he shared with his mother until her death, he had one drink of Jack Daniels Black Label and branch water, sometimes two, but never more. He might stop for a moment in the foyer before the Roman bust of himself, regarding it with a glint of pleasure and amusement in his eye.*

If the weather was good, he puttered in his garden. (He was very proud of his roses.) Once, like all Washingtonians, he had to contend with soil that is resolutely unfriendly to lawns. Then he put down artificial turf—"the stuff is wonderful"—and was spared the chore. Or, of an evening, he read his favorite magazines—*Reader's Digest* or *U.S. News & World Report*—a Western novel, or dip into his favorite moralistic writers, Norman Vincent Peale and Ralph Waldo Emerson. He enjoyed the poetry of Kipling, of Robert W. Service, because it said something to him and because it scanned.

In his middle years, he had enjoyed the night club scene. On his inspection trips, he would frequent Toots Shor's or the Stork Club in New York. In Chicago, he liked the Pump Room at the Ambassador East, in Los Angeles Chasen's or Romanoff's. Like a small-town boy, he was secretly thrilled by the company of the big newspaper names—Walter Winchell in his heyday, Quentin Reynolds—or the once great prizefighters—Gene Tunney and Jack Dempsey. His name was romantically linked with those of Lela Rogers, Ginger's mother, and Cobina Wright—and he was friendly with the reigning sirens of the period, Dorothy Lamour included. But he was never serious in his attentions. "I was in love once when I was young," he would say, though

*At a party given by Martha Mitchell, wife of the Attorney General, shortly after *Life* had celebrated him in a cover painting depicting him as a marble bust of a Roman emperor, he apologized to those who might not have recognized him. "We emperors have our problems," he said. "My Roman toga was not returned from the cleaners."

never naming the object of his affections. "But then I became attached to the Bureau. What wife would have put up with me then?" He had met Desi Arnaz, and it was Hoover who told him that Lucille Ball, Desi's wife, was having a baby.

Hoover loved practical jokes, and Julius Lulley, owner of Harvey's, was a consistent foil. Taking off for the West Coast, Lulley was told by Hoover that he was alerting FBI offices to his itinerary so that he would be looked after. When the restauranteur arrived in San Francisco, there was a call from the FBI field office that Hoover was in the city, that he would meet him in the lobby of the St. Francis Hotel at 11 a.m. Lulley was there on time, but it was not until noon that he was paged by the local FBI. Would he meet the Director at the Fairmont Hotel at 1 p.m.? At 2 p.m., Lulley was again called by the FBI. Hoover hadn't been able to make it, but he would definitely be able to be at the Top-of-the-Mark at five. At six o'clock, there was a phone call from Hoover. "I hear you've been waiting for me, Julius," Hoover said. "That's right," Lulley answered. "But where are you?" "In Washington," Hoover said cheerily.

Among Washington officialdom, he had warm and lasting friendships. Harlan Fiske Stone, of course, was his hero, and after Stone became Chief Justice of the United States, he would drop by Hoover's office from time to time to say in smiling ritual, "Well, Edgar, I've come to get an accounting of your stewardship." Frank Murphy, Franklin D. Roosevelt's controversial Attorney General was, as Hoover noted, "so opposite philosophically." But when Murphy went to the Supreme Court, Hoover would visit him on the Hill and share the long walk down Pennsylvania Avenue to the Washington Hotel where Murphy lived, chatting with his old boss. There was a long relationship with Richard Nixon, dating back to the Hiss case, and when the President announced his trips to mainland China and the Soviet Union, Hoover was one of the few ranking anticommunists who expressed his approval. His friendship with William P. Rogers antedated the period when Rogers was Attorney General under Eisenhower. And he was close enough to Lyndon Johnson in his Senate days to socialize informally with him. When one of President Johnson's beagles died, Hoover presented him with a beagle pup which LBJ named Edgar.

He had his troubles with Harry S. Truman, but there was no acrimony and, in fact, the President asked him to take on a full investigation of the Federal Establishment when the "Truman scandals"filled the newspapers. Hoover declined the assignment. "It would put the FBI in politics," he told Truman, "and how would I go about investigating the Justice Department." He resented the Central Intelligence Agency, a Truman creation—and he lost few opportunities to decry indirectly its secret funds. "Every penny the FBI gets," he would say, "it accounts for to Congress. Everything the FBI does operationally is known to Congress and to the Attorney General. A lot of the talk about confidential operations is nonsense. A few things like files must be kept secret, but Congress and the taxpayers have a right to know how the money is spent."

"The FBI," he said on one occasion, "is not an independent entity . . . I must explain every item in our budget and how the money is used. I never want any secret fund, a lump-sum appropriation for which I don't have to account. I want to account for every cent because an unexplained fund is dangerous. As it stands, we don't have to apologize for being in the FBI. This standard we live by has paid off. There never has been a scandal involving the FBI [in all its years]. We are fair and we are hard, but that's the way it should be." He did not make excuses for his toughness, though he repeatedly told friends that there was nothing more difficult for him than to fire those who did not meet up to FBI standards. He would point out that even his own office was inspected for irregularities—a claim which was true but impressed few. And he felt no embarrassment at quoting Scripture in defense.

"I find my own rules of conduct laid down in the sixth chapter, eighth verse of Micah," said the man whose boyhood ambition had been to be a preacher. "This says, '. . . and what doth the Lord require of thee, but to do justly, and to love mercy, and to walk humbly with thy God.' That is a philosophy all of us should have—a philosophy that brings a deep sense of humility. We need it in the country as well as in the FBI." But his was an Old Testament sense of mercy and justice: "We must pay the penalty for the wrongs we do."

In his last report to Congress, as he spoke up for the FBI's annual appropriation, he rang the same changes that had echoed in all his previous reports:

. . . The $318,646,000 requested for the fiscal year . . . is an increase of $30,931,000 above the $287,715,000 required for 1971. The staff of 20,727 full-year employees provided for 1972 will represent an increase of 2,251 full-year employees over the staff of 18,476 (7,837 agents and 10,639 clerks) full-year employees provided for in 1971.

. . . Regarding the tenure of service of many of our personnel, I am pleased to report . . . the low turnover among our agent staff which averaged under one-half of 1 percent per month during the 1970 calendar year.

. . . The fingerprints of criminals and suspects identified with fingerprints on file reached an all-time high of 2,223,189 . . . (Our) searches resulted in the identification of 37,646 fugitives.

. . . Notable progress has been made in our research to develop automatic equipment which will read and identify fingerprints. FBI research projects have successfully demonstrated that identifying characteristics of fingerprints can be detected and recorded through the use of an optical scanner and computer equipment.

. . . Of 18,567 offenders released from the Federal criminal justice system in 1963, [our] study shows that 65 percent had been rearrested . . . by the end of the sixth calendar year after release.

. . . A record of 882,254 investigative matters were received during the fiscal year 1970, an increase of 22,588 matters over the 1969 volume . . . The pending work has increased 24 percent in the last three years . . . The average assignment per agent is now 31 matters . . . greatly in excess of 18 matters per agent which I would prefer to see.

. . . A new peak was reached . . . as fines, savings, and recoveries in FBI cases totaled $410,974,099 . . . This accomplishment represents an average return of $1.60 for each $1 of direct funds appropriated to the FBI.

. . . A record 13,245 convictions were recorded in Federal courts . . . Convictions were obtained [by the FBI] of over 90 percent of the persons brought to trial.

. . . The success of the FBI's stepped-up drive against organized crime is apparent in the sharp rise in convictions recorded in Bureau-investigated cases since the fiscal year 1964 . . . an all-time high of 461 convictions . . . This represented an increase of 45 percent . . . Among the rings broken up were a number handling between $50 million and $100 million a year in wagers.

. . . A new record was established . . . with the location of 17,885 deserter fugitives.

. . . Civil rights investigations continue to require a significant portion of the FBI's investigative resources. The volume of cases involving interference with Constitutional rights matters reached 5,619.

This was the serious, the business side, of John Edgar Hoover, the stern law-enforcement officer. This was the side of him that much of the public saw—the Director who had no life except the FBI's, who took work home every night and sometimes on weekends. He appeared as the government official *par excellence,* the man whose life reflected his background, his training as a child, the sense of duty inculcated in his formative years. But even a political enemy like Drew Pearson could see that there was another side, could write that Hoover was "a boon companion who relishes a good joke, a lively conversationalist who can discourse on an astonishing range of subjects, a genial host who personally attends to the wants of his guest."

Hoover could laugh at himself, and at the image he had helped create of the super-sleuth. He told the story repeatedly of how he had been bilked not once but twice. "Yes," he would say, "this man came by door-to-door selling fertilizer at $30 a ton. I bought a load of it from him for my roses. Then Clyde Tolson, who is a farm boy, came by. 'You were taken,' he said to me. 'That stuff is black sawdust.' And there was the time I visited the 'Birdman of Alcatraz.' He had two cells—one in which he lived and the one where he kept his birds. My mother was still alive. She loved birds and liked to keep them. So I bought a canary from the Birdman. It turned out to be a sparrow, dyed yellow. You can see I've been conned twice in my life. I guess that shows I'm human."

2.

In the Beginning

THE LIFE OF JOHN EDGAR HOOVER IS A MONOLITH. AS HE WAS IN THE beginning, so he was at the end. Through childhood, boyhood, adolescence, and young manhood, he epitomized the now-embattled values of a middle-class America, the Puritan ethic which found its apotheosis in Horatio Alger's evocations. He was genuinely what every mother wanted her son to be—and it is this, perhaps more than the derring-do tales of FBI achievement, which gave him the solid hold on the American imagination. And it is this, too, which in a changing and battered culture earned him the ironic disdain of an other-oriented intellectual community. Those who stood in opposition saw what they considered his "righteousness" as a pose, and derided him as an Elmer Gantry in lawman's clothes. The story of his early years belies this.

John Edgar Hoover was born in small-town America—a sleepy southern town named Washington, D.C.—on New Year's Day, 1895. His family, of Swiss stock, had settled in the nation's capital in the early 1800s when it was a morass of muddy streets and new buildings, in which a fledgling government was attempting to establish a new system. It would be well over a hundred years before the city became the bureaucratic center of the country and its major power source. One of Hoover's great uncles worked as a stonemason on the Capitol. His father and grandfather were minor officials in the United States Geodetic Survey. His great grandfather on his mother's side was John Hitz, the first Swiss consul-general to the United States, who had settled in Washington when his term of service ended. On neither side had Hoover's family accumulated money or achieved a status beyond that of middle echelon government.

The house where John Edgar grew up, in Washington's Southeast at 413 Seward Square, was a monument to the family's station. It was comfortable, solid, stone, two-and-a-half stories, in the shadow of the Capitol, of Grant-era design, its tall, narrow windows properly lace-curtained. In the other houses on Seward Square lived the families of equally middle-rank government officials. The atmosphere was pleasant and friendly, with none of the tensions which today mark Washington urban life—or any of its heterogeneity. The neighborhood was self-contained and of a piece culturally and religiously.

In the Hoover family, the dominant—and dominating—influence was John Edgar's mother, Annie M. Scheitlin Hoover—a woman of determined piety and uncompromising morality, whose love for her children did not allow her to deviate from precepts learned in childhood and at church which she labored to instill in those about her. She was, some would say, a bit of a martinet in the way she ran home and family—but there was also a softness about her which found a response years later in J. Edgar's FBI associates, frequent visitors to the Seward Square house, who unabashedly called her "Mother Hoover."

Dickerson Hoover Sr., Edgar's father, did not die until his son was twenty-six. But though the boy sometimes visited him at the Coast and Geodetic Survey offices where Dickerson was chief of the printing division, and though the relationship between them was a kindly one, the major influences on young Hoover's life were his mother and Dr. Donald Campbell McLeod, pastor of the church which the Hoover family attended. It may or may not be of any significance that John Edgar was awarded a Bible for attending Sunday School fifty-two weeks without a single absence.

In 1934, when the *Washington Post* interviewed Dickerson Hoover Jr.—the story ran under the head "Capital's Famous Hoover Brothers/John Edgar Leads Nation's Crime Detection Work;/Dickerson H.'s Genius Has Made the Seas Safer"—the "fat, fifty-ish, and extremely affable" older brother reminisced: "I guess that I have wheeled Edgar a thousand miles around Capitol Hill in one of those old-fashioned high-wheeled baby buggies that mother bought for him . . . It was my daily chore to take Edgar out for an airing. I'd tuck his bottle under the pillows of the baby carriage and sometimes we would be gone for hours." It must have been an onerous chore for a fifteen-year-old to play nursemaid, but Annie Hoover was a strict disciplinarian.*

There is little of moment in John Edgar's elementary school days. Perhaps it is significant that he picked up a nickname then which still is used by some of his very old friends—Speed. It came as a result of his first venture into the world of labor. "I started earning money," he recalled, "when I was twelve years old by carrying groceries. In those days, markets did not hire delivery boys, but I discovered that if one stood outside a store, a customer laden with purchases would happily accept a helping hand and gratefully tip anyone who aided with a heavy load. The first such commission I got was to carry two

*Dickerson Hoover was in the news in 1934 as Inspector General of the U.S. Steamboat Inspection Service, investigating the tragic fire on the S.S. *Morro Castle.* He had also investigated the sinking of the S.S. *Vestris,* and was known as an outstanding expert on sea safety.

baskets two miles for which I received a tip of ten cents. I realized that the quicker I could complete each chore, the more money I could earn, so I spent most of my time running. Because I ran back to the market and was outside the Eastern Market every day after school and from 7 a.m. to 7 p.m. each Saturday, I could earn as much as two dollars a day. In those times, that was a king's ransom."

In a sense, "Speed" Hoover had been running ever since. This is not written in any pejorative sense. It merely records the fact that John Edgar Hoover always exerted himself to the utmost in any context of his life, devoting all of his waking hours to the attainment of the goals in mind. His high school career, exceptional and outstanding both for its nature and its achievement, is a case in point. He was then, under the influence of Dr. McLeod, already thinking of going into the ministry, yet there was nothing contemplative about his activities. A critic would have said that he was in training to be the All-American Boy.

In 1909, Edgar Hoover did not step from elementary school into the neighborhood high school, as did most of his classmates. He chose Central High, three miles from his home, because it was a better and a bigger school. This meant walking six miles a day in good weather and bad, but he considered it no sacrifice. Central High was known for its excellence, and in the student body were ambitious youngsters from Maryland and Virginia. And the curriculum he chose for himself clearly demonstrated that he saw high school as an opportunity to receive as much instruction as it was humanly possible to get —not merely as an interval before college. That he was absent only four days in the four years is a sign of his determination as well as his good health.

The course of studies he chose tells the story. He took four years of mathematics when only two were required. He took four years of history, though this, too, was not required. When current events classes were discussing topics he was interested in, he would show up several times a day, though he received no extra credit. Physics was Central High's toughest course, and J. Edgar took it. Latin was not a requirement, but he chose it. French and English were also on his list of studies. Though his uncle, Halstead Peirce Hoover was the head of the music department at Central, Edgar was not attracted by the subject. On his graduation, Hoover was among those at the top of his class, which elected him valedictorian.

But John Edgar did not merely distinguish himself academically. As a freshman, he went out for the football team, but to his chagrin he was turned down because he was too light. He went out for track, but his running days in elementary school did not serve him sufficiently to make the team. He found his way to high school eminence on the debating team and in the cadet crops. The gusto he brought to his cadet training comes to light in "Company Notes" of Central High's *Review* for February 1911: "Citizen to C.H.S. pupil, 'Is that noise a lion coming roaring down the street or is it an approaching thunderstorm?' Pupil, 'O, no, sir; it's just Hoover counting cadence for Company B.'"

That same issue of *Review* reports: "In consideration of the rivalry which exists in the Junior Class, Mr. Hoover and Mr. Eggleston, guided by the suggestions of the faculty committee, have undertaken to select teams for a Junior Class debate. The subject selected is an interesting one, namely, that 'Cuba should be annexed to the United States.' Mr. Hoover will uphold the affirmative of the proposition while Mr. Eggleston will support the negative." A subsequent issue reported: "The judges decided unanimously in favor of the affirmative, first honors going to Mr. Hoover."

In October 1912, John Edgar took the officers' examination and was appointed Cadet Captain of Company B. His great day came on March 4, 1913, when President Woodrow Wilson was inaugurated. One of the units marching down Pennsylvania Avenue was Captain Hoover's Company B. After it was over, *Brecky,* the school newspaper, would write of the company that "Army and Navy men, critical to the last degree . . . have been unstinting in their praise of the appearance made by it, some officers even going so far as to say that in point of military excellence the High School Cadet Regiment was second only to the West Pointers among all the marching organizations in that immense martial array."

In March, Hoover wrote for the *Review* his thanks to the school officials for offering medals to the best drilled team in an article whose tone predestined many to come in the FBI days: "We trust this innovation has come to stay. Officers meetings are held weekly, convening early in the evening and often adjourning early in the morning. Now that the programs are in our hands, it means work all the time. Attendance, fight, and set-up are the three essentials." His farewell to his cadet company demonstrated again how the child is father to the man. For he was at once full of pride of outfit, pride of leadership, and sense of responsibility—despite the unmeant condescension—for those he had led.

"I want to take this opportunity of thanking and complimenting the men of Company A," he wrote.

The Company is accredited on all sides for being the best six-squad company on the field . . . There is nothing more pleasant than to be associated with a company composed of officers and men who you feel are behind you heart and soul. The saddest moment of the year was . . . when I realized that I must part with a group of fellows who had become a part of my life. And in conclusion, let me say that I want every man in Company A of 1912–13 to look upon me as their friend and helper wherever we might go after this year.

Hoover's debating record was equally outstanding—twelve victories in twelve starts. In his major high school debate, he argued successfully the affirmative: "Resolved, that the Wisconsin system of direct primaries for the nomination of Presidential candidates should be substituted for the convention system"—a proposition which still invites political battle. The negative was taken by the debating team of Baltimore City College, and when the rhetoric was over, it was the consensus that the debate had been won by J.E. Hoover "whose cool and relentless logic overturned point after point" of the collegians' argument.

For the *Review,* he wrote his views of the importance of debating as a training for life superior to "book learning." Debate, he said, "teaches one to control his temper and free himself from sarcasm; it gives self-possession and mental control; it brings before the debater vividly the importance of clean play, for debate . . . offers loopholes for slugging, but when the referee is composed of three lawyers, slugging in the form of false arguments and statements proves of little use; and lastly, it gives . . . a practical and beneficial example of life, which is nothing more or less than the matching of one man's wit against another."

When John Edgar Hoover was graduated from Central High School, the 1913 *Annual* published under his picture, as part of his school biography, these laudatory sentiments: "A gentleman of dauntless courage and stainless honor, 'Speed' is one of the best Captains and Captain of one of the best companies that have ever been seen at Central . . . He is some debater, too . . . 'Speed' intends to study law at college, and will undoubtedly make as good in that as he has at Central . . ."

For Hoover, the way ahead seemed clear. He had a running start on the collegiate life with a scholarship at the University of Virginia, long noted for its excellent law school. But like his brother Dickerson, fifteen years before, he could not accept. Hoover's father could not afford the cost of keeping a son in an out-of-town college. If J. Edgar wanted a higher education, he would have to work for it. Had he gone to the University of Virginia, then a school of gracious and gentlemanly leisure, his life might have developed differently. For away from the disciplinary atmosphere imposed on his home by Annie Hoover, J. Edgar might have stopped running and become a successful lawyer, perhaps ending up in the House of Representatives or the Senate.

Instead, he accepted a life of continued hard work which perpetuated an early pattern. To earn a living, he took a job as clerk at the Library of Congress at a salary of $30 a month. To continue his studies, he enrolled in George Washington University, an institution with little luster, as a night-school law student, bypassing undergraduate courses. As in high school, his social life was almost non-existent. He had an occasional date, but he never "went steady" nor did he become emotional involved. For one thing, he was too busy, at work during the day, in school at night. For another, the job at hand was his prime consideration. In high school, his friends had teased him that he was "in love with Company A." At the Library of Congress, he exceeded the call of duty by mastering for himself the intricacies of card-index systems, an expertise which he took with him to the FBI. At George Washington, he joined the Kappa Alpha fraternity, where he became "No. 1"—but one of the members remarked years later that he "took a dim view of such antics as crap games, poker, and drinking bouts." That he was not thrown out of the fraternity bodily speaks well for his ability to get along with people—or for the subduing influence of morality.

Hoover earned two degrees at George Washington—Bachelor of Laws in 1916, with honors, and Master of Laws in 1917. Taking the small step instead of the big one, Hoover went to work for the Justice Department as a law clerk, helping prepare cases for Assistant Attorney General Francis P. Garvan. That he should have started so modestly is interesting, for Annie Hoover was a cousin of Judge William Hitz, who in turn was distantly related to Supreme Court Justice Harold Burton. But perhaps Hoover preferred to start small—he had been the runt of Company A when he joined it—and to work his way up. In a notable series for the *New Yorker,* Jack Alexander has described how Hoover made it at the Justice Department:

From the day he entered the Department, certain things marked Hoover apart from scores of other young law clerks. He dressed better than most, and a bit on the dandyish side. He had an exceptional capacity for detail work, and he handled small chores with enthusiasm and thoroughness. He constantly sought new responsibilities to shoulder and welcomed chances to work overtime. When he was in conference with an official of his department, his manner was that of a young man who confidently expected to rise. His superiors were duly impressed, and so important did they consider his services that they persuaded him to spend the period of the World War at his desk.

In this description of Hoover, admiration jostles gentle irony. That combination is always there for those who accept the belief that hard work and diligent application are mandatory concomitants of success. But those whose duty it is to see that the work gets done are appreciative of the men who do it, particularly in a Federal bureaucracy whose performance never quite matches the demands of office. Hoover rose in the Justice Department because he labored long hours and took his duties seriously. But this was only one of the ingredients of his success. He was, in a sense, born into the middle reaches of government. He knew the pitfalls, the rewards, and drawbacks of Federal service. He also knew the opportunities of Federal service as no tanktown lawyer or Harvard graduate could on arriving in Washington. And he was determined to rise.

Like all ambitious men, moreover, he realized that it is often necessary to guide opportunity's knocking hand to the proper door. At the time Hoover was making his way up in the Justice Department, Washington was living through its first surge of excitement, of expansion, and of national importance since the days of the Civil War. Men of stature in the world of public affairs, of industry, of the professions, roamed the corridors of the Federal City. The pressure of war, impending or actual, extended the scope of government and the size of its bureaucracy. Temporary office buildings, barracks-like and shoddy— the "tempos" that did not finally fade from the Washington landscape until the late 1960s—were being thrown up to accommodate the influx of men and women ranging from clerks to dollar-a-year men.

But more than the elephantiasis of war had seized the national capital. For the first time in its history, the United States was feeling the hot and cold winds of international change.

The "splendid isolation" that marked American history since the inconclusive termination of the War of 1812 was being breached. There were some who saw the country, just a few years past the inclusion of its forty-eighth state in the continental jigsaw, threatened from within and without. German imperialism was on the march and threatening the shaky structure in Europe which had allowed America to go its way alone. At home, revolution seemed to be around the corner. Militant and bellicose anarchist and socialist movements were using the divisions among the American people to mount raucous and violent attacks on "American capitalism," on the "system," and on the government.

At this juncture in American history, moreover, the American people were bewildered by the onslaught, outraged by the attacks on principles and values which they had considered beyond question, and frightened by manifestations of lawlessness which, in certain areas, far exceeded what was to come in the Sixties. In such a political context, a young man so patently dedicated to the patriotic virtues and so willing to put his administrative and intellectual powers to their defense was bound to rise. But Hoover aided that rise by being one of the first in government to make a serious study of both the structure and the philosophical underpinnings of the radical movement, from anarchist to communist. It was no easy task, for the vast scholarship which has since been brought to bear on American radicalism and its foreign inspiration was not available. Edgar Hoover had to cope with the raw files of history to arrive at his conclusions. But he was not satisfied with the study of documents, tracts, or the incunabula of the Third International, the organizational arm of Communist revolution.

Among the first in this country to realize what the Communists and their allied revolutionary dupes were about, he wanted to know why. He did not have a scholarly bent of mind nor the research tools of those who, even in that time, had begun to criticize him and sneer at his efforts. But he did what they failed to do. For hours on end, he talked to those of the extreme left who came within the purview of his work. He was not questioning them, in the police meaning of that word, but seeking to discover what it was in their thinking which turned them against those verities which he held eternal. He was trying to find that twist in the revolutionary mentality which turned people against their countries and which saw violence as the key to domestic tranquility. Like others before and after him, he was defeated, but his efforts were sufficiently humane to lead Emma Goldman, one of the people he would help deport, to say, "At least, Hoover was fair."

From other sources, he was learning a second lesson—that innocent men and noble purpose could be employed as effectively as fire bombs and explosive charges in the sabotage of the national purpose. The memoirs of Franz von Rintelen, a German Navy officer who worked as secret agent in the days before America's entry into World War I, tell a story which, sadly, Hoover saw repeated many times in the long years of his tenure in government. Rintelen had, among other subversive acts, organized an organization named Labor's Peace Council. Years later, in his memoirs, the German spy described one of his many successes:

> The first thing I did was to hire a large hall and organize a meeting, at which well-known men thundered against the export of munitions (to the Allies). Messrs. Buchanan and Fowler, memboers of Congress; Mr. Hannis Taylor, the former American Ambassador in Madrid. ... together with a number of university professsors, theologians, and labor leaders appeared and raised their voices. I sat unobtrusively in a corner and watched my plans fructifying. None of the speakers had the faintest suspicion that he was in the service of a German officer sitting among the audience.

It was the Bureau of Investigation, forerunner of the FBI, which with small resources, further limited by the number of political hacks who were in its ranks, uncovered the Rintelen conspiracy. It was not until America's entry into the war that the BI could move against Rintelen and his agents, since there were then no laws against espionage or sabotage. But the record

of the German operation was known to Hoover and never forgotten. In a few years, the Kaiser's agents were able to plant
timed explosives on vessels carrying supplies to Britain and
France—damaging or destroying cargoes worth an estimated
$10 million. Business fronts were set up which siphoned addi-
tional millions in defense contracts, holding back desperately
needed armaments and supplies to the Allies.

This was all part of the education of Edgar Hoover in those
years of crisis.* It not only conditioned his thinking when other
threats to national survival loomed, but it also instructed him
in the modus operandi of revolution and subversion. His role in
the crisis, however, was less important than some would have
it, more involved that he would in later years admit.

*Though Hoover had wanted to enlist when war broke out, he was declared
"essential" by the Attorney General and did not serve.

3.

An America in Turmoil

THE YEAR 1919, FOR AMERICAN CITIZENS AS WELL AS THEIR GOVernment, was one of crisis, turmoil, and bitterness. Not since the Reconstruction had the social fabric been so tattered—and not until the 1960s would Americans look about them with equal cause for despair for the future. The war years had brought their share of internal troubles—treason and sabotage which had doused the euphoria of the first days when every red-blooded American had visions of himself yanking the Kaiser's whiskers.

The draft, which came as a shock to some, had led misguided young men, purportedly inspired by enemy agents and the growing radical movement, to defy their government and to take to the fields in open battle. "Slackerism"—the less violent but more pernicious form of avoiding military service—became an issue when Secretary of War Newton D. Baker informed the Attorney General that there had been, as of June 10, 1918, a "known desertion" under the draft of 308,489 young men.

The Bureau of Investigation, born under President Theodore Roosevelt, could muster only 300 agents to cope with the million-plus enemy aliens, the draft dodgers, the skilled and ubiquitous spies and saboteurs of the Central Powers, militant pacifists intent on hamstringing the war effort, and revolutionary organizations like the Industrial Workers of the World which saw the dislocation of normal life which war brings as an opportunity to strike at the "capitalism" and the "imperialism" of the "ruling class.

That tiny component of law enforcement agents had been increased to 400, but this was hardly enough, and the Bureau's chief, A. Bruce Bielaski, was encouraged by Attorney General Thomas W. Gregory to accept the suggestion of A. M. Briggs, a Chicago advertising executive, to set up a volunteer auxiliary to aid the Bureau of Investigation in its work. But the American Protective League, which grew to an estimated 250,000, proved to be more an embarrassment than a help. Many of its members pinned on the APL badge and, like so many Kentucky colonels, did nothing. Others were overzealous and made illegal arrests which blew up in the face of the Bureau.

The mass media of the day, moreover, was horrified when the Bureau of Investigation, working with the APL and local police units, set up a dragnet to haul in all men of military age who were not carrying their draft cards. Young and old, hale and infirm were arrested in mass raids if they could not produce the cards which, under law, they were required to carry at all times, and the outcry over this blunderbuss approach echoed in the halls of Congress.

The war's end brought only a momentary breathing spell. And then, in almost every sphere of the national life, the country quaked. For the average citizen, the cost of living was a serious irritant. The index of food prices had risen from 100 in

1913 to 168.3 in 1918, 185.9 in 1919, and would pass the 200 mark in 1920. (It would not be until 1921 that prices showed any perceptible decline.) Sugar was selling at 30 cents a pound, a $3 pair of shoes cost $12. Though the government attempted to impose make-shift controls, inflation continued—and the consumer retaliated with "buyers' strikes" and "rent strikes."

But these spontaneous and unorganized "strikes" were of small impact compared to the real strikes which shook the nation's economic structure. On January 9, 1919, the harbor workers in New York City walked off their jobs. Less than two weeks later, 35,000 clothing workers went on strike, again in touchy New York City. On February 6, striking shipbuilders in Seattle called for a "general strike" to halt the American economy. On March 12, all the local transportation in New Jersey ground to a halt. On April 11, workers on the still-nationalized railroads were able to exact payraises of $65 million. On July 17 and 18, cigar workers in New York and construction workers in Chicago hit the bricks. On August 1, 70,000 men in the railroad yards walked out, and were joined by subway workers in Boston and other cities. In the days that followed, railroad shopmen in Washington, D.C. left their jobs, and Brooklyn's local transportation ground to a halt. Pressmen, carpenters, even actors went on strike. On October 1, every bituminous coal mine in the United States was shut down, crippling transport and industry. The greatest strike of all, in the steel industry, lasted from August 27 to January 8, 1920, marked by violence and death. One of its leaders was William Z. Foster, later to head the Communist Party of the United States.

But the most shocking of all the strikes occurred in Boston, where 1,117 of a 1,544-man police force deserted their posts. With no policemen on the streets, there was looting and violence. As a contemporary reporter described it, "In the following morning a sight not beautiful met the eye; lawlessness continued; license ran wild; daylight robbery . . . the voluntary police were assaulted." Only the stern call of Governor Calvin Coolidge to the citizenry to resist, after the use of militia had led to bloodshed, broke the strike. To the appeals of Samuel Gompers, president of the American Federation of Labor, that the striking policemen be returned to their jobs, Coolidge replied, to applause from President Wilson and the public: "There is no right to strike against the public safety by anybody, anywhere, anytime."

The country could find some justification for the wave of strikes. But it was shaken to the core by a series of events which the passage of time and the selective reporting of historians has dimmed.

As a backdrop to these events, there was the world-shaking drama of the Russian Revolution. Begun as a democratic overthrow of the Tsar and the assumption of power by Alexander Kerensky, the Revolution had been suppressed by V. I. Lenin and Leon Trotsky who restored the knout and the firing squad to Russian politics, in the name of communism and proletarian democracy. The United States was as horrified by Communist ideology as it was by the separate peace which Lenin and Trotsky made with the German Empire—a peace which released troops for battle on the Western Front where Americans were fighting. The average citizen did not take kindly to the statements made by Eugene Victor Debs, the leader of the Socialist Party, convicted of violation of the Espionage Act, who proclaimed Lenin and Trotsky the "foremost statesmen of the age."

On April 30, 1919, sixteen dynamite bombs were discovered in the New York City General Post Office, and eighteen other infernal machines throughout the country, addressed to Supreme Court Justice Oliver Wendell Holmes, the postmaster general, Federal Judge Kenesaw Mountain Landis, the secretary of labor, the governor of Pennsylvania, the mayor of New York, and Attorney General A. Mitchell Palmer. On June 2, a bomb wrecked Palmer's home in Washington and shattered the windows of one of his neighbors, Assistant Secretary of the Navy Franklin Delano Roosevelt. Three other bombs exploded at roughly the same hour at the homes of a Cleveland mayor, a New York judge, and a Roxbury, Massachusetts judge. In November, three ex-soldiers, attempting to raid an IWW headquarters in Centralia, Washington, were shot to death. Along with these overt acts, the Wobblies and the Communists were calling for immediate revolution in an overblown rhetoric designed to frighten and anger citizens and to lead to a public clamor for strong countermeasures.

In June 1919, the Congress had responded to public clamor and press attack—the liberal New York *World* roared that "murder is being preached in the United States openly and defiantly" and the New York *Times* described the bombings as "plainly of Bolshevik or I.W.W. origin"—by ordering the Attorney General of the United States, A. Mitchell Palmer, to put an end to the violence and radical activity which was shaking the country. To this end, Palmer appointed Francis P. Garvan to the post of Assistant Attorney General in charge of all investigations and prosecutions in the subversive field. He also put William J. Flynn, former chief of the Secret Service, in charge of the Bureau of Investigation. Within Garvan's "radical division'" Palmer created a new General Intelligence Division under Special Assistant to the Attorney General John Edgar Hoover, then 24 years old. Hoover's major mission was to study subversion in the United States and recommend ways and means to contain it. In the course of his researches, Hoover was to receive all reports from the special agents of the Bureau of Investigation.

The task was a difficult one. On the one hand, an inflamed public opinion saw the Communists and other radicals as beyond the pale, to be dealt with summarily with no necessity for the color of law to justify restraints or punitive action. On the other hand, the liberal intelligentsia and its friends had begun their long love affair with the Soviet Union and saw communism as the instrument of high-minded men seeking answers to the problems of society. Professors at Harvard and Yale law schools lectured their students and argued from public platforms that the Communist Party was simply a pacifist organization dedicated to peaceful change. Their point of view was summed up by Federal Judge George W. Anderson of Massachusetts who likened the Communist Party to "a fraternal society constituted on the lodge system . . . Its whole scheme is for propaganda by words, not by deeds" lacking "weapons of the cutting or exploding kind . . . There is therefore not a scintilla of evidence warranting a finding that the Communists are committed to the 'overthrow of the Government of the United States' by violence . . . Its methods are those of ordinary political and social propaganda" couched in "the language of exaggeration."*

In reports to the Attorney General and to the Congress, Hoover set out to lay a legal basis for action against the Communist Party and its contemporary cousin, the Communist Labor Party. More than two decades later, his pioneer work would be embodied in the Foreign Agents Registration Act, drawn up in part by Representative Jerry Voorhis, a California Democrat who lost his seat in the House in 1946 to Richard Nixon. But beyond this, Hoover also attacked the Communist philosophy on moral grounds and in terms of its threat to American freedom. Tracing the evolution of communism from the theories of Marx to the realities of Lenin and Trotsky, Hoover cited extensively from Communist literature. Today, much of what Hoover wrote has become the sad commonplace of this century's history. But in the waning days of its second decade, when some saw the Soviet revolution as the first step toward utopia and others saw the revolutionists as only unkempt and bushy-haired bomb-throwers, Hoover realized that it was a conspiracy of a small, hard-headed elitist group, working extra-legally and in contempt of all the standards by which

*It should be noted, however, that at roughly the same time, Federal Judge John C. Knox in New York was ruling that "the manifesto and program of the Communist Party . . . are of such character as to easily lead a reasonable man to conclude that the purpose of the Communist Party is to accomplish its end, namely, the capture and destruction of the state as now constituted by force and violence . . . The question here is not one of degrees of imminence of overthrow . . . but, rather, whether that it is the ultimate purpose of the organization."

American society had attempted to regulate man's baser impulses—faith in an ethical God, love of country, truth and honor in the dealings of men, respect for the family unit. Lenin had boasted that the Communists would use cunning, lies, falsification to destroy democracy and to establish a totalitarian dictatorship. The manifesto which created the Third (or Communist) International said it all, though in language dulled by Marxist rhetoric.

That manifesto, Hoover wrote, "specifically states that it does not intend to capture the bourgeoisie . . . but to conquer and destroy it, and that the final objective of mass action is the medium intended to be used in the conquest and destruction of the bourgeoisie state to annihilate the parliamentary state and introduce a revolutionary dictatorship . . . There is no effort to accomplish in this instance the ultimate aim by parliamentary action, but it is conclusive that in order to attain the aim desired that force and violence will be resorted to as a means of acquiring the desire . . . There can no longer remain any doubt in even the mind of a reader who gives but casual note to the manifesto of the Communist International, that it openly advocates the overthrow of the Government . . . by force and violence."

Hoover noted, moreover, that the American Communist Party had agreed to Point 16 of the "21 Points" adopted by the Third International: "All the resolutions of the congresses of the Communist International, as well as the resolutions of the Executive Committee, are binding for all parties joining the Communist International." Point 16 was very much in Hoover's mind when he wrote the legal brief on which the proceedings to deport Ludwig C. A. K. Martens were based. Martens, in the guise of the trade representative and unofficial ambassador of the Soviet Union, had arrived in the United States late in 1919. His appearance on the American scene was hailed by the Russian Bolshevik Federation in America as offering the "American proletariat . . . an opportunity of revolutionary activity in direct contact and cooperation with the Russian proletariat and the Soviet Government of Russia." His function, as the world would later learn, was to coordinate Communist subversion and agitation in the United States. Under an Act of Congress, approved on October 16, 1918, any alien who advocated the overthrow of the United States government by force and violence was subject to deportation.

With direct logic, Hoover argued that the Soviet government was a creature of the Communist Party of the U.S.S.R. So, too, was the Third International. Since the CPUSSR and the Third International advocated the overthrow of the American government by force and violence, then any member of that party, subject as he was to its discipline and to its decisions, was similarly tainted. "Having established the above points," Hoover wrote, "the conclusion necessarily follows that if Ludwig C. A. K. Martens is a member of the Communist Party of Russia . . . Martens falls within the class of persons subject to deportation under the Act of Congress." Carrying the argument further, in other briefs, Hoover used Point 16 to demonstrate that members of the Communist Party in the United States were equally committed to the advocacy of violent overthrow.

But Hoover's studies covered a wider field than the Communist Party. He assiduously collected the newspapers and handbills of the nonaffiliated radicals who urged revolution on the country. An organization grandiosely called the American Anarchist Federated Commune Soviets circulated leaflets the like of which were not again seen in the United States until the rise of the New Left in the Sixties. "We have paid the price in streams of blood for generations," it told "all the workers" of America. "Now it is time to put a stop to it, and this we can do only by arming ourselves, learning how to shoot, organizing secretly, educating ourselves, forming reading groups, etc., and then we can answer and attack the white terror until we are either victors or the vanquished."

But Hoover and the General Intelligence Division did more than collect the outpourings of radical groups—collated and summarized in confidential weekly reports detailing radical activity—for the use of high Federal officials. The GID worked actively against IWW and other elements in the labor movement which were fighting a two-front war, attacking both the employers and the American Federation of Labor, under Samuel Gompers. Reporting to the Congress on the great steel strike of 1919, Hoover and the GID contended that its main thrust was "to rid the American Federation of Labor of its so-called conservative leadership and form the greatest revolutionary labor movement the world has ever seen . . . Through the action of the Department of Justice in exposing the plan, this strike was terminated with, in reality, a complete victory for the American Federation of Labor." Despite the hyperbole, there was an element of truth in this. The strike, as has already been noted, was led by William Z. Foster, later to head the CPUSA, against the wishes and with the opposition of the AFL leadership. Its motivation was completely political, with, as the GID noted in reporting on one IWW-led strike, "the first of their ten demands being the freedom of all political and industrial prisoners, which demand is not a proper strike demand, being entirely beyond the control of the employers."

Hoover, of course, was accused of running a strike-breaking operation, and there is little doubt that his reports to the Attorney General and the Congress helped to solidify governmental opposition to the IWW strikers. But it is also true that the AFL made full use of the information turned up by Hoover's GID in its battle against infiltration by the Wobblies and the Communists. In fact, there was more than casual cooperation between the GID and the AFL, which began keeping files of its own on radicalism. This interest continued long after J. Edgar Hoover had turned to other activities and lasted well into the Thirties, when AFL officials testified before the forerunner of the House Un-American Activities Committee on activists of the left, from Communist militants to Walter Reuther.

One aspect of Hoover's researches, however, lingered on and was the seed for later charges that he was racist. At the time, the Communists and their friends were making a concerted effort to win over America's Negroes, which they saw as the dregs of the "proletariat" and therefore the ripest for revolutionary activity. It was during this period that the Communists were distributing maps showing a substantial portion of the South crosshatched to set off a future Negro "republic." With typical thoroughness, Hoover collected copies of Negro newspapers, the statements of black and white organizers seeking to mobilize the Negro into a revolutionary army, and a record of radical activity in the race field. Contrary to the myth, however, Hoover was not stigmatizing Negroes, but merely those who were attempting to use them as pawns. In two reports, one submitted to the House and the other to the Senate by Attorney General Palmer, Hoover made his point very clear. "The Reds," he wrote, "have done a vast amount of evil damage by carrying doctrines of race revolt and the poison of Bolshevism to the Negroes." And he noted that much of the Negro press was "naive rather than malicious" in its coverage.

But the historical significance of Hoover's work with the General Intelligence Division of the Justice Department was in his briefs and memoranda on the hopes and plans for a violent overthrow of the American government by the Communists and their allies. Much has been written of the Palmer raids, whose legal justification was based on Hoover's analyses, but of that outpouring little will stand the test of objective investigation. Those who defended Attorney General Palmer and those who belabored him were alike in their sweeping and undocumented accusations. On the one hand, the Justice Department and those members of the Wilson Administration involved presented one set of arguments, "facts," and conclusions. On the other hand, individuals and organizations pointing a finger of horror were also *parti pris* and willfully jumbled together the acts and alleged acts of local police forces, vigilantes, and the Justice Department, dedicating themselves to the proposition that any acts against radicalism were *ipso facto* vicious and unconstitutional. In the investigations that followed, the Congress was deeply divided, and proponents as well as antagonists marshaled "evidence" which was sometimes contradictory and for the most part hearsay.*

In the 1950s, when the FBI's success in infiltrating the Communist Party became known as a result of the Smith Act trials —and when controversy swirled about him—Hoover was depicted as the "master mind" of the raids and, in William Z. Foster's words, "Palmer's hatchet man." Hoover's comments to Fletcher Knebel, in an interview for *Look*—"They arrested a lot of people that weren't Communists. I was sent up to New York later . . . and reported back that there had been clear cases of brutality"—and his expressions of repugnance were brushed aside as self-serving. A check of the record would have disabused those who asserted his complicity. It was there, 788 pages of testimony taken in 1921 by a Senate Judiciary subcommittee headed by Senator Thomas Walsh of Montana who bulldogged a thorough, sometimes harsh, investigation of *Charges of Illegal Practices in the Department of Justice.* Nowhere in the occasionally acrimonious exchanges between witnesses and members of the subcommittee is there even a suggestion that Hoover had anything to do with abuses of law or the planning of the Palmer raids. In fact, he was called to the stand only to testify on the veracity of some of the testimony and to validate documents.

The record, moreover, would show that Hoover, as head of the GID and as an assistant to the Attorney General, had warned that there was "no authority under the law permitting the Department to take any action in deportation proceedings relative to radical activities." That authority resided in the Labor Department which was almost as zealously anxious as Palmer himself to conduct the raids and was embodied in a 1918 law, duly enacted by Congress "to exclude and expel from the United States . . . aliens who believe in or advocate the

*According to one charge, frequently repeated, six-man teams of Bureau agents arrested 10,000 people in one nightly sweep of their dragnet. Mathematics falters when these figures are set alongisde another: The entire Bureau consisted of 400 agents, many of whom were not involved in anti-alien activities.

overthrow by force or violence of the United States or all forms of law . . . aliens who advocate the unlawful destruction of property . . . aliens who are members of or affiliated with" any organization which advocated, believed in, or taught such actions or practices.

It was Hoover's role as a Justice Department lawyer to prepare the briefs which established that the Communist Party, the Communist Labor Party, and various anarchist groups *did* teach and advocate violent overthrow and destruction or property—hardly difficult to do since their literature and the speeches of their leaders loudly proclaimed these purposes. It was he who forwarded these briefs to the proper officials of the Immigration Service and the Labor Department, both of which worked with the Justice Department. As head of the GID, moreover, he served as liaison. But it was also Hoover who helped draw up the orders for the Bureau of Investigation under which arrests were to be made, stressing the legal safeguards and the rights of those arrested. That these orders were in a considerable number of instances ignored or changed by the Bureau was the fault and responsibility of Frank Burke, then its chief, as the Walsh committee discovered.

Many years later, Hoover would be held responsible for a change in a section of Rule 22 of immigration regulations. It had read: "At the beginning of the hearing under the warrant of arrest the alien shall be . . . apprised that he may be represented by counsel." This had been revised by Immigration Commissioner General Anthony Caminetti, after consultation with the Labor Department, to withhold advice of counsel until "such hearing has proceeded sufficiently in the development of the facts to protect the Government's interests." If Hoover had been responsible for this change, it would have indicated at least a cavalier attitude toward the civil rights of arrested aliens, and the Walsh committee delved into it with considerable care. The exchange between Senator Walsh and Hoover spelled it out.

Walsh. I would like to hear Mr. Hoover tell us about that Rule 22.

Hoover. You mean the change of Rule 22?

Walsh. Yes.

Hoover. My recollection in regard to the change of that rule is substantially the same as Mr. Abercrombie (Solicitor General of the Labor Department) stated before the committee when he appeared last week. There had been considerable comment in the Immigration Service as to the handicap under which they were working under the rule permitting the alien to have counsel from the beginning of the hearing. I know of one inspector at Ellis Island who came to Washington and spent three days here in Washington to protest about that rule as it then stood.

Mr. Parker (law officer of the Immigration Service) had prepared, I am informed, the memorandum, I think in June 1919, before any of those raids were made, and recommended that the rule be changed to its original form which permitted counsel only at such stages of the proceedings as it was deemed for the best interests of the Government.

Walsh. Is your recollection quite clear about that?

Hoover. My recollection is quite clear about that. I have discussed the matter with Mr. Caminetti, Commissioner General of Immigration.

Walsh. I asked Mr. Parker to come up here, and he told me that the rule had been changed at his instance . . .

Hoover. Exactly . . . Now, in so far as the Department of Justice is concerned in the change of Rule 22, it had no part whatsoever. The rule was changed at the instance of the immigration officers. I shall be glad to produce for your examination a copy of Mr. Parker's memorandum.

Walsh. That is all I care for.

There was only one area in which Hoover pushed hard. He wanted bail set high for arrested aliens since he believed that once released they would disappear—as some of them did. He shared both the official and the popular view of the Communist and anarchist threat.* He also believed that it was his duty to enforce the statutes written by Congress, and to enforce them

*Writing of that period in *The FBI in Our Open Society,* the Overstreets did not find it offensive to their liberal principles to note that "The anti-radicalism of that period was not much ado about nothing. Rather, it was too much ado about something . . . Radical violence existed. . . . The hopes to which revolutionary radicals geared their actions were wildly unrealistic. There was no danger of their overthrowing the Government. But there was danger of their causing an intolerable destruction of life and property."

fully. He parted company with Frank Burke, the Bureau's chief —and did so strenuously—in the illegal methods and the brutality sometimes employed in rounding up aliens. And he was appalled, as he later confided to the Attorney General who appointed him head of the Bureau, at the activities of agents who lacked any knowledge of the rules of evidence and who made arrests which could not stand up in court.

But in assessing Hoover's role in the Palmer raids, a distinction must be made. The early arrests of aliens under the 1918 statute were reprehensible only to those who took exception to the law. Those early "raids" were later lumped together with the mass raids, and Hoover's involvement in legal activities were lumped together with those abuses and excesses by Palmer and the Bureau of Investigation which marked the later dragnet approach. In the first of the carefully conducted arrests of the early period, all following due process, 250 members of the Union of Russian Workers were, after court review, ordered out of the country.

In the last of these early actions, Alexander Berkman and Emma Goldman were caught in the Bureau of Investigation's seine. Berkman and Goldman were the biggest fish in the anarchist movement—and though they claimed to be "anarchists of the thought" (as opposed to "anarchists of the deed"), their records belied it. Emma Goldman's diatribes, it had long been believed, had inspired Leon Czolgosz to assassinate President McKinley. In 1892, Berkman had walked into the office of Henry Clay Frick, who headed a vast steel empire, and shot him. "The removal of a tyrant," Berkman wrote after he was released from prison, "is not merely justifiable; it is the highest duty of every true revolutionist. Human life is, indeed, sacred and inviolate. But the killing of a tyrant, of an enemy of the people, is in no way to be considered the taking of a life."

When deportation hearings were held on Ellis Island, it was John Edgar Hoover who presented the government's case, and he marshaled his evidence so effectively that the deportation ordered was sustained by the Supreme Court. On December 21,

1919, Berkman, Goldman, and 247 other deportees were loaded on an Army transport, the U.S.S. *Buford*—the "Soviet Ark" it was immediately nicknamed. As guests at this event, Hoover invited a group of congressmen to witness the departure. On hand as well was Bureau of Investigation Chief Flynn. When Berkman spotted him, he shouted, "We'll be back. And when we do, we'll get you bastards." Amused, Flynn handed Berkman a cigar.

What impressed Hoover was that the deportees, presumably downtrodden workers, were plentifully supplied with money. One man, in fact, turned to Hoover and asked him to cash a $3,000 check. Hoover offered to turn the check over to friends of the deportee, but the man said, "I wouldn't trust you." "Very well," Hoover said. "Take it to Russia and trust the Bolsheviki."

But the Palmer raids which were to stir up such violent and long-lasting controversy did not come until much later. They were not sparked by fear of radicalism as a philosophy but by fear. One year and fifteen days after the Soviet Ark had sailed, that fear found its justification in a brutal and senseless bombing.

Shortly before noon, on September 16, 1920, a horse-drawn wagon drew up to the curb in front of the United States Sub-Treasury building at Broad and Wall Streets, across from the J. P. Morgan Company, in the heart of New York's financial district. The streets were crowded with Stock Exchange personnel and traders, clerks, stenographers, messengers, and other passers-by on their way to lunch. No one paid any attention to the vehicle or to the man who had been driving it and who disappeared into the crowd. What followed was dramatically described by Mark Sullivan in *Our Times*:

Suddenly the wagon seemed to disintegrate with a crashing roar that reached for miles about. Up from the street swept a wall of flame which thrust fiery tongues into windows lining both sides of Wall Street, setting desks afire and burning the hair from the heads of office workers; people at windows six stories from the ground were badly burned. Even more destructive than the flames were the thousands of fragments of iron, later found to be parts of sash-weights, which the explosion drove in a deadly rain in all directions. The immediate dead, for the most part passers-by in the street, numbered thirty-eight. Hundreds were injured, fifty-seven badly enough to require hospital treatment. The damage to property was estimated at between half a million and two millions and a half. For several blocks plate glass windows in stores were shattered and the facades of buildings were badly pitted.

The Wall Street bomb explosion shook the country. Unlike most of the attempted terrorism of the year before, it had succeeded. The country was aroused and demanding action. So, too, was the United States Senate. In 1919, it had forcefully ordered the Attorney General to take immediate and drastic action to prevent any recurrence of terror. The Wall Street bombing made it mandatory for Palmer to move. His hands tied by judicial decisions, and lacking the investigative forces necessary to solve the crime, he decided to move against all aliens belonging to revolutionary societies and parties. Bureau of Investigation agents who had infiltrated Communist organizations were alerted and ordered to prepare lists of suspects. A date was set for the dragnet raids and careful instructions drawn up by an assistant to BI chief Flynn for the use of all agents taking part in the operation:

All literature, books, papers, and anything hanging on the walls should be gathered up; the ceilings and partitions should be sounded for hiding places . . . Violence towards any aliens should be scrupulously avoided . . . If found in groups they should be lined up against the wall and searched . . . I leave it entirely to your discretion as to the method by which you gain access to such places. . . . If it is absolutely necessary for you to obtain a search warrant for the premises you should communicate with the local authorities . . . Grounds for deportation . . . will be based solely upon membership in the Communist Party of America or the Communist Labor Party. . . .

Special agents were also instructed: "If possible, you should arrange with your undercover informants to have meetings of the Communist Party and the Communist Labor Party held on the night set." All agents were further advised that "On the

evening of the arrests this office will be open the entire night
... Communicate by long distance to Mr. Hoover on all matters
of vital importance or interest which may arise during the
course of the arrests . . . The morning following the arrests you
should forward to this office by special delivery, marked for the
'Attention of Mr. Hoover' a complete list of the persons arrested,
with an indication of residence, or organization to which they
belong, and whether or not they were included in the original
warrants." These warrants had been prepared from files on
Communists and other radicals which the General Intelligence
Division had collected under Hoover's supervision.

The arrests were made simultaneously in thirty-three cities.
Agents bearing an estimated 3000 warrants rounded up some
2500 aliens. Of these, 446 were deported. The deportees were
exclusively members of the Communist Party. On a ruling by
Assistant Secretary of Labor Louis Post that the Communist
Labor Party did not believe exclusively in violent overthrow of
the government—he argued that it did not bar change by parliamentary means—its members were released, though Hoover
urged that there was no difference in ideology between the two
parties and found support in his contention from Communist
leaders like William Z. Foster.

That there were abuses in the Palmer raids is beyond question. Local police forces were in some cases called in to help,
and available evidence indicates that they were responsible for
most of the excesses. In the months and years of charge and
countercharge, tales of horror proliferated, and these were
broadcast in the hearings that were held by the Senate. Much
of the proceedings were screaming contests in which Assistant
Secretary Post blamed the press for inspiring a "great terroris-
tic scare" and Palmer accused Post of protecting the Communists and making "outrageously false statements." Hoover was
called to the witness stand and averred that he had urged the
Labor Department to deport any Communist alien arrested,
regardless of later protestations that he had no knowledge of
the aims of the Communist Party. "The fact remains that he is

an alien," Hoover said, "and a member of an organization declared to be unlawful, and the same is sufficient grounds to warrant deportation."

But the most honest defense of the raids was made by Palmer in an anguished moment on the stand:

I say I was shouted at from every editorial sanctum . . . I was preached at from every pulpit; I was urged . . . to do something and do it now, and do it quick, and do it in a way that would bring results . . . I accept responsibility for everything my agents did. If one or two of them, overzealous or perhaps outraged . . . stepped over the bounds and treated them a little roughly, or too roughly, I forgive them. I do not defend it, but I am not going to raise any row over it.

J. Edgar Hoover defended the need for the Palmer raids and furnished the Attorney General, through his General Intelligence Bureau, the legal underpinnings and the investigative resources to carry them out. If he felt repugnace at the time, he kept it to himself—if only because it was always his philosophy, both as Indian and as chief, that it was not the duty or the right of those in subordinate position to interpose their own judgment where the decisions of a superior were in question.

There is a footnote to Hoover's conduct during that confused era. On November 22, 1950—during the controversy over Max Lowenthal's attacks on Hoover in *The Federal Bureau of Investigation*—Chairman Emmanuel Celler of the House Judiciary Committee, a New York Democratic liberal, placed in the *Congressional Record* a letter from Morris Katzeff, counsel for some four hundred aliens who had been arrested and interned at Deer Island in Boston Harbor in 1920. Katzeff had worked on the cases with Professor Felix Frankfurter. In introducing the letter, which had been in Celler's files since 1940, he pointed out that in the most scathing criticism of the Palmer raids, written by former Assistant Secretary of Labor Louis Post, *The Deportation Delirium of 1920,* Hoover was not even mentioned. Katzeff's comments were more positive than that:

I want to say that I have personal, first-hand knowledge of that part that Mr. J. Edgar Hoover played in the so-called New England raids upon alleged Communists in 1920 . . . I was personally present at all of the hearings, after [the aliens] were allowed to have counsel. I had numerous conferences during these months with local immigration authorities . . . At several of these conferences, Mr. J. Edgar Hoover was present, but I never received the impression that he was the man who gave instructions to the . . . Department of Justice agents or immigration inspectors . . . We obtained and read into the record [of the trial] the original instructions given by the Department of Justice in Washington to the local Department of Justice agents, and it appears unmistakably that these orders were issued by one Burke, who was then the chief of some department, ...

I spoke to Mr. Hoover once or twice at Washington in 1920 about the manner in which the raids were carried out, the utter lawlessness of the entire transactions, and I do recall distinctly that he deplored these conditions as much as did counsel for the defense.

Since there are so few persons who were intimately connected with the case who could speak of it with any degree of personal knowledge, I feel it my duty to send this letter to you for such use as you can make of it.

4.

The Great Job Begins

ON MARCH 4, 1921, WHEN WARREN GAMALIEL HARDING BEGAN HIS
sorry tenure in the White House, the Bureau of Investigation
was—as one writer would later call it—"a national disgrace."
Appointment as a special agent was political, with senators and
congressmen paying off favors by placing their friends and
supporters on the BI's rolls. The Bureau's work was sloppy and
the cases it presented to the Justice Department for prosecution
were lacking in solid evidence and sketchily prepared. Repeatedly, the U.S. attorneys entrusted with cases submitted by the
Bureau would never even take them to court. Rumors of bribery
and corruption were rife, and there was talk in the press of
abolishing the Federal government's major law enforcement
agency.

But the situation would get much worse before it got better.

President Harding, with his propensity for taking the worst possible advice and making the worst possible appointments, placed an old Ohio crony and political supporter, Harry M. Daugherty, in the post of Attorney General. When it was rumored that Daugherty was planning to replace William J. Flynn, Wilson's director of the Bureau, with William J. Burns, there was a flurry of opposition. The labor movement, with support from the press, noted that the William J. Burns International Detective Agency had a long strike-breaking record and had been involved in a jury-rigging incident in 1912. But protests to Harding were futile. Daugherty was his friend and Daugherty wanted Burns.

Five months after taking over the Justice Department, Daugherty brusquely fired Flynn, a man more bumbling than venal, and turned the Bureau over to Burns. At the same time, he transferred John Edgar Hoover from his job as a Special Assistant to the Attorney General to one where the 26-year-old lawyer would presumably not witness what went on in the Justice Department—as the $4,000-a-year Assistant Director of the BI.

Hoover was not particularly happy with the appointment, though he made no objections. Within two months, however, he was clashing with Gaston B. Means, a friend of Daugherty who had been appointed special agent. Means had a lurid record: An agent for the Imperial German government before United States entry into World War I, tried and acquitted of murdering a rich widow, and exposed by the courts for filing a false will in a related case. He was an adventurer and a braggart, with a penchant for self-publicity. Hoover was unable to control Means, Daugherty's favorite investigator, but he did tell the Attorney General that he wanted no part of him and would not tolerate him in his office.

While Director Burns and many special agents devoted themselves to the task of breaking a railroad strike in which 400,000 shop workers were opposing a 12-percent wage cut, Hoover turned to another matter, more in keeping with his opinion of what activities the BI should investigate—a renascent Ku Klux Klan which was terrifying the South. Reports of KKK terrorism had been crossing his desk, but the agents he assigned to these cases somehow failed to find any violations of Federal law. The break came when Paul Wooton, Washington correspondent for the New Orleans *Times-Picayune,* bypassed Burns and Daugherty and took a sensational story to Hoover.

Wooton had a letter from Governor John M. Parker of Louisiana. It was addressed to the Attorney General. "I'm bringing you this letter personally," Wooton told Hoover, "because the Governor can't trust the the people around him. His mail is watched by the Klan and his telephone is tapped. And he needs help badly."

"Do you mean to tell me that the Governor of Louisiana can't use the telephone or the U.S. mails because of the Klan?" an incredulous Hoover asked.

"That's exactly what the Governor told me when he sent for me to come to Louisiana," Wooton answered.

Hoover decided to take personal charge of the matter. He called Louisiana Attorney General A.V. Coco who confirmed Wooton's story. Though Klan violence was a local police matter, Hoover found justification for Bureau intervention under Article IV, Section 4 of the Constitution which gives a state governor the right to Federal aid if he specifically requests it. At Hoover's suggestion, Governor Parker made this request directly to President Harding, in a letter dated October 2, 1922.

"Due to the activities of an organized body reputed to be the Ku Klux Klan," Parker wrote, ". . . two men have been brutally murdered without trial or charges . . . My information tonight is that six more citizens have been ordered to leave their homes under penalty of death. These conditions are beyond [my] control . . . A number of law officers and others charged with the enforcement of law in this State are publicly recognized as members of the Ku Klux Klan." Invoking the Constitution, Parker asked for Federal help.

The case Governor Parker referred to was one of particular

brutality. Two men, Watt Daniels and T.F. Richards, had been kidnapped by the Klan because they had been alleged to be witnesses to a KKK beating. Released with a warning to keep their mouths shut, they nevertheless told friends that they recognized the kidnappers. A week later, as they returned from a baseball game and barbecue, they were seized by armed men wearing white hoods. And that was the last of Daniels and Richards.

Working with local authorities, a group of BI agents selected for their trustworthiness by Hoover began an investigation. There had been a gasoline fire on the banks of Lake La Fourche on the night of the kidnapping—and divers were sent down to search the waters. Two mutilated bodies were found, their heads severed from their bodies. There was evidence that the victims had been horribly tortured, their bones broken on improvised racks made of wagon wheels. An autopsy indicated that the mutilation had been performed by a skilled surgeon. But when a local doctor and a deputy were brought before a grand jury, no indictments were returned: a majority of the jurors were Klansmen.

But Hoover was not discouraged. The publicity had hurt the Klan, turning some of its more prominent supporters and members against it. A telling blow was struck when, on the basis of continuing BI investigation, Imperial Kleagle Edward Y. Clarke was indicted in Texas on white slavery charges and pleaded guilty. Under Hoover's orders, moreover, the Bureau had moved into Georgia, uncovering the then common practice of "selling" Negro prisoners on road gangs to local farmers. Conviction of one farmer who had killed twelve Negroes in order to hide the evidence broke the back of that practice.

But there were still bad days ahead for the Bureau of Investigation and the Justice Department. Though Gaston Means had been forced out of his job as special agent by pressure from Congress, Burns had rehired him as a paid informer. His major job was to investigate members of Congress. When this was discovered, and when the Teapot Dome oil scandal involved

Attorney General Daugherty, the fat was in the fire. Early in March 1924, the Senate began its sensational investigation of BI director Burns, Daugherty, and Means, on a resolution sponsored by Senator Burton K. Wheeler of Montana. When an attempted frame-up of Wheeler, leading to an indictment on charges that he had accepted bribes from the oil interests, blew up with Burns admitting BI participation, the Bureau's days seemed numbered. Wheeler was, of course, acquitted. And only the death of Harding saved the BI from a death of its own.

There was sufficient cause for questioning the usefulness of the Bureau. The Justice Department, snared by Teapot Dome, was being widely called the Department of Easy Virtue, and of all its adjuncts, the BI had shown itself to be no better than the other fallen sisters. In his hard-headed New England way, however, President Calvin Coolidge realized that extinction was no answer. The Justice Department and the Federal government needed an investigative arm. What was called for at both Justice and the Bureau was a thorough housecleaning which would restore them to public confidence, and Coolidge turned to another strong-minded New Englander to clean out the Augean stables.

That man was Harlan Fiske Stone, a classmate at Amherst, an attorney of unquestioned integrity, and the former dean of Columbia University's School of Law. It was a choice that took courage, for Stone had been under attack for his defense of conscientious objectors during the war and for his criticism of the Palmer raids. But only that kind of man could sanitize the Justice Department and resist political pressures. Confirmed overwhelmingly as Attorney General by the Senate, Stone moved cautiously. He waited just over a month before he fired Burns, the BI director. That was easy. The problem was to find a successor he could trust. His first impulse was to pick someone who had never been tainted by association with the Bureau. But in searching for the right man, he mentioned his problem to Secretary of Commerce Herbert Hoover. Hoover in turn discussed it with his assistant, Larry Richey.

"Stone doesn't have to go searching," Richey told Hoover. "He's got the man he needs right there. He's young and he has a good legal background. And his name is Hoover, too."

"Can he do the job?" the Secretary asked.

"Of course he can," Richey answered. "I know him very well."

Herbert Hoover's recommendation was good enough for Attorney General Stone. On May 10, 1924, he summoned J. Edgar to his office. As Hoover tells it, he faced the interview with trepidation, expecting to be fired. The Attorney General—a big, rugged man with a perpetual frown on his face—"looked like solid stone. He told me brusquely to sit down and looked at me intently over his desk. Then he said to me 'Young man, I want you to be Acting Director of the Bureau of Investigation.' "

Hoover was twenty-nine then, and in a less youth-oriented time, this was considered very young. "But what impressed me the most," Hoover would recall, "was the recognition that I had not been responsible for the policies which had made the Bureau what it was." He thought for what must have been a minute but seemed like an eternity. Then he said:

"I'll take the job, Mr. Stone, but only on certain conditions."

"What are they?" the Attorney General snapped.

"The Bureau must be divorced from politics and not be a catch-all for political hacks," Hoover said. "Appointments must be based on merit. Promotions will be made only on proven ability. And the Bureau will be responsible only to the Attorney General."

"I wouldn't give it to you under any other conditions," Stone said curtly. "That's all. Good day."

But that was not all. Hoover wanted it in writing. He wanted the Bureau to be staffed by men trained in law and accountancy. But most of all, he wanted a free hand, subject only to the Attorney General's veto, to build up the kind of organization which the country needed. It would have to be an organization responsible to him and reflecting his moral views, almost paramilitary in its discipline and not bound by the usual civil service restraints which, in his view, encouraged laxity and inefficiency. Without a written commitment from Harlan Fiske Stone, he would be at the mercy of the politicians. At Hoover's urging, the Attorney General laid the groundwork in a Memorandum of Instructions which the Acting Director drafted for the Attorney General's signature.

The Memorandum stressed six points: The Bureau would be limited to fact-gathering functions rigorously confined to Federal law violations. It would act under the direction of the Attorney General. Stringent reduction of personnel, "consistent with the proper performance of its duties" would be sought. The incompetents and time-servers would be fired in quick order. All the political appointees and those attached under irregular working circumstances to the Bureau would be summarily dropped. In hiring new personnel, training, good character, and ability would be the guiding principles.

Hoover moved quickly to get rid of the corrupt and the undesirable. Perhaps his first act was to fire Gaston Means, who had been retained under dubious circumstances by Burns. In this, he had the hearty concurrence of Attorney General Stone. But he was equally energetic in taking command of the Bureau, and in a series of directives, he began establishing the rules under which the Bureau, for the rest of his lifetime, operated. On May 6, 1924, for example, he informed Stone of his first administrative action:

I have . . . instructed the heads of the respective Divisions of the Bureau that the activities of the Bureau are to be limited strictly to investigations of violations of the Federal statutes . . . I have already commenced an examination of the personnel files of each of the employees of the Bureau and have already recommended a number of Special Agents whose services may be discontinued for the best interest of the service . . . Every effort will be made by the employees of the Bureau to strengthen morale.

The reaction in Washington, official and unofficial, to Hoover's appointment was mixed. The *Literary Digest,* a precur-

sor of today's newsmagazines, took a sanguine view in its
report:

A young lawyer has succeeded William J. Burns, the prominent and
much discussed detective, as the head of the United States sleuthing
business. So the days of the "old sleuth," the man of "shadows" and
"frame-ups" and "get the goods" in any way you can . . . are past so far
as the present administration of the United States Department of Justice is concerned. The new chief detective, John Edgar Hoover, is a
scholar, a gentleman, and a scientist . . .

But the *Literary Digest* also quoted Robert T. Small, a correspondent for the Consolidated Press Association, who noted
some opposition:

Attorney General Stone cast aside all of the ancient notions of how a
bureau of investigations . . . should be conducted. Detectives of the old
school the whole world over, from Scotland Yard to Tokyo, will be
watching this new idea in Washington. Naturally they are skeptical.
They look askance at the appointment of a young lawyer . . . to head
one of the most important branches of the Government's system for
the control and apprehension of criminals.
    But John Edgar Hoover, the disciple of Blackstone, who has suc-
ceeded Billy Burns, the reincarnation of the Old Sleuth, has gone
calmly about his work in a manner which has given the Justice officials a feeling that they need worry no more about the affairs of the
investigation bureau . . . Young Mr. Hoover, of the new school of crime
detection, has no entangling alliances. Among his friends he is known
to be as clean as a hound's tooth. He looks at detective work from a new
angle. Instead of "getting the goods" he is concerned with making the
"goods" stick in court . . . He is striking out along new and clean lines
. . . He is going to try to do his government work in a big and legitimate
way.
    Perhaps that sort of thing is too idealistic. Perhaps the old third-
degree style will come back. But anyway, we shall see . . . *

But Hoover continued to make his point very clear. In special
instructions to the agents, he stated flatly: "This Bureau is to
operate solely upon the basis of efficiency. Influence, political

*The New York *Times* reported Hoover's appointment in a one-paragraph
story buried away on the financial page.

or otherwise, will not be tolerated and any agent or employee of this Bureau resorting to same will be disciplined." Those employees and agents who saw this as window dressing, an effort to placate public opinion, learned otherwise very quickly. There were some who tried to bypass Hoover by writing to their senators or to other politically influential people. They found themselves out in the cold the moment Hoover discovered what they had done.

Administratively, Hoover built up both morale and efficiency by decentralizing the operations of the Bureau and giving the Special Agents in Charge of field offices greater authority. In the past, agents had undercut their SAC by going over his head with complaints and recriminations addressed to the Director and the Washington office. Hoover put a stop to this, at the same time making the SAC accountable for the activities of his office. Two months after taking over as Acting Director, he informed the Special Agents in Charge that "I look to you . . . as my representative and I consider it your duty and function to see that Special Agents and other employees assigned to your office are engaged at all times upon government business." And he advised them that they were to "exercise even closer supervision over the work of the Agents under you." At the same time, he put a stop to another practice prevalent under his predecessors—the filing of bad efficiency reports on the work of an agent without notifying him first. This hurt morale, he realized, and he made this clear in a directive which went to every SAC.

"I do not desire to be embarrassed as I have in the past by incidents [of this kind]," he wrote. " . . . I desire that absolute frankness be maintained in all dealings with Agents by Agents in Charge. The same frankness will continue to be observed by the Bureau in its dealings with all Bureau employees."

To make sure that his instructions were being carried out and that the field offices were being run properly, Hoover set up an inspection system, with a corps of inspectors which moved from office to office and reported directly to him. Office routines were standardized, and working hours were set—tough ones which matched Hoover's own work habits.

All of this could fall into the category of administration. But Hoover went far beyond this, taking steps which won him the opprobrium or the ridicule of Bureau critics. He decided from the start that those who worked for the BI were to be like Caesar's wife—beyond all suspicion—and that this would have to carry over beyond the performance of Bureau duties. He wanted the Bureau's agents and employees to represent the best in middle-class values. They were to be neat, to be moral in their private relations, to be sober. There was to be no one under him who, however efficient, fell into the pattern of the sloppy, unkempt flatfoot. Drinking, in violation of the Prohibition statutes, nonpayment of debts, easy sexual practices— these were all banned and led to summary firing. The way of this Hoover set forth in a confidential letter to the Special Agents in Charge one year after he took over the Bureau—seven months after he was promoted from Acting Director to Director by an approving Attorney General.

... I am strongly of the opinion that the only way whereby we can again gain public respect and support is through proper conduct on our part ... I am determined to summarily dismiss from this Bureau any employee whom I find indulging in the use of intoxicants to any degree or extent upon any occasion. This, I can appreciate, is a very drastic attitude and I shall probably be looked upon by some elements as a fanatic. I am not, however, one of those who may be classed as a "white ribbon" advocate, but I do believe that when a man becomes part of this Bureau he must so conduct himself, both officially and unofficially, as to eliminate the slightest possibility of criticism as to his conduct or actions ... I, myself, am refraining from the use of intoxicants ... and I am not, therefore, expecting any more of the field employees than I am of myself.

This Bureau cannot afford to have a public scandal visited upon it in the view of the all too numerous attacks made ... during the past few years. I do not want this Bureau to be referred to in terms I have frequently heard used against other government agencies ...

What I am trying to do is to protect the force of the Bureau of Investigation from outside criticism and from bringing the Bureau of Investigation into disrepute because of isolated circumstances of misconduct upon the part of employees who are too strongly addicted to their own personal desires and tastes to properly keep in mind at all times and upon all occasions the honor and integrity of the service of which they are a part.

He protected the integrity of the Bureau in another fashion. Several months after his appointment, he wrote to all employees that rumors had come to his attention that "former employees and officials of the Bureau may be able to obtain information of the Bureau's work and activities and may be shown special consideration in their dealings with the Bureau . . . I want to make certain that all employees of the Bureau understand that there is to be no special consideration shown to anyone whether or not he has been previously connected with the Bureau . . . and, further, that the files, records, and activities of the Bureau . . . are not to be discussed with or disclosed to anyone not officially connected with the Bureau or [Justice] Department." In subsequent years, there would be criticism of the Bureau's files and of what they purportedly contained. But there has never been a substantiated case that they were bandied about, or even unofficially leaked.

In his successful effort to eliminate politics from the Bureau, Hoover had some bad times. At the start, though he had the full assurance of Attorney General Stone, he did not know how far he could go. When he transferred an agent to the Southwest because he persisted in political activity, Hoover received an angry call from a prominent senator who wanted the agent transferred back so that he could help in the upcoming campaign.

"I'm sorry," Hoover said, "but I feel it would be best for the agent and best for the Bureau if he gets away from his political ties. This will give him a new chance."

"I'll take this up with the Attorney General," the senator stormed.

Within fifteen minutes, as Hoover would later tell it, he had been called to the Attorney General's office. "Stone gave me a long look and then asked me, 'Hoover, what are the facts in the case?' He listened to what I had to say and then said, 'I think you are not entirely on sound grounds.' I stiffened and said to myself, 'This is it. This is where I resign.' And then the Attorney General said, 'You should have fired the fellow at once.' "

It took many years before senators and congressmen realized that they were wasting their time when they interceded for an agent who had been found wanting or who had been transferred to a field office which he thought undesirable or inconvenient. In all these cases, Hoover wrote to the interceding politicians, "I sincerely regret that I am unable to accede to your interest" in whoever the agent may have been. If there were mitigating circumstances, he sometimes relaxed his rules, but in time he learned that this did not pay. After a particularly troublesome episode in which he had offered to discuss an agent's discharge with him, only to have charges of bigotry hurled at the Special Agent in Charge, he confessed his error in a letter to an associate. "It convinces me all the more," he said, "that once we let a man out, we should never effect his reinstatement unless we are absolutely certain that an injustice has been done." He stuck by that rule to his dying day, unimpressed by political pressure or by threats of "exposure" from those who were about to be fired.

Arriving early and working late—and putting in as many hours as any agent working on a difficult case—Hoover painstakingly reorganized the Bureau of Investigation, establishing order out of chaos, systematizing its routines, clearing out the deadwood and bringing in the earnest young lawyers and accountants who later gave it its reputation. In this, he had the wholehearted support of Harlan Fiske Stone—the "father" of the FBI by Hoover's account and, in time, a close friend. By 1928, he began to feel that he had accomplished his mission. Though Stone had moved up to the Supreme Court, he still kept up his interest in the Bureau, still visited Hoover from time to time, always saying with paternal affection, "Edgar, I came by to inquire into your stewardship."

Among Hoover's prized possessions was a letter from Stone,

written in 1932. "I often look back to the days when I first made your acquaintance in the Department of Justice," Stone wrote, "and it is always a comfort to me when I see how completely you have confirmed my judgment when I decided to place you at the head of the Bureau of Investigation. The Government can now take pride in the Bureau instead of feeling obliged to apologize for it."

Still ahead for John Edgar Hoover were the days when "G-man" would become a household word, when his name would become as well-known to the American public as that of Presidents and film stars, and when the FBI would be held up to the world as the finest and most incorruptible law enforcement agency history had known—in many respects the superior of Scotland Yard.

5.

From the Official Reports, 1924–28

IN THE ANNUAL REPORT OF THE ATTORNEY GENERAL OF THE UNITED States, filed with the Congress on December 4, 1924, the twelve pages allotted to the Bureau of Investigation are preceded by two lines in 6-point type:

(William J. Burns, Director from August 22, 1921, to June 14, 1924; John Edgar Hoover, Acting Director since June 15, 1924)

The account was all Hoover's, however, and a recitation of his achievements in the first six months of his tenure. There would be forty-eight such reports from Hoover. They would grow longer with time, and with the increasing duties of the Bureau. An element of the hortatory would creep in, commensurate with Hoover's importance as a Federal official and a public figure. But in the five years from 1924 through 1928, the tone and the methodology of Hoover's reports to Congress were set.

Each report was designed to convince the Congress of the Bureau's efficiency, its continually improving methods of serving the Federal goverment's law-enforcement needs, the increasing scope of its activities, and its successes as the only arm of government which brought in more money than it spent. Significantly, it was in that five-year period—before the Bureau had achieved its national popularity—that Hoover created a solid foundation for Congressional support and approval. The adulatory stories and the gang-busting headlines came after Hoover had established the Bureau as a vital and essential part of the Justice Department.

The activities of the Bureau for those five years make an interesting contrast to charges by critics that Hoover's unique position in the governmental structure had been achieved not by solid accomplishments but by the astute use of publicity techniques and a personality cult. The 1924 report begins to tell the story and it merits substantial quotation.

"Of the total appropriation [for] detection and prosecution of crime for the fiscal year 1924, the Bureau of Investigation spent $2,058,493.49 as compared with $2,447,104.16 for 1920, a reduction in expenditures of $388,610.67," Hoover told the Congress. "Following strictly the policy of retrenchment, the regular or payroll personnel has been reduced by approximately 150 over 1920, 61 reductions in personnel having occurred within the last six months. The work of the Bureau of Investigation has, however, materially increased.

"... A number of changes have been made in the administrative work of the Bureau and in the policies of operation, resulting in increased efficiency and improvements of the service generally. A system of inspection has recently been established under which all field offices of the Bureau of Investigation are inspected at intervals, thereby effecting closer contact and the exercise of personal supervision ... Numerous savings in the cost of operating of the Bureau have already been effected even in the short period of time since the establishment of the inspection system. Eight of the field offices have saved $950 per annum in telephone service alone. Economies which have been effected in office rentals total approximately $8,000 to date . . . Employees whose services were no longer necessary or who were not properly qualified for the duties which they were called upon to perform have been removed, and a number of field offices have been completely reorganized and some discontinued. On May 10, 1924, there were in operation 53 field offices, while today there are in operation 48.

" . . . The entire field service has been reclassified. Every employee has been graded according to his ability and efficiency, and promotions are being based solely upon the efficiency attained by the individual employee. The bureau at the seat of government has been reorganized and divided into six major divisions, as follows: Division No. 1, director's office; division No. 2, assistant director's office; divisions Nos. 3 and 4, supervision of certain classes of investigations; division No. 5, chief clerks office; division No. 6, identification . . . All files have now been coordinated into one division . . .

"Another substantial step forward has been the establishment of a rule under which preference for appointments of special agents is given to men with legal training. More than one third of the force of agents now possess such qualification. The 'paper work' has recently been reduced to approximately one-third of its former proportions. There formerly existed in practically all of the field offices different filing systems. This has been corrected by establishing a uniform filing system."

Hoover's 1924 report then carefully broke down the functions of the various divisions of the Bureau. Division No. 2 "handles among many classes of investigations the following subjects: Alaskan matters, arms and ammunition running, civil rights and domestic violence, crimes on the high seas, Indian and Government reservations, impersonations, intimidation of witnesses, jury matters, espionage, naturalization frauds, translations [for other government departments], passport frauds, and miscellaneous matters." The report then noted the various cases in those categories which it had handled. These included breaking up attempts to smuggle arms, ammunition, and planes out of the country for revolutionary groups in Mexico, China, Honduras, and Cuba; investigation of 92 cases of peonage in the South; investigation of 25 cases of intimidation of witnesses and 17 cases of jury fixing; 1,145 investigations conducted for other departments and agencies of the Federal government.

Division No. 3, Hoover stated, "directs approximately 55 accountants, covering violations of the national-bank laws, using the mails to defraud, bankruptcy act, thefts from interstate shipments, thefts and embezzlements from the government, violations of the war risk insurance act, false claims and miscellaneous frauds against the Government. Out of a total of 3,659 cases handled during the fiscal year, 2,212 were concluded. Of those closed by prosecution, there were 511 convictions and 112 acquittals." And, of some interest to sociologists and government corruption watchers: "The many Government agencies created during and immediately subsequent to the war period have contributed largely to the work of the Bureau, particularly in the cases of conspiracies either to defraud these agencies or to violate the provisions of the act creating them; for instance, the War Finance Corporation has referred several major investigations to this Bureau. The War Minerals Relief Commission is another agency which has turned to this Bureau for the investigation of conspiracies to defraud . . .

"In the summer of 1923 the department [of Justice], with the aid of the Post Office Department, inaugurated a drive on many alleged oil companies found using the mails in furtherance of their schemes to defraud and concentrated their efforts in Texas and California, the two most prolific centers for this kind of offenders. A staff of [Bureau] accountants, working with Post Office inspectors, prepared evidence which resulted in the conviction of numerous promoters, among them Dr. Frederick Cook, who first became internationally famous when he claimed to have discovered the North Pole. Cook had been active for some time in Texas in promoting various alleged oil companies, and at the trial of the offense for which he was indicted with 23 others, 21 of the defendants were convicted ... Cook himself receiving [14 years and 9 months] together with a $12,000 fine."

In reporting on the work of Division No. 4, Hoover wrote that "the Bureau of Investigation has investigated 189 suspected violations of the Sherman antitrust law." In this, the Bureau was swimming in dangerous waters. For, as Hoover added, "The most extensive investigation was that of the suspected combination to enhance the price of oil and gasoline, while that of the lumber industry was a close second."

The increasing ubiquity of the automobile shows up in the statistics offered by Hoover on the enforcement of the National Motor-Vehicle Theft Act: 12,628 reported violations, with 136 investigations which involved both that statute and the Mann Act, which prohibits the transportation of females across state lines for immoral purposes. Hoover's feeling of repugnance for the violators of the Mann Act—or White Slave Traffic Law—comes through in a single paragraph: "Reports show that of offenders punished this year by the courts 65 of their victims were under the age of 18 years, 2 being only 13 years of age. Thirty victims were induced to leave their homes under promise of marriage and 50 were commercialized. In 70 percent of these cases there were families involved, including children who suffered from the resuls of the violation of this law." Hoover added with some satisfaction that since the inception of the act, there had been 4,427 convictions, with "imprisonment imposed, 2,840 years 11 months 9 days 5 hours, and fines assessed $475,800.64."

Division No. 4 also had under its jurisdiction Selective Service Act violations, lottery cases, railroad and other interstate commerce law cases, the unlawful wearing of Army, Navy and Marine uniforms, the tracking down of deserters, income tax law cases [eight in those days of low taxes], a case where a Census Bureau official divulged information, and so on. But there was an area of crime which today has the patina of nostalgia. Congress had passed a law prohibiting the shipment of prize-fight films in interstate commerce. Hoover, therefore, solemnly notes that "In the Dempsey-Carpentier prize fight film case over 30 defendants were arrested for transporting the film interstate . . . In the Dempsey-Gibbons case 15 individuals have been investigated . . . In the Dempsey-Firpo case over 25 persons have been arrested . . . At the last prize fight of any prominance, held at Michigan City, no moving pictures of the actual combat were taken."

J. Edgar Hoover's first report stressed what would become one of the Bureau's more publicized activities—close to the Director's heart because it brought order to the chaos of identification of victims and malefactors—the formation of a National Division of Identification. In time, there would be some carping over the vast files of fingerprints and other identifying marks kept by the Bureau. But when Hoover created it, a fortnight after taking over as acting director, it was highly praised by law enforcement officials and by the Congress.

"Not only did the Federal authorities take a keen interest in the matter of bringing about the establishment of such a division," Hoover wrote, "but the police authorities throughout the United States have, through the International Association of Chiefs of Police (IACP), rendered material assistance and aid in bringing about [its creation], which, it is recognized, will serve as one of the most powerful influences in not only bringing about a more effective detection of crime but also an influence in the way of prevention of crime."

For police officials, the Bureau's central file of fingerprints and other identifying marks—it eventually included such things as a catalogue of laundry and dry cleaners' marks—helped track down criminals who had left behind so much as a handkerchief in earlier crimes of local jurisdiction. A fingerprint on file in, let us say, San Francisco was of no value to New York police. With a central file, this record was available to any police force in any part of the country. And, as Hoover repeatedly argued, the central fingerprint file was of great value in identifying people who died in accidents where the body might be unrecognizable, as well as in cases where no local identification was possible.

In his report Hoover recounted how identification records maintained by the Justice Department at Leavenworth Penitentiary were transferred to Washington, D.C. These were combined with other such records collected by the IACP which had contributed them to the Bureau. "As soon as the appropriation granted by Congress became available," Hoover reported, "the Division of Identification was formed and now is progressing rapidly toward bringing up to date its work . . . It is expected that no later than the end of 1924, the work of the Division of Identification will be up to date and the close cooperation thus established between the Federal authorities and the police authorities throughout the United States will tend to exert a powerful influence in deterring criminal elements in their pursuits." There were already 835,000 fingerprints on file as Hoover reported, and "approximately 750,000 had been classified and filed and 930,000 index cards on identifications made and filed. The daily average of prints received is 286 and the number of regular contributors is 1,200."

In what became a regular feature of Bureau reports to the Congress, Hoover wound up his report with a tabulation of the sentences imposed as a result of its work—4,126 years 11 months 9 days. "The total amount in fines and recoveries is $2,786,622.83, which is $728,129.34 more than the year's expenditures for the Bureau of Investigation [$2,058,493.49]. In considering this comparison sight should not be lost of the enormous amount of work performed and splendid results obtained in cases either remaining to be tried or the results of which can not be figured in dollars and cents."

In 1925, the Bureau's share of the Attorney General's Report to the Congress had increased to 22 pages from the previous year's 12. Hoover could report that the percentage of agents with legal training had risen from one-third to a half. Field offices were cut down from 48 to 36 "with a resulting reduction in personnel. There has, however, been a considerable increase in the demands made upon the Bureau . . . but notwithstanding the reduction in personnel and the increase in investigative demands, the summary of the work performed for the past fiscal year shows an increase in results obtained," Hoover reported—which was exactly what the Congress liked to read.

Prohibition was beginning to plague all law-enforcement agencies, and Hoover noted a sharp increase in impersonation cases. "In many of these investigations"—there were 803 in all—"there developed cases of impersonation of a Government officer by persons who represented themselves to be Federal prohibition agents and who thereby secured sums of money from various persons upon a promise of protection from prosecution." Peonage in the South was also a problem, and Hoover reported, as a result of 99 investigations, convictions totaling "15 years 6 months and 1 day" and fines of $3,700. Hoover added, in one of his few understatements, that in these cases "successful conclusion involved work of a most difficult character, and in one case resulted in the indictment and conviction of a number of county officials." In the South of that period, it was indeed difficult for the Bureau—or anyone—to prosecute white men who were holding Negro prisoners in virtual bondage.

Hoover, moreover, did not make friends among some of the big city police forces when his investigators disclosed the existence of a ring of 48 police and 23 prohibition agents who were shaking down violators in Cincinnati, Ohio. "Seventy-one persons were indicted and all but one, who had fled to Canada, apprehended. So complete was the evidence obtained that 59 of the defendants entered pleas of guilty." This was in sharp contrast to the experience of the Bureau in the past when untrained agents failed to collect admissible evidence. The increasing effectiveness of the Bureau was demonstrated by its investigation and arrest of former United States Attorney Frank Boykin, who was convicted of bribery and sent to the penitentiary.

"A thorough investigation of the conditions existing in the

Atlanta Penitentiary by agents of this Bureau," Hoover also reported, "resulted in the exposure of extensive graft and corruption existing upon the part of certain officials of that institution. The evidence obtained resulted in the conviction of the warden of the penitentiary. In this investigation the agents also gave attention to administrative features of the operation of the penitentiary and their report was the basis of instituting extensive reforms in the operation and management of the Atlanta Penitentiary."

The 1925 report also cited Bureau work involving the protection of Indians in Oklahoma who had been intimidated, assaulted, blackmailed, and even murdered by criminals such as the notorious "Blackie" Thompson; indictments of publishers of obscene materials sold to children; disclosure and prosecution of postal frauds; the indictment of 263 furniture dealers in Chicago for violation of the antitrust statute; a sharp increase in the uncovering of crimes of embezzlement by bankers. Lawyers who were taking the lion's share of settlements made to widows and orphans of servicemen came under the Bureau's scrutiny and led to convictions. In auto theft, the Bureau submitted statistics showing a sharp rise in cases reported—the car was coming into its own—indictments (2,046 over 1924's 1,923) and convictions (1,435 over 1924's 895). Hoover also made his tabulation of Mann Act cases: 528 convictions, 117 acquittals, 62 cases in which nolle prosequi was entered, and 842 pending cases. Reports showed, Hoover wrote, "that of the offenders given prison sentence . . . 37 of their victims were under the age of 18 years, 21 of their victims were under the age of 15 years, 3 of their victims were under the age of 12 years, and 1 of their victims was 10."

Of the Division of Identification, it was proudly stated that the "physical consolidation" of its records was an accomplished fact. In the process, more than half a million fingerprints were reduced to the standard 8 × 8 Bureau cards, 930,000 alphabetical index cards had been made out—most of this work having been done in the last six months of the fiscal year. The

Bureau now had on file 914,848 fingerprint records, 1,051,347 alphabetical index cards, and approximately 225,000 Bertillon photographs. The Identification Division occupied 21 rooms, or 5,492 feet of space—an increase of 9 rooms over the previous year.

The conclusion of the report offered a summation of the Bureau's work for the year: prison sentences of 3,572 years 85 months 167½ days, with fines and recoveries of $3,063,540.78— or $874,678.78 more than the Bureau's entire appropriation.

The 1925 report had listed J. Edgar Hoover as "Acting Director to December 15, 1925: Director from December 16, 1924." The 1926 report covered his first full year as Director. And there was a perceptible note of added confidence in Hoover's account of the Bureau's achievements and increased efficiency. Though he had eliminated two more field offices, he could assert in the second paragraph of a 17-page statement:

"The sentences and fines imposed in cases investigated by the agents of the Bureau for the year ended June 30, 1926, amounted to 4,494 years (exclusive of two life sentences) and $1,038,856.42, respectively. The Bureau also aided in obtaining recoveries amounting to $6,652,619.59. The expense of the Bureau for the fiscal year ended June 30, 1926, totaled $2,023,-561.83—the smallest expenditure for Bureau operations since the fiscal year 1923." In his introduction to the general report, he once more justified his policy of securing "the services of men who have had legal training in order that the investigators of this Bureau might have a proper understanding of the value and weight of evidence." During 1926, moreover, "there was added to the examination made of applicants for appointment . . . a requirement for a physical examination."

The report covered the gamut of cases in which the Bureau had jurisdiction, and noted that the net increase in cars recovered under the National Motor Vehicle Theft Act had increased by 453, to 2,492, with a value of $1,930,709.86; that there had been 528 arrests for white slavery involving "the debauchery of previously virtuous women or of young girls and children";

that the Bureau of Identification now had 1,052,852 classified fingerprints on file, with a resultant ability to identify 29 percent of all fingerprints received from local police and other authorities, a jump of seven percentage points over the previous year; and that the "most modern methods" were being employed by the Bureau in this highly technical field.

In 1927, Hoover was still whittling down the size of the Bureau—by sixteen agents. For some reason, Hoover did not give a figure for the number of prints then in the files of the Bureau of Identification. He simply reported the number of prints received and classified, the number of identifications, and the rise by 31 percent of identifications made. His report was but seven pages long, but he found room in it for the other constant in his messages to Congress:

"The sentences imposed in cases investigated by the agents of the Bureau amounted to 10 life sentences, 7,090 years, and $1,149,045.55. The Bureau also aided in obtaining recoveries amounting to $6,014,483.47. The expenses of the Bureau during the year totaled $2,012,860.06—the smallest expenditure for Bureau operations since the fiscal year 1923."

By 1928, Attorney General Harlan Fiske Stone, Hoover's mentor, had been appointed to the Supreme Court. His successor, John G. Sargent, was cut to the noncharismatic and terse Coolidge style—and Hoover's section of the Annual Report of the Attorney General of the United States reflected the atmosphere of the Justice Department. It was the shortest statement of his administrative husbandry yet, and it lacked the details of prosecutions and investigations that had marked Hoover's earlier product.

In his prefatory remarks, he stated that the number of agents had been further reduced, by 17, though the number of field officers still held at 30. But he had made a significant administrative change by reforming the territorial jurisdiction of these offices so that they matched those of Federal judicial districts. This, he explained, would "assure a closer relationship of each field office with the United States attorneys. The effect of this was to bring about increased economy in field operations [and] greater dispatch in administering the Bureau's investigative work in the field." Hoover had also prepared and issued to every investigator a Manual of Rules and Regulations covering all aspects of Bureau procedures and practices, codifying the circular letters which he had been sending out in a steady stream to his special agents. Every employee was "charged with the duty of being thoroughly familiar with the contents thereof."

His now-traditional statement followed: "The sentences imposed in cases investigated by the agents of the Bureau during the year amounted to 2 death sentences, 11 life sentences, 7,921 years 7 months 8 days, and $492,187.31. The Bureau aided in obtaining recoveries amounting to $3,589,467.77. The expenses for the Bureau year totaled $2,092,773.28." Perhaps sensitive about the increase in expenditures over past years, Hoover added: "In connection with the expenses of operation, the Bureau was required by law to pay an increase of 50 percent in per diem expenses incurred by its employees over that paid in the previous year." Hoover then ticked off the various activities of the Bureau in 1928, usually in single paragraphs:

Larceny of goods in interstate commerce—283 indictments returned, 261 convictions;

National Motor Vehicle Theft Act—2,549 indictments returned, 2,-055 convictions, 3,455 cars worth $1,391,371.12 recovered;

White slave traffic—602 indictments, 469 convictions.

Deserters from the armed forces—127 apprehended;

Crimes on the high seas—20 indictments, 13 convictions;

Impersonation of government officers—212 indictments, 135 convictions;

Bribery—23 indictments, 10 convictions;

Crimes on government reservations—144 indictments, 99 convictions;

Interstate commerce (except thefts from)—19 indictments, 39 convictions;

Pardon, parole, and probation matters—The Bureau had made "many" investigations to determine the fitness of those applying for parole, to locate parole and probation violators, to determine if the conditions of parole and probation had been violated;

Bondsmen and sureties—4 indictments and 5 convictions in cases involving the financial standing and reliability of bondsmen;

Miscellaneous—130 indictments, 119 convictions, in cases involving investigations of applicants for the Prohibition Unit and in those of Justice Department personnel;

The National Bank Act (mostly embezzlement)—312 indictments, 213 convictions;

Use of the mails to defraud—110 indictments, 85 convictions;

National bankruptcy laws—421 indictments, 159 convictions;

Antitrust laws—63 indictments, 237 convictions;

Theft, embezzlement, and illegal possession of government property —112 indictments, 101 convictions;

Frauds against the government—71 indictments, 35 convictions;

Election fraud—Investigations and reports to prosecuting officers, particularly concerning charges "that in certain Southern states political influence has been sold to seekers for appointments to Federal positions";

Fugitives from justice—923 apprehended;

Identification and information—1,440,099 fingerprints, 2,314,713 index cards.

The Bureau had become what Harlan Fiske Stone had envisioned—efficient and enforcing the laws without fear or favor, apprehending embezzling bank officers and army deserters with equal zeal, apprehending antitrust violators and mail thieves, and becoming part of the Justice Department machinery. These things the Bureau had never been since its flamboyant beginning under President Theodore Roosevelt or its shoddy and corrupt days under Woodrow Wilson and Warren Gamaliel Harding. No one had yet risen in Congress to compare it favorably to Scotland Yard or to the Deuxième Bureau—nor to the Tsarist Okhrana and the GPU. Little children did not say, "Bang! bang! I'm a G-Man!" John Edgar Hoover, in fact, was one more bureau head—more efficient and harder working than his colleagues, better liked on Capitol Hill by legislators he did not ruffle or court more than was absolutely necessary. His brother, investigating disasters at sea, was far better known to the public at large, to the press, and to the men of place in the higher echelons of government. Hoover's day was yet to come as the country skipped into crime and depression.

6.

The Crime Years

IT WAS A TIME OF NATIONAL HANGOVER, OF LAWLESSNESS, OF IRRE-
sponsibility. The country had learned cynicism in the years
after World War I. The Harding Administration scandals had
struck the country just as revisionist historians were diligently
arguing that the United States and President Wilson had been
dragged into the bloody conflict by the munitions makers and
the international bankers. And Prohibition, which had promised to make the nation safe for sobriety, had made millions of
otherwise law-abiding citizens into lawbreakers. Thwarting
the law became a national pastime, supporting the bootleggers
a national avocation. What had begun as simple bootlegging—
almost a family-store business—organized itself into powerful
gangs and combines which branched out into such fields as
gambling, robbery, prostitution, and dope peddling. And as a

concomitant to these, there grew up the most noxious activity of all—the protection racket. This involved a whole subculture of mobsters, crooked officials, "mouthpieces" or "lips" to handle pay-offs and keep criminals out of prison, and a small army of people to provide logistical support—doctors, tailors, prostitutes, bought police, hotel owners, and provisioners of every kind. The take ran into billions, with the income of the Al Capone gang in Chicago alone being estimated at more than a quarter of a million dollars. The cost of Prohibition in dollars and social deterioration, however, did not seem excessive to a citizenry convinced that prosperity was as perpetual as the stock market's cornucopia.

But though John Edgar Hoover spoke out repeatedly against the lawlessness that afflicted the country, his Bureau of Investigation was powerless to act. Murder, theft, and most other crimes against the person and/or property were out of the Federal jurisdiction. Prohibition enforcement had been assigned to the 4,000 agents under the Treasury Department. Corrupt political machines were the rule rather than the exception—and no one really cared. "Going for a ride" became as much a part of the national idiom as "taking a trip" is today, as the gangs fought murderous wars for control of liquor sales and the rackets. The Bureau, moreover, not only lacked jurisdictional access. Its agents were not permitted to carry weapons and they had no more right to make an arrest than an ordinary citizen.

Nevertheless, in 1925, when Hoover began to get complaints from Cincinnati that saloons were doing business openly next door to the Federal Building, that the city government was allied to the underworld, and that narcotics sales were booming, he asked Attorney General Stone for permission to look into the situation. "If Federal laws are being violated," he told Stone, "then we can move." "Go ahead," Stone said. A team of Bureau investigators was sent into the city. In short order, the special agents discovered ties between the police department and Federal Prohibition and narcotics agents. This gave Hoover the handle he needed.

Working alone, since the police could not be trusted, the Bureau began piecing together the evidence needed for presentation to a grand jury. Affidavits were taken from narcotics peddlers whose annual gross ran into the six figures. Saloonkeepers confessed that they had been paying protection money to the police. An extortion racket run by Prohibition agents was uncovered. These agents made arrests on a quota system, then released their prey for substantial bribes. Under Hoover's direct supervision, the Bureau agents prepared their case in several months. Forty-eight Cincinnati policemen and two dozen Prohibition agents were indicted. Some fled the city, certain that they could hide out once they had left the state. But the Bureau pursued them to Los Angeles, to Miami Beach, and to Syracuse, New York. All of them were apprehended except one man who was able to leave the country. Sixty-four were convicted.

It was not long after this that the Bureau faced a crisis of another kind. One of its special agents, Edward B. Shanahan, was killed by a professional car thief, Martin James Durkin. Shanahan, unarmed, had stopped Durkin to question him. Durkin calmly shot him through the breast with an automatic pistol. Hoover called in his assistants. "We've got to get Durkin," he said. "If one of our agents is killed and the killer is permitted to get away, it will be open season on all our agents. We can't let Durkin get away with it. Get him."

The trail ran through Illinois, California, Arizona, New Mexico, and Texas. In Chicago, Durkin killed a policeman and wounded a second. In San Diego, with Bureau agents on his trail, Durkin stole a Cadillac. He was traced from city to city. In Pecos, Texas, a sheriff noticed an automatic on the seat of a Cadillac, next to the driver. Questioned, Durkin said that he was a deputy sheriff from California and had the right to carry the gun. "Let me go back to my hotel," Durkin told the sheriff, "and I'll show you my identification." When the sheriff agreed, Durkin stepped on the accelerator and took off into the desert. The sheriff notified the Bureau field office in El Paso. A wrecked Cadillac was found in the desert. Fanning out, agents found a rancher who had given a man and a woman a lift to a nearby railroad station. The man's description fitted that of Durkin. At Alpine, Texas, a ticket agent reported to Bureau investigators that Durkin had bought a ticket for San Antonio. In San Antonio, the fugitive had boarded a train for St. Louis. But having located Durkin, the Bureau could not arrest him for the murder of Shanahan. (It was only later that Congress made it a Federal crime to kill a Federal officer.) On instructions from Hoover, the agents pursuing Durkin called St. Louis police authorities and arranged to have the train on which the fugitive was riding stopped outside of the city. If Durkin resisted arrest and escaped from the train, the Bureau reasoned, he would have to make his way over open fields. If there were a gun battle, no bystanders would be hurt. But these precautions were not necessary. When Bureau agents and local police boarded the train, they were able to push into Durkin's compartment before he could reach for the gun in his overcoat pocket.

But this exercise in pursuit was child's play compared to the mystery, drama, and controversy that would involve Hoover and Bureau in a case that shook the nation—the kidnapping of the Lindbergh baby. Before the dust of time had settled on that tragedy, Hoover would become a household word. He would be denounced on the floor of Congress for persecuting Bruno Richard Hauptmann, convicted of the kidnap-murder. And he would find Congress thrusting new and important duties on him—duties which would make "G-Man" and "FBI" synonymous with all the virtues. For it was the Lindbergh case that projected the Bureau onto the national stage. Prior to that, it was known only to criminologists, to law enforcement officials, and to Washington's official enclave.

Ironically, the Bureau's role in solving the kidnapping was no more than routine.

In every respect, the kidnapping of the Lindbergh child was horror compounded. Colonel Charles A. Lindbergh, a national hero, and Anne Morrow, the lovely and sensitive girl who married him, had attempted to withdraw from the public gaze by living in the seclusion of the New Jersey foothills, near Hopewell. On the night of March 1, 1932, between 8 p.m., when his nurse had left Charles Lindbergh Jr. asleep in his room, and 10 p.m. when the crime was discovered, a kidnapper had propped a crudely made ladder against the second-floor window of the nursery and taken the twenty-month-old child. On the window sill, the kidnapper left a note:

Dear Sir
Have 50000$ ready 25000 in 20$ bills 15000 in 10$ bills and 10000$ in 5$ bills. After 2–4 days we will inform you were to deliver the mony. We warn you for making anyfing public or for notify the police. The child is in gut care. Instruction for the letters are singnature.

The letter was signed with two overlapping circles, punched by three holes.

The kidnapping struck the country hard, bringing out the worst and the best in people. For the newspapers it was a sensational story, and they milked it mercilessly, hounding the grieving parents and pawing every shred of evidence. While the nation sorrowed, gangsters with hearts of gold offered their services to police, press, and the baby's family. Gaston Means, an intimate of former Bureau chief William J. Burns and an agent himself until Hoover turned him out, returned from "retirement" to "help" in the search. And Dr. John F. Condon, a retired school teacher, found himself the center of notoriety when he offered to act as intermediary for the Lindbergh family.

Through an advertisement in a Bronx, New York, throwaway newspaper, Condon—using the name "Jafsie"—made contact with "John," the kidnapper. A month and a day after the kidnapping, "Jafsie" met "John" in St. Raymond's cemetery in the Bronx to give him $50,000 in the denominations dictated by the kidnap note. In return, he was told that Charles Lindbergh Jr. was alive and well on a boat named "Nellie," at anchor in Martha's Vineyard, an island off the coast of

Massachusetts. There was, of course, no such boat.

But before this, Gaston Means, known as a crook in Washington, was summoned by Mrs. Evelyn Walsh McLean, who wanted to put her millions to work at solving the case. Mrs. McLean reasoned that it takes a thief to catch a thief. Would Means help? It so happened, Means told her, that he could. Just a few days before the kidnapping, Means confided, he had run into an ex-convict he had gotten to know during an enforced stay at the Atlanta Penitentiary. His friend had tried to enlist his aid in a big kidnapping job. When he learned that the Lindbergh baby had been snatched, Means told Mrs. McLean, he had been able to discover through his underworld contacts that the kidnapper was a member of the gang which had pulled off the job. He was sure he could break the case.

In short order, Means was back with great news for Mrs. McLean. The gang would deliver the Lindbergh baby to him for $100,000. Less than a week after the kidnapping, Means had the money and she had his promise that it would remain safely with him until the baby was returned. So that all parties could communicate without police interference, a code was devised in which the gang leader was the "Fox" and the Lindbergh child the "Book." There were long-distance phone calls and the "Fox" even visited Mrs. McLean's home. But even after Mrs. McLean had given Means another $4,000 and was on the verge of giving him still another $35,000, Means had not produced the child. The police, he claimed, were interfering, frightening off the "gang." Finally, Mrs. McLean's attorney notified Hoover and the Bureau.

Means, of course, persisted in his story that he was dealing with an underworld gang. But his protestations came to nothing when the FBI tracked down the "Fox." The only clues Hoover had were the long-distance calls made by Means and the "Fox" to Mrs. McLean. But these were all made from pay stations in South Carolina, New York, Maryland, and New Jersey. Painstakingly, the Bureau's agents began checking out all long-distance calls made in the immediate area of the pay station on the days that calls were made to Mrs. McLean. They discovered two long-distance calls, made back to back, from the same pay phone—one to Means and the other to the home of one Norman T. Whitaker. In investigative parlance, Identification Division records "reflected" that Whitaker was an ex-convict and a disbarred attorney. When he was identified by Mrs. McLean as the "Fox" the sordid case was solved. Means was sentenced to fifteen years, Whitaker to eighteen months, for conspiracy to commit larceny.*

On May 12, 1932, the body of Charles A. Lindbergh Jr. was found by a truck driver's helper, not far from the Lindbergh home. The discovery was accidental. Three weeks later, Congress passed the so-called Lindbergh Law which gave the Federal government jurisdiction in kidnapping cases and imposed a death penalty for transporting a kidnapped person across state lines. On September 15, 1934, the first solid lead in the case fell into the hands of local police authorities and the Bureau.

In the Bronx, a motorist paid for gasoline with a $10 gold certificate. The attendant noted the license of the car on the bill, suspicious because all gold certificates had been called in by the Treasury some eighteen months earlier when the United States went off the gold standard. A bank teller realized that the bill was part of the Lindbergh ransom money, the Bureau was notified, and a check with the New York State Motor Vehicle License Bureau showed that the license number belonged to the car of Bruno Richard Hauptmann. When he was arrested, one of the ransom bills was found in his pocket and $13,000 of the ransom money was found in his garage. Hauptmann was identified by "Jafsie" as the "John" who received the ransom in the cemetery. Other damning evidence was turned up by the Bureau and local police, linking Hauptmann to the homemade

---

*On the witness stand, Means stuck by his story that he had tried to ransom the Lindbergh baby. After his testimony, he sat down next to Hoover. "Well," he said, "what did you think of that?" Hoover looked at him coldly, "It was all a pack of lies," he answered. Means grinned. "But you've got to admit it was a whale of a good story."

ladder used in the kidnapping. He was convicted in a trial that was a Roman holiday for the press* and electrocuted on April 3, 1936—four years and thirty-three days after the crime.

The Lindbergh kidnapping aroused the public and changed national attitudes toward crime and violence—at least for a while. But before the Bureau could take advantage of public revulsion, both Hoover and the Bureau were confronted by a crisis which might have changed the course of history for them.

In November 1932, Franklin Delano Roosevelt was elected President of the United States. As the incoming Administration began making its plans, Washington was filled with rumors that there would be a general housecleaning to sweep out of government service all those known to have had the confidence of the outgoing President. Among those being widely nominated for governmental oblivion was J. Edgar Hoover, who was considered a protégé of Herbert Hoover. It was no secret that Louis McHenry Howe, whose behind-the-scenes influence on Roosevelt was great, wanted J. Edgar out and a more manipulatable man put in his place. President Hoover, however, heard the rumors. Roosevelt had held him off from the moment of election to the hour of Inauguration, refusing to confer with him. But as the two men were riding down Pennsylvania Avenue, after the swearing-in ceremony, Hoover brought up the subject.

He remarked to Roosevelt that he had been "somewhat responsible" for J. Edgar's appointment, that he was a lawyer of "uncommon ability and character," that he had eliminated politics from the Bureau and staffed it with excellent and trained men. And he urged President Roosevelt to retain "young Hoover" in his post. Roosevelt was noncommittal, but he promised to give thought to Hoover's advice. Perhaps because the New Deal Administration had other fish to fry, and matters of

*The press did not cover itself with glory in its coverage. One piece of evidence —Jafsie's phone number written on a panel in a closet of Hauptmann's house —was planted by an overzealous newspaperman who led police to it.

greater importance than the political ax-job desired by Howe, nothing was done. But the rumors persisted. In June 1933, Washington's leading political gossip columnist predicted:

The Bureau of Investigation, a little known department to the general public, will be abolished, and in its place will be set up a small, compact, and efficient organization charged with making all investigations for the various government departments. Instead of the 800 investigators now serving under J. Edgar Hoover, bureau chief [there were in fact only 326 investigators at the time], it is probable the investigatory personnel will be no larger than 350 or 400.

This item, based on more solid ground than the columnist's usual output, had been planted by Louis Howe. A wave of kidnappings troubled Roosevelt, and he had asked one of his chief brain-trusters, Raymond Moley, to suggest ways in which the Justice Department and the Bureau could be strengthened so that they could better handle the situation. This, Howe believed, was a good time to deliver the *coup de grace*.

"Part of what was in Roosevelt's mind," Moley has said, "I knew was a doubt about the desirability of continuing J. Edgar Hoover in office—a doubt put there by Louis. When the Administration had come into office in March, there were many rumors that Hoover was to be ousted in favor of a Democratic politician. I had vehemently defended the magnificent work of Hoover to the President and Louis. I like to think that what I did in August 1933 gave me the opportunity to strengthen Hoover still more and to work with him in the development of plans that proved to be successful."

As director of the Bureau, Hoover had served under two Republican presidents. The changeover to a Democratic president had come at a time of great national travail and dislocation in which old values and old traditions were being questioned and discarded. He was aware of the anomaly of his position, but that was not the only thing he had on his mind. On June 10, 1933, Roosevelt had merged the Bureau of Investigation and the Prohibition Bureau into a single Division of Investigation in the Justice Department. Administratively, and from a public relations viewpoint, that spelled trouble. The Prohibition Bureau was corrupt, discredited, and hated. As a law enforcement agency, it was worthless, as were its more than one thousand agents. "They would have swamped us," Hoover remarked years later, "and undone all the work we had done to make the Bureau honest, sound, and efficient."

Under the previous Administration, there would have been no executive order such as Roosevelt had signed without some consultation with Hoover, if only as a matter of courtesy. Hoover was therefore compelled to take his objections to Roosevelt's first Attorney General, the capable and conscientious Homer S. Cummings. He discovered that Cummings was not only sympathetic but understood the nature of Hoover's objections. If it was necessary to put the Bureau of Investigation and the Prohibition Bureau under one head, Hoover urged, his organization should remain a separate entity—maintaining the independence of its personnel, its files, and its general mission. This was a retreat on Hoover's part, since one of his conditions for taking the directorship had been that he would report only to the Attorney General. But he argued further that merging the two bureaus would make no sense. In a memo to Cummings, he noted that the Prohibition Bureau, "by reason of the forthcoming repeal of the Eighteenth Amendment, will necessarily recede in size and diminish in importance"—in fact, would no longer have any reason for being. Hoover won over Cummings and Moley won over Roosevelt. The executive order became a dead letter, and Hoover was not replaced. What in two years time would become the FBI was saved.

7.

Enter the G—Man

PERHAPS IT WAS HIS UPBRINGING. PERHAPS IT WAS THE WHIM OF IRON
which he inherited from his mother. Perhaps it was only a
lawman's normal tilt. But the fact, simple or complex, was that
John Edgar Hoover deeply and harshly hated crime and criminals. Both struck at his Old Testament belief that man must
earn his bread by the sweat of his brow, that to do otherwise
was both sinful and vicious. He had no patience with the Robin
Hood *mythos,* and he saw no glamour in the forcible seizure of
what other people, whether rich or poor, had amassed. Nor had
he any patience with the reformer's view that society was responsible for the criminal. He saw criminals as people apart,
much as the criminologist Cesare Lombroso had held years
before.

It was this view which, perhaps subconsciously, brought him

to that metaphor of a city of criminals which he used in his speeches and in the first chapter of his book on the gangster era, *Persons in Hiding.*

"If every house in a city of more than four million were occupied by thieves and thugs and murderers," he wrote in 1938, "if the street cars and subways were manned by kidnappers, and patronized only by people with criminal records,—if every office building were filled with the spawn of the cell block, of the prison yard and the reformatory . . . if every baseball park, every stadium, and every motion picture theater were filled with nearly a quarter-million potential murderers, and with the half-million or more potential car thieves and more than a million petty crooks, grafters, chiselers, confidence and bunco men who live by stealing what we have earned . . . in fact, if every inhabitant in that city were one of the vicious lawbreakers whose fingerprints now repose in the Identification Unit of the Federal Bureau of Investigation, then and only then would we have a concentration of our lawless army . . ."

He could not understand why so many people could be tolerant of crime and solicitous of criminals. "Even with this illustration before one," he continued, "there might be a temptation to view it as something apart, something to concern another, but not to be considered as a matter of importance to one's household. Until this viewpoint can be changed, that City of Crime will continue to grow; and all the law enforcement in the world can only besiege it, without hope of its annihilation. Only one person can eliminate crime. That is the honest citizen. And he must do more than be appalled by it. Thus, crime eradication is more than a task of man-hunting. It concerns itself greatly with enlightenment."

Hoover saw himself not only as the scourge of the criminal. It was his responsibility to overcome the reluctance of the average citizen to become involved in the assault on the City of Crime.

One of the difficulties which law enforcement men encounter in attempting to make crime understandable to the honest person is that of correctly revealing the criminal brain. It is so hard to persuade the average person that its working is different from that of our own minds, that it reasons by different standards . . . It must be remembered that the true criminal, being nearer to the beast than others of us, also is nearer to the instincts by which beasts live—the predatory habits of depredation and seizure, plus the inherent instincts of escape. In animal life, these take the form of visual camouflage. In the criminal, the transposition is mental. He changes his viewpoint to suit his desires. And since there are certain traits necessary to crime, such as selfishness, ego, the easy ability to regard as persecution anything which conflicts with personal desires, he is almost invariably self-centered enough to regard anything as fair as long as it attains his desired object . . .

Therefore, if you want to understand the criminal brain, you must become a momentary actor . . . Tell yourself that if you have a gun in your hand and the man at whom you point it is unarmed, then you are a brave man and he is a coward. School yourself to think that you amount to something if you can get away with murder . . . Look upon all law enforcement officers . . . as inherent crooks who would be stealing, as you are doing, if they "only had the nerve." Tell yourself that persons are fools to work for money and that you are smart because you . . . can take the fruits of toil from those who have labored for it . . . Be maudlin concerning yourself and cynical about the feelings of others. Believe yourself fine and noble if you indulge in cheap sentimentalities . . . if "you have always been good to your mother." However, should these components become impedimental, have no compunction whatever about deserting your sweetheart, using your mother's home as a hideout, shooting down a baby or choking your dog, all to the purpose that you hate to do it, but after all, you've got to live . . . And no person who cannot understand that this is the lawbreaker's mind should have any part whatever in dealing with the persons who constitute our army of more than four million enemies of society.

In some of his speeches, Hoover could say in referring to the high incidence, even in those years, of youthful crimes that "only in the rarest of instances of diseased minds can we say that the first offender commits crimes out of sheer antisocial sentiments. Children are driven to crime because of deep-laid faults in society such as poverty, degeneracy, and because their elders neglect them. When youth commits a crime, generally it is because . . . of laxity in early discipline . . . because of distorted views held by those who should know better and who have allowed adolescent minds to take a downward direction." But he still lashed out at criminals as "blots of scum from the boiling pot of the underworld" or "public rats." And he still centered his fire on the "sentimental yammerheads" and "moronic adults" whose "idiotic idolatry of cowardly outlaws" encouraged crime.

He took particular pride in the fearsome reputation that the Federal Bureau of Investigation, as it was officially designated in 1935, had among members of the underworld. In articles, in speeches, and in conversation, he delighted in telling how the Bureau's agents had gotten the nickname of G-Men. "Back in September of 1933," Hoover would recount, "a group of our special agents surrounded a house in Memphis where George 'Machine-Gun' Kelly was hiding out. For two months FBI had been trailing this gangster and his wife. As the FBI agents and local police surrounded the house and entered, one of them called out, 'We are Federal officers. Come out with your hands up.' 'Machine-Gun' Kelly's hands were trembling as he reached for the ceiling. 'Don't shoot, G-men! Don't shoot!' That abbreviation of 'Government men' passed along the grapevine of the underworld. It was both a nickname and a warning."

Behind the very real fear of the FBI felt by lawless elements, there was more than Hoover's determination to extirpate the "public rats." Congress, at the urging of President Roosevelt and based on recommendations that grew out of Raymond Moley's study of the crime problem, had enacted a series of laws which broadened the FBI's jurisdiction and opened the Federal courts' powers to prosecute—the Federal kidnapping statute, the Federal Bank Robbery Act, the Federal Extortion Act, the National Stolen Property Act, the Unlawful Flight to Avoid Prosecution Act, and the Federal Anti-Racketeering law. Of considerable importance to Hoover and the FBI, moreover, the Congress had authorized the Bureau's agents to carry guns without getting special authorization and to make arrests as

Federal officers rather than relying on local police who sometimes had ties with the very criminals the FBI was trailing.

This meant greater emphasis on what can only be called the combat training of FBI agents. Representative Wright Patman, in a long account of the Bureau's work, explained it to Congress in 1935. Though the Bureau had high educational requirements, he said, "to Mr. Hoover they are not sufficient to enable an agent to start the work of investigating ... Hoover, therefore, instituted a training school for agents. Here, over a period of 14 weeks, the newly appointed agent receives an intensive course in all phases of law enforcement work. He studies the elements of each of the offenses against the United States; he becomes thoroughly versed in the methods of scientific crime detection; he becomes an expert in the science of fingerprinting and a qualified handler of all types of firearms." Added to the training in firearms, special agents were required to develop proficiency in the techniques of hand-to-hand and body-to-body fighting— all necessary if they were to carry out their new role.

In the fight against crime, Hoover also created an FBI National Academy to train local police officials in modern techniques, to help establish uniform police methods, and to bring local authorities within the ambience of the Bureau, thereby laying a groundwork for future cooperation between the Federal agency and state and city police. Testifying before the Senate Appropriations Committee years later, Hoover said:

The reason that National Academy was created in 1935 was that at the time . . . there were demands that we set up a national police to stamp out kidnapping. I have always been vigorously opposed to anything savoring of a national police force. There was then a gap between the local and Federal authorities. There was jealousy, incompetence, and inefficiency at the local level. . . .

In one particular city we were in pursuit of John Dillinger, and we had advance word that he was coming to that city to visit a doctor for the purpose of having a bullet wound treated. We went to the local authorities, as we usually did, and asked their cooperation . . . We surrounded the block . . . An hour before his time for arrival the afternoon paper came out stating that Dillinger was due for treatment.

Of course, Dillinger never showed up in that town. It was two or three months later when we had the gun battle in Chicago and had to kill him.

That sort of thing prevailed in those days, but we do not find a similar situation today. That has been largely done away with due to the fact that for a period of years our Academy has been in operation and these officers have come here ... These graduates [of the Academy] work with us in full cooperation and harmony. That is the American way of avoiding any resemblance of national control or of a national police system to which, as I say, I am very much opposed.

But mechanisms and organizational charts are never enough. The major factor had to be leadership and dedication—and these Hoover had, as even his strongest critics conceded. At the height of the "G-Man" years, Courtney Riley Cooper, then writing extensively about the FBI for *American Magazine* and other publications, described Hoover at work:

Everything which J. Edgar Hoover does is directed. The man is almost fanatical in his energy, the strength and the time which he gives to his job; it is nothing for him to work fourteen to sixteen hours a day. His brain is one of the most rapidly functioning mechanisms I have ever encountered; I have seen him direct the handling of four big criminal chases simultaneously, veering from one phone to another as he commanded the hunt, instantly freeing his mind from the concentration of one case that he might give his entire attention to the other. His associates believe that he possesses a sixth sense which allows him instantly to find the flaw in seeming perfection; often a few scribbled words in red ink, written down instantly after the reading of an investigative report, will be the starting point of a new line of investigation which will close an important case, resulting in the conviction of an offender.

Because of his involvement in the minutiae of the Bureau's work, the movement of its special agents, and the handling of every case, the FBI record of crime detection was in a very real way, the record of John Edgar Hoover, even if he was not personally present at the arrest or solution. The Bureau was an extension of himself. In those days particularly, nothing happened within the FBI that escaped his notice or attention. No word of approval or opprobrium went by him—and his letters of thanks to newsmen and writers who commented favorably on the FBI were a steady flow. With bank robberies occurring at a rate of two a day and kidnappings continuing despite passage of the Lindbergh law, Hoover needed sixteen hours of each day to get his work done. He expected the same of his agents.

The public outrage over the Lindbergh kidnapping helped win over the public to more active law enforcement. But the Kansas City Massacre sent waves of horror through the country and won over many who had been dismayed by the thought that the Federal government, not the states, should be involved in the sordid business of running down—sometimes shooting— bank robbers and killers. The Kansas City Massacre, in one of the quirks of history, took place just at the time when Drew Pearson was predicting Hoover's imminent departure from the Washington scene—and when Louis Howe was working from his tiny White House office to speed that day. It shook President Roosevelt and opened the door of the Oval Room to Hoover.

FBI agents had climaxed a three-year search for Frank Nash, ex-convict and gunman, by capturing him in Hot Springs, Arkansas. With them, and an invaluable collaborator in the exploit, was Police Chief Otto Reed of McAlester, Oklahoma. On information that Nash's mobster friends were planning an ambush to free him, Reed and the agents secretly moved Nash from Hot Springs, then an underworld resort, to Fort Smith where they boarded a train to Kansas City. But there was a leak somewhere along the line, and a gangster "posse" made of Vern Miller, Charles "Pretty Boy" Floyd, and Adam Richetti—all vicious killers—was organized to meet the train when it arrived at 7:15 a.m. At Union Station, Nash and his guard were met by two more FBI agents and two Kansas City detectives. The seven men guarding Nash walked rapidly to the east end of the station where an FBI car was parked.

As Nash and his guards were piling into the car, the outlaw "posse"—armed with two submachine guns and an automobatic—burst upon them with shouts of "Up! Up! Up!" As the

agents and officers not yet in the car wheeled around, the outlaws opened fire. Reed, the two Kansas City detectives, and an
FBI agent were killed in the first burst of bullets, two agents
were wounded—one of them with two .45 slugs in his spine and
another in the pelvic cavity. One agent was unharmed. And
Nash was killed by a bullet to the brain, leading Hoover to
believe that the mob wanted him dead, fearing that he would
talk when questioned by the FBI.

A month and six days later, the FBI's special "kidnap line,"
National 8–7117—publicized by Hoover and Attorney General
Homer Cummings—flashed at headquarters in Washington. It
was after midnight, and Hoover was at home asleep. But following his instructions, the FBI operator switched the call to
him. The caller was Mrs. Charles F. Urschel of Oklahoma City,
and in tears she reported to Hoover that her husband, an oil
man, and his friend, Walter R. Jarrett, had just been kidnapped.
Mrs. Urschel said that she and her husband had been playing
bridge with the Jarretts when two armed men had walked into
the house and demanded, "Which one of you is Mr. Urschel?"
Neither man had answered, so the kidnappers had taken both
of them.

Hoover immediately called the Special Agent in Charge at
the Oklahoma City field office and ordered him to take over.
The SAC began calling up special agents, giving them orders to
go to the Urschel home, to cooperate fully with local authorities, and to follow FBI policy on kidnapping: Do nothing that
will endanger the life of the victim; give no advice to the family
on whether it should or should not pay ransom for his release.
An hour after the first FBI man had arrived at the Urschel
home, Jarrett was back. He had been driven to the outskirts of
town with Urschel, his money taken from him, and he had
watched the kidnap car as it headed south. It was not until four
days later that the kidnappers made contact.

A Western Union messenger delivered a package to one of
Urschel's friends. It contained a letter in Urschel's handwriting
and instructions to E. E. Kirkpatrick, another friend, demand-

ing $200,000 and giving him the wording of the advertisement he should place in the *Daily Oklahoman* if he was ready to pay the ransom. When the advertisement appeared in the paper's classified pages—it read:

FOR SALE—160 Acres land, good five room house, deep well, Also Cows, Tools, Tractor, Corn, and Hay. $3750 for quick sale. TERMS. Box H-807.

Kirkpatrick received instructions to register at the Muehlebach Hotel in Kansas City and wait for a telephone call. That call gave Kirkpatrick further instructions. He was to take a taxi to the LaSalle Hotel and walk west, carrying the ransom money. (The FBI had made a record of the serial numbers of all the bills—$20 bank notes.) As Kirkpatrick walked down a Kansas City street, a man approached him and said, "Mr. Kincaid, I'll take that bag. The deed to the farm will be delivered in twelve hours."

When Urschel arrived at his house the following night, unharmed, the FBI questioned him closely. "Tell us everything you remember, no matter how unimportant it may seem to you." Urschel had a good memory for detail, but what he had to tell seemed of little use to him. He had been blindfolded with gauze, cotton, and adhesive tape. At what he thought must be daylight, following the abduction, the kidnap car had been driven into a barn—or perhaps a garage. There he had been moved to what seemed to be a larger and heavier car—perhaps a Buick, perhaps a Cadillac. He had been made to lie down on the floor of the back, and something had been thrown over him. At what he thought must be three hours later, the car stopped for gas. The attendant was a woman because he heard her voice.

"How are the crops doing," one of the kidnappers had asked her.

"The crops are burned up," she had answered, "but we may make some broom corn."

When the kidnappers stopped again, at a barn—or perhaps a

garage—one of them said that it was 2:30 p.m. They had re-mained there until nightfall, and Urschel was given a ham sandwich and coffee. He and his captors walked to a nearby house. The next day, he was taken to another house, a short driving distance away. It had to be a farm, Urschel reported, because he could hear the barnyard noises of cows, chickens, and hogs. A tin cup from which he drank had no handle. The water had a mineral taste. Though he was handcuffed to a chair, he was able to lift his blindfold enough to see his watch. Every morning at about 9:45 and every afternoon at about 5:45, he could hear a plane, except on a Sunday, when there was a heavy rainstorm and no plane passed overhead. On the day of his release, he was taken to Norman, Oklahoma and left in a field.

It seemed like very little to go on, but Hoover—directing the search for the kidnappers from Washington—was optimistic. And he was right. The schedules of all airlines passing within six hundred miles of Oklahoma City were studied. United States Weather Bureau meteorological records for the area were also studied. And with this, the case was solved. American Airways records showed that on the Sunday of Urschel's cap-tivity, a plane on the Fort Worth-Amarillo run had changed course to avoid a rainstorm. Weather Bureau records showed that this Texas area had been severely hit by drought until the Sunday downpour. Plane speeds showed that the Fort Worth morning plane and the Amarillo afternoon plane passed over an area near Paradise, Texas, at the times mentioned by Urschel.

Like the "deductions" of Sherlock Holmes, it looked simple in retrospect. But simple or not, careful reasoning gave the FBI the information it needed. The house where Urschel had been held belonged to Robert Shannon, stepfather of Kathryn Kelly, wife of "Machine Gun" Kelly. FBI agents found the tin cup with no handle, the chain that Urschel remembered, and the water that tasted of minerals. Confronted by Urschel, Shannon and his wife confessed that they had guarded him for "Machine

Gun" Kelly and an accomplice, Albert Bates. The FBI found Bates in Denver. "Machine Gun" and Kathryn were tracked down in Memphis. On September 26, 1933, FBI agents and local police surrounded the house where the Kellys were hiding out. It was at the moment of this arrest that Kelly contributed to the American language with his famous plea, "Don't shoot, G-Men!" And Hoover proved that kidnapping and the other gangster depredations were "in interstate commerce" and could not be handled by local police forces, each working in its own jurisdiction. As Don Whitehead pointed out later in his book on the FBI:

> The oil man was kidnapped in Oklahoma City, Oklahoma. He was held captive near Paradise, Texas. The ransom demand was mailed from Joplin, Missouri. The money was paid in Kansas City, Missouri. The "hot" money was circulated in St. Paul, Minnesota, and some of it was found in Oregon. Part of the money was dug up in a cotton patch in Texas. One of the kidnappers was caught in Denver, Colorado, and the other in Memphis, Tennessee.

The FBI haul was a big one in the Urschel case. Twenty-one people were convicted, with life sentences for the Shannons, the Kellys, and Bates. Crooked lawyers, underworld operators who circulated the ransom money, and others who played a part in the kidnapping received sentences of up to ten years. And the gangs developed a new respect for Hoover's G-Men.

8.

Dillinger Et Al.

JOHN DILLINGER COULD HAVE BEEN A SUCCESSFUL LAWYER, BUSINESS-man, or master mechanic. He had more than average intelligence and great manual dexterity. He liked people and people liked him—until he was crossed, and then he became dangerous. He wanted what he wanted when he wanted it—and he wanted to come by it easily. He was not driven to crime by his environment or by his associations but sought it out and let it lead him. These aspects of the Dillinger personality had a repugnant fascination for J. Edgar Hoover. He kept the memorabilia of the desperado's capture on view in the outer room of his office on Pennsylvania Avenue, and he referred to him with more than coincidental frequency.

For to Hoover, Dillinger represented the enigma of the criminal mind, an enigma he could no more fathom than he could that of Soviet agents like Alger Hiss or Harry Dexter White. Hoover could understand though not forgive the slum child who grew up surrounded by crime and slipped into it. But Dillinger had no excuse except his own perversity. For Hoover, moreover, Dillinger was the prime catalyst for attitudes in America he found reprehensible and inexcusable. To the very end of Dillinger's life, and after his death, he won the solicitous help and sympathy of well-meaning people who saw him as the victim. This was infuriating to Hoover, and his speeches during that period were heavy with fulminations against those who, in his mind, encouraged crime by coddling the criminal. After Dillinger's death, Hoover was roundly attacked, criticism even coming from associates in the Justice Department, for saying, "There is no romance in a dead rat."

In the days when the "dead rat" was a legend-in-reverse, sob sisters and their brothers created the myth that he had been born on a poverty-stricken dirt farm and had soured on the world after watching his father working from dawn to dark in a losing battle against drouth and a hard-hearted local banker. In fact, however, Dillinger came of a reasonably prosperous middle-class family and lived his childhood in a comfortable residential section of Indianapolis. His father, a grocer, held strong religious and moral views which he attempted to pass on to John. As John Toland, in his account of the Dillinger days, reports, "It was Johnnie Dillinger who had the first bicycle on the block, who spent the most on fireworks, who always had enough money to treat the other children to candy."

He had strange ideas of fun. When he was still a small boy, he piled rocks on the roof of a friend's porch—and then dumped them off on the head of the friend's drunken father. On another occasion, he tied a friend to the carrier of a lumber mill, threw the switch, and allowed the screaming boy to come within a yard of the whirling saw before turning off the current. When he was twelve, he organized his own gang, the Dirty Dozen. One of the gang's activities was to steal coal from the Pennsylvania Railroad and sell it in town. Caught and required to appear in

Juvenile Court, he stood before the judge refusing to remove his slouch cap, chewing gum, and grinning defiantly—the lopsided grin that became a kind of trademark. At thirteen, he committed his first rape, then turned the girl over to his companions while he stood guard.

Refusing to go to high school, he moved from job to job—always doing well—"very fast and accurate . . . sober, honest, and very industrious," one of his employers said of him—but quitting out of boredom.

When his father retired, selling his store and the four houses he owned, the Dillingers moved to a farm in Mooresville. There, young Dillinger joined the church, went to high school though under protest, and was popular with the boys and girls who enjoyed riding in his father's Apperson "Jack Rabbit." But in school, he failed almost every subject. He was also staying out all night, becoming a poolroom hanger-on, and after having run through all the girls in Mooresville and neighboring towns taking up with prostitutes, one of whom gave him gonorrhea. Quitting high school, he got a job in Indianapolis. His first serious run-in with the law came in July of 1923, when he stole a car. To get away from his family, he joined the Navy, went AWOL, and then deserted. Back in Indianapolis, he got a job in a machine shop and lived with a woman by whom he had two children.

In time, Dillinger left his woman and children and returned to Mooresville and his father's farm. Shortly thereafter, he married a sixteen-year-old girl. A few weeks later, he was arrested for stealing forty-one chickens, but his father was able to convince a friendly judge to quash the case. In September of 1924, he attempted to rob a grocer, striking him on the head with a large bolt and, in the struggle, firing a .32 revolver at his intended victim. For this, he was sentenced to ten to twenty years at Pendleton reformatory. To the superintendent of that institution, he said defiantly, "I won't cause you any trouble except to escape." And true to his word, he made three unsuccessful attempts. Dillinger's job in the prison was making manhole covers. This was hard work. To get out of it, he poured hot steel into one of his work shoes, then poured acid on his injured foot, ulcerating the wound. At his own request, he was transferred to the Michigan City penitentiary, where two men whose friendship he had made, hardened criminals, were incarcerated. At the penitentiary, he alternated between good behavior and bad—caught gambling, caught in bed with another inmate, caught stealing melons and tomatoes. When he wanted to, he could turn out twice the work of any other man in the shirt shop where he had been assigned. He even invented a gauge for the machine he used. Then, suddenly, Dillinger's behavior became all good. He had decided to get a parole.

What galled J. Edgar Hoover was not so much that Dillinger succeeded in getting Governor Paul McNutt's signature on the parole papers but that otherwise responsible citizens could conspire to bring this about. Dillinger's father, who knew the nature of his boy and what direction his life had taken, nevertheless used the excuse of his second wife's impending death to plead with the Michigan City warden to release the convict. There was an element of irony in this, since Dillinger had never been close to her and had, in fact, resented her deeply. The grocer he had beaten and attempted to rob, along with some two hundred of Mooresville residents, petitioned for his release, though they knew that he had been a thief and a hellmaker before incarceration. A doctor in Mooresville wrote to Governor McNutt that Dillinger "was never in trouble until this unfortunate circumstance placed him in the condition he is now." And when Dillinger returned home and wept at a church service, he became a hero to the 1,800 inhabitants of the quiet Quaker community. This was several weeks after his release, and in that time he had already held up a bank, two supermarkets, and a drugstore.

What the authorities would not know until much later was that Dillinger's good behavior and the release which it earned him had been part of a plot of a group of accomplished bank robbers and stick-up men with long sentences. Dillinger was to get out and raise the money for a prison break. And this he did, being captured almost at the time that his accomplices were breaking out of the Michigan City penitentiary. They were grateful and rescued him from the smalltown jail where he was being held—killing a sheriff in the process. From that point on, Dillinger embarked on a career of murder and robbery that carried him around the country.

Ten men died in that spree, and seven others were seriously wounded. To Hoover, these deaths were directly attributable to the "yammerheads" who let Dillinger loose with no effort to discover whether or not he had been rehabilitated. But neither Hoover nor the FBI could do a thing to move against Dillinger and his murderous gang. He had violated no Federal laws, and the state and local authorities wanted no help from Washington. It was Dillinger himself who gave the FBI its opportunty. Wanted in Indiana for the murder of a policeman, he was spotted in Tucson, Arizona and picked up by local authorities with three members of his gang. At his hideout, the police found three submachine guns, several rifles, five bullet-proof vests which had been stolen from police arsenals in Indiana, and $25,000 in cash.

Dillinger was brought back to Indiana and locked up in the escape-proof Crown Point country jail to await trial. To while away the time, he took up whittling, carved out a wooden gun, and frightened his guards into releasing him. Picking up two Tommy guns along the way, he put his guards behind bars and headed for Chicago in the sheriff's automobile. This was his fatal mistake. Crossing a state line in a stolen car was a violation of the Dyer Act, and this gave the FBI authority to begin its relentless pursuit of Dillinger.

Hoover had been waiting for some slip, some event which would allow him to enter the pursuit of Dillinger. He called in one of his best agents, Samuel P. Cowley, to give him a green light and to reassure him that all the Bureau's resources were at his disposal. "Stay on Dillinger," he said. "Follow the trail wherever it takes you. Find everyone who was ever connected with the gang, no matter how remotely. Take Dillinger alive if you can, but take him. And protect yourself." It was a big order. For following Dillinger's second escape, Hoover's office was flooded with tips from people who reported that they had seen him here or there at widely separated parts of the country. On a single day, there were two hundred such tips, all contradictory. But all the tips were investigated—they had to be—by the FBI and by local authorities. And one tip almost paid off. The FBI was informed that Dillinger had arranged for treatment of a wound he had received in one of his escapades. Cowley knew the time and the place—staking out his men to capture Dillinger. But the press, then as now, was more interested in a good story. A local police officer passed the word on to a reporter and, hours before Dillinger was to show at the Starks Building in Louisville, the *Herald Post* appeared on the streets with a screaming page one headline:

U.S. LAYS DILLINGER TRAP AROUND
STARKS BUILDING

Dillinger found another doctor.

On the day that Dillinger was rescued from the FBI trap by a Louisville newspaper, a group of Mooresville citizens were circulating a seven-point petition to Governor McNutt. Point two stated that "John Dillinger has never manifested a vicious, revengeful, or bloodthirsty disposition, there being considerable doubts as to whether he has ever committed a murder." Point five argued that Dillinger should be pardoned if he surrendered to law enforcement officials, and point six added: "It is our opinion that many of the financial institutions of the state have just as criminally robbed our citizens without any effort being made to punish the perpetrators." It did not take long before Governor McNutt's secretary, Wayne Coy, took up the refrain. "There does not seem to me to be any escape from the fact that the State of Indiana made John Dillinger the Public Enemy that he is today," he said. There is no exact record of how Hoover responded to this, but according to all reports he was vitriolic.

It was this kind of public attitude which permitted Dillinger to spend a weekend with relatives and friends in Mooresville, an event reported only to the press which did not inform the police until Dillinger had moved on, or to take vacation jaunts to the north woods of Wisconsin for weekends of poker and fishing. At Little Bohemia, a Wisconsin lake resort, the FBI thought they had him surrounded, but he escaped, along with the rest of the gang, leaving their women behind. But the ring was closing. The press could rail at the FBI for letting Dillinger slip through its fingers at Little Bohemia, and Will Rogers could write, "Well, they had Dillinger surrounded and was all ready to shoot him when he came out, but another bunch of folks came out ahead, so they just shot them instead. Dillinger is going to accidentally get with some innocent bystanders some time, then he will get shot."

Congress, of course, was up in arms over the "blunder," but President Roosevelt called in the legislative leaders and reminded them pointedly that twelve anticrime bills had been languishing in committee. The bills were reported out the next day and ten of them were passed within the week. Hoover and Attorney General Cummings pressed the President to do more than that, to call on the people to cooperate with law enforcement agencies, and he complied in a personal message to the country. "I ask citizens, individually and as organized groups, to recognize the facts and meet them with courage and determination . . . ," he said. "Law enforcement and gangster extermination cannot be made completely effective while a substantial part of the public looks with tolerance upon known criminals, or applauds efforts to romanticize crime."

At the time, the reward offered for Dillinger's capture—for violating his parole—was $25. The Justice Department raised the ante, offering a reward of $10,000 for Dillinger, $5,000 for information leading to his capture. Dillinger joked about it, flattered by the sum. But it pushed him into plastic surgery which he thought would change his appearance—it didn't—and to clumsy efforts at erasing his fingerprints. He was rapidly running out of money, and he needed at least $50,000 to hole up in Mexico. Every holdup was more dangerous than the previous one, and Dillinger knew that somewhere along the line the reward money would tempt one of the people around him. "My time's coming," he said, "but I don't know just when it'll be."

Unable to find reinforcements for his gang as the FBI devoted manpower and ingenuity to his capture, Dillinger dropped out of sight. Hoover pressed Cowley who pressed the agents under him. They knew Dillinger was in Chicago, but he had removed himself from those underworld contacts which might deliberately or inadvertently betray him. Hoover conferred on an almost hourly basis with his agents in Chicago. Like Dillinger, he felt that the time was coming. And then the break came.

Using the name of Jimmie Lawrence and posing as a Board of Trade clerk, Dillinger had taken up with Polly Hamilton, an attractive twenty-six-year-old divorcee who worked as a waitress in a Chicago restaurant. She was a roomer at the North Side apartment of Mrs. Anna Sage, a bawdyhouse madam who, after three convictions, faced deportation to her native Romania. Through Polly, Dillinger had become a part of the Sage household, and in time he admitted to Anna (her real name was Ana Cumpanas) that he was the famous outlaw. He became known in the neighborhood as an affable man who ate strawberry sundaes at the corner ice cream parlor, patronized the local bookmaker, and liked to go to the movies. Ana was not particularly troubled by the identity of Polly Hamilton's boy friend. But as deportation loomed, she decided that she might make a deal with the Justice Department.

Through intermediaries, she made contact with Special Agent Cowley and Melvin Purvis, the Special Agent in Charge of the Chicago field office. If she had firm assurances from the FBI that it would block her deportation—and that she would get the reward money—Mrs. Cumpanas said, she could lead them to Dillinger. Purvis could not guarantee the entire reward, but he promised her that she would get a substantial part of it. As to the deportation, he could make no commitments for the Immigration Service. But he convinced her that he would do his best for her. Ana Cumpanas agreed to the deal. Then she informed Cowley and Purvis that Dillinger was taking her and Polly to the movies the next day, a Sunday. She wasn't quite sure what movie they were seeing—she thought it would be at the Marbro—but she agreed to notify the FBI the following day, the moment she knew.

An elated Purvis immediately phoned Hoover who had given instructions that he was to be informed immediately if there was any break in the case. He was at home in Washington reading a novel when the call came through, transferred to his direct line by the FBI switchboard operator. He would later recall that as he reached out to pick up the phone, the thought flashed through his mind, "It's about Dillinger. The madam has come through." Purvis's excited voice confirmed his thought. "He's going to the theater tonight," said Purvis without using any names. "We think it will be the Marbro Theater, though it may be the Biograph. There will be two women with him. The boys are looking over the land right now. We'll get him when he goes in or goes out."

"Take him alive, if it's at all possible," Hoover ordered. "Take him when he comes out. It will be safer that way. No attempt is to be made to arrest him in the movie house. Innocent bystanders might be hurt. And no agent is to draw a gun unless it's absolutely necessary. It you close in on him quickly enough, he won't have a chance to get at his own gun. There are to be no mistakes this time."

That Sunday morning, in sweltering record heat—there were twenty-three deaths by heat prostration that day—every available special agent was crowded into the field office. Using a diagram of the Marbro Theater, Cowley assigned each agent his post and gave him very careful instructions. There was to be no failure this time. "If he makes his escape, it will be a disgrace to the Bureau," he said. ". . . This is the opportunity we have all been waiting for and he must be taken . . . If Dillinger offers any resistance, each man will be for himself. It will be up to each of you to do whatever you think necessary to protect yourself in taking Dillinger."

At 5:30 P.M., Anna Sage called to tell Crowley that they would be going to either the Marbro or the Biograph. Agents were immediately sent to the Biograph to make a map of the theater and its environs. At 7 P.M., she called again to say that he had arrived. But she did not know which movie house he would be taking them to—and Cowley divided his forces to cover both. It turned out to be the Biograph. Dillinger was spotted entering the theater with Polly and Anna. Anna was wearing a red dress —the Woman in Red of the sensational news stories. The agents at the Marbro were recalled and took up their stations at the Biograph. For ninety minutes, FBI agents waited for Dillinger to emerge. But there was one contretemps which might have saved Dillinger. The theater manager, seeing men loitering in the alley near the rear entrances, across the street from the box office, and almost everywhere he turned, suspected a holdup and called the Chicago police. A squad car was dispatched, and two agents were being questioned—arguing with the local gendarmerie that they were Federal agents when the crowd began to leave the theater. Other police had also attempted to arrest the FBI "loiterers" but accepted the explanation that the FBI was after "a fugitive" and departed before Dillinger, Polly Hamilton, and Anna Sage strolled out.

For a minute, Cowley and Purvis thought they would be able to take Dillinger without any violence. He seemed unconcerned and smiling, one more moviegoer discussing the plot of the murder thriller he had just seen. (It was a Clark Gable–William Powell film, *Manhattan Melodrama*.) But he had spotted the agents. Suddenly, he whipped a Colt .45 from his righthand trouser pocket and made a dash for a nearby alley, running at a crouch. Three agents fired—at head, body, and legs—and the most notorious outlaw of the era, Public Enemy Number One, was dead. Two bystanders were hurt—one by a stray bullet, another by a bullet that had passed through Dillinger's body.*

Through the day, Hoover had been getting reports from Purvis and Cowley. But for the one hour and a half of the stakeout, he had paced anxiously, from phone to chair, waiting and wondering. The call from Purvis came at 10:30 P.M. "We got him," Purvis said. "Dead or alive?" Hoover asked. "Dead," said Purvis. "He pulled a gun." "Were any of our boys hurt?" "Not one," Purvis told him. "A woman in the crowd was wounded, but it doesn't look bad." For the first time in many hours, Hoover relaxed. "Thank God," he said.

Dillinger's body was rushed to the hospital where a Bureau fingerprint expert identified the body. The attempt to obliterate Dillinger's fingerprints had failed. And at the end, the press had the last word. The young doctor who took over in the basement of the hospital was a stringer for the *Chicago Tribune*. The paper had notified him that Dillinger was dead and he had gone to the hospital, short of doctors on a Sunday, and offered to help with the autopsy. Throughout the grisly proceedings, he never removed the straw hat casually cocked on the back of his head.

In short order, the FBI began its roundup of the members of the Dillinger gang—the lawyer who had been his intermediary in making arrangements for the plastic surgery with which he had tried to disguise himself, the doctor who had performed the surgery, the people who had harbored the fugitive, accomplices in bank robberies, the fences who handled the stolen money,

---

*The day after the FBI cornered and killed Dillinger, Hoover dictated a "Dear Sam" letter to Cowley expressing his "commendation and pleasure last evening upon the excellent results which you attained in the Dillinger hunt ... To you, as one of those who has actively participated in the planning and direction of this must go a major portion of the credit. Your persistence, patience, and energy have made it possible for the Division of Investigation to attain this success, and I am proud and grateful to you. . . ." Four months later Cowley was facing "Baby Face" Nelson—real name, Lester J. Gillis—murderer of three FBI agents and "Public Enemy Number One" at the time, and another member of the Dillinger gang, on an Illinois highway. Nelson opened fire, and in the gun battle Cowley and Special Agent Herman Hollis were killed. Nelson died a few hours later of his wounds, and his body was dumped naked in a ditch by his wife who had been with him. As for Anna Sage, she was deported despite FBI efforts in her behalf.

the tough and tawdry gang molls who consorted with members of the gang and acted as lookouts or helped case the banks the gang was planning to rob. The FBI also closed in on the other gangs. On October 22, 1934, "Pretty Boy" Floyd, a participant in the Kansas City Massacre, was killed on an Ohio farm resisting arrest. Adam Richetti surrendered to the FBI and ended up in the gas chamber. On November 27, 1934, "Baby Face" Nelson was fatally wounded. On January 8, 1935, Russell Gibson of the Barker-Karpis gang was shot to death in a Chicago alley while resisting arrest. On January 16, 1935, "Ma" and Fred Barker died in a gun battle with FBI agents in Florida. And on May 1, 1936, Alvin "Old Creepy" Karpis, inheritor of the Public Enemy Number One honor, was captured in New Orleans by Hoover himself.

9.

Hoover's "Own" Cases

IN THE BURST OF LAWLESSNESS WHICH FOLLOWED THE PROHIBITION era, the FBI handled many cases. The headlines highlighted the capture of bank robbers, kidnappers, and the "Public Enemies" who, one by one, were tracked down and eliminated in shoot-outs or by the slower process of law. But these cases were merely the tip of the iceberg. Under John Edgar Hoover, the FBI was also rounding up and handing over for prosecution the hundreds of criminals and semi-criminals who made the depredations of the headliners possible. The gangsters and racketeers of the time had created a veritable underground railroad so that when the heat was on for high man or low in crime's hierarchy, he could move from hideout to hideout. The mobs had their own kind of group health system—doctors on call to patch up bullet-ridden fugitives and take care of their other health needs. Men on the lam needed women, so prostitutes were recruited to make a temporary home away from home for the mobsters. And at all times, lawbreakers needed lawyers—"lips"—to employ the tricks of law against the uses of justice.

It was the FBI's task to eradicate this peripheral army and its camp followers, and Hoover pressed his agents as hard in this battle as he did in nailing the headliners. Unfortunately, courts and juries often saw the underworld in B-movie terms, glamourizing the culprit while deploring the crime. Hoover found himself under attack by sentimentalists after every gun battle. He was under fire by the Ku Klux Klan, by columnists like Westbrook Pegler and Drew Pearson, and by the Thirties version of the little old ladies in tennis shoes. To Hoover, whose life was dominated by the religious precepts he had learned and taught in his youth, the FBI's drive against crime was not merely a war against particular criminals but a moral crusade. In a cold kind of way, he seethed at toleration of criminality more than at crime itself. The cases that exacerbated his sense of outrage the most were those of John Dillinger, because he had the background and the ability to excel in the overworld; of "Ma" Barker because she degraded motherhood by leading her own sons in their outlaw activities; and of Bonnie Parker and Clyde Barrow, because they made a game of murder.

Hoover bore an almost personal grudge against some of the predatory gangs of those turbulent days. Contrary to popular belief, most of the principals came from old American stock, from families which had settled the country and given it its character—and Hoover saw in their criminality a betrayal of America. "Let us look," Hoover told Frederick L. Collins, "at the entire list of principals, assistants, hideout owners, harborers, and messenger boys in the Barker-Karpis crew . . . The names are monotonously of a type we have come to classify as 'American,' against the Latin or north of Europe 'foreigners.' Here we have Barker, Wright, Delaney, McLaughlin, Gibson, Bolton, Davis, Campbell, Farmer, Weaver, Sawyer, Harrison, Wilson,

Murray, Eaton, Alderton, and a dozen more which would pass anywhere as 'American.' The only person in the whole crew who might possibly be classed as foreign was Alvin Karpis, and that is stretching matters a point, since he was reared from childhood in the United States." And the case of "Ma" Barker particularly rankled.

"It was at 'Ma' Barker's knee," he would say, "that her brood became the most vicious and cold-blooded crew of murderers and kidnappers we've known in our time. In the case of the Barker gang, you can say that the major criminal factors were home and mother. She had the most resourceful criminal brain of any man or woman I have observed, and she passed it all on to her sons."

"In her sixty or so years," he wrote after her bloody demise, "this woman became a monument to the evils of parental indulgence. Of her four sons, one became a mail robber, another a holdup man, and the remaining pair were highwaymen, kidnappers, wanton murderers . . . to her they looked for guidance . . . She kept open house for big-time criminality. With the calm of a person ordering a meal, she brought about bank robberies, holdups or kidnappings and commanded the slaying of persons who, only a short time before, had enjoyed what they thought was her friendship. Yet withal, she shuddered in jealous trepidation when a new gun moll threatened to steal the love of one of her boys, and she was one of the easiest weepers in the history of criminality. She liked now and then to hum hymns . . . She gave half her lifetime to a defiance of the law and died . . . a bullet-heated machine gun in her aged hands."

The Barker-Karpis gang was a crime wave in itself. During its heyday, its members killed ten people, wounded many others, and stole more than $1 million—in less than five years. Her four boys moved in and out of the penitentiary, but she was never caught. In fact, getting caught was the one thing about which she belabored her sons and the other members of the gang. Her major contribution to the gang's efforts was to "case the joint" before a bank robbery and then prepare the detailed plans which the gang followed. Describing her techniques, Hoover wrote:

A "nice little old woman" easily can enter a bank, ask questions, seek the advice of bank officers or their assistance in cashing a check. She can observe what are the peak hours of business, learn something about the cash on hand, what police protection is afforded . . . When Ma "cased a joint" nothing was left unnoticed. Her eyes were keen, her ears sharp, her appearance and mannerisms of a type which dulled suspicion . . .

She used the same care in the making of the "getaway charts" . . . In Ma's case, the procedure would be to sit in a car with one of her boys, marking down in code every turn and twist of the road, every obstruction, every dangerous curve, every place where it was possible to take a side road and thus defeat pursuit. Speeds were catalogued, so that the bandit car might know more than its pursuers about road conditions—whether a curve could be taken at sixty miles an hour, or fifty, whether the pavement was safe in wet weather, and when to slide to the "cat" or back roads in order to skirt a town instead of being forced to stop for traffic lights.

Ma was an expert at this. But of course Ma never went out on the actual robberies. Enough that she should sit in at the rehearsals before the robbery, when every gangster went through his part and Ma, from her expert knowledge of the situation, could make suggestions regarding better methods. A smoothing of the hair, a clearing of the throat, and then—"I believe you boys would get along better at that place with machine guns. Flash them the minute you step into the bank. It's close quarters, you know—you could cover everybody easily."

It cannot be said that the Barker gang went about its business with impunity. From time to time one of its members was arrested, convicted, and sent to prison. But parole was easy to get, and there was always "Ma" Barker to petition governors, to cry out that her boys had been framed, and to charge prison brutality. "They've got Arthur hanging by his thumbs in that Oklahoma prison," she told reporters, "and rats are gnawing at his feet." It made a good human interest story. But the gang's ace-in-the-hole was simple bribery. Wherever they were hiding out, "Ma" Barker would buy protection from police officers and from municipal or country officials. Time after time, honest cops would move in on a hideout only to find that the Barkers had moved out hours ahead of them. A member of the gang, "Ma" Barker's lover, was suspected of tipping off the police, and she ordered his execution. He was not "taken for a ride" but for a row. He went fishing with two of the Barker boys and never returned. "We didn't get him," they boasted. "The fish did."

But "Ma" got careless. She and "Old Creepy" Karpis decided to kidnap a prosperous banker. They succeeded, releasing Edward G. Bremer for $200,000. But under the Lindbergh Law, this brought the FBI into the case. Bremer led the FBI to a barn near Rochester, Minnesota where, following Ma's careful plan, the kidnap car had refueled. On an empty gasoline can, FBI agents found part of a latent fingerprint. It was a gargantuan job to identify this partial print among the hundreds of thousands in the FBI's Identification Division. Fingerprint files usually contain all ten fingers, but Hoover had the division break this down into single print files for all known criminals. The partial print was found to belong to one of the Barker boys. When the FBI began picking up members of the gang, Ma Barker panicked and she ordered the execution of one hanger-on whose ability to remain silent was questioned. And then, coincidence took over.

The FBI had been receiving reports of a strange kind of hunting at Lake Weir, Florida. Townspeople had complained that a group of people, living in a luxurious establishment on the shores of the lake, were dragging live pigs, roped to speed boats, through the waters and shooting the alligators which attacked the pigs with machine guns. The FBI had no jurisdiction over this barbarous sport. But when one of the minor members of the Barker gang was arrested, a map of the area with Lake Weir circled in pencil was found in his possession. "This must be it," Hoover said.

Within hours, he had dispatched a chartered plane to Florida. On board was one of the Special Squads he had organized. At nightfall, they surrounded the mansion. At Hoover's orders, five agents guarded the highway to warn off motorists who might get caught in the fire fight. Eight agents took their places around the house. Just before dawn, the Inspector in Charge approached the house. " 'Ma' Barker," he shouted, "we are Federal officers. We want you to come out one at a time. You will not be hurt." There was no answer, but the agents could hear movement in the house. "Unless you come out, we'll use tear gas," the Inspector called out. Other agents repeated his words so that the Barker gang would know that they were surrounded.

"All right," "Ma" Barker called out.

The Inspector thought that this was capitulation. "You won't be hurt," he repeated. "Come out one at a time. You first, Fred Barker." He was answered by bursts of machine-gun fire which amazingly did not hit him. There were wild exchanges of fire, which the FBI agents believed would exhaust the besieged gang's ammunition. They did not know that Ma Barker, as logistics officer, had made an arsenal of the building with two machine guns, several hundred-shot drums, two shotguns, three automatic pistols, cartons of ammunition, a rifle, and five bullet-proof vests. Obviously, the gang could hold out for a long time. The Inspector then moved to the second phase of the assault, according to Hoover's instructions. Bursts of fire from the house had disclosed to the agents where the members of the gang were stationed. They put down their submachine guns and picked up rifles. Then, sighting carefully, they began shooting into the frame structure at those points. When, after this, there was no answering fire, agents crawled close to the house and fired tear gas shells through the shattered windows. Then they cautiously entered the building. At an upstairs window, they found "Ma" Barker dead, pierced by three rifle slugs. Her machine gun, still hot, was clutched across her breast. In her pocketbook was $10,200 in large bills. Her son Fred had stopped eleven bullets.

But that was not the end of the Barker gang. Alvin Karpis was still loose. He had not been in Florida during the FBI raid. "Old Creepy" considered himself one of Ma's adopted sons, and when he learned of her death, he declared a vendetta on the

FBI. His first plan was to fly from city to city, killing the Special Agents in Charge of field offices. But he put this aside for an even better one. He sent word to Hoover that he intended to kill him, thereby avenging "Ma" Barker's death. The threat was not an idle one to Hoover. An associate later explained:

We knew that the gang leaders and lone-wolf desperadoes were convinced that with the Director dead, there would be a letup in the campaign against them. We knew, too, from the wild boasting that Karpis was given to that he believed he would achieve a kind of royalty status in the underworld if he could knock off the top man in the FBI and get away with it. So the Director followed the pursuit of "Old Creepy" with even greater care than he would have in any other case.

This special interest was put into direct instructions to field offices. Karpis was "the Director's man" and any leads, any information, no matter how tenuous, was to be relayed to Hoover instantly so that he could participate in the capture personally. What seemed like a solid lead came when Hoover was in New York on FBI business—"inspecting the posts"—and also taking a little leisure time for himself. An inspector in the Washington office called to say that Karpis was holed up in Hot Springs, a favorite gangster resort at the time. Hoover immediately chartered a special plane and flew directly to Washington to pick up some of his best agents. But somewhere there had been a leak and the local police, which played hand in glove with the underworld, had tipped off Karpis.

This was in March 1936. A month later, Hoover was testifying before the Senate Appropriations Committee. A member of that committee was Senator Kenneth McKellar, a crusty veteran of Capitol Hill wars who had a strong dislike for both Hoover and the FBI and represented the ultraright's antagonism to Hoover. In what was more a grilling than an appropriations hearing, McKellar taunted Hoover for not knowing very much about crime detection and for never having caught a criminal himself. The implication was that Hoover was a coward who let his agents do the dirty work of running down criminals and of risking their lives in capturing them. As *Time* put it, "McKellar wanted to know why G-man Hoover wasn't out risking his own neck. Hoover had to admit that he had never personally made a pinch. Boiling mad, he returned to his office and demanded the latest reports on Alvin Karpis, the last of the Barker gang. Then he flew down to New Orleans, personally led the raiding squad into Karpis' hideout. . . ." *Time* had the story —and had it wrong.

Hoover *was* boiling mad. He felt that his manhood had been impugned. And he felt that McKellar's accusation was deliberately unfair, as if a commanding general showed cowardice if he didn't go out as point in a patrol action. He was doubly angered because he had been planning to be on hand for the capture of Karpis, a fact he did not mention to McKellar.* "I just had to sit there and take it," he said. "But there was nothing else I could do."

Hoover was again in New York, some days later, when he received another flash that pursuing FBI agents had trailed Karpis from Hot Springs to Corpus Christi, and then to New Orleans where he was living in a house on Canal Street with Fred Hunter, another fugitive. This time Hoover wanted no slip-ups, and he gave strict orders that the New Orleans police were not to be alerted. It was to be stricly a Bureau operation. Then, boarding a plane, Hoover flew directly to New Orleans. This was to be his answer to Senator McKellar, and as he told the story over the years, there were few words changed in his account.

"When I got to Canal Street," Hoover recalled, "I told the boys how desperate Karpis was and I gave them all a chance to back out if they wanted to. Not one of them made a move. Then I said that they could put on bullet-proof vests. Not one of them made a move. When we began moving in on Karpis, there were agents on the roof, agents on the fire escape, agents at the back

---

* For the record, when McKellar learned more of Hoover and the Bureau's work, he publicly apologized.

door." Hoover, Assistant Director Earl Connelly, and two agents from Oklahoma were to advance on the front door. "We had made our plans carefully," Hoover would continue, "Everyone was to move in simultaneously on signal. It would have worked perfectly but for one thing. Just as we started, Karpis and Hunter came out of the front door and walked toward their car. And before we could do something about it, a mounted police-man came galloping down the street on a white horse. We had to wait until he went by because he wouldn't have known what the shooting was about and opened fire on us. Then a little boy on a bicycle came pedaling by in front us, and that held us up again." But Karpis and Hunter were taking their time. As they climbed into their car and slammed the doors, Hoover dashed to the driver's side and grabbed Karpis by the shirt collar before he could reach for the rifle that lay behind the front seat. Con-nelly had approached the car from the other side, grabbing Hunter, and FBI agents converged on it from their posts. "Keep your hands on the wheel," Hoover ordered. He had made his arrest.

"Put your cuffs on him, boys," he said. And at this point in his account, Hoover would smile broadly.

"Then it turned out that there wasn't a pair of handcuffs among us. So we improvised. The two Oklahoma agents took off their neckties and used them to bind the hands of our prisoners. 'To the Post Office Building,' I told the driver when we had Karpis in one of our cars. After we had gone for a few blocks, I asked the agent who was driving, 'You know how to get there in a hurry, don't you?' "

"No, sir," he told the Director. "I was never in New Orleans before in my life."

"Mr. Hoover," said Karpis, who had been silent, "if it's the *new* Post Office you want, I know how to get there. I was going to hold it up."

"Fortunately for the dignity of the Bureau," Hoover re-counted, "it was the *old* Post Office to which we were bound, and we didn't have to get help from Karpis. We stopped to ask the way from a pedestrian. I wonder how frightened he would have been had he known that Alvin Karpis was in the car, restrained only by an Oklahoma necktie." At this point in telling the story, Hoover would laugh. "Maybe not the only thing. We had our guns."

From the Federal Building, Hoover and his agents took Karpis to the airport where they boarded a chartered TWA plane for St. Paul where he was eventually tried, and sentenced to life imprisonment for two kidnappings. On board the plane, Hoover noticed that Karpis was literally shaking, his face white. "Are you sick?" Hoover asked him. A hysterical Karpis shouted out at him, "Go ahead! Do it! Do it! Get it over with!"

"What are you talking about?" a puzzled Hoover asked him.

"I know what you're going to do," Karpis screamed. "You couldn't kill me on the street. You guys are going to throw me out of the plane and then say I did it myself."

"You're a fool," Hoover said. "We don't do things like that. You're going to St. Paul. You're going to stand trial. And you're going to be convicted. Nobody's going to hurt you while you're with the FBI."

For the first time since his capture, Karpis began to relax and seemed ready to talk. "How did you know who I was when we were in the car?" Hoover asked him. Karpis, who was a passionate fisherman answered, "I saw a picture of you after you caught a sailfish. Your luck is better than mine. I've been trying to catch one for three years." In recounting this conversation, Hoover later remarked, "If he'd spent as much time fishing as he did kidnapping people and robbing banks, his luck might have been a little better."

On the trip to St. Paul, there was one small irony. As the DC-3 put down in Kansas City for refueling, sandwiches, coffee, and newspapers were handed out to the passengers. The newspaper headline for that morning read, KARPIS ROBS BANK IN MICHIGAN. Hoover laughed and showed the newspaper to Karpis, who also laughed. "This is one time I've got a perfect alibi," he said.

In 1971, paroled from his life sentence and living in Canada,

Karpis "wrote" a book. He denied that Hoover was in on the capture, insisting that Hoover did not approach his car until all danger was past, that he had no rifle behind the front seat of his car, and that he had been threatened with aerial defenestration on the trip to St. Paul. But his description of the man who had grabbed him fitted J. Edgar Hoover completely. And the last three sentences of the book told the story completely: "I have nothing but contempt for J. Edgar Hoover. For the rest, there are no apologies, no regrets, no sorrows, and no animosity. What happened happened." This could have been his epitaph.

The case of Bonnie Parker and Clyde Barrow did not touch Hoover as personally as the Karpis episode. But his reactions, as reported by friends long after the "G-Man era" was history, were more complex than those of a law man. To him, Bonnie and Clyde were symbolic of a moral decay, of the criminality which lodges itself in the human spirit and brings tragedy to the world. There are killers who sentimentalize over each murder, who can rationalize their crimes until the switch is thrown in a death house. There are gun molls, the consorts of these killers, who proclaim that it was all for love. But Bonnie and Clyde killed because it was a lark, and fornicated afterward because they had beaten death. Clyde Barrow was a small man, prissy in his manners, whose slicked-down hair, parted in the middle, made him look like the floorwalker in a small-town department store. Without a qualm, he could chop off two of his toes to avoid penitentiary work which he considered onerous. When he picked up Bonnie Parker on a Dallas street, she was a small, yellow-haired girl, flat-chested as a boy, with a husband and several men who shared her favors.

A psychiatrist would have said of them that they got more release from the Tommy-guns, automatic rifles, shotguns, and pistols which they fondled than from normal sexual encounters. They also loved fast cars. Clyde was, in fact, bisexual and he enjoyed sharing Bonnie with whatever partner they had in tow, even if it involved incest. Their hobby was taking pictures of each other, displaying the major arsenal they always carried with them. Bonnie also wrote ballads deriving from the old Wild West style. It was not Pulitzer Prize material, but it had a certain folk reality. After a shoot-out in which Barrow killed one police office, an unfinished poem was found in the Barrow-Parker hideout, *The Story of Suicide Sal:*

> We, each of us, have a good alibi
> For being down here in the joint;
> But few of them really are justified,
> If you get right down to the point.
>
> You've heard of a woman's glory
> Being spent on a downright cur.
> Still you can't always judge the story
> As true being told by her.
>
> As long as I stayed on the island
> And heard confidence tales from the gals,
> There was only one interesting and truthful,
> It was the story of Suicide Sal.
>
> Now Sal was a girl of rare beauty,
> Tho' her features were somewhat tough,
> She never once faltered from duty,
> To play on the up and up.
>
> Sal told me this tale on the evening
> Before she was turned out free,
> And I'll do my best to relate it,
> Just as she told it to me.
>
> I was born on a ranch in Wyoming,
> Not treated like Helen of Troy,
> Was taught that rods were rulers
> And ranked with greasy cowboys . . .

The FBI was in on the pursuit as Bonnie and Clyde, with confederates who were killed or dropped away, shot and killed —moving from state to state. But it was the local law, working on FBI tips, which eventually tracked Bonnie and Clyde. Companies of the National Guard, posses that numbered into the hundreds, and law enforcement officers repeatedly converged on the couple only to allow them to make incredible escapes.

One by one, the members of the Barrow gang were killed or arrested, but Bonnie and Clyde seemed to slip through the net miraculously. It was not until Hoover assigned Special Agent L. A. Kindell to work full time with local police that the net around them began to close. It was through Kindell that the locals learned that the couple was hiding out in the vicinity of Arcadia, Louisiana, and an elaborate ambush was set up. The idea of catching them alive had been rejected; too many law men had already died in that kind of attempt.

It was getting dark on a side road near Arcadia when a Ford V-8 came over a rise in the road and into the ambush area. Bonnie was wearing a red dress and red shoes. Clyde, "disguised" by sun glasses, was driving shoeless. In the car, they had fifteen sets of license plates, a shotgun, three Browning automatic rifles, a revolver, eleven pistols, and two thousand rounds of ammunition. Bonnie's overnight case lay on the back seat with a saxophone and a small pile of sheet music. As Clyde stopped the car to talk to a man changing a tire—an accomplice who had gone over to the law—a sheriff stood up and shouted. "Put 'em up, Clyde! You're covered." Clyde grabbed a shot gun, Bonnie a pistol, but before they could fire, the five local law men and the special agent shook the car with a broadside. The Barrows were dead. In the car, they did not find *The Story of Bonnie and Clyde,* a ballad that Bonnie Parker had been writing to tell the world their story. She had mailed it the previous day to a Texas newspaper. She had begun writing it months before in Minnesota when they were on the run, fleeing police. It was a sad tale as she told it, a fit epic for the age of violence and lawlessness which the FBI had effectively closed:

> You have read the story of Jesse James,
> Of how he lived and he died.
> If you are still in need of something to read,
> Here is the story of Bonnie and Clyde.
>
> Now Bonnie and Clyde are the Barrow gang.
> I'm sure you all have read

How they rob and steal
And how those who squeal
Are usually found dying or dead.

There are lots of untruths to their write-ups,
They are not so merciless as that;
They hate all the laws,
The stool-pigeons and rats.

They class them as cold-blooded killers,
They say they are heartless and mean.
But I say this with pride,
That I once knew Clyde
When he was honest and upright and clean.

But the law fooled around,
Kept tracking him down,
And locking him up in a cell,
Till he said to me,
"I will never be free,
"So I will meet a few of them in hell."

This road was so dimly lighted
There were no highway signs to guide,
But they made up their minds
If the roads were all blind
They wouldn't give up till they died . . .

The road gets dimmer and dimmer,
Sometimes you can hardly see,
Still it's fight, man to man,
And do all they can,
For they know they can never be free.

If they try to act like citizens,
And rent them a nice little flat,
About the third of the night they are invited to fight
By a submachine-gun rat-tat-tat.

They don't think they are too tough or desperate,
They know the law always wins,
They have been shot at before
But they do not ignore
That death is the wages of sin.

From heartbreaks some people have suffered,
From weariness some people have died,
But take it all in all

Our troubles are small,
Till we get like Bonnie and Clyde.

Some day they will go down together,
And they will bury them side by side.
To a few it means grief,
To the law it's relief,
But it's death to Bonnie and Clyde.

When the law, in relief, found them dead, Bonnie's pistol had three notches carved on the grip. The shotgun Clyde was still clutching had ten notches on the stock. They were not buried together.

But the success of the FBI in ending the rash of gangland bank robberies that had plagued the Midwest also won for Hoover the enmity of local police forces which felt that they had been made to look bad. And it even stirred up a rhetorical backlash in the halls of Congress. In 1936, during debate on an increase in Hoover's salary, Representative Marion A. Zioncheck of Washington rose to attack the Federal Bureau of Investigation in scathing terms:

Apparently, Mr. Speaker, one of the most popular illusions that the American people are suffering from today is the illusion that has been deliberately created and built up by the master of fiction, J. Edgar Hoover, the great "G-man." Mr. Speaker, since Congress was kind enough to favor him by allowing his men to run around with guns, machine guns, and sawed-off shotguns, four "G-men" have been killed and eight gangsters, and we cannot find out how many innocent people were killed in the process. Dillinger! Dillinger did not know that about seventeen young boys with shaking hands were all leveled on the place where he was to come, and they let him have it. He looked like a sieve when they got through with him. That is law and order. That is effective justice. Incidentally, Mr. Speaker, if you had happened to have been at that theater at the same time and if you had gone out, you would have been killed. They did hit an innocent person.

But that is not the only case, Mr. Speaker. That was fine. Even Mr. Hearst praised [the FBI] for it. So they continue to do that. An automobile with a gangster—it happened to be a gangster this time—tried to get away, so they sneaked up behind him and got him in ambush and they loaded that car up with holes. They killed the fellow all right. Real American justice! What if that had been a kidnapper? What if the little Lindbergh child had been in the bottom of that car in a sack? They would have gotten the Lindbergh baby. They could not have missed it. The dictator, J. Edgar Hoover!

It has been said, Mr. Speaker, or it has been rumored that he may know the answer to the Hauptmann murder . . . Mr. Speaker, it is rumored that the great "G-man"—"G" not standing for God—may know under whose direction the ladder was built that convicted Hauptman; that he may know why Hauptmann did not talk, because Hauptmann had nothing to say. He did not know anything.

The Zioncheck attack was roundly denounced by both Democrats and Republicans alike, as had an attempt by Senator McKellar to reduce the 1936 FBI appropriation. But on the political front, there was one threat which deeply worried Hoover and his friends in the Roosevelt Administration. After the Roosevelt Inaugural in 1933, it had been the New Deal contingent which wanted to effect Hoover's ouster. But four years later, the right wing of the party, led by Postmaster General James A. Farley, dispenser-in-chief of patronage, took out after Hoover. In the Harding era, the Bureau of Investigation had been second only to the Post Office Department as an agency in which to plant deserving friends of the politicians in Federal jobs. Farley could not understand why the men he sent to Hoover for jobs were turned down if they did not meet the stringent requirements of the FBI.

Farley, therefore, began a campaign to replace Hoover with an FBI Director more amenable to the needs of the Administration's patronage. His candidate, as Jack Alexander would later report in *The New Yorker,* "was the late Val O'Farrell, who ran a private detective agency in New York. Besides sleuthing, O'Farrell used to analyze sensational crimes for a New York tabloid. His articles were ghost-written, and frequently his analyses were so inept that the ghost disregarded them and analyzed the crimes himself."

The attack from the left had also continued, directed by a group that had infiltrated the Treasury Department under Secretary Henry Morgenthau. A team of Secret Service agents was quietly assigned to "investigate" the by-then historical deaths of John Dillinger and a member of his gang, Eddie Green, shot in an escape attempt, though he was unarmed. The thrust of the investigation was to prove that the FBI's agents were trigger-happy. But when word of this investigation leaked out, Roosevelt's Attorney General Homer Cummings told the press, "Hoover has my entire confidence and if anybody thinks he's going to get him out of his office, he'll have to get me first." Morgenthau apologized to Cummings, demoted the Secret Service agents involved, and censured "the irresponsible action."

Hoover had also run head-on into the National Probation Association by pointing out in speeches and other public statements that the criminals the FBI was apprehending were, almost to the man, out of prison on parole. He insisted that the whole system of probation and parole needed rehauling, that the "sob-sister" mentality which had gotten Dillinger and other criminals out of the penitentiary was wrong, and that abuses in the system were the cause for the current crime wave. Counterattacking, the National Probation Association demanded of Roosevelt that Hoover be silenced and that he be compelled to "refrain from issuing statements which are derogatory and destructive to the advancement of [the system] of probation."*

Hoover's defense was one which he repeated over the years. In a memorandum to the Attorney General, he pointed out that

*It is an interesting commentary of the period that while Hoover was being attacked for demanding fewer parole and probationary loopholes in the law, H. L. Mencken was writing, "When a conspicuous criminal is at large, [the police] are denounced for not taking him at once, and not uncommonly it is hinted that they are afraid to tackle him or have been bribed to let him go. But in nearly every such case they have actually taken him already, not once but half a dozen times . . . He is loose because getting loose, with the grotesque system which now prevails among us, is at least twice as easy as staying in jail . . . When a bold and atrocious crime has been committed normal people are not interested in hearing a long discourse on his psychology, couched in muddy, pseudo-scientific language; what they are interested in is hearing that he has been promptly and adequately punished . . . that he has got what he gave, and that the account is squared."

he had never criticized "the theory or principle of parole" but only "the administration of those systems by venal politicians and by inefficient and corrupt influences in some of our states." He offered to supply Cummings and the President with "not dozens, but literally hundreds and running into thousands of cases to prove my point." The National Probation Association continued to demand that Hoover be "gagged," but the FBI Director had one friend on his side whose judgment and support meant everything. His name was Franklin Delano Roosevelt.

Where Hoover ran into difficulties was in his relations with some police departments. Over the years, corrupt politicians had infiltrated these departments to protect criminal elements of value to them on election day. (Hoover's troubles were duplicated when Senator Estes Kefauver's investigation of crime had to cope with local police forces, many years later.) In many instances, Hoover and the FBI found good and honest cops who would cooperate fully in the apprehension of criminals. But in all too many cases, Hoover also found that the local police leaked information to politicians and favored newspapermen or tried to beat the FBI to the punch, once they had been alerted, in order to make the headlines and grab the glory.

The catalogue of the FBI's controversies with local police forces is long and dreary. But the most newsworthy and colorful ones concerned the New York City Police Department. New York had known its share of police corruption, just as its "finest" could move superbly when free of political interference. But the police felt that they were being upstaged by an FBI which garnered an ever-greater share of newspaper headlines and public adulation. And this provoked a vendetta. Three cases in particular nettled the New York police.

Case One. In December 1934, $590,000 in Treasury notes had been stolen from the United States Trust Company on Wall Street. The New York Police Department had insisted that there had been no robbery but that the notes had been "mislaid"—until two of them turned up at a Federal Reserve bank.

But police efforts to find the money or the thieves proved futile. Then, in April 1936, Hoover announced from his office in Washington that a gang of eight men had been rounded up and $310,000 of the Treasury notes recovered. To add to the embarrassment of the New York police, five of the robbers had been arrested in New York City. The police accused the FBI and Hoover of secrecy and lack of cooperation, implying that the theft would have been solved sooner had they been in on the investigation.

Case Two. Several months later, Harry Brunette, wanted for kidnapping a New Jersey state trooper, was discovered to be hiding out in a house on New York's West Side. The FBI notified the New York police and set up a stake-out. Two detectives were assigned to work with the FBI. On the evening of December 13, at about 8 p.m., the two New York detectives took off—"for coffee," they later said. At 11:55 p.m., the detectives had not returned, but Brunette was seen entering the brownstone house which was his hideout. An agent immediately called Hoover, who was directing operations from a midtown hotel. He took a taxicab to the scene, and personally led the raid on Brunette's apartment. There was a heavy exchange of fire, which brought radio squad cars, but the police restricted themselves to holding back the crowd that had gathered. Tear gas brought Brunette, unharmed, and his wife, shot in the thigh, out of the building, with Hoover personally making the arrest. New York's Police Commissioner immediately charged Hoover with "heroics," "small-town stuff," and "headline hunting"—and claimed that the original tip had come from his own men.

Case Three evolved from the warm friendship that developed between Hoover and Walter Winchell, then at the height of his fame (or notoriety) as a show business and political gossip columnist. Contrary to the popular account, Winchell began his glorification of the FBI and its exploits long before he had met Hoover. And as the record will attest, on occasion he held back from publishing what would have been an important newspaper "beat" because it would have hindered the FBI in the solution of a crime.* The two men met when Hoover was going through a relatively brief nightclub fling. He enjoyed being wined and dined at the Stork Club by Sherman Billingsley and he reveled in the company of noted Broadway characters like Damon Runyon, Quentin Reynolds, and other who dominated New York's night life.

In 1937, the Hoover-Winchell friendship produced page one news which again infuriated the New York City police. Louis ("Lepke") Buchalter, one of the most dangerous of New York's gangsters and rackets bosses, had been indicted for murder, narcotics trafficking, and extortion through unions he controlled in the restaurant, theater, fur, baking, and garment industries. Lepke went into hiding, while he systematically directed the murder of potential witnesses against him. When the police failed to locate him, after a two-year search, Thomas E. Dewey, then in his racketbusting phase, offered a $25,000 dead-or-alive reward for Lepke. On his Sunday night broadcast, Winchell announced the reward and appealed to Lepke to surrender to the police if he wanted to stay alive.

Within hours, Winchell's phone rang, and a voice he recognized said: "Lepke wants to come in." But he would surrender only to Hoover, fearful that a New York cop would shoot him for the reward. Would Winchell tell Hoover? "Do you trust me?" Winchell asked. "Yes," the voice said. "I'll tell Hoover." Hoover agreed to go to New York to make the arrest, which would have put Lepke in a Federal prison where he felt his life would not be in jeopardy. For two weeks, Hoover waited, convinced with every passing day that it had all been a ruse and accused Winchell of being a "hot air artist." Finally, Winchell got the word —another phone call. "Lepke will surrender to Hoover, but only

*Winchell prized a letter from Hoover on official stationery, reporting on a speech he had made to an editors' convention in Washington. "I pointed out, without, of course, mentioning the name specifically, how a well-known columnist had refrained from printing a truly national and international scoop in the Lindbergh case for twenty-four hours, in order not to harm the investigation which was being conducted in that case. Of course, you know who that person is. . . ."

if you're there," the caller said. "But why me?" Winchell asked. "If Hoover's with you, Lepke knows they won't start shooting," the caller said.

Late that night, Winchell, in a borrowed car, drove to a Yonkers theater. A stranger climbed into the car and told him to drive to 19th Street and Eighth Avenue in New York City. There, another stranger got into the car and gave Winchell further instructions. He was to call Hoover and tell him to walk alone to 28th Street and Fifth Avenue—a neighborhood deserted after nightfall. Hoover was to be at the designated street corner between 10:10 and 10:20 p.m. At 10:15, at a street corner off Madison Square, Winchell dropped his second passenger and picked up a third, Louis Buchalter. A few minutes later, at 28th and Fifth, the two men alighted from the car and approached Hoover, standing alone. "Mr. Hoover," Winchell said, "this is Lepke." "Glad to meet you," said Lepke.

Dewey, of course, was able to win jurisdiction of the Lepke case, and the notorious racketeer was sentenced to death and executed. But the story goes, and it may be apocryphal, that when Winchell phoned in the big story to his paper, the *Daily Mirror*, the editor said, "That's real good, Walter—but Hitler just invaded Poland." True or not, the story had its poetic significance. For like the news, the FBI and John Edgar Hoover had already moved from their gangbusting days to investigative labors that far transcended their war against crime.

10.

A Shift in Direction

IN ITS ISSUE OF MARCH 11, 1940, *TIME* REPORTED, IN A STORY HEADED "Policeman's Lot": "Periodically there erupts in the U.S.A. a campaign to smear John Edgar Hoover. Among his ill-wishers are some newspapermen who believe Hoover is conceited, arrogant, publicity-hungry. They do not like him any better because Columnist Walter Winchell is continually claiming the inside track on crime stories. Last week, newshawks and other critics erupted again." Of this there was no doubt, as the week's budget of Hoover news easily demonstrated. For again, as it had repeatedly happened over the years, both right and left were taking pot shots at Hoover. And like many of the attacks of the past, the March quota was based on "facts" that existed less in reality than in the mind of the accuser.

That week, the *New York Daily News,* whose competition

then was the *New York Daily Mirror,* Winchell's home paper, reported that Hoover was having a high old time in a swank Miami hotel, though he had complained to Congress that because of a shortage of personnel, the FBI had a backlog of 7,448 unassigned cases and another 7,736 on which no substantial work had been done for over a month. Representative Vito Marcantonio, whose politics were redder than the rose and who habitually referred to Hoover as "the Stork Club detective," was reversing his field and charging the FBI with being too zealous in its pursuit of criminals. Hoover, Marcantonio proclaimed, "should be stopped from engaging in inquisition-like tactics in handling crimes no more serious than stealing a bag of peanuts."

There was a widely publicized complaint that Hoover was staying at the Nautilus hotel and paying $175 a week for a villa there. Senator George W. Norris, grown old and crotchety, took to his feet in the Senate to say that he was "frankly worried about the activities of the Bureau" which had arrested sixteen people in Detroit who had, in violation of the law, recruited volunteers to fight for the Abraham Lincoln Brigade, a Communist fighting force in war-torn Spain. Westbrook Pegler, who had not yet begun to specialize in Mrs. Eleanor Roosevelt, echoed barroom rumors that the FBI had dossiers on every official in Washington, that it tapped "wires of family telephones and even, in one incredible case . . . took phonograph records and moving pictures, on suspicion, of conversations and scenes within the bedroom of husband and wife"—a lip-smacking morsel for his readers.

As usual, Hoover wasted no time in making his rebuttal. Showing not a trace of suntan for his time in Florida, he reported that he had been there on business. An FBI roundup of more than thirty persons, part of a Federal drive against interstate vice and prostitution, announced at the time, bore him out. His room at the Nautilus, far from costing $175 a week without meals, cost $12.50 a day with meals, of which the government paid only $5. The rest came from his own pocket. The

Pegler charges—said Hoover, "Pegler has mental halitosis"—of pervasive surveillance of Washington officials had been made before and continued to be made until the day of Hoover's death. His most detailed answer would not come until several years later in an interview with Bert Andrews, a veteran Washington correspondent and bureau chief for the *New York Herald Tribune:*

We have less than 3,800 special agents in the FBI who are required to investigate violations of more than 120 Federal laws in the entire United States and its territories. In addition to investigating [these laws], which last year resulted in 11,812 convictions, we have the responsibility of investigating candidates for appointment in the Department of Justice, Federal judgeships, United States attorneys, United States marshals, and, likewise, we make 6,000 applicant-type investigations for the Atomic Energy Commission each month. We have less than 200 special agents assigned to handle all types and classes [of investigations] in Washington.

As to the Detroit case, Hoover could point to the complete bill of health given to him by the then Attorney General Robert H. Jackson, a public official of high reputation for probity. Hoover took cognizance of the gossip that he was orgying in New York by announcing that "Communists at a meeting yesterday have instructed two of their writers to portray me as a Broadway glamor boy and particularly to inquire into my affairs with women in New York"—the last a monumental exercise in futility since Hoover had never been a womanizer. ("His reason," *Time* stated solemnly, was "his dread that someone, some day, somewhere, will plant a naked woman in his path, to try to frame him"—a piece of journalistic invention which delighted Hoover.) With hardly less license, Winchell later "revealed" what he chose to believe was Hoover's only romance: "The only girl he really adores and sends gifts to is a famous movie star who makes more in a fortnight than he does in a year"—Shirley Temple.

At that time, Hoover had much more on his mind than the perkiness of little Miss Temple, and only his obsessive need for answering any and all criticism led him into tangle with those who assailed him. His small force of FBI agents, sometimes working in tandem, and sometimes at cross-purposes, with the military intelligence services, were fighting a deadly battle against forces of subversion, espionage and sabotage in the United States. The world was at war, though the United States was still technically neutral, and the entire Western Hemisphere had become a theater of operations for Japanese, Soviet, German, and Italian agents. In that Spring of 1940, moreover, home-grown Communist elements were using American labor unions to block the production of armaments and thwart President Roosevelt's promise that this country would be the "arsenal of democracy." Since September 6, 1939, the FBI had been charged by Presidential directive "to take charge of investigative work in matters relating to espionage, sabotage," etc., and all law-enforcement agencies had been ordered by Roosevelt to "turn over to the nearest representative of the Federal Bureau of Investigation any information obtained by them relating to espionage, counterespionage, sabotage, and subversive activities." In addition, Roosevelt had alerted the heads of Allied governments to the FBI's new role, and for the first time in his career, J. Edgar Hoover found himself dealing directly with Scotland Yard, with MI-5, with the French Deuxième Bureau, and with our own Office of Naval Intelligence and G-2. He was also thrust into direct relationships with Latin American governments which had been targeted by the Axis powers as sources of raw materials and centers for the dissemination of propaganda—not to mention espionage.

In these areas of enemy activity, Hoover quickly learned, there was "no such thing as a domestic field—it is international." As he pointed out after the war's end, the FBI had to be everywhere.

Germany, lacking an ever-necessary supply of platinum, turned to the black market of South America. One arch platinum smuggler was arrested in California. His trail led through several South American countries. In each, the facts were communicated by the FBI to the established law enforcement agencies in these countries and the holes were plugged. In one espionage case which centered in New York, shipping information was getting out of the country. Contacts of the enemy were spotted in Brazil and Chile. There the authorities quickly moved into action. Twenty-four clandestine radio stations were put out of business, 30 short-wave transmitters were seized, and, in all, 335 espionage agents were arrested in South America alone through the fine cooperation of the countries of that continent . . . We not alone averted enemy sabotage at home—none occurred in the entire Western Hemisphere throughout the entire period of World War II.

That this should have been achieved with the limited resources of the FBI underscored Hoover's ability to cooperate with other intelligence agencies. In the war years, he was even able to manage a polite coexistence with the Office of Strategic Services, a catch-all Intelligence organization which combined the best and the worst in American secret service methodology and included in its ranks some of the most professional Soviet agents of the period. It was in cooperation with the OSS that the infamous *Amerasia* case was broken—and then unbroken by political pressures.

But there was another aspect of FBI work which had begun years before at the behest of Franklin D. Roosevelt. It was a touchy area, and one that the President wanted kept secret from the public and, if discovered, not associated with him. For many years, therefore, Hoover accepted both the credit and the blame for the program—a concerted surveillance and infiltration of Communist and Fascist (both German and Italian) groups in the United States. There is debate even today as to why FDR wanted the FBI to keep a finger on Communist subversives. He had from the start expressed a kind of amused tolerance for the Communists, feeling—as he would later feel toward Stalin—that he could outwit and outmaneuver them. He was, moreover, paradoxically maintaining a highly secret liaison with the top leadership of the CPUSA through such couriers as Josephine Truslow Adams, member of a historic Boston Brahmin family, whose focus of loyalty had at the time not been determined.

In 1936, as the Fascists and the Communists began feeling out each other's strength—and testing their own weapons—in the bloody Spanish Civil War, and as the forces of Hitlerism began to gather strength, Roosevelt began to ponder the effectiveness of local subversion in pushing the country in directions which he did not favor. The American left, led by the Communists, was pushing hard to involve the United States directly in support of a Spanish government slipping gradually into the hands of the Soviet Union—and this Roosevelt objected to strongly. There is reason to believe, moreover, that he was aware of the Communist infiltration in his Administration— though hardly its extent—and that he was troubled not at the ideology but at his inability to control these elements as he successfully played off other warring factions in the Federal Establishment.

Whatever his motivation, President Roosevelt summoned Hoover to the White House on August 24, a little more than a month after the outbreak of the Spanish Civil War. It was, though neither man knew it, just about the time that the first really effective Communist cell in the American government— a cell including Alger Hiss, Harry Dexter White, and other rising civil servants—was beginning to go into high gear. When Hoover was ushered into the President's office, Roosevelt put down the papers he was studying, smiled, said. "Sit down, Edgar," and slipped a cigarette into his cigarette holder. "I asked you over," he said, "because I want you to do a highly confidential job for me. I've become increasingly worried about the activities of the Communists in this country—for reasons which I cannot discuss. And I think it is of great importance that I have more information than I am getting from my staff. What I need is a broad Intelligence picture of what the Communists and the Fascists are up to, particularly as their activities affect the political and economic life of the country."

"Mr. President," Hoover said, "there is no government agency which has the jurisdiction to compile the kind of Intelligence you want. It is not a violation, of course, to be a member of the Communist Party or the German-American Bund. We in the FBI have had no specific authorization to investigate these groups unless we have probable cause to believe that they are violating the law."

"Well, Edgar," Roosevelt said, "it seems to me that there must be some way that this could be done, some law to make it legal. You must have some suggestions."

Hoover thought for a few minutes. "Yes, there is a way," he said, and Roosevelt smiled again. "Under Title II and Title V of the United States code, the FBI is authorized to make investigations of 'official matters' for the Department of State when there is a request from the Secretary of State. If the Secretary requests the Attorney General to make the kind of general investigation you have in mind, Mr. President, then we could move ahead."

Roosevelt frowned. "You mean, Edgar, that the Secretary of State can make the request but the President of the United States cannot? This is rather strange." Hoover explained that it was relatively simple. The President could direct the Secretary of State to make the request. But Roosevelt was still dubious. "If I make a formal request to the Secretary, there will be a leak from the State Department. I think it would be wiser for me to put a handwritten memorandum in my safe stating that I instructed Secretary Hull to ask the Attorney General for FBI information on subversive activities. Come back tomorrow and we'll talk it over with Cordell."

The following day, Hoover was in Roosevelt's office. Cordell Hull arrived a little later, and Roosevelt explained that he was worried about the lack of information he had about what Fascist and Communist organizations were up to. "I feel that the FBI should take over this investigation for me," he told Hull, "but Edgar says he can do this legally only if the request comes from you." Hull turned to Hoover and said, "Go ahead and investigate the cocksuckers." Roosevelt leaned back in his chair and laughed. He enjoyed salty language, and the only other one of his advisers who used it was Anna Rosenberg. Then Hull asked, "Do you want the request in writing?" This, of course, was precisely what Roosevelt did not want. Nor did he want the FBI to deliver hard evidence, legally admissible in court. He wanted facts, he wanted attitudes, and—as later evidence indicates—he wanted to know which of the people in the far-ranging bureaucracy with whom he dealt had ties, tenuous or otherwise, with the Communist apparatus. In this, the Office of Naval Intelligence (ONI), G-2 (Army Intelligence), and such trustworthy members of the State Department's own intelligence division—the men who worked directly under Hull and had no contacts with Undersecretary Sumner Welles—were to coordinate their activities and investigations. On September 1, 1936, Roosevelt, Hull, and Hoover met again in the President's office, and Hoover was authorized to pass the word on to the Special Agents in Charge of the FBI's new mission. It was not until September 10 that Attorney General Homer Cummings was informed, and he gave Hoover a full-speed-ahead signal.

But Hoover's orders were already in the works. His memorandum to the SACs had stated the President's purposes succinctly:

The Bureau desires to obtain from all possible sources information concerning subversive activities being conducted in the United States by Communists, Fascists and representatives or other organizations or groups advocating the overthrow or replacement of the government of the United States by illegal methods. No investigation should be initiated into cases of this kind in the absence of specific authorization from the Bureau.

This, of course, was in a sense Hooveresque double-talk. It was duplicated in a subsequent memorandum to the higher echelons of the Bureau which spoke of handling the investigation in "a most discreet and confidential manner." Hoover, as those who were close to him at the time knew, was aware that an investigation which delved into that black-gray-white area of ideology-cum-action could be discreet only as to the findings of the FBI men who were assigned to the task. That the investigation was taking place could never be hidden. Franklin Roosevelt knew this, which is why he wanted his directive to the FBI hidden in his own private safe. The lightning would strike both Edgar Hoover and the Bureau, and Roosevelt knew that Hoover would not take to the fireside chat to justify himself. As for Hoover, it can be stated categorically that he was of two minds on the subject. He understood the threat of Communist and Fascist subversion. He knew that other agencies of government were not capable of handling it. The New Deal had brought in too many people, in every agency but the FBI, who were to varying degrees committed to the Marxist-Leninist rationalization for communism. He knew, too, that in the country at large, there were opposite forces which could be vastly patriotic about communism but saw no harm—and often much good— in the activities of the Fascists. He knew that the Bureau would be hurt by this shift in direction, but he felt too strongly his responsibility as a civil servant to dodge the assignment.

For the FBI, as for Hoover, it was a great wrench. They had been fighting the kind of crime which makes headlines and arouses the citizenry. Now they were to move into an area in which the Bill of Rights did not spell out what was wrong and what was right, what was permissible and what was actionable. He had the full legal support of the Attorney General and the moral support of such liberals in the Justice Department as Francis Biddle, then an Assistant Attorney General and later to take over the department's helm.

The first part of the task was one of education. Hoover had done his homework on communism in his days as head of the Justice Department's General Investigation Division. But his agents had not. For many of them, communism was something you hated, along with Hitler, Mussolini, and sin. But if you asked them just what a Communist was, how you identified him, and what you did about it after these first steps had been taken, he would have been baffled. It is significant, as those who were about in those days can attest, that Hoover did not send his special agents for their schooling to the far right but to the anti-Communist left, which had fought communism with little recognition from the public and much criticism from the ritualistic liberals since the days of the Second International. The editors of such repositories of information on the Communists as the *New Leader*, then a Social Democrat weekly in New York, found themselves visited by FBI agents who approached them with schoolboy earnestness. The FBI also turned to knowledgeable people in the labor movement, experts who worked for David Dubinsky in the International Ladies Garment Workers Union, for the names, dates, and places which eventually became an integral part of the FBI record. In those days, people like Sol Levitas, the manager of the *New Leader*, and Victor Riesel, its managing editor, or Benjamin Stolberg, a free-lance writer of both knowledge and intuition on the subject—not to overlook others in that periphery—supplied the FBI with voluminous material on both Communist and Fascist incursions into the American body politic.

It was Hoover's view, moreover, that whatever came to the Bureau would be the Bureau's exclusively. He wanted no joint efforts with other agencies of government and released information only under direct orders of the Attorney General, or the President through the Attorney General. He was criticized considerably for this within the Administration—and also by those who felt that the investigation of subversion should not be the exclusively property of the one branch of the Justice Department which was free from political controls. But in this, Hoover's judgment proved to be correct. Not too many years later, when the war had reached American shores, the wisdom of his insistence on a role for the FBI which did not rely on the cooperation of other intelligence agencies was confirmed when the Office of Naval Intelligence was ordered to close down its Red Desk and destroy its files.*

But it was not a battle that Hoover won easily. The State

---

*ONI's Red Desk had earned the enmity of Mrs. Eleanor Roosevelt when it refused to clear Joseph Lash for a Navy commission. Typically, the Navy ostensibly bowed to the order, but it never destroyed its files.

Department, then as now jealous of its prerogatives and tilting heavily against security measures, fought tooth and nail through Undersecretary Sumner Welles, who had Roosevelt's ear far more than the tough but aging Secretary Hull. There was a cabal within the Department of State which knew that Ambassador William Bullitt had returned from a tour of duty in Moscow with reports not only on Soviet espionage methods but also with the names of several agents of the Kremlin in the Federal government—among them the Hiss brothers, Alger and Donald. He had also brought back information which in the late thirties shocked members of Roosevelt's White House staff—some of whom remained unbelieving—namely that the Soviet Embassy staff did not comport itself along diplomaticly approved lines but was nosedeep in espionage. Bullitt, who won many enemies for his forthright disclosure of what he had learned in Europe, did not carry his information to the State Department but—after the customary discussion with the President—to Hoover and Attorney General Cummings.

The state of American official naïveté in those days is apparent in a memorandum which Hoover dictated for his own files after talking to Bullitt:

He [Bullitt] stated he knew at first hand that Stalin, who heads the Russian government, is also the one who issues orders to the Third Internationale, and so, consequently controls the activities of the Third Internationale ... Mr. Bullitt told me that the Communist leaders in Russia make every effort to put spies in all foreign government agencies, and particularly those agencies which are engaged in or charged with the responsibility of knowing about subversive activities ... I think it is time to take steps to endeavor to ascertain more definitely the activities of [Soviet Ambassador to Washington] Oumansky in view of the fact that Mr. Bullitt tells me he is the direct contact in this country for organizations and individuals who are engaged in the subversive movement against the Government of the United States.

Contrary to current popular belief, however, Hoover's main concern in those prewar days was not the Communist Party or its underground apparatus but those organizations and individuals which had been proliferating in the country since the rise of Hitlerite Germany.

The crescendo of impending war, however, had not been the original motive for Hoover's interest in subversion and espionage—however little his admiring public might have known about it. In 1934, an intra-Cabinet group made up of Secretary of Labor Frances Perkins, Secretary of the Treasury Henry Morgenthau, and the Attorney General had met with Hoover to discuss with him reports of rising pro-Nazi and pro-Fascist efforts in the United States. At this meeting, Hoover was told to zero in on these groups and on any espionage apparatuses that might be in existence or a-borning. Hoover made it clear that, where espionage was concerned, he had no problems of authority or justification. But he wanted it known that until there was a finding by the Attorney General, the President, or the Congress that anti-American groups of any stripe were operating in violation of law, he could do little more than keep an eye on them.

In this, the Attorney General concurred. In 1937, after Heywood Broun and other columnists made serious charges against the German-American Bund, FDR asked G-2 to "make a definite check" on their allegations. The War Department, however, passed the buck to Justice which told Hoover, in effect, to look but don't touch. It was at this time that Hoover began using the infiltration method of investigation. Special agents were assigned to join the Bund, to become active in its work, and to keep accurate records of its behind-the-scenes doings. On the basis of this information, Hoover reported regularly to the Attorney General. Justice Department lawyers decided, however, that though the Bund's philosophy and its actions were repugnant, they did not violate any laws of the United States.

Espionage was another matter. Though Hoover had his jurisdictional difficulties with the State Department and occasionally with the War or Navy Department, his agents maintained a careful surveillance of all suspected espionage agents. The measure of his interest—and success—can be found in the simple statistic: In 1934, the FBI handled a baker's dozen of espionage cases, but by 1938, it was handling an average of 250 a year. The tips came from everywhere. Americans were jittery and suspicious of the world. In the political struggle between interventionists and isolationists, the interventionists believed that a Nazi spy lurked under every isolationist bed. Hoover, therefore, had to act with circumspection, and as a policy matter did nothing to antagonize either group.

But when Fulton Lewis Jr., the radio commentator, went to Hoover with information of Japanese espionage, Hoover listened intently. Lewis was under attack from the left and was considered to represent an isolationist viewpoint. Therefore what he had to say was doubly valuable. "I've got enough material for a broadcast," Lewis told Hoover. "But this is explosive material and it touches on the national interest. I think it should be handled by the FBI. If I expose one man, I may be allowing a whole ring to escape." His story concerned one John Semer Farnsworth, a graduate of the United States Naval Academy. Farnsworth had been dishonorably discharged from the Navy and had fallen on bad days. He was a heavy drinker —"a drunk," Lewis put it—but he obviously knew much that no private citizen should about the Navy. And a check by Lewis had shown that Farnsworth had demonstrable ties with the Japanese. On this information, Hoover ordered an investigation. It proved that Lewis had been doubly right—once in suspecting Farnsworth and again in not broadcasting his knowledge. For Farnsworth was a highly paid agent of Tokyo and had turned over to its agents in the United States Navy codes, blueprints, signal books, and plans.

II.

All This and Espionage Too

IN ANY RETROSPECTIVE VIEW OF JOHN EDGAR HOOVER'S LIFE, IT becomes clear that probably its most rewarding and most relaxed period was during the administrations of President Roosevelt. That this was so may seem odd since Hoover was under the most concerted liberal attack of his career in the late thirties and early forties. But he was serving under attorneys general who were ready to stand by him, and who also knew that he was liked by FDR. In fact, it can be said that President Roosevelt was most responsible for making those the best years in Hoover's life. Roosevelt enjoyed Hoover, though the two men were in background, character, and personality completely antithetical.

Critics have analyzed Roosevelt's actions in sinister terms, depicting him as a ruthless powerbroker, a man who deliberately violated moral precepts, and who had "sold out" to the liberal/left for reasons ranging from traitorous to self-serving. In point of fact, Franklin Roosevelt was a man who enjoyed life, enjoyed power, enjoyed people, and enjoyed manipulation of events for the sheer mental muscularity it required. On his staff and in his entourage, he had men and women of violently disparate views, each of whom approached the throne with one thought in mind—to win over Roosevelt to their ideologies and to make him serve their purposes. In the long run, of course, he used them.

From all the available evidence, based on written records and the conversation of those who knew both men, Roosevelt particularly delighted in Hoover because the FBI chief embodied all that we now describe as the "Puritan ethic." Roosevelt himself was neither moral nor immoral; he was the happy pragmatist. Hoover's every act was based on moral precepts which, like all highly moral men, he could compromise to achieve a moral result. If the ideological and intellectual prima donnas who surrounded Roosevelt complained that Hoover was keeping tabs on their activities, Roosevelt could never be sure that they were correct—but he liked the thought that Hoover might be keeping an eye on Harry Hopkins or any one of the palace guard, just so long as Hoover delivered whatever information he gathered to Roosevelt, for Roosevelt's personal use. And so these complaints served to strengthen Hoover, rather than to weaken him. Roosevelt, whose feel of the public pulse was remarkable, knew that Hoover was not strong enough to defy the Presidential power, as some others attempted to do. He also knew that Hoover's loyalty to him was not negotiable.

Hoover, moreover, was the kind of man who delivered his loyalties to people—not to ideologies. Of the attorneys general he worked for during the Roosevelt administrations, he was therefore most comfortable with Francis Biddle, perhaps the most "liberal" of all. And Biddle liked him, respected him, and defended him. That Biddle was to the manner born, a true American aristocrat, did not stand between the affection of a man born into a bureaucratic middle class and the object of that affection. Hoover had idolized Harlan Fiske Stone, but he was truly comfortable with Attorney General Biddle. A notable passage in Biddle's autobiography, *In Brief Authority,* may explain why.

It was largely to bring Edgar Hoover more into the center of things that I arranged weekly policy conferences (in the Justice Department). . . . He was not concerned with policy decisions and eschewed them, taking the position that the investigator should not draw conclusions from the evidence. This constituted a broad and safe defense against criticism, and tended, I think, to add to the efficiency of his work, and to take it out of the temptations of politics. But he was too valuable a man not to use in discussing and determining departmental policy. . . .

Hoover's character interested me . . . Chief Justice Stone had appointed him when Stone was Attorney General; and Stone gave me a key to Hoover's complex character: if Hoover trusted you he would be absolutely loyal; if he did not, you had better look out; and he had to get used to his new chief each time.

I had come to office with the stamp of "liberal," and Hoover must have suspected that I would be too soft, particularly now that a war was on; too soft with Communists—so many liberals had not yet realized what the Communists were after. I think the word "liberal" included in his mind a large number of individuals whose views were considered radical by the conservatives of church and state, and carried a sense of irresponsibility. Temperamentally, Hoover was a conservative, although such an easy classification hardly describes a temperament which was clearly not reflective or philosophical. Edgar Hoover was primarily a man of immediate action.

I sought to invite his confidence; and before long, lunching with him in a room adjoining my office, he began to reciprocate by sharping some of his extraordinarily broad knowledge of the intimate details of what my associates in the Cabinet did and said, of their likes and dislikes, their weaknesses and their associations. It was as if he were saying to me that he trusted me enough to know that I would not repeat information which, except to his Chief, it would have been highly indiscreet of him to communicate, and would have been embarrassing had his revelation been communicated to the V.I.P. whom it concerned. Edgar was not above relishing a story derogatory to an occupant of one of the seats of the mighty, particularly if the little great man was pompous or stuffy . . .

I suppose these things are trivial, and I cite them to show a human side of Edgar Hoover with which he is not always credited. To be efficient to a degree not achieved by other men has built up a figure in the public imagination that excludes the warmth as well as the weaknesses of other men. And his absolute self-control strengthens the image. Behind the control is, I suspect, a temper that might show great violence if he did not hold it on a leash, subject to the domination of a will that is the master of his temperament. Of course, like all men of action, he cares for power and more power; but unlike many men it is power bent to the purpose of his life's work—the success of the Federal Bureau of Investigation.

The "information" that Hoover gave his superiors was not, however, all derogatory or malicious. In 1941, when Roosevelt was building his bridges to Britain in anticipation of American involvement in the war, he sent Harry Hopkins to London to confer with various British officials. By this time, the FBI had been authorized to have its men scattered abroad for intelligence purposes. After a dinner given by Lord Beaverbrook, the leading newspaper publisher in England and then Minister of Aircraft Production, Hoover wrote a letter to Roosevelt's aide, General Edwin "Pa" Watson, reporting on the events at Claridge's that evening. When Roosevelt was shown the letter he was, according to Robert Sherwood, "delighted."

"At the conclusion of the dinner it appeared from facial expressions that all the guests were quite happy at the result of the dinner and discussions," Hoover wrote. "Small groups of them stopped in the coffee room, where representatives of this Bureau were seated at the moment, and the gist of the conversations related to the very charming manner of Mr. Hopkins, his keen insight into current problems and the very remarkable fact that he combined a very charming but almost shy personality with a very vigorous and dynamic personality. In no instance was any unfavorable comment made and the entire gist of their conversations relative to Mr. Hopkins was positive and commendatory."

When shown Hoover's letter to "Pa" Watson, the President was fully aware that the FBI men had not been in the coffee room by chance, and that they took note of far more than the remarks about Harry Hopkins. But this is precisely what Roosevelt wanted of Hoover. What the FBI men reported of British reactions to Harry Hopkins or to anything or anyone else might be no more than chitchat, but it reflected attitudes which it was important for the President of the United States to take into account at that time. Roosevelt found the State Department totally inadequate, as other Presidents have also found, in giving him the delicate sense of what friend and foe were thinking, and he knew that the voluminous reports that passed across Hoover's desk in those days, when the essence was extracted for him, were of considerably greater value. Secretary Hull could resent being by-passed, and he let his feelings be known. But he himself had reservations about the judgment and the objectivity, to put it mildly, of some of his subordinates.

In writing of this period, Sherwood, whose source of information was Hopkins, would list among the major achievements during this period of growing American preparedness, the contribution of Edgar Hoover in that early, sub rosa, and quasi-illegal period of "common law marriage" between the United States and Britain. Said Sherwood:

There was, by Roosevelt's order and despite State Department qualms, effectively close cooperation between J. Edgar Hoover and the FBI and British security services under the direction of a quiet Canadian, William Stephenson. The purpose of this cooperation was the detection and frustration of espionage and sabotage activities in the Western Hemisphere by agents of Germany, Italy, and Japan, and also of Vichy France, Franco's Spain and, before Hitler turned eastward, the Soviet Union. It produced some remarkable results which were incalculably valuable, including the thwarting of attempted Nazi Putsches in Bolivia, in the heart ot South America, and in Panama. Hoover was later decorated by the British and Stephenson by the U.S. Government for exploits which could hardly be advertised at the time."*

*When the Office of Strategic Services (OSS) was organized under General William "Wild Bill" Donovan, the British neither respected nor trusted the organization and cooperated with it only when ordered to by the highest authority. They preferred to work, whenever possible, with Hoover and the FBI, believing, as one Englishman put it, that the "OSS leaked like a sieve, whereas the FBI was tight as a drum."

Relations with the British were not all sweetness and light, however. On one occasion, Hoover reported to Biddle that Scotland Yard had violated its territorial jurisdiction by picking up two British navy deserters in a Baltimore bar, handcuffing and tossing them into a waiting car, then driving off to New York where the men were delivered to their ship. Hoover was not so outraged as worried over the precedent. He had no desire to make waves with the British by doing the arresting in a case like this. Biddle, however, was shocked, and with Assistant Secretary of State Adolph A. Berle, one of the few men in the State Department trusted by Roosevelt on security matters, protested to Lord Halifax. The British ambassador apologized for the incident and then confessed that he knew nothing about it because his government never informed him of its secret service work.

That the relationship between Hoover and Roosevelt was a relaxed one is no better demonstrated than in the controversy that arose over wiretapping in the now-forgotten deportation case against Harry Bridges, the West Coast Communist labor leader who controlled the International Longshoreman's and Warehouseworker's Union. The law stated clearly that if Bridges were a Communist, he was deportable. Hoover was asked to investigate and submitted his report to the then Attorney General, Robert Jackson. Roosevelt opposed the litigation, so that nothing was done. But when Biddle was named Acting Attorney General, on Jackson's departure to the Supreme Court, he moved ahead with the prosecution. In the course of further investigation, the FBI had employed wiretaps and one of Hoover's agents had been discovered at this work.

The episode became a matter of testimony when Biddle came up before the Senate Judiciary Committee for confirmation as Attorney General. There was some newspaper comment, deriding the FBI for getting caught and raising the issue of the legality of wiretaps. On the second point, Hoover was in the clear. In a Justice Department safe was a letter from FDR to Attorney

General Jackson, dated May 21, 1940, which stated categorically:

> You are . . . authorized and directed in such cases as you may approve, after investigation of the need in each case, to authorize the necessary investigating agents that they are at liberty to secure information by listening devices directed to the conversation or other communications of persons suspected of subversive activities against the Government of the United States, including suspected spies. You are requested furthermore to limit these investigations so conducted to a minimum and to limit them in so far as possible to aliens.

What the newspapers did not know at the time was that the FBI agent had so bungled his job that he had left behind identifying papers when he was discovered and fled from the scene. Biddle, who knew this would come up in the hearings on his confirmation, urged Hoover to visit the President with him and to tell him all the details. Roosevelt listened to Hoover's account with a small grin on his face, then broke out into a roar of laughter. Slapping Hoover on the back, he said: "By God, Edgar, that's the first time you've been caught with your pants down!"

There were, of course, more serious attacks on Hoover during this period. The most prolonged of these attacks concerned the arrest of a group of Communists who had recruited troops for the Abraham Lincoln Brigades and for the Spanish Loyalist army during that country's sanguinary civil war. The case was an explosive one. American liberals, almost to the man, had united behind the Spanish Loyalists and saw the war as a titanic struggle between the forces of good and evil. Millions of dollars were raised for the Loyalists, though much of that money remained in Communist Party coffers. In Detroit, the drive to recruit men for the Abraham Lincoln Brigades had been a little more blatant than in other cities, however, and this brought the Federal government into the picture.

The facts were these: In 1937, Philip Raymond, then the Communist Party's candidate for governor of Michigan, had publicly directed the recruitment program. He had offered $300 a month in pay to any young man who volunteered to fight in Spain. Physical exams were conducted by three doctors connected with the staff of the Detroit Health Department who collected the bills for these examinations from the City of Detroit. Successful candidates were sent to New York where they reported to Jacob Golos, heading a special front named World Tourists, Inc.—a sideline to his regular work, espionage for Red Army Intelligence.

Routine reports of this were filed by Hoover with the Justice Department's Criminal Division. When it showed no interest, Hoover informed his field office in Detroit to spend no more time on a continuing investigation. In September 1938, however, Hoover was told by the Criminal Division that to proceed with further inquiries would be "highly desirable." Secretary Hull had prompted the request for further information. In April 1939, Hoover forwarded a detailed report to the Justice Department which told him to forget it. But on July 28, Attorney General Frank Murphy, who served briefly between the tenures of Homer Cummings and Robert Jackson, ordered the United States Attorney to prepare for prosecution. On December 18, O. John Rogge, head of the Criminal Division, ordered the United States Attorney in Detroit to "proceed with prosecution in that case immediately." On February 3, 1940, a grand jury handed up secret indictments and the FBI was ordered to proceed with the arrests.

Hoover, as he remarked to friends at the time, was not happy with the assignment. He knew that there were powerful forces within the Administration, some reaching into the White House, that would bitterly oppose prosecution. He knew, too, that much of the media would label the arrests "political persecution" and hold him responsible. "I knew that no matter how carefully I handled it," he would confide, "I would be accused of brutality, of repeating the Palmer raids, of violation of civil rights. I wanted no slip-ups, no acts that would give the supporters of these men any grounds to attack the Bureau." He therefore called in Inspector Myron Gurnea, in whom he had considerable confidence, and, in a telephone conference with Special Agent in Charge John Bugas, his Detroit man, they worked out the details of arrest procedures.

In his most decisive machine-gun delivery, Hoover gave Bugas his instructions: All the arrests were to take place at 5 a.m. The indicted people were to be taken immediately to the FBI office. A physician was to be present who would examine them on the spot and as they left, "so none of them can claim that he has been beaten, mistreated, or taken into custody when he is ill." The suspects were to be kept in separate rooms, but all doors were to be left open, for questioning, fingerprinting, and being photographed. Since they could not be arraigned until 3 p.m.—the first hour at which a Federal judge would be available, they were to be fed breakfast and lunch. If they wanted other food or drink, it was to be sent for. At the time of the arrests, no agent was to remain alone with the one woman defendant. While she was being held at the FBI office, she would be in the custody of a matron. Arresting agents were not to argue with the suspects or to bring up the subject of communism. The arrests had nothing to do with communism but with a violation of the Neutrality Act. No Communist material discovered was to be brought to the FBI office, and all seizures should relate specifically to the crime charged, namely recruiting for a foreign army.

Everything went smoothly and exactly as Hoover had directed. In two instances, suspects had refused to open the door for the FBI. In one of these cases, the agents showed the suspect their warrant through a window, shining a flashlight on it so he could read it. In another, the suspect received a phone call informing him the FBI agents were at his door. Two men refused to admit the agents and their doors were forced open. That afternoon, the suspects were taken before a Federal judge, where they stood mute. Placed under bond, they were turned over to United States marshals—and Hoover breathed a sigh of relief.

But the marshals, following a local custom where multiple defendants are being led away, handcuffed them to a chain. When newsphotos of this appeared in the papers, there was an outcry—against the FBI. Hoover was accused of Gestapo tactics. The entire left-wing press turned on Hoover and the FBI and when one of the suspects, in a by-line story for the Communist *Daily Worker,* "quoted" an FBI agent as having stated that "We only take orders from the FBI chief here, Mr. Bugas. The Bill of Rights does not mean a thing," the fat was in the fire. The *New Republic,* as usual letting its indignation outstrip the facts, devoted a full-page editorial to the "American OGPU": "In foreign countries people are forced by their governments to submit to their Gestapos," the magazine stated. "In this country, Hoover has the voluntary support of all who delight in gangster movies and ten-cent detective magazines." And then it cited Harlan Fiske Stone, the man who had made Hoover the head of the Bureau of Investigation, in its argument against Hoover and the FBI.

Under this pressure, Jackson, who had succeeded Murphy, ordered the indictments dismissed, arguing that he could see "no good to come from reviving in America at this late date the animosities of the Spanish conflict so long as the conflict has ended and some degree of amnesty at least is being extended in Spain." But the cry against the Hoover "chain-gang" had been taken up by the Congress. Representative Vito Marcantonio, who followed the Communist line without deviation, was calling for the decapitation of John Edgar Hoover. Others in the Congress, equally incensed, reached the aging Senator George W. Norris, a man whose lofty principles so often led him into bad causes. In his indignation, Norris wrote to Jackson and then took to the floor of the Senate, conceding that he had no more knowledge of the facts than what he had read in the *New Republic*—and that Jackson would have facts at hand to determine whether the *New Republic* were right. He also insisted that the crimes charged against the now-released defendants were "technical" and not of "malice." On his own, Jackson made a careful study of the record, the photographs, the allegations of those who claimed they had been mistreated, and wrote to Norris stating that "having reviewed the facts, I find nothing to justify any charge of misconduct against the Federal Bureau of Investigation." Norris persisted, agreeing that he would stand by the conclusions of a formal investigation. But when the investigators, having visited the scene and interviewed non-FBI or government individuals who had been present, concluded that "the conduct of the agents is not subject to justifiable criticism," Norris brushed it aside as a "whitewash" and labeled Hoover the "greatest hound for publicity on the American continent today."

The campaign against Hoover put on a personal and subjective plane what he had always objectively known—how the Communists could take a spurious case and build it up into a national issue. At the time he received one of Norris's early letters, Hoover had also read a report from an informant within the Communist Party that its National Committee had decided at a secret meeting that the Norris complaints could be pumped up into a nationwide campaign against the FBI. Hoover had brushed this report aside, convinced that Senator Norris would accept the evidence rather than rely on propaganda. But in a couple of months, mimeographed resolutions from groups scattered geographically were pouring into Washington, all bearing a telltale similarity. A seventy-six page memorandum charging the FBI with investigating "opinions" was being circulated in Washington, unsigned and scurrilous in nature. And Professor Franz Boas, an innocent and gentle scholar whose knowledge of life extended little beyond his field of anthropology, solicited support for a full investigation of "the dangerous nature and scope of the FBI's activities as recently exposed by Senator Norris" on the letterhead of the Communist-front American Committee for Democracy and Intellectual Freedom —an organization which he nominally headed. The questions Norris had asked, by some alchemy had been transformed into an "exposé."

To make matters worse, other rumors were lapping at the FBI's door. A demand made by Senator Theodore Green of Rhode Island for an investigation of all wiretapping was being widely interpreted as being directed at the FBI. When the Senate Judiciary Committee voted to hold the investigation, this was held to be proof positive. The truth was that Senator Green was interested in a wiretapping case involving private individuals during a Rhode Island election campaign. The evidence of this wiretapping had been turned up by the FBI itself and delivered to the Justice Department. But even Senator Green's statement that, as a matter of fact, this investigation into wiretapping practices was "partly the result of evidence uncovered by the Federal Bureau of Investigation in my state," did not quiet the rumors or weaken the attacks.

Several factors saved Hoover and the FBI. The first was the climate of the times. Most Americans saw the war reaching ever closer to their homes. There was a general fear of Nazism, and the Communists, defending the Hitler-Stalin Pact, were repeating Molotov's phrase that "fascism is a matter of taste." Therefore, the support that critics of the Bureau would normally have gotten in those years was missing. Secondly, the great mass of Americans still remembered the gangbusting Hoover. But most important of all was President Roosevelt's continuing support.

In his book on the FBI, Don Whitehead recalls a typically Rooseveltian gesture. The scene was the annual White House Correspondent's Dinner. The date was March 16, 1940. "President Roosevelt was the guest of honor," Whitehead wrote. " . . . Roosevelt spotted Hoover among the press and called to him. 'Edgar,' he said, 'what are they trying to do to you on the Hill?'

"Hoover shook his head and replied, 'I don't know, Mr. President.'

"Roosevelt grinned and turned his thumbs down. 'That's for them,' he said."

But Roosevelt's liking and trust of J. Edgar Hoover sometimes went beyond what the FBI director wanted. He saw the functions of the Bureau in severely delimited terms, and in the areas of his concept would accept any and all responsibility and power. It was, after all, for the Bureau. But he wanted no extension of these responsibilities into other areas, no matter what the need, and fought strongly against them. Shortly before the Pearl Harbor attack, for example, Roosevelt had asked Hoover to work out plans for press censorship should war break out. The President also let it be known that he would like Hoover to take over that chore when the time arrived. Both earnestly and jokingly, Hoover tried to dissuade the President by suggesting what the press would have to say were he made the censorship boss. But Roosevelt, perhaps enjoying this aspect of it, merely smiled.

Hours after the Japanese had struck, Roosevelt called Hoover and gave him oral instructions to handle all press censorship on an interim basis. Then he issued a brief memorandum to the Secretaries of War, Navy, State, and Treasury, and to the Postmaster General and the chairman of the Federal Communications Commission announcing: 'I have today directed J. Edgar Hoover, Director of the Federal Bureau of Investigation, to take charge of all censorship arrangements pending such further measures as I shall presently take."

Hoover's own plans, however, were already drafted—based on studies he had directed his agents to make of the British system. On December 8, the day after the attack, Hoover invited the secretaries and the heads of agencies named in the Roosevelt directive, plus the chairman of the Office of Facts & Figures—an early propaganda organization—to meet with him. At this conference, and to the surprise of all present, Hoover outlined his plan.

First," he said, "any office of censorship and any director of that office should be a civilian directly responsible to the President and to no one else. Secondly, the military services, the FBI, and other concerned civilian agencies should have no participation in any office of censorship but only advisory capacities. Thirdly, the director of that office should address himself to the problem of getting voluntary censorship from the press and radio. Fourthly, the director of that office should be a man with newspaper experience who is respected by the press, not a government official. And fifthly, the public should be mobilized behind a censorship program, otherwise it will never work.*

There was some debate over the Hoover proposal. Secretary of the Treasury Morgenthau believed that the responsibility for censorship should be vested in his office, as it had during World War I. After some debate, the meeting adopted Hoover's formulation and gave approval to a recommendation which went to the President. It stated:

The Director of Censorship and the censorship organization should be under no existing governmental agency and should be free from the control of the Military, Naval or any existing civilian establishments inasmuch as many governmental departments will be "customers" of the censorship organization, and no customer should control the administration of the organization. Experience in England has proved particularly that it should be free from Military and Naval control.

Then, to make sure that no pressure on him would be applied to accept the post, Hoover saw to it that the meeting recommended that "a permanent Director of Censorship be promptly designated and that he be a civilian, preferably with newspaper experience and very definitely with executive capacity."

Hoover had spelled out the qualifications with one man in mind—Byron Price, executive news editor of the Associated Press—and Hoover had his way. The country got a good man, and Hoover's hands were freed to take on the job he had in mind for the FBI—counterespionage.

*These suggestions were embodied in a formal memorandum which was sent by Hoover to the President.

12.

Roundups and Spy Scares

THE FULL TRAGIC STORY OF PEARL HARBOR—OF HOW THE UNITED
States slipped into World War II—may never be known. The
Intelligence records of the countries concerned are incomplete.
Many of the diplomatic records were deliberately destroyed.
But there are certain acts, germane to this account, which are
incontrovertible. The first is that the Office of Naval Intelli-
gence had broken the Japanese code and therefore had laser-
like insights into Japanese plans. By mid-November of 1941,
U.S. Intelligence knew that the message "East Wind Rain" on
a Japanese regular short-wave news broadcast would mean
"War With England. War with America. Peace with Russia."
That message, the Army Board which investigated the Pearl
Harbor attack reported, "was received and translated on 3

December 1941, and the contents distributed to . . . high authority."

Another incontrovertible fact is that when Secretary of State Cordell Hull rejected a modus vivendi which would have led to the withdrawal of some Japanese forces from the Asian mainland and opened the way for negotiation of the Sino-Japanese war, he "had no serious thought" that Tokyo would accept American counterproposals which were in reality an ultimatum. In fact, on November 26, when Hull discussed the ultimatum with President Roosevelt, FDR's response was that "we are likely to be attacked, perhaps next Monday." It was common knowledge in Washington, and reported by the press, that the Hull ultimatum had closed the door permanently to any agreement or understanding with Japan. The only other alternative, barring a status quo which neither Japan nor the United States wanted, was war. This, at least, is how the highest echelons in Washington were talking.

In this context, the question arises, where was the FBI in those critical days? Why did it not alert the President, the Army, and the Navy of the impending attack on Pearl Harbor? Was its counterintelligence force asleep or incompetent? Such charges were made and have been since. But the fact is that Hoover and the FBI were as much the victims—though not with such horrifying consequence—of a breakdown in American communications as the men who were showered by an East Wind Rain at Pearl and in the Philippines. For the War Department, the Navy Department, and the White House did not expect a direct military attack on Pearl Harbor as the signal that hostilities were beginning. They were convinced that the first aggressive acts of the Japanese would be sabotage. So pervasive was this belief that the military forces at Pearl were put on a sabotage alert, pulling their planes and ships together, thus making them more vulnerable to bombing.

The FBI was not then part of the military aspects of counterintelligence. Its job was to prevent sabotage and to run down spies in the United States, and even this assignment was of a limited nature. In 1940, for example, Hoover had turned down a suggestion from Roosevelt that he take over primary responsibility for investigations of sabotage, subversive activities, and espionage in Hawaii. "I have only nine special agents in the Honolulu office, and five stenographers," he told the President. "ONI has several hundred people there. In time and with proper appropriations, the Bureau could take over. But right now, it would be folly." Roosevelt agreed, and at a meeting with Admiral Walter Anderson, director of ONI, and Brigadier General Sherman Miles, who was assistant chief of G-2, it was agreed that Hoover's role would be minimal until such a time as he had the trained manpower to handle it. Late in 1940, moreover, Hoover had made it plain that "the Bureau does not consider it advisable or desirable at this particular time" to "assume responsibility for the supervision of all Japanese espionage investigations in the Territory of Hawaii." At the time of the Pearl Harbor attacks, the Army and the Navy shared the responsibility of "coverage of Japanese espionage," with the FBI a very minor partner.

Hoover, in point of fact, was having difficulties enough meeting his mandate from the President within the continental United States. He maintained that the FBI had the right and the duty to intercept and investigate coded messages being sent from the United States to the capitals of the Axis powers. He had argued this point from the day that war had broken out in Europe, only to meet the determined opposition of Federal Communications Commission Chairman James L. Fly whose somewhat bifurcated rebuttal was that (1) such intercepts were illegal, and (2) that they should be handled by the FCC alone. Hoover carried the debate to the White House where he was reassured that Roosevelt would issue the proper Executive Order untying the FBI's hands. That order still had not been issued when the bombs fell on Pearl Harbor.

Fly was in Hoover's ointment on another matter. Hoover had requested that the fingerprint cards of over 200,000 licensed radio operators, as well as those of employees of the FCC—men in sensitive positions—be turned over to the Bureau for checking. Fly refused, holding that it would be a breach of faith with those fingerprinted, a violation of their civil rights, and anathema to the leaders of unions holding jurisdiction in the communications field. Almost a month after Pearl Harbor, Fly was still refusing to turn over the fingerprints, and even the energetic intervention of Attorney General Biddle would not budge him. The United States was well into the second year of its direct involvement in the war before Fly retreated.

Hoover's battle with Fly over FBI intercepts of coded messages was not an academic one. Had the White House acted less lethargically in granting Hoover that authority, Pearl Harbor might well have been averted. For immediately after the bombing, on Hoover's instructions, the Special Agent in Charge in Honolulu had asked the local police to station an officer at the Japanese Consulate. The police guard noticed that papers were being burned, and he was able to seize a code book and a thick wad of transmitted messages from the Consul, Nagao Kita. Those messages were not only of the movement of United States Navy vessels, particularly aircraft carriers, but gave away Japanese intentions and plans. One message addressed to "Foreign Minister, Tokyo" and to "Chief of Third Section, Naval General Staff" spelled out signalling codes to Japanese fleet fliers:

". . . 2. Signal

"Light in Lanikai beach house at night.

"One light from 8 p.m. to 9 p.m. indicates '1.' From 9 p.m. to 10 p.m. indicates '2' . . . When not in accordance with above 1 full automobile headlight and one half light indicates 1, 2, 3, 4 . . .

"On Lanikai coast during daytime from 8 a.m. until noon every hour 1 piece linen cloth indicates 1, 2, 3, 4 . . .

"In Lanikai bay during daytime in front of harbor a star boat with one star on sail indicates 1, 2, 3, 4; a star and 'III' indicates 5, 6, 7, 8 . . .

"Light in dormer window of Kalama house from 7 p.m. to 1

a.m. every hour indicates 3, 4, 5, 6, 7, 8 . . ."

The numbers referred to a code, detailing the ships of the United States Navy and their dispositions. A December 3, 1941 message was an even greater giveaway:

FROM: FOREIGN MINISTER, TOKYO
TO: KITA, CONSUL, HONOLULU
STRICTLY SECRET
WOULD LIKE YOU TO HOLD ON TO YOUR LIST OF CODE WORDS (ALSO THOSE USED IN CONNECTION WITH RADIO BROADCAST) RIGHT UP UNTIL LAST MINUTE. WHEN THE BREAK COMES BURN IMMEDIATELY AND WIRE US TO THAT EFFECT.

TOGO

Another message, dated December 6, 1972, stated:

FROM: TOGO, FOREIGN MINISTER
TO: CONSUL, HONOLULU
PLEASE INFORM US IMMEDIATELY OF ANY RUMORS OF THE MOVEMENT OF WARSHIPS AFTER THE 4TH.

TOGO

General George C. Marshall was horseback riding when the Japanese attacked Pearl Harbor. J. Edgar Hoover was in New York. Edward A. Tamm, one of the top Assistant Directors, was in Griffith Stadium watching the Washington Redskins play the Phildelphia Eagles. At 2:30 Eastern Standard Time, following a brief delay, Special Agent in Charge Robert Shivers was able to get through from Honolulu to FBI headquarters in Washington. The telephone operator reached Hoover almost immediately on the FBI private line in New York. Tamm had left his seat number at the stadium with the operator, and he was also reached in very short order. As he picked up the phone, he could hear Shivers say, "The Japs are bombing Pearl Harbor. It's war. Listen, you can hear the explosions yourself."

Hoover immediately ordered Tamm and Shivers to put contingency plans, worked out previously, into operation. Then he was driven to LaGuardia airport in New York and flown back to Washington. Attorney General Biddle was in Detroit, addressing a Slav-American defense savings meeting. He rushed to the airport to fly back to Washington on an Army plane. The Cabinet was meeting at eight that night. The President, Biddle would write later, was "deeply shaken, graver than I had ever seen him before . . . The congressional leaders joined up, and the President told them the story. They were silent for a tense moment; and then Senator Tom Connally of Texas, who had recently been made chairman of the Foreign Relations Committee, sprang to his feet, banged the desk with his fist, his face purple. 'How did they catch us with our pants down, Mr. President?' he shouted. And the President, his head bowed, his assurance at low ebb, muttered, 'I don't know, Tom, I just don't know . . .' "

Meanwhile, the FBI had been at work. Just days before, Hoover had instructed all special agents to be prepared to move immediately for "the apprehension of Japanese aliens in your district who have been recommended for custodial action." This order had been based on a prior Hoover directive to his agents, ordering the compilation of a list of all aliens who might prove dangerous in time of war. Included were Japanese, Germans, Italians, and even some Spanish—members of the Falangist wing of the Franco government who were working with Nazi agents. The list was relatively small, some four thousand individuals, of which less than eight hundred were Japanese. But Hoover could take no action until he was given specific authority by the Attorney General. Biddle, in turn, had to wait for a Presidential order which he did not receive until after the Sunday night Cabinet meeting. But Hoover was not taking any chances; through Louis Nichols, his de facto second-in-command, he had ordered an immediate surveillance of every person on the list. "Don't take anybody into custody until we get the green light," Nichols told impatient SACs. "But don't let any of those people get away from you even if you have to plant yourself on their doorsteps."

The moment the orders had been signed, the FBI teletype began clacking away with Hoover's message: "Immediately take into custody all Japanese who have been classified in A, B, and C categories in material previously transmitted to you. Take immediate action and advise Bureau frequently by teletype as to exact identity of persons arrested. Persons taken into custody should be turned over to nearest representative of Immigration and Naturalization Service." Hoover was working under direct orders to make arrests without warrants, a wartime measure that both Biddle and the President felt were necessary—but he wanted no charges of new Palmer raids.* It was a part of his plan, therefore, to have suspected subversive aliens brought immediately before a civilian board for a hearing where they were represented by counsel.

With the help of FBI-trained local police, the Bureau went into high gear. In less than 72 hours, 3,846 aliens were quietly taken into custody. (In the course of the war, some 16,000 enemy aliens were arrested.) With the tacit approval of Roosevelt, moreover, he moved into areas which were strictly not part of the FBI's jurisdiction. The airlines were requested not to carry any Japanese passengers until events dictated a different course. Air express packages addressed to or sent by Japanese were barred. Sabotage and espionage alerts were sent to defense industries. And he banned all press and other communications to Japan and occupied territory which again brought him into conflict with FCC Chairman Fly, who told the communications industry to disregard the FBI stop orders. The companies heeded Hoover, not Fly.

In those first days of the war, another problem arose. Hoover held a reserve commission of lieutenant colonel. Clyde Tolson, technically second man in the Bureau, was a reserve Navy commander. Other agents of all ranks held reserve commissions. Many wanted to see active service. The decision was made for all of them by Secretary of War Henry L. Stimson and Secretary of the Navy Frank Knox who asked them to resign

*Roosevelt was worried about the Japanese and the Germans. But as he told Biddle, "I don't care about the Italians. They're a lot of opera singers."

their commissions and remain in the FBI in order to utilize "every man in the capacity in which he can contribute most to the defense effort."

There were certainly enough "contributions" for Hoover and the FBI to make. As the number of war prisoners in the United States rose to well past the 400,000 mark, with escapes numbering seventy-five a month, the FBI was assigned the task of tracking down escapees. There were literally thousands of reports of sabotage, most of which proved to be individual acts perpetrated by men angry at their employers and not motivated by anti-American feelings. It was Hoover's view that these acts, which could lead to death and destruction for Americans in combat, should be punished as stringently as those of enemy agents—but he was overruled in this by the Justice Department.

Hoover was also under pressure to repeat the mass roundups of draft dodgers that had been conducted during World War I. (One such raid in 1918 had dragged in fifty-thousand young men in New York alone, the majority of whom were guilty only of not carrying draft cards.) It was Hoover's position that the important thing was to get men into uniform, not create mass hysteria, and he refused to let the FBI be used for this latter purpose. Each case of draft evasion was carefully investigated before action was taken, and the largest single sweep, in thirty-nine cities, netted less than eight hundred culprits, with more than 150 in New York City.

Hoover was also entrusted with investigating war contractors who falsified tests of military material in order to make a bigger profit. Faulty hand grenades with insufficient charges, shells that were not properly armed, bad wiring for field telephones and ships—all these were turned up by FBI agents who proved the value of the laboratories set up by Hoover to aid in peacetime law enforcement. Of a far touchier nature was the FBI's role in helping to determine whether a conscientious objector was sincere or simply trying to evade military service.

Among the vaster operations conceived by Hoover and

turned over to the FBI was the Special Intelligence Service. The Germans and the Italians, who had long prewar contacts and business relations with Latin America, were using them as a means of building up espionage apparatuses which, hopefully, could penetrate the soft underbelly of the United States. The problem was a sensitive one because countermeasures would have to be taken in countries of varying friendliness to the United States. Hoover, therefore, took up the question with Assistant Secretary of State Berle, a trusted expert on Latin American matters. With Roosevelt's approval, Berle invited Hoover to discuss the problem with the heads of ONI and G-2. There was agreement on the need for an SIS which would funnel information to the State Department, to G-2, and to ONI on the financial, political, economic, and espionage operations of the Axis powers in Latin America. A directive by Roosevelt, assigning to Hoover and the FBI all nonmilitary intelligence functions south of the border—with G-2 and ONI continuing to handle the strictly military aspects of this work—was issued. It took Hoover, who had blueprinted the plan carefully before proposing it, thirty days to set it in motion.*

In the light of later attacks on Hoover, his one major stand during the war years against the White House assumes considerable significance. It was a stand shared with Attorney General Biddle and with a few courageous souls on the West Coast, including Mayor Harry P. Cain of Tacoma who as a senator in the Fifties was strongly attacked as an enemy of civil liberties, and Senator Sheridan Downey of California. (These two men, Biddle would write years later, were the only two elected officials on the West Coast who strongly opposed mass evacuation of Japanese-Americans and their confinement to "relocation" camps.)

*The story of the SIS, its daring operations, and its successes in keeping Axis agents off balance would require a book in itself. It was for many years kept secret by Hoover and Berle, and only a small part of it has ever been made public. "I do not think a similar operation has ever been carried on," Berle wrote Hoover in 1946, "and I can personally attest to the brilliance of the results."

Pressure to root out Japanese-Americans from their homes and away from their businesses began almost after Pearl Harbor. On December 10, Hoover received a call from Secretary of the Treasury Morgenthau requesting that he meet with him at the Treasury Department. At this meeting, according to Hoover's memorandum to Biddle, Morgenthau stated "that he had been in communication with his representatives in San Francisco and as a result had ascertained that the task they were carrying out" of freezing Japanese assets "was an enormous one and that he believed more drastic measures should be taken to adequately cover and complete it. The Secretary then put in a call to . . . one of his representatives in San Francisco . . . It was the opinion of Mr. X that there should be a round-up of Japanese in San Francisco, as well as in certain sections of the San Joaquin Valley . . .

I told the Secretary that I felt you would be reluctant to approve any such program unless there were sufficient facts upon which to justify the cases of the persons arrested, as I believed you would be opposed to any "drag-net" or "round-up" procedure. I pointed out to the Secretary that in the arrests which had already been made of the Japanese, German, and Italian alien enemies, factual cases had had to be prepared on each one of them prior to their arrests and that these had to be approved by the Attorney General, and that of course citizens of the United States were not included in any arrests as the authority to make arrests was limited to alien enemies . . . unless there were specific actions upon which criminal complaints could be filed . . . .

At that time, the major thrust was against the Japanese. But Hoover was aware that the intent was to include Japanese-Americans as well, for reasons ranging from hysteria to a greedy desire to take over going businesses at a miserable fraction of their worth. He hinted at this in his memorandum to Biddle, noting that "the necessity for mass evacuation is based primarily upon public hysteria and political pressure rather than on factual data." But the pressure mounted and what had been demands for the evacuation of Japanese nationals spread to include Japanese-Americans. Statistics were falsified to "prove" the threat posed by these Japanese-Americans. The Army general who conducted the evacuation justified it by announcing that "more than 60,000 rounds of ammunition and many rifles, shotguns and maps of all kinds" had been found in a single raid. What the public was not told—but Biddle learned from Hoover—was that this "arsenal" came from a sporting goods store owned by a Japanese alien and from a warehouse of the owner of a general store. Such explosives as were found had been taken from those using them for legitimate industrial purposes.

Those pressing for the evacuation charged that "substantially every ship" leaving a West Coast port after December 7 was attacked by enemy submarines and that this pointed "conclusively to the existence of hostile shore-to-ship communication." However, after Hoover had investigated he was able to report categorically to Biddle that there had been no submarine attacks on West Coast shipping following Pearl Harbor. Every complaint of signaling had been investigated, Hoover added, but in no case "has any information been obtained which would substantiate the allegation that there has been signaling from shore-to-ship since the beginning of the war." In fact, as later careful inquiries determined, there was no proven instance of espionage among the Japanese population after Pearl Harbor in either Hawaii or the United States mainland.

But the forces pressing for the unconstitutional acts which ended with the "relocation" in concentration camps of innocent Japanese-Americans—and these included men like Walter Lippmann and Earl Warren—were not interested in acts. When they had convinced Franklin D. Roosevelt, who, as Francis Biddle would write, "thought that rights should yield to the necessities of war" even if this meant the rape of the rights of American citizens, then it became a fait accompli. Hoover always considered himself a "good soldier" so he stood mute before the bar of his conscience. He could salve that conscience by arguing to himself, and to friends, that the Bureau had not been a part of the decision. And it can be added in his favor that the "relocation" fight was but a small part of his duties. Facing him then was the grand design of espionage from both Communist and Fascist sides—and here he did not have to face any personal recriminations.

13.

The Enemy Spies

TESTIFYING BEFORE THE ROBERTS COMMISSION, DURING THE FIRST
civilian inquiry into the Pearl Harbor tragedy, Special Agent in
Charge Robert Shivers, of the Honolulu field office, said flatly:
"If we had been able to get the messages that were sent to Japan
by the Japanese consul, we would have known, or we could
have reasonably assumed, that the attack would come, somewhere, on December 7; because if you recall, this system of
signals that was devised by Otto Kühn for the Japanese Consul
Generals simply included the period from December 1 to
December 7."

Had the FCC not intervened, the FBI would have had those
messages, and there is little doubt that John Edgar Hoover
would have gotten them to the President immediately. With the
intercepted messages, moreover, the FBI would have been able

immediately to pick up the man who was to send the signals. For Otto Kühn was one of the group of pro-Nazis in Hawaii which its small office had singled out for investigation. The Bureau put its finger on Kühn on the slim lead from G-2 that the Japanese Foreign Office was interested in a couple named "Friedell." Friedel, Bureau agents discovered was Mrs. Otto Kühn's maiden name. Names and address had gone into the files when spot checking had turned up no evidence against the couple. Espionage in Hawaii, moreover, was a military responsibility, and the FBI's minuscule forces were alerted to watch out for sabotage.

The moment the intercepts reached Washington, Hoover gave the signal for the Honolulu office to swing into action, and Kühn was arrested in short order. And in his confession, Kühn acknowledged that he had given the Japanese a full report on the number of battleships, cruisers, aircraft carriers, destroyers, and submarines clustered at Pearl Harbor or cruising in nearby Hawaiian waters. Kühn was convicted of espionage by a military court—one of the ninety-one persons so convicted between 1938 and 1945—and sentenced to death, but this was commuted to fifty years of hard labor. (In 1948, he was released for deportation to Argentina.)

But the FBI had been busily penetrating Nazi espionage long before Pearl Harbor. "Even before the outbreak of hostilities in 1939," Hoover recalled after the war, "we knew that the Nazis were training spies at the Klopstock Pension in Hamburg for service against the United States. We knew, too, that the *Abwehr,* the vast German espionage organization, considered the FBI a bungling organization and was convinced that its agents were operating with immunity among us. They learned in time how efficient we were." Hoover was right in this, though he exaggerated the FBI's role in frustrating the Nazi espionage machine by implying, but never quite saying, that he had infiltrated the Klopstock school with his own agents. There was no need for this little fiction. Through his official ties with MI-5 and other allied Intelligence organizations, he received the tips which were the basis for the FBI's indubitably brilliant performance.

The major Nazi spy caught in the FBI web was Karl Frederick Ludwig. American-born and of German parents, Ludwig had lived most of his life in Germany, though he had returned frequently to the United States. In 1940 Ludwig was sent to the United States by the *Abwehr* at his own suggestion. His cover name was "Joe" in the files of Nazi espionage. His operation was smooth and daring, and the information he sent his spymasters was of great value.

The first clue to Ludwig's activities was a letter, read by a British censor in January 1941, which seemed suspicious. She turned it over to William Stephenson, head of the British Secret Service in the Americas—a Canadian who liked to refer to Hoover as the "formidable halfback." When his own operatives failed to trace "Joe," Stephenson turned over a number of intercepted letters to Hoover. But the FBI found itself equally defeated by the elusive spy. The break came in March 1941, when one of Joe's letters was intercepted by the FBI. It reported a fatal accident to "Phil" who was struck down in New York's traffic, and told of notifying "Phil's" consulate. When the letter was treated for secret ink, it disclosed a telltale message:

"Date of the accident 18 March about 20:45 . . . The hospital where he was taken to and died is Saint Vincent's Hospital. Phil died on Tuesday, 16:30 o'clock (March 19, 1941). The Consulate mentioned is the Spanish."

This was enough for the FBI. A check at St. Vincent's showed that a "Julio Lopez" was the accident victim. He had arrived in New York two days previously from the Far East, having made a stopover at Pearl Harbor, where he had checked in at the Taft Hotel.* Among the papers found in Julio Lopez's rooms were

*Searching through *Abwehr* records which he had unearthed after the fall of the Third Reich, Ladislas Farago came across a record of what "Lopez" had been doing in Hawaii: drawing up detailed plans of Pearl Harbor which he had forwarded the the *Abwehr* as "of certain interest to our Yellow allies."

letters addressed to Carl Wilhelm von der Osten of Denver, Colorado, the dead man's brother. Hoover and the FBI knew then that one of the *Abwehr's* most important agents had been killed on a New York street. This was the first real lead to the identity of Joe. Within two days, Hoover was able to inform Stephenson that "investigation has disclosed that 'Joe' is identical with one Frederick Ludwig."

With "Joe's" identity in its possession, it was only a matter of time before the FBI was able to track him down. He had operated openly as a businessman in New York, and as he fled to the West Coast, he left an incriminating trail. When he was picked up, trying to board a Japanese freighter, he implicated other German agents—and an important spy ring was broken.

Of perhaps more significance than the arrest of Ludwig was the FBI's success in solving the mystery of the "little dots." In January 1940, the FBI, by means Hoover has never disclosed, made contact with a young man who had just been graduated from the Nazi espionage school at the Klopstock Pension in Hamburg. In a New York hotel room, hours after the young man had landed in this country, he told two FBI agents a puzzling story.

My class was graduated two weeks ago. In a farewell speech, the principal, Dr. Hugo Sebold, said, "The greatest problem of the Führer's agent in North and South America is keeping in touch with us. The Americans have given us a great deal of trouble. But before long we shall be communicating back and forth throughout the world with impunity. I cannot explain the method now but watch out for the dots —lots and lots of little dots." I have been sent to America with my orders—and was told nothing more.

Was this a ploy—part of the game of misinformation which espionage services play to deceive the enemy? It did not seem so to Hoover. As he would later tell it, "Until this time, we had kept German and Japanese espionage backed into a corner by constantly uncovering every new enemy communications technique. . . . Once we took from a spy's pocket a box of safety matches. Four of them, looking just like the others, were actually little pencils that wrote invisibly, the writing later to be developed by a solution made from a rare drug. This story-book contraption we exposed . . . All these devices and more we had detected. But what was this matter of 'lots of little dots'?"

Working in the FBI laboratory was a young physicist who was a expert in microphotography. Hoover repeated the story to him and assigned him to undertake certain experiments, based on his guesses as to what the "little dots" might signify. Agents were also told to keep their eyes open for "dots"—an order that must have led some to believe that the Director was cracking up. But what seemed like a wild chase after a wilder story paid off.

In August 1941 the FBI "met" a traveler from the Balkans on his arrival to the United States. "There was reason to believe that he was a German agent," Hoover has since recounted.

We examined his possessions with meticulous care. While a laboratory agent was holding an envelope so that the light slanted obliquely across its surface, he saw a sudden tiny gleam. A dot had reflected the light. A dot—a punctuation period on the front of the envelope, a black particle no bigger than a fly speck.

With infinite care, the agent touched the point of a needle under the rim of the black circle and pried it loose. It was a bit of alien matter that had been driven into the fiber of the paper, where it looked like a typewritten period. Under the microscope it was magnified 200 times. And then we could see that it was an image on film of a full-sized typewritten letter.

The message, in clumsy English, was a chiller:

There is reason to believe that the scientific works for the utilization of atomic-kernel energy are being driven forward into a certain direction in the United States partly by use of helium. Continuous information about the tests made on this subject are required and particularly:

1. What process is used in the United States for transporting heavy uranium?

2. Where are tests being made with uranium? (Universities, industrial laboratories, etc.)

3. Which other raw materials are being used in these tests? Entrust only best experts with this.

Confronted by the FBI with this evidence, the agent eventually explained the microdot process in detail to the FBI. Armed with this knowledge, the Bureau began examining all suspect mail for the microdots. "On one spy," according to Hoover, "we found what seemed like an innocent telephone message on a crumpled memo form from a switchboard. But the printing of that blank contained two periods which, when enlarged, contained several messages."

Discovery of the microdot technique proved one of the most important finds for FBI counterespionage. It was particularly useful in the FBI's work against Axis agents in Latin America, where they maintained numerous letter drops. The FBI discovered microdots in all sorts of letters from all sorts of people— as Hoover described it, "love letters, family letters, business communications, all seemingly harmless. But their microdot messages were full of information about war production, about blowing up seized Axis ships in South American harbors, and about penetration of governments. Those letters were written or typed by different people, but the microdots were all produced by the same machine and the signatures on the secret messages were all in the same handwriting. So we knew that they came from a single source. As a result of having these messages, we were able to make one great round-up, handled by South American authorities but with the aid of the FBI—and we were able to seize a great interlocking ring of Nazi agents south of the border."

Ironically, one of the most celebrated "feats" of the FBI during the war period was one in which it played a relatively routine role—the case of the saboteurs who landed on Long Island, in Florida, and in Maine from Nazi submarines with explosives to blow up major American industrial plants. What broke up this sabotage attempt was the incredible stupidity of the Nazi agents and the eagerness of some of them to avoid a dangerous mission by spilling all to the FBI. Once the saboteurs had given themselves away by the clumsiness of their landings, it was a matter of detection work to round them up—and when two of their number made contact directly with the Bureau, the discovery and arrest of the other saboteurs was a foregone conclusion.

The drama in the case was not in the details of the arrest, but in the worried hours shared by Hoover and Attorney General Biddle as one question pressed in on them: Would the saboteurs be able to carry out any of their plans before they were rounded up? Biddle describes those hours and days vividly:

All of Edgar Hoover's imaginative and restless energy was stirred into prompt and effective action. His eyes were bright, his jaw set, excitement flickering around the edge of his nostrils when he reported the incident to me. He was determined to catch them all before any sabotage took place. He had steadily insisted that this war could be fought without sabotage. But he was, of course, worried. The immediate problem was whether the Coast Guard and patrols along the Atlantic beaches should be alerted, indeed whether the public should not be told—other submarines might be landing as we talked; or whether FBI agents alone should work on the capture of the eight, and every effort made to prevent the news of the landings getting into the papers and being read by the quarry. We both thought the latter course was preferable; but I wanted the President's approval, and telephoned him. He agreed.

When Hoover called Biddle to tell him that all but one of the saboteurs had been caught and the eighth was being cornered, Biddle's worries continued. What if there were others caches of explosives? What if the last of the saboteurs eluded the FBI? Would there be another Black Tom explosion, such as the one which devastated New York harbor in World War I? Biddle was dining with Constantine Fotich, the Yugoslav ambassador, that night and when he received a call from Hoover informing him that the last of the saboteurs had been taken, Biddle felt, as he later recalled, "a flood or relief." Biddle immediately called Roosevelt, who was at Hyde Park, to give him the news. He also reported that the caches of explosives and other paraphernalia had been found and that $715,000 had been taken from the arrested men.*

"Not enough," Roosevelt said. "Let's make real money out of them. Sell the rights to Barnum and Bailey for a million and a half to exhibit them around the country in cages at a dollar a head." And, Biddle later commented, "I think he would have enjoyed doing it."

The next greatest contribution to the counterespionage effort —and one which contributed substantially to the Allied victory —was in the Sebold case, and in its twin, the ND98 case. In both these cases, it was not merely detection and apprehension which counted. Of far more significance in assaying the FBI's role was its ability to meet head-on the *Abwehr* and the brains of Nazi espionage, fool them, and put them to Allied use.

William George Sebold—born Wilhelm George Debowski— was of German birth. When he was twenty-three, he had jumped ship in Galveston. Liking the United States, he changed his name, married, and became a citizen. He held a series of odd jobs—dishwasher, bartender, mechanic at an aircraft plant —until 1938 when, after an illness, he decided he wanted to see his family in Germany. Even after the war broke out, he remained in Germany, working as a mechanic. The United States was neutral, and he felt no compulsion to return. But the Gestapo had singled him out as a man who could be sent back to do undercover work for the Third Reich in the United States. The first approaches failed, until the Gestapo discovered that he had run afoul of the law as a young man in his home town of Muehlheim—a fact Sebold had failed to disclose to naturalization authorities when he got his citizenship. He was also threatened with imprisonment in a concentration camp. Thereupon, Sebold agreed to work for the *Abwehr*.

*One by-product of the breakup of the sabotage attempt was not known until after the war. When Berlin learned of the arrests, Admiral Doenitz, who commanded the Germany navy, flew into a rage that his submarines had been put into jeopardy by being sent right up to the American coast for the landings— and without his knowledge. His anger added to the infighting in the German High Command and therefore indirectly served Allied purposes.

But before Sebold reported for training at the Klopstock Pension, he visited the American Consulate in Cologne, with the knowledge of the Gestapo, ostensibly to arrange for sending money to his wife in the United States. But what Sebold "arranged" with Vice Consul Dale W. Maher was something entirely different. He confessed to Maher that he was being blackmailed into accepting an *Abwehr* espionage assignment and that, following his training as a radio operator, he would be sent to the United States. This information was immediately passed on to the FBI by Maher. Sebold returned to Hamburg where, in a seven-week course, he was throughly trained in radio telegraphy, Morse code, the operation and construction of short-wave transmitters, and the use of codes.

At the FBI, however, the question of Sebold became a high-level problem. Could Sebold be a plant? Hoover wondered. And if he was sincere, to what use could he be put? If the FBI made use of Sebold and he was a plant, would he learn more about the Bureau's operations than it would learn about Nazi espionage? Hoover decided to take the chance. Sebold, he reasoned, would be in the United States and under constant FBI watch. His first misstep would, therefore, be discovered. And he could be invaluable in giving the FBI leads on other Nazi agents, whether sincere or not.

On February 6, 1940, Sebold arrived in the United States. He carried with him the names of four "collectors" whose reports he would transmit, an American passport in the name of William G. Sawyer, five pieces of microfilm hidden in his watch case—instructions for the collectors—$1,000 in cash, and orders to open an office in midtown Manhattan and set up a transmitter. In his head, he carried precious information on the *Abwehr* and on Major Nikolaus Ritter, spymaster of the apparatus in the United States. By this time, Hoover had decided that Sebold could be used for transmitting false information to the Nazis and as a magnet which would attract other Nazi agents into the view of the FBI.

The FBI was waiting for Sebold. To have absolute security in the midtown office Sebold had been instructed to open, Hoover turned to Vincent Astor, an officer in the Office of Naval Intelligence. Astor provided the FBI space in the Knickerbocker Building on 42nd Street and Broadway—once the historic Knickerbocker Hotel at which Enrico Caruso lived and later to become the Newsweek Building—which Astor owned.

Sebold's office—the Diesel Import Company—was converted into a counterespionage agent's dream. There were two-way mirrors behind which the FBI could film every visitor. The rooms were wired for sound. The FBI portion of the office was in direct telephone contact with the New York field office and with FBI cars which could tail those who did business with Sebold. At the same time, a radio transmitter was built to the *Abwehr*'s specifications in Centerport, Long Island, but Sebold was never permitted to visit it or even know where it was. Recordings were made of Sebold's "fist"—a term for the individual touch which every telegrapher develops and which is recognizable to experts. Two FBI agents were painstakingly trained to duplicate what was, in effect, Sebold's telegraphic handwriting.

Two months after his arrival, Sebold was prepared to begin operations. He had contacted his collectors, and he was ready to start. The *Abwehr* in Hamburg gave him—the FBI really— a schedule, a code name (Tramp), and the key for the messages he was to send, Rachel Field's *All This and Heaven Too*. All urgent messages were to be transmitted by Tramp and as communications with other agents became more difficult, the *Abwehr* transferred them to Sebold. And in Hamburg, he was the wonder of the *Abwehr*. Documents found after the war indicate the delight and respect the Nazis had for this agent who was so brilliant and so shrewd that he was able to evade FBI surveillance for so long.

To maintain Sebold's cover, the FBI had to transmit all the messages brought by Nazi agents. Had it not, word might have gotten back to Germany, compromising Sebold's position. Among those he sent back were some of tremendous military significance—that Roosevelt had ordered the Army to deliver the highly secret and highly effective Norden bombsight to the British and that the British would be manufacturing them in England; the movement of ships in and out of New York harbor, technical information. But Hoover was also working with G-2 and ONI, preparing false information which would mislead the Nazis. The Nazi agents also did some of their own, though unwitting, misleading. In February 1941, Tramp radioed Hamburg with the message:

CHURCHILL HERE IN BATTLESHIP KING GEORGE V. VISITED ON SHIPBOARD BY ROOSEVELT AND KNOX.

The information was somewhat off. Lord Halifax, the British ambassador, was on board when the King George V docked at Annapolis. But the Nazis did know that this battleship was in American waters on its maiden voyage, and that the President had visited it—something which only the highest echelons of the United States government knew.

Then, on June 29, 1941, Hoover announced the "greatest spy round-up in a series of raids." There was consternation not only in Hamburg, at *Abwehr* headquarters, but throughout the German High Command. The German Foreign Office was also up in arms. The United States and Germany were still technically at peace and this made diplomatic relations more difficult. But what hurt the most was the effect of the FBI dragnet. Thirty of Germany's best agents were rounded up. Five different spy rings were smashed. The only consolation for the *Abwehr* was that Sebold was not among those arrested. Then, during the trial of the spies, Sebold surfaced, as a witness for the government. And there was worse news for the Nazis. The FBI had been able to infiltrate a sixth important Nazi apparatus and compromise its members. As Ladislas Farago would write in his encyclopedic account of Nazi espionage, *The Game of the Foxes,* "The FBI—which even a few months before seemed so indolent and ineffective—was now suddenly revealed as the world's most effective counterespionage force."*

ND98 was another kind of agent. Trained by the *Abwehr,* he was sent to Montevideo as a spy, to set up a radio transmitter and to transmit "information from America concerning war production and military installations." Once in Montevideo, ND98 came to the conclusion that life would be pleasanter and more profitable in New York. Through an American Embassy official in Montevideo, he made contact with the FBI which concurred in at least one part of ND98's aspirations—that he come to the United States. Hoover hoped that he would now have another Sebold. On FBI instructions, therefore, ND98 wired Hamburg that it was "impossible to obtain information desired" in Montevideo and that he was going to the United States "where I will be able to operate more freely."

In February 1942, when the United States was at war, ND98 began transmitting information from the short-wave radio built for Sebold on Long Island. Every scrap of information sent out by ND98 was prepared by the FBI, under Hoover's careful supervision and the screening of Joint Security Control at the Pentagon. The major effort was to mislead the enemy—the trickiest form of counterintelligence since enough truth must be mixed with falsehood to deceive. Enough of what the enemy wants to know must be in the package to make him buy it all. Hoover also hoped to make ND98's operation seem so foolproof to the Germans that they would use him as a central transmitter, thereby bringing other important Nazi agents into the FBI net. What Hoover did not know at the time was that the FBI had so devastated the Nazi apparatus in the United States that, except for a handful of unimportant agents, the only one left was working for him.

At Hoover's orders, therefore, ND98 began to send complaints that he "urgently" needed help, and requesting that

---

*It might be added that it was probably the only one that showed some financial return. At the end of the war, the FBI had turned over to the Treasury $366,125 in cash and valuables taken from Nazi espionage agents who defected or were arrested.

other agents be assigned to him. The *Abwehr* consistently replied that ND98 was "too valuable" to be exposed to other agents and that the operation was already too expensive. When ND98 threatened to quit because "strain and danger are great," the *Abwehr* immediately gave him a bonus of $20,000—in addition to the $34,000 it had already paid him—money which was turned over by Hoover to the Alien Property Custodian.

In November 1942 Hoover and the Joint Chiefs of Staff decided to gamble by ordering ND98 to report to Hamburg that the United States planned a major attack on the Northern Kurile Islands. There was some danger in this, because an attack was being mounted on the Kuriles. But it was to be diversionary, while the main United States forces attacked the Marshall Islands. The *Abwehr* dutifully passed ND98's message to the Japanese who reinforced the Kuriles at the expense of the Marshall Islands, thereby guaranteeing the success of the major American thrust, as the Joint Chiefs of Staff acknowledged to Hoover.

But ND98 really came into his own in the days before the Allied invasion of the Normandy coast on June 6, 1944. It was of utmost importance that Hitler and the German High Command be kept in a state of confusion as to the exact place where the Allies were to open the long-awaited Second Front. This, it was hoped, would force the Nazis to scatter their forces. It would also cast doubt on whatever solid intelligence they had as to the target of the major invasion thrust. The date of the attack was also to be kept from the Germans by the use of applied disinformation.

Working in tandem with the British, Hoover contributed conspicuously to that confusion. The *Abwehr* was given statistics of military production which showed that there had been bad delays in the production of invasion craft. And five days before D-Day, ND98 wired the *Abwehr:*

NEVI REPORTS THAT EXPRESS LINERS ILE DE FRANCE AND NEW AMSTERDAM WILL LEAVE NEW YORK HARBOR FOR UNDISCLOSED MEDITERRANEAN DESTINA-

TION WITHIN NEXT FEW DAYS APPEARING OF HIGHEST IMPORTANCE INDICATING
SOME PLAN CHANGE IT APPEARS THAT A FORCE CONSISTING OF A NUMBER OF
INFANTRY AND ARMORED DIVISIONS ORIGINALLY SCHEDULED FOR UNITED KING-
DOM ARE BEING DIVERTED FOR A SPECIAL OPERATION. WILL MAKE EVERY EF-
FORT TO ASCERTAIN FURTHER DETAILS

This was the last truly significant message sent by ND98,
though he continued to file to Hamburg until the city fell to
Allied forces in May 1945. It gave Hoover particular pleasure,
in his postwar recounting of the exploit, to point out that the
entire ND98 operation had been financed by the Nazis themselves.

The one other major Nazi spy working within the United
States was Walter Koehler. Though well on in years—he had
been a spy for the Kaiser in World War I—he was one of the few
agents of any ability left to the *Abwehr* who knew the United
States. His physical characteristics, moreover, were a plus factor—as was his background. Hoover described him as "a
swarthy, short, heavy-set man with thick-lensed glasses who
walked with a stoop—hardly the spy type." He was a bona fide
Dutchman and a Roman Catholic, which would give him protective coloration as a refugee of Nazi terror in the United
States. Though a jeweler by trade, he had a fairly good grasp
of technical and scientific matters.

The *Abwehr* picked him, after months of ignored warnings
to the German General Staff that something was afoot in the
nuclear physics field in America, to acquire "additional information about American plans and of the progress made in the
United States in the field of nuclear research." After a crash
course in the fundamentals of nuclear physics, Koehler and his
wife, who was part of his cover and also an assistant in his
espionage work, were sent to Madrid. Their instructions were
to apply for a visa to the United States at the American consulate there, posing as refugees. The *Abwehr* was convinced that
the "stupid" Americans would fall for the trick. The city was
crowded with refugees clamoring for admittance to the United
States, and the Koehlers would appear as just two more unfor-

tunate people seeking asylum. The *Abwehr* had little doubt that Koehler, who was famous in the German secret service for his persuasive ways, would succeed in getting a visa. But Koehler, whose strength and weakness as a spy had always been that he worked things out for himself, decided on another strategy.

When he was ushered into the vice consul's office, Koehler immediately put aside all pretense that he was a refugee. He confessed he was an agent for the *Abwehr,* assigned by the Nazis to spy on the United States. To prove it, he pulled out of his wallet a series of microphotos which he thrust at the vice consul. As Hoover later described it, "They dealt with every detail of building and operating a shortwave radio, frequency tables, ciphers, hours of transmission on a copy of the Dutch national anthem, and a copy of the Dutch-language prayer book, on which his code was based. Koehler pleaded that he had never intended to work for the Nazis and that he had gone through with it just to get out of Europe. He insisted that he loved the United States and would willing serve it as a counterspy."* Koehler also produced $16,230 in cash, travelers checks, and gold coins, as well as several pieces of valuable jewelry. The vice consul told him, in effect, "Don't call us, we'll call you" and through the State Department notified Hoover. A check of the espionage files which the Bureau had been collecting for years disclosed immediately that Koehler was lying when he posed as a man caught in the toils of the *Abwehr* and ready to betray his masters. Most of Koehler's record was there for Hoover to ponder. The question for him was: "Can we use Koehler to double-cross Hitler, as he is attempting to double-cross us, or will it be too risky?"

It was a decision Hoover had to make, consulting no one outside of the FBI. In such a sensitive area, he could not count

*Whenever Hoover told this story, he referred to Koehler as "Albert van Loop" to protect his identity. But since analysis of *Abwehr* records has identified Van Loop as Koehler, the true name of the agent has been substituted in this account.

on the security of any other government agency. After all, Secretary of State Hull had violated security on the most important military secret of the war—that we had broken the Japanese code. This had reached the Germans who passed it on to Tokyo which, as a postwar search of the records showed, fortunately did not believe it. After some intensive soul-searching, Hoover decided that it was worth the risk to give Koehler his visa and to put him to work for the United States. "Send him along," he cabled the Madrid consulate. Hoover was one of the few Americans who knew what was going on at Los Alamos, and he wanted to make sure that the Germans learned as little as possible of the scope and success of American efforts at producing an atomic bomb.

When Koehler arrived in the United States, he was questioned at some length about his past and forced to admit that the story he had told in Madrid was a fabrication. Then, in mid-July 1942, the Koehlers were moved to a New York hotel where they could be kept under strict surveillance. Hoover was taking no chances. A secret inspection of Koehler's baggage had led to the discovery of items which he had not mentioned —equipment for microphotography, chemicals for making secret inks, a miniature Leica camera. Koehler was confronted with this, as well as the information that his wife had paid what she thought was a secret visit to a minor Nazi agent to pick up money.

While the FBI constructed a transmitter on Long Island for Koehler, special agents studied his sending idiosyncrasies, as they had with Sebold. This was particularly important since the FBI knew that Koehler would be transmitting directly to a radio operator who, as Hoover would relate, "could identify the sending style of anyone with whom he had even once communicated." Other agents were also analyzing the idiomatic oddities of Koehler's German so they could reproduce it in phrasing his messages. On February 7, 1943, Koehler made his first radio contact with Hamburg. Until May 1945 Koehler sent a steady stream of messages to the *Abwehr,* though he was never allowed to visit the transmitting station on Long Island.

"We gave the Nazis industrial and military information on a week-to-week basis," Hoover has written. "Most of the information we gave them was true, because we wanted to give Koehler a high degree of credibility. It was a touchy situation because we did not want to give away anything of real importance and also because we could not let it appear that Koehler knew too much. After all, he was a single agent working alone in the United States. If he had been too knowing, the Germans would have suspected us. Really, what we wanted out of the Koehler operation was to prevent the Nazis from sending others to pry into our nuclear activities. But we also wanted to learn how Nazi agents on the American continent were being paid. And of considerable importance in an operation of this kind, we wanted to know what the Nazis wanted to know." In counterespionage, the last point is an invaluable aid.

But Hoover was also using Koehler for another purpose of vital importance to the United States. While ND98 was sending messages that indicated the opening of a Second Front in southern France, Koehler was hinting at another target. As Hoover told it, "The Germans wanted descriptions of the insignia on troops taking pre-overseas furloughs in New York. They wanted the Army serial numbers of trucks being shipped overseas. They wanted to know where our troops were going. We gave them enough so that Koehler would be given a high efficiency rating. But we also fed them bits of information about the Second Front. In the messages Koehler was sending, Iceland kept cropping up, with the clear indication that the Allied landing target was Norway. On March 3, 1944, we sent this message to Hamburg."

LAST SUNDAY WAS IN A HOTEL BAR WHERE A GROUP OF OFFICERS WERE DRINKING AND CONVERSING QUITE LOUDLY. ONE OF THE GROUP WORE A FIVE-SIDED BLUE-AND-GOLD DEVICE I HAD NEVER SEEN BEFORE. IN REPLY TO A REMARK ABOUT SERVICE IN ICELAND, THE OFFICER WITH THE FIVE-SIDED EMBLEM TOLD THE OTHERS THAT THEY SHOULDN'T LAUGH TOO SOON BECAUSE IT WAS ENTIRELY POSSIBLE THAT SOME OF THEM MIGHT ALSO BE SENT THERE, AS, PRIOR

But did Koehler, having "betrayed" Germany, betray the United States? In 1971 the claim was made that Koehler, in addition to the messages which went out over his name from the FBI's Long Island transmitter, had also been making contact with a Nazi agent who journeyed periodically from Rochester to New York, picked up messages for the *Abwehr,* and transmitted them when he returned home. In certain quarters Koehler became known as "the spy who fooled J. Edgar Hoover"—a contention based on the fact that messages presumably from Koehler, in a code different from the one the FBI used in its communications to Hamburg, had been found among the *Abwehr*'s records. But there is evidence which would question this contention.

For one thing, shortly after Koehler's "Iceland" message, German reconnaissance planes flew over that island for the first time in months to photograph fake barracks and other installations built there to deceive the German High Command. Secondly, none of the "Rochester" messages contradicted what Koehler had been sending from Long Island. Thirdly, both the FCC and the FBI were monitoring the radio waves for enemy transmissions. If a clandestine station were sending as regularly as Koehler's alleged Rochester contact, it would have been heard and, by the process of triangulation, traced to its source. Fourth, Koehler was under constant FBI surveillance since Hoover did not trust him. Koehler might have eluded the FBI tails once or twice, but never systematically. Fifth, though Hitler was faced by increasing demands to strengthen his defenses throughout France for the impending Second Front invasion, troops were sent to Norway in anticipation of an Allied landing there.

A long time after, Hoover could express his pride for having done his bit, through the FBI, in confusing the Nazis. "The armed services," he would report, "felt the same way. I am very proud of their commendations for the part we played in the successful invasion of Normandy." Had Koehler been a triple agent, the British, whose intelligence agents had thoroughly infiltrated *Abwehr* operations, would have gotten some hint of it. The FBI, clearly, had fought Nazi espionage to a standstill, with the help of the British, our own G-2, and ONI. It would not be able to say the same about its frustrating work against another enemy.

14.

Spies in the Parlor—I

ON FEBRUARY 10, 1944, JOHN EDGAR HOOVER SENT A CONFIDENTIAL messenger to the White House with a letter to Harry Hopkins, then one of the men closest to President Roosevelt. It read:

Dear Harry:

I have just learned from a confidential but reliable source that a liaison arrangement has been perfected between the Office of Strategic Services and the Soviet Secret Police (NKVD) whereby officers will be exchanged between these services. The Office of Strategic Services is going to assign men to Moscow and in turn the NKVD will set up an office in Washington, D.C. . . .

I wanted to bring this situation to your attention at once because I think it is a highly dangerous and most undesirable procedure to establish in the United States a unit of the Russian secret service which has admittedly for its purpose the penetration into the official secrets of various government agencies. The history of the NKVD in Great

Britain showed clearly that the fundamental purpose of its operations there was to surreptiously obtain the official secrets of the British Government . . .

I feel that it will be highly dangerous to our governmental operations to have an agency such as the NKVD officially authorized to operate in the United States where quite obviously it will be able to function without any appropriate restraints upon its activities. In view of the potential danger . . . I will advise you of any further information which I receive about this matter.

Hoover also sent a copy of this letter to Attorney General Biddle with a covering letter in which he added that "secret agents of this agency (NKVD) have been engaging in attempting to obtain highly confidential information concerning War Department secrets. I think that the establishment of a recognized unit of the NKVD in the United States will be a serious threat to the internal security of the country. . . ."

There was, of course, more than one "confidential but reliable source" for the information which Hoover had forwarded to Hopkins and Biddle. The British, with whom Hoover was in close touch, had made no bones of their suspicion of OSS. So, too, had G-2 and the Office of Naval Intelligence. MI-5 maintained a careful watch of OSS agents in London and behind enemy lines. There had literally been fist fights between OSS personnel and G-2 operatives over the exchange of information. Hoover knew, moreover, that OSS had recruited heavily from among Communist veterans of the Spanish Civil War; that Allen Dulles, heading the OSS operation in Switzerland, was funneling money through Noel Field and other Soviet agents into Communist Party channels in Germany; that security within the vast OSS was virtually nonexistent; and that in General "Wild Bill" Donovan's outfit, anti-Communists were systematically weeded out. Word of the plan to give the NKVD official status in the United States had come from high-level sources in the War Department, from the British, and from one good friend in the State Department.

In the matter of the OSS-NKVD exchange, the matter was quickly settled. Hopkins showed President Roosevelt the

Hoover letter. A few quiet words were said to Donovan, who was also admonished for embarking on such a project without first consulting the White House or the Joint Chiefs of Staff. The matter had been even more quietly dropped, not to the surprise of the Kremlin which had never seriously believed that the Americans would be stupid enough to give such solicitous shelter to a Trojan Horse in their midst. But Hoover's success in this instance was a lonely one. Though he had been instructed by Roosevelt since 1936 to "keep an eye" on Communists—and though FBI agents had gathered fully documented information on Soviet espionage in the United States—in this area Hoover had moved from one frustration to another.

Since 1938, FBI files had held evidence of Communist cells within the Federal Establishment, particularly within the Treasury and State Departments. In 1939, Assistant Secretary of State Berle, one of the few high-echelon people at State who cooperated fully with the FBI, had confided to Hoover that he had presented the President with damning corroboration of this infiltration only to be silenced with a pleasant smile. Since the inception of the Manhattan Project which developed the first atomic bombs, Hoover had known, through the reports of FBI agents, as well as those at G-2, that Communist agents and sympathizers were delivering vital material on the developing nuclear processes to the Soviet Union's agents in the United States and Great Britain.

In fact, a not-inconsiderable part of the FBI's strained resources had been employed to keeping the Soviet espionage apparatus in the United States off balance. But all attempts at developing cases for prosecution had been thwarted at the White House level on the grounds that the Soviet Union was our "ally" in the war against Hitlerism and therefore should not be "upset" by the kind of exposure which open litigation would entail. Since it was the FBI's function to gather information and not to act upon it, Hoover had harbored a growing frustration which did not come to light until the Eisenhower years, when he was ordered by Attorney General Brownell to tell a small part of the story to a Senate investigating committee.*

At Hoover's direction, the FBI had begun a systematic infiltration of its own into the ranks of the Communist Party, working at all levels. It had also maintained a surveillance of Communist functionaries and recorded their secret meetings, gathering the evidence for the Smith Act "Trial of the Eleven" which led to the conviction of the party's highest leadership in 1950 for conspiring to teach and advocate the violent overthrow of the United States government. The Trial of the Eleven demonstrated the care with which the FBI had planted its people in the Communist Party and the painstaking way in which it had gathered its evidence. As each new informant took the witness stand, the party's officialdom was shaken to the core— and behind closed doors one leader accused another of having "sold out to the FBI." But nothing that happened in that court —or in the appeals which led to the Supreme Court—really impinged on Hoover's main concern: the failure of high government officials to recognize communism for what it was and to extirpate its agents from the government service.

In the case of atomic espionage, the FBI's role was tangential. The atomic bomb project, known as the Manhattan Engineer District (MED), was under the Army Corps of Engineers, and G-2 had told Hoover to "stay out of our business," confident that its Counter-Intelligence Corps could handle all security problems, but the FBI was working night and day to contain general Soviet espionage, and since there was an overlap in personnel, it repeatedly came up with material which it forwarded to G-2. CIC would also frequently ask the Bureau for help, which was usually forthcoming. And G-2 had certain obligations, under a Roosevelt directive, to keep the FBI abreast of what it was doing and learning. As a result, Hoover was probably the most in-

* Even a once-over-lightly account of the full extent of Soviet espionage and infiltration would fill a shelf of books. The interested reader can turn to *The Greatest Plot in History* for probably the most complete account of Soviet atomic espionage, to "The Case of the Reluctant Prosecutor" in *America, I-Love-You* for a detailed account of the *Amerasia* case. Both books are by Ralph de Toledano.

formed man in America on the network of atomic spies and their scientist sources. But he was helpless to act.

The extent of his frustration can be measured by some of the evidence which FBI agents were able to gather. In the broad panorama of atomic espionage, they made up part of the canvas. For example:

On March 29, 1943, at 11:15 p.m., the telephone rang at 3720 Grove Street, Oakland, California. This was the home of Steve Nelson, political commissar in the Spanish Civil War, high functionary in the underground Communist Party, and part of the far-flung efforts of a Soviet apparatus determined to steal the nation's atomic secrets. Nelson was not at home, but his wife answered the phone, telling the caller, Dr. Joseph Weinberg, a scientist at the Radiation Laboratory in Berkeley that "he won't be home until late, but if it's important, you can come here and wait for him."

It was not until 1:30 a.m. that Nelson arrived at his house. Weinberg was waiting for him, and the two men got down to cases immediately. "I have some information for you that may be very useful," Weinberg said. "I can't leave it here because it must be back at the Radiation Laboratory the first thing in the morning. It belongs to someone else, and it's in his handwriting." (This is no "reconstruction" of the conversation but his exact words.) Then Weinberg proceeded to read aloud while Nelson took down a complicated formula dealing with the Radiation Laboratory's research into the military use of atomic energy. The FBI heard and took down the entire exchange.

Several days later, Nelson made his regular phone "contact" with Peter Ivanov, nominally the Soviet vice consul in San Francisco, but actually one of the Soviet agents assigned to spy on the atomic project. The two men agreed to meet at the "usual place." Late that night, Nelson and Ivanov met briefly in an open field on the grounds of the St. Francis Hospital. An FBI agent, crouched behind a bush, saw Nelson give Ivanov an envelope. Twelve days later, Vassili Zubilin, an NKVD agent well-known to the FBI, visited Nelson's home. He counted out ten bills, denomination unknown, and thanked Nelson for a job well done. "Jesus, man," Nelson exclaimed, "you count out money like a banker."

Hoover was informed of these meetings and of what had occurred. Under normal circumstances, this would have been the beginning of an ever-widening surveillance which would have thrown a net over the apparatus and terminated in the Federal courts. But Hoover, to his deep annoyance, could only report the facts to the MED's security officers. He could continue his watch over Nelson and other of his associates since their activities were multifarious. But wherever the FBI ran into the atomic project, it was under orders to simply report and ignore.

There was the case of Clarence Hiskey. He was a young scientist with a long Communist record who worked at the Metallurgical Laboratory in Chicago, doing work for the Manhattan Project. Hiskey was under surveillance by CIC, but when he met Arthur Alexandrovitch Adams, a Soviet spy master, in Chicago's Lincoln Park, there was an overlap with the FBI. Hiskey was seen giving Adams a large envelope. Adams continued under FBI surveillance when he boarded the New York train. The envelope Hiskey had given him was now in a briefcase, and an FBI agent employed an old but effective trick, the switch. When Adams got off the train, he was carrying a briefcase stuffed with newspapers, whereas the FBI had his in its custody. Hiskey's envelope was turned over to the MED. "My God," said one of the scientists who examined its contents, "this is part of the formula for the atom bomb." This again should have been grounds for an all-out FBI drive, but Hoover was told not to interfere.

Hoover, however, had the authority to continue his surveillance of Arthur Adams, and he ordered his agents in no uncertain terms to spare no effort. As a result, Adams was put under 24-hour surveillance. An agent with technical equipment was stationed in the room next to the one occupied by Adams at the Peter Cooper Hotel. Half a block away, at another hotel, the FBI set up a 60-watt broadcasting station to direct the radio cars being used in the Adams surveillance. Those who contacted Adams were in turn put under FBI surveillance. Steve Nelson arrived in New York and was picked up by a Soviet consulate limousine which in turn picked up Adams. The two took a meandering drive around the city. Then Nelson got out of the limousine and, at another corner, Pavel Mikhailov, a Soviet vice consul, was picked up. After more aimless driving, Adams was dropped. When the limousine returned to the Soviet consulate, Mikhailov was carrying the briefcase Nelson had brought with him from the West Coast.

The FBI observed that Adams frequently visited a jewelry store on Madison Avenue. Once a week, Marcia Hiskey, wife of the scientist, picked up mail at a post office box in Brooklyn and delivered it to the jewelry shop. The FBI, of course, had full access to the box and, presumably, to the contents of the "letters" Mrs. Hiskey was receiving. In time, the Bureau put together a strong case against Adams. But with no clearance from the Justice Department, Hoover could not proceed or make an arrest.

Then Adams returned the favor of the briefcase switch by employing a trick as old and as effective against the FBI. At 1 a.m., he stepped out of the apartment house of one of his "contacts." He was bareheaded and leading her dog. Two FBI agents, standing by their car, followed him on foot. Adams strolled casually down the empty street, then suddenly hailed a passing cab, letting the dog go and leaping in. Having eluded the FBI, he called a confederate who met him at Grand Central Station with a suitcase.

A call to Hoover, who was at home sleeping, gave him the bad news. His reaction was typical: "Get him if you have to get every agent out of bed." FBI teletypes began to clatter and agents began fanning out to every major railroad and bus terminal in the country. When Adams got off the train in Chicago, two FBI men were waiting for him. Nevertheless, Adams continued his westward trek. He tried to break free in Denver, failed, and moved on to Portland, Oregon. Hoover believed that Adams would try to board a Soviet freighter and leave the country, and the Attorney General was so warned. Normal procedure would have been to arrest Adams for espionage, but the State Department objected. Instead, the FBI was given orders not to let him leave the country unless he boarded a ship. Even then, the charge was to be violation of the immigration statutes or the Selective Service Act, not espionage.

In Portland Adams went directly to the docks where a Soviet freighter was loading—as Hoover had predicted. But when he saw FBI agents at the gangplank, he walked quickly away, returning to the railroad station. Back in New York, the expensive game of keeping him under 24-hour surveillance continued, and with the State Department remaining adamant in its objections to his arrest, his eventual escape was a foregone conclusion.

Meanwhile, piece by piece, the secret of the bomb was being stolen and sent to the Soviet Union. Security at Los Alamos was feeble though Army Counter-Intelligence, armed with FBI reports and the results of its own investigations, attempted to plug the loopholes. If any concrete proof of this fact is needed at this time, it can be found in this: When the Soviets built their first reactor it was almost identical in size and layout to the "secret" reactor 305 at Hanford, Washington. The specifications:

	Reactor 305	*Soviet Reactor*
Power	10 watts	10 watts
Diameter	19 feet	19 feet
Lattice spacing	8½ inches	8 inches
Loading	27 tons uranium	25 tons uranium
Rod diameter	1.4 inches	1.6 inches

("The odds," Admiral Lewis Strauss would remark, "are astronomical against such a neat series of coincidences.")

Then, the war over and a new kind of warfare begun between

the free world and the Soviet Union, the case of Klaus Emil Fuchs, a nuclear scientist out of the top drawer, broke on the world. And ironically, when it became known how thoroughly the NKVD had plundered the chest of America's nuclear secret, the first criticisms were leveled at Hoover and the FBI. How, it was asked, could an organization so adept at tracking down the enemies of the country have failed so signally? Hoover bitterly resented this criticism but could say nothing. He could not tell the country that the many leads the FBI had developed (only a few are cited here) had been ignored or that his men had been specifically barred from participating in the security of Los Alamos and the Manhattan Project. To have done so would have been to attack openly the policies of his government and of the Roosevelt-Truman administrations. Quietly, he could explain to friends what his situation had been, and this was passed on even more quietly by the Bureau to trusted newspapermen. But only a detailed statement of the record could have laid the story before the American people, and this Hoover would not and could not do.*

What the public did not know until a long time later was that leads to Fuchs had come directly from Hoover in detailed information he had supplied MI-5. With the war's end and the passage of the Atomic Energy Act, the FBI had been given jurisdiction over security in the nuclear field. Hoover had immediately assigned some of his best investigators to go through the personnel files of the Manhattan Project, as well as the CIC's investigative reports which had been gathering dust for years. Every iota of incriminating evidence that was found was to be correlated with materials in the FBI's carefully cross-indexed records.

In Gestapo records turned over to the FBI at the war's end, researching agents found a reference to Klaus Fuchs, tagging

---

* When this writer was working on *The Greatest Plot in History*, the FBI continued to stand on the public record, and such theretofore unpublished material on the FBI's role as the book brought together came from other sources.

him a Communist student. An address book, found by the Royal Canadian Mounted Police among the effects of an atom spy arrested after the disclosures of Igor Gouzenko, a Soviet Embassy code clerk who had broken with his country in 1946, listed Klaus Fuchs and gave his address. And, of course, the name Fuchs was in the personnel records at Los Alamos. Hoover not only turned this information over to MI-5, he urged British Intelligence to institute a watch on Fuchs. This surveillance had, in turn, developed enough evidence to make Fuchs crack and confess his complicity. But beyond this, Fuchs was singularly uncooperative.

To the FBI agents who questioned him in England, Fuchs would only say that the "contact" to whom he had turned over important information used the cover name of Raymond, that he was of average height, round-faced, given slightly to fat, no physicist but probably a chemist. They had met in New York, in Cambridge, in Santa Fe. And that was all. (Fuchs, in fact, refused to identify "Raymond" until after the FBI trap had been sprung and "Raymond" confessed.) "Find him," Hoover told his top aides. "Do you know how many chemists there are in the United States?" Hoover was asked. "Find, find!" Hoover repeated. The assignment seemed impossible. But Hoover was adamant. The solution, if one there was, would have to come from the caverns of FBI files. One by one, in a long and dusty process, the thousands of chemists on whom the FBI had a file were eliminated. But "Raymond" would never have been found if not for that one devastating fact that espionage agents never follow their own rules.

The first principle of espionage is that each operation must be hermetically sealed. But this seldom happens. Spies are lonely people, and among their own they talk. When Elizabeth Bentley, a prim, New England school teacher, had given her heart to the Soviet Union, she had risen in the *apparat* to the position of courier. That is to say, she was entrusted with meeting the various "contacts" and in getting from them the material they had gathered. She had learned much about these people, in and out of the government, who supplied her with the information which was transferred to microfilm and shipped to Moscow. Among those who had broken his cover by letting her know his real identity and something about his background was Harry Gold, a chemist. In those long debriefing, almost psychoanalytical, sessions she had had with the FBI after she broke with the Soviet underground, Elizabeth Bentley had mentioned Harry Gold.

It was not very much to go on, but the FBI had its instructions from Hoover, "Find him!" The Bureau knew only that Gold lived in Philadelphia or its vicinty, but this was enough. When two agents visited him, he was friendly and frank. But when they showed him a picture of Klaus Fuchs, they sensed a heightening of tension. In the end, it was not their suspicions or their questions that broke Harry Gold but, as he later wrote in a long and tragic confession, his own sense of guilt.

The details of that confession are a twice-told tale. Harry Gold not only admitted that he had been the man to whom, in his days with the Manhattan Project, Klaus Fuchs had turned over detailed drawings of the atom bomb as well as production details. He also gave the FBI leads to other atom spies. For the FBI wanted to know much more than what Gold knew about Fuchs. That was a case closed, from an investigative standpoint, by the confession Fuchs made to British security officers. Important to Hoover were the ramifications of the plot, the other contacts, and as much of the atomic spy ring as remained within the FBI's jurisdiction. "We want them all," he told his aides.

Harry Gold confessed everything, in a sad and tragic document. Among other episodes in his life of espionage, he told of traveling to Albuquerque where he had gone to the home of an Army technician named David Greenglass. The recognition signal was a simple one, often used by agents. He had said, "I bring regards from Julius." Greenglass had picked up his wife's purse and rummaged in it for a portion of a Jello box side, cut in a zig-zag pattern. Gold had produced the other part of the piece of cardboard, and they matched. He had returned that afternoon to be given several sheets of paper on which Greenglass had made drawings of the high-explosive lens mold being used at Los Alamos as well as a description of the progress of the research in cylindrical implosion—a process in which the Soviets were particularly interested.

It was no problem to locate Greenglass, now back in New York, and he was put under surveillance, leading the FBI to Ethel and Julius Rosenberg. When two FBI agents visited him, Greenglass was pleasant but noncommital. But pictures of him were rushed to Harry Gold, who was being held in Philadelphia. When Greenglass was told that a positive identification had been made, he confessed his own role but refused to implicate the Rosenbergs. But in the FBI files were a few entries which pointed to the Rosenbergs as espionage agents, though only tenuously. Then Greenglass broke, describing in a long, written confession how Ethel Rosenberg, his sister, and Julius had recruited him for espionage, the material on the atomic bomb he had given them, their plans for flight when they learned that Harry Gold had been arrested. In the trial, he turned state's evidence, presenting the judge and jury with that most lethal of combinations—both direct and circumstantial knowledge of the Rosenberg's complicity. The government presented 102 witnesses in all. They nailed down the defendants' Communist activities, their efforts at recruiting others into their spy ring, the whole sordid story. The Rosenberg defense consisted of flat denials and frequent use of the Fifth Amendment against self-incrimination. The Rosenberg lawyers also argued that the material Greenglass described as having given to the Rosenbergs was inconsequential. Convicted, they were sentenced to death. Had they spoken, that sentence would have been reduced to life imprisonment. But Ethel and Julius Rosenberg went to the electric chair silent and unrepentant.

It had all come about because the FBI had been able to find a needle in a haystack—one chemist in the many, many thousands in the United States. As it had from the start, the filing system begun by Hoover paid off.

But there was another case of espionage with which Hoover and the FBI had to deal, in which evidence was meticulously gathered, arrests made, and nothing happened. In *The Forrestal Diaries,* under date "28 May 1945" and headed "Lieutenant Andrew Roth" there is the following interesting entry:

Major Correa [Matthias F. Correa, at the time a special assistant to the Secretary of the Navy] reported to me that the Department of Justice has evidence to the effect that Lieutenant Andrew Roth has been furnishing confidential and secret documents to a man named Jaffe, head of a publication named *Amerasia* in New York City. Jaffe has had intimate relations with the Russian Consul in New York.

Other Departments of government involved are the Office of Strategic Services, the Department of State, and the Foreign Economic Administration.

Major Correa reported that it was proposed that Lieutenant Roth should be taken into surveillance Wednesday. He said that the FBI thought that unless speedy action were taken important evidence would be dissipated, lost and destroyed. I pointed out that the inevitable consequences of such action now would be to greatly embarrass the President in his current conversations with Stalin, because of the anti-Russian play-up the incident would receive out of proportion . . .

I asked Captain Vardaman [Naval Aide to the President] to see to it that the President was informed in this matter and I then called Mr. Edgar Hoover and suggested that he advise Mr. Tom Clark [then an Assistant Attorney General] and have him also see that the President is in full information of all the facts in the matter as well as their implications.

Forrestal was referring to the controversial *Amerasia* case. It had all begun when an OSS Far East analyst, reading *Amerasia,* a publication with less than two thousand circulation but considerable influence in the State Department, had lifted verbatim several paragraphs from a highly secret report he himself had written. OSS—called by some "Oh So Secret" and by others "Oh So Subversive"—had been plagued by leaks of vital information, and Frank Brooks Bielaski, Director of Investigations for OSS, was asked to look into the matter. The *Amerasia* office, on New York's lower Fifth Avenue, was put under surveillance and a study of Philip Jaffe, its editor, was begun. It was discovered that Jaffe was a high-ranking member of the U.S. Communist Party, and that he was in frequent association with those members of the Soviet Consulate in New York who were known to carry out its espionage assignments. It was also discovered that the staff of this small magazine worked night after night until the small hours.

Bielaski decided to search the *Amerasia* offices. On March 11, 1945, he and a group mostly of former FBI men who made up his investigative team, entered the *Amerasia* offices. The first thing that startled them was the extensive photocopying equipment, hardly commensurate with the magazine's circulation and scope. The next thing that shocked Bielaski and his men was the profusion of government documents, most of them stamped top secret and all of them bearing the notation that possession was in violation of the Espionage Act. There were documents from almost every department in the government with the exception of the FBI. There were cables to the Secretary of State "for eyes only"—originals and photocopies. One of the military documents was a detailed plan for the bombing of Japan, another gave the disposition of ships in the Japanese fleet. A third dealt with an "A" bomb, about which OSS knew nothing. A fourth gave the order of battle of the Chinese armies. Bielaski picked out from the three hundred or so documents a baker's dozen that came from OSS. The OSS papers were, however, damning enough, including one on what was then of highest secrecy in the services—that the United States Navy had broken the Japanese code.

A full report was prepared for the OSS chief, General Donovan, and after he had read it, he took it personally to Secretary of State Edward Stettinius. Horrified, Stettinius promised to present the evidence to his colleagues at the highest level of government. Six days later, Hoover was called in and told to act. But before he was given the green light, the White House had given full approval. For Hoover, the assignment was made to order. Supervising his agents every step of the way, he broke down the job into two parts. One, of course, was surveillance. The other was a close look at the agencies that had been pillaged on such a large-scale basis.

Surveillance is an expensive and wearing business, and in the *Amerasia* case it was particularly so since Jaffe and his coeditor, Kate Mitchell, led very busy lives. Every person they met had to be checked out. But by studying the daily reports, Hoover was able to weed out the casual or nonbusiness contacts and those people who came within the FBI's ken. Eventually, he was able to narrow the focus of FBI scrutiny to six persons: Jaffe, Mitchell, Roth, Emanuel Larsen of the State Department, Mark Gayn, and John Stewart Service, an old China hand who as a Foreign Service Officer had been a thorn in the side of his superiors. FBI agents, tailing the six, noted a frequent exchange of large manila envelopes in out-of-the-way places. When Jaffe was on one of his frequent trips to Washington, the FBI also planted a bug in his room and recorded some startling conversations.

Among them was one in which Service said to Jaffe, "Well, what I said about the military plans is, of course, very secret." In another conversation, Service had been pressed to get a particular classified document. Service had answered, "It will be hard for me to get this report because it's kept in a section where I am not assigned. If I can dig up a copy, it will be the Far Eastern Division's copy, and they may not be willing to part with it. But I'm sure I'll be able to run off a copy for you."

On June 5, 1945, Jaffe, Mitchell, Gayn, Service, Larsen, and Roth were arrested for violation of the Espionage Act. A raid, with warrant, on the *Amerasia* offices at the time of these arrests gave the FBI all the evidence it needed—some 400 secret documents along with photocopies. Other documents were found in Gayn's possession, two hundred in Larsen's home, and a number in Kate Mitchell's file cabinet, which included one so secret that Army officers who mislaid their copies were subject to court martial.

Hoover was justifiably pleased with the job that the FBI had done. In short order, the Bureau had been able to bring to justice men who had been involved in a systematic violation of the Espionage Act, and some who had perpetrated a wholesale theft of sensitive and classified documents. Instead both the FBI and the State Department found themselves the targets of a concerted attack. Hoover was charged with attempting to curtail the "freedom of the press." The State Department was accused of using the prosecution as a means to fight those who opposed official policies on China. Had Roosevelt been alive, the outcome of the case would have been different. But Harry Truman had succeeded to the Presidency, and in those first floundering months, he was subject to many political pressures. As the press outcry against the arrest grew, he washed his hands of the affair and let the Justice Department handle it. And handle it the Justice Department did. Hoover was not consulted on the evidence. Instead, a Justice Department attorney handling the presentation of the case to a grand jury argued that the documents "could be seen in almost every magazine and newspaper office in New York." Somewhere along the line, the charge of conspiracy to commit espionage was dropped, and in its place was substituted illegal possession of government property. The Justice Department also decided that Kate Mitchell's only culpability—she belonged to a politically powerful Buffalo family—was that she shared offices with Jaffe.

Under the new charges, Service was automatically eliminated. The grand jury, on the basis of the evidence presented by the Justice Department, indicted only Jaffe and Larsen. A deal was made between Jaffe's lawyer and the Justice Department that he would plead guilty if there was a guarantee that he would pay a fine but serve no prison sentence. In court, during proceedings that lasted some five minutes on a Saturday morning, with no press present, Jaffe's lawyer eulogized his client as a patriotic American, and the prosecution agreed "in substance." Then the government told the judge that Jaffe had sought and used the documents for journalistic purposes. The fine was $2500—exactly half of millionaire Jaffe's annual contribution to the Communist Party. At a subsequent appearance in court, the government exculpated Larsen and he was fined $500.

In the years that followed, there were congressional investigations of the *Amerasia* affair, but they raised far more questions about the Justice Department's conduct than were ever answered. For John Edgar Hoover, however, this was academic. He had neatly wrapped up an espionage case and then seen the government throw it away. He could explain it in only one way, "Politics!"—the kind of politics he had fought so successfully to keep out of the FBI. The next time around, he swore, there would be a difference.

15.

Spies in the Parlor—II

ON SEPTEMBER 2, 1939—THE DAY AFTER HITLER INVADED POLAND—
four people sat down to dinner at Woodley House, the Henry L.
Stimson mansion in fashionable northwest Washington. They
were Assistant Secretary of State and Mrs. Adolf A. Berle, the
hosts; Isaac Don Levine, a free lance writer with an imposing
reputation in the anti-Communist field; and Whittaker Chambers, a minor editor on *Time*. The meeting had been arranged
by Levine at Chambers's request, with the understanding that
what was said to Berle would be conveyed to President Roosevelt. After dinner, Mrs. Berle retired and, while an agitated
Berle took notes, Chambers told of serious Communist infiltration in the Federal government. Berle's notes, headed "Underground Espionage Agent," listed many names and some details.
Among the names were those of Alger Hiss, then a rising offi-

cial in the State Department, and Harry Dexter White, who was destined to become Assistant Secretary of the Treasury under Henry Morgenthau.

Berle's agitation was understandable. Hitler and Stalin had joined forces, and as an expert on security, Berle knew that as long as this partnership existed, what the Communists had the Nazis would know. Before Levine and Chambers had departed, Berle was on the phone to the White House, seeking an appointment with the President. How the conversation between the two progressed is locked in the tomb. From what Berle confided to friends years later, however, Roosevelt was tired and edgy. The world was on the brink of World War II and he could not be bothered by what seemed to him like unimportant details. When Berle pressed his point, the Roosevelt cigarette holder clenched between his teeth made its characteristic upward lunge. Roosevelt smiled in tight dismissal, and he said, "Adolf, go fuck yourself." (In later accounts, Berle softened that to: "Adolf, go jump in the lake.")

Chambers, whose own role in the Soviet underground espionage group he had described had been explained to Berle, expected to be arrested with the members of his apparatus. But he heard nothing more of his disclosures. Berle made a copy of his notes for J. Edgar Hoover and put the original in his safe. If Roosevelt did not want to move, neither he nor the FBI could. But the matter did not die. In 1943, Hoover prepared a memorandum on Communist infiltration of the United States government which was again ignored by the Attorney General and by the cabinet members whose departments were involved. Among those mentioned was Alger Hiss. Again, there was no action from above—and Hoover, whose FBI was at a straining point preventing Axis espionage and keeping an eye on Soviet agents seeking to ferret out America's defense secrets, let the matter rest. However, with the war's conclusion, he sent highly confidential memoranda to the White House warning President Truman of the existence of Communist apparatuses at high levels in the Federal government. These were based on the confessions of Elizabeth Bentley, a Soviet spy courier, and on some thirty other sources who had voluntarily approached the Bureau to tell their stories. Again, there was no significant response from on high.*

But with the passage of time, Hoover's concern over the Communist cells in the Federal government slightly diminished. Hiss and White had left it for posts beyond the FBI jurisdiction, and those who remained did so, Hoover could only reason, with the blessings of the Truman Administration. He was occupied, moreover, with a reorganization of the Bureau and with holding off attempts by well-meaning friends to put him in charge of what later became the Central Intelligence Agency. Hoover did not want this assignment. It would have taken the FBI out of his hands, divorcing him from his life's work. In the intramural battles over the creation of a super-spy agency, moreover, Hoover was attempting to keep the jurisdictional areas granted him by Franklin Roosevelt intact, and he could not afford to enter into controversy with the White House. To Hoover's chagrin, he lost at least part of the war when Truman, one of whose confidants and advisors was the violently anti-FBI New York lawyer Max Lowenthal, took from the FBI jurisdiction over the Latin American operations which had so successfully held the Axis in check during the war years, giving it to the CIA.

This was the state of affairs in the early summer of 1948 when Washington correspondents like Jerry Greene of the *New York Daily News* and David Sentner of the Hearst newspapers began to report that the House Committee on Un-American Activities was preparing to put on the stand a former Soviet agent who would reveal the existence of a wartime Soviet spy ring in Washington. Elizabeth Bentley's testimony—though vitiated by lurid newspaper stories that she was a "beautiful blonde spy queen," which she was not—caused a sensation. For with that meticulous memory which espionage agents seem to

* See Chapter 16 for the sequel to these attempts by Hoover to alert Truman.

develop, she gave chapter and verse on a spy ring which included Harry Dexter White and others in high places who had systematically fed the Soviets precious American secrets and—of more consequence—bent American policy to Communist purposes.

Almost by happenstance, Whittaker Chambers was subpoenaed to corroborate some of the Bentley testimony. By this time he was a senior editor on *Time* and a power in that organization. Robert Stripling, research director of the House committee, had heard rumors about the Chambers involvement in a Washington apparatus and felt that another witness covering some of the same ground might strengthen the Bentley testimony. Stripling did not expect anything very startling would come from Chambers. But for the new witness, the subpoena came as a bombshell. Following his conversation with Berle, he had thought the matter dead. In 1943, he had been visited at his Maryland farm by Raymond Murphy, a State Department expert on communism and internal security. That same year, he had been questioned by the FBI, but other than the memorandum circulated by Hoover, the Bureau had done nothing.

His appearance, however, made blacker headlines than those of Elizabeth Bentley. For not only did he corroborate what she had said of Harry Dexter White's involvement in a Soviet ring, he also named Alger Hiss. To the average newspaper reader, that name meant little or nothing. But the Washington press corps knew him as the man who had accompanied Franklin Roosevelt to Yalta, who had been secretary-general of the San Francisco Conference at which the United Nations Charter had been drafted, and a rising star in the State Department who had abruptly resigned his job as director of the Office of Special Political Affairs to become president of the Carnegie Endowment for International Peace. (The press did not know that he had quit his job after being questioned by the FBI about the charges in the 1946 Hoover memorandum.)

The nation, the committee, and the press were more shocked at the allegations of Chambers than they had been at those made by Elizabeth Bentley, even though he was speaking of events which had taken place in the mid-thirties. Perhaps it was the flat, almost noncommittal manner in which Chambers gave his testimony that made the impact. A factor, also, was the question immediately asked: Why would a senior editor on *Time*, making $30,000 a year—a sizable salary in 1948—jeopardize his job and compromise his reputation by making the charges and admitting his role in an underground Communist cell in the Federal government?

What followed has been a many-times told tale: Hiss's appearance before the committee two days later, on August 5, 1948; his categorical denial of what Chambers had said and even that he had ever laid eyes on his accuser; the consternation of the committee; the determination of Richard Nixon to get to the bottom of the case; the further questioning of Chambers; the mass of lies and self-contradictions in Hiss's subsequent testimony; the dramatic confrontation between the two protagonists in which Hiss finally admitted that he knew Chambers but continued to deny any association with the underground cell; Hiss's demand that Chambers repeat his charges where they would not be privileged so that he might file a libel action; the Chambers appearance on *Meet the Press* in which he stated, unprotected by any immunity, that Alger Hiss "was and still may be a Communist"; the suit filed by Hiss after he had been prodded into it by faithful friends.

Up to that point, it was a duel between two men, with a Greek chorus in the form of the press chanting, "Who is lying—Hiss or Chambers?" But when, in the course of pretrial examination, Chambers produced secret State Department documents and four memoranda in Hiss's handwriting—and subsequently six rolls of microfilm, the famous "pumpkin papers" so named because he had hidden them in a pumpkin on his farm when he heard that Hiss's investigators were on the prowl—the case assumed a new proportion. It was no longer a case of infiltration and subversion but clearcut espionage. The pressure of public opinion forced a foot-dragging Justice Department to place the evidence before a grand jury. This, of course, made the FBI an active participant in the case.

It was said at the time and has been repeated since that the FBI was remiss in not having pursued the Hiss matter from the moment it learned from Berle of Hiss's involvement in a Communist underground cell in the State Department. Until the State Department opens its files to researchers, the world will never know just how much damage was done by Hiss in the seven years between the Chambers-Berle meeting in 1939 and Hiss's departure from the State Department in 1946. But it remains a fact that Hoover did not mount any investigation of the Chambers disclosures when his responsibilities clearly demanded that he should have. The excuse he made was that the Bureau was overburdened with its work against Axis spies and the espionage activities of Soviet espionage rings such as those headed by Arthur Alexandrovitch Adams. He was also aware, though he never mentioned it in extenuation of his lapse, that President Roosevelt had been briefed by Berle but had turned away investigative action.

Once the Justice Department had taken up the case, however, Hoover moved with decision and dispatch. Every scrap of information passed across his desk, and at one point he assigned 263 agents to the case. The first step was to drain Chambers of every fact, every memory, in the hope that a scrap of recollection could be turned into a lead in a case more than ten years old. Chambers spent long and weary days dredging up the past for the agents assigned to the case. Names, addresses, details of his life and what he knew of Hiss's life, conversations he could recall—it was all taken down and thoroughly analyzed. But the key to the case, as Hoover saw it, were the documents. If those could be linked to Hiss, then the government had a case. If not, it boiled down to the question, "Who is lying?" And this was not enough. The statute of limitations had run out on espionage, leaving only perjury as an indictable offense. And the perjury law required two witnesses or one witness and documentary evidence.

Had Chambers simply microfilmed the State Department documents, the FBI would have been in bad trouble. Anyone might have stolen them for Chambers. But what was on the rolls of microfilm and in the actual papers presented by Chambers were typewritten copies. And every typewriter is unique, like a fingerprint. If the FBI could prove that the material presented by Chambers had been typed by Hiss or his wife, Priscilla Hiss, then the government would have a solid case. Chambers had already testified that Hiss had brought home classified documents and that they had been copied there, but that had been in the Thirties. Hoover wanted to be absolutely sure, and agents were assigned to the painstaking task of checking the Chambers documents against every piece of paper typed in every State Department office during that period. Satisfied that the documents had not been copied in the State Department, Hoover pushed in a more significant direction. Find out, he ordered, whether Hiss had a typewriter at home during the crucial period, what kind of a typewriter, and what happened to it.

Hiss had already been nailed on one lie. He had told the House Committee on Un-American Activities that he had prepared the handwritten memoes for his superior, Assistant Secretary of State Francis Sayre. But Sayre, under oath, had categorically denied this. And Sayre and other State Department witnesses had also testified that some of the documents were so sensitive that even making copies of them would have been in violation of the department's security and of the Espionage Act. If it could be proved that Hiss or Mrs. Hiss had done the document copying at home, it would be sufficient to prove that Hiss had, indeed, been a spy. But when agents questioned Hiss about his typewriter, he was very vague. Yes, he did have a typewriter during that period. He "believed" it was a Remington, but he had given it to a Negro servant in 1938. The servant said he had sold it. What the FBI did not know was that the Hiss defense had recovered the typewriter and was holding it secretly pending further developments.

But, as Hoover realized, the typewriter itself was not essential if other "standards"—that is, letters written by the Hisses during that period could be found and compared with the characteristics of the typewriter which had been used to copy the documents. On the face of it, this looked like another "needle in the haystack" assignment. Hoover had, however, grown dubious of the Hisses when, by checking the types of all typewriters, the Bureau discovered that the documents had not been run through a Remington, as Hiss had said, but a Woodstock. He therefore insisted on an all-out search for the "standards" that would either destroy the case against Hiss or sustain Chambers.

Where would a letter written by one or another of the Hisses in 1938 still be in existence? Hoover called in his top assistants to give them his best thinking on how to go about it. "The typewriter must have been used for letters to organizations the Hisses belonged to—or to schools attended by the Hiss children. People destroy or lose correspondence, but organizations tend to file it. That's where to look." He also pointed a finger in one other direction. "Mrs. Hiss says she's not a good typist. Did she ever study typing? Did she ever pass a typing test? Find out!"

The agents fanned out, seeking answers. And it was their investigation which gave the Justice Department the documentary evidence it needed if a case was to be made. FBI agents found a report that Priscilla Hiss had written for the Bryn Mawr Alumnae Association during the period that Chambers had testified were the espionage years. They found a letter she had written to the University of Maryland. And they found a letter signed by Hiss in 1936 to the Landon School in Bethesda, Maryland. Microscopic examination of the report and the two letters proved conclusively that they had been typed on the same machine as the copies of the State Department documents. This destroyed any possibility that Hiss could suggest to negate the Chambers account.

The Bureau was also busy investigating Chambers. But in every one of his statements concerning the relationship with

Hiss, the facts sustained him. The 1934 Ford Hiss had transferred to him, the $400 Hiss had given him as a loan so the Ford could be traded in for a new car, the Bokhara rug Chambers had presented to Hiss—these and other corroborative evidence were translated into legal evidence by FBI investigation. The FBI even went into tangential areas such as who had done the microfilming for Chambers. He told them of a man named "Felix" who lived in Baltimore and had once worked for an electrical appliance shop. That was all the FBI had to go on. But with dogged determination, they eventually found Felix Inslerman. He denied knowing Chambers, but his camera gave him away. Microscopic marks detected on blow-ups of the microfilm matched those on the lens of Inslerman's Leica.

The first Hiss trial resulted in a hung jury, for reasons which are not germane to this account. Between the termination of the first trial and the beginning of the second trial, however, the FBI continued to search for additional evidence. What was needed was one witness who could challenge Hiss's statement that he had never visited the Chambers home. That they did find such a witness is, in Hoover's words, "one of the finest examples of the FBI's investigative techniques." For the FBI started out with almost nothing—and turned up the witness, Edith Murray, who had worked for Whittaker and Esther Chambers at the time of their greatest intimacy with the Hisses. This is Hoover's account of the search:

Chambers told us that in August 1934, during his Communist espionage activities, he and his wife and their infant daughter, Ellen, lived in an apartment at 903 St. Paul Street, in Baltimore. They used the name of Mr. and Mrs. Lloyd Cantwell. Chambers was able to remember the name of the landlady. In the spring of 1935, the Chambers family moved to the Washington apartment lent to them by the Hisses. In October of 1935, Chambers recalled, the family moved back to Baltimore, to an apartment on Eutaw Place. Both Mr. and Mrs. Chambers were positive that the Hisses visited them several times at their apartment. And the Chamberses mentioned a maid who had worked for them then. They were sure that this maid had met the Hisses. In particular, they recalled one occasion when Priscilla Hiss had taken care of the Chambers baby while Esther Chambers was in New York for a physical check-up.

The Chamberses remembered that the maid's name was Edith. Her surname might have been Brown or Brun or Brunner. They were certain that her husband's first name was Ellwood and that he had worked as a mechanic just off Greenmount Street. Our job was to find Edith. We worked on all facets of the investigation simultaneously. It took us some time to find the landlady of the St. Paul Street apartment. We traced her from Baltimore to a town near the Pennsylvania border to Florida, but she could remember nothing of the 'Cantwells' or any maid they might have had. By checking old city and business directories, we located several former neighbors of the 'Cantwells' at the St. Paul Street address but they remembered nothing. The garage where Ellwood worked had gone out of business some fourteen years before. The manager, when we finally found him, said that all records had been destroyed and he could remember no one named Ellwood.

Finally, we found two tenants at the apartment who had lived there during the tenancy of the Chamberses. They remembered an Edith, but that was all. The owner of the apartment had died, but we located his son. He was able to give us the name of the janitor who had worked for his father from 1927 to 1944. The janitor, when we found him, identified photos of the Cantwells but couldn't recall any maid.

Agents handling the questioning of both Whittaker and Esther Chambers continued to press for details, anything. In the course of one long session with Esther Chambers, a painter before her marriage to Whittaker, she mentioned that during that period of their lives she had done several oil paintings. Whom had she painted? Mrs. Chambers was not sure. But that was the big break. Pressed for the names of the people she had painted, as Hoover told the story, "she vaguely remembered actually doing a portrait of the maid. She thought she had given the painting to Edith, but perhaps she hadn't." If she hadn't? Where would it be? At this, she drew a blank. But she suggested that if she still had the portrait, it would be in the attic of the Chambers farm in Maryland. Two agents went through the clutter, looking for the painting. In a dark corner, festooned by cobwebs, they found an unfinished painting of a young Negro woman. Now, at least, the Bureau knew what Edith had looked like fourteen years before, or at least "a fair likeness" in Esther Chambers's words.

With the date for the second Hiss trial approaching, Hoover leaned on his agents: "Find Edith! Find her now!" At the first trial, both Hisses had testified categorically that they had never visited Chambers in Baltimore, that he was but a casual acquaintance, an impecunious free-lance writer who had taken advantage of them. Daily conferences were now called by Hoover to sift what little the previous day had produced. At the same time, the endless dredging of such memories as the Chamberses had continued. And once again, in what was almost a psychoanalytical process, the FBI was able to discover another few nuggets of information. Mrs. Chambers seemed to remember that Edith had lived on Madison Street in Baltimore, that she had a friend named Missouri who sometimes substituted for her. Once again, the special agents fanned out, this time bearing photocopies of Esther's painting.

"We contacted every conceivable source of information. We searched city and phone directories. We interviewed managers of employment agencies and checked every maid whose name was Edith. This meant tracing hundreds of people, from house to house, from city to city. In each instance, we encountered dead ends," said Hoover. In mid-September, less than two months before the second trial was scheduled, Hoover and the special squad conducting the search huddled once more. They could find no holes in their investigation. But Hoover was implacable.

"We'll start all over again," he said.

"We decided to reinterview every person who had lived or worked in the vicinity of the Chambers apartment during the time that he and his family had lived there. Having been questioned once, it was just possible that they had continued to think about it. We had no luck at all until we talked to the former janitor and showed him a picture of Edith. Since the first interview, he admitted, he had recalled Edith. In fact, he had seen her on the street, talked to her, and found out her last name—Murray—and her address." Why hadn't he come forward? "I didn't want to get involved," he said. The agents decided that it would be best to let Hoover know before they proceeded any further. He might have new instructions. And Hoover did. "Don't mention any names. Just let her volunteer any information she may have."

The agents knocked at Edith Murray's door and identified themselves. "Do you know who this is," one of them asked, showing her a reproduction of the Esther Chambers portrait. The woman smiled. "Why, sure," she said. "It's me."

Then, according to Hoover,

She told the agents that she had worked for a family named Cantwell and volunteered the information that they had a little girl named Ellen. She said her husband's name was Ellwood and that he had been employed at a gasoline station. She identified photographs of Mr. and Mrs. Chambers as those of Mr. and Mrs. Cantwell. She had gotten her job with them through a friend, Missouri Diggs. Edith was asked about visitors to the apartment. She volunteered that she remembered a "lady from Washington" who had visited on several occasions.

Specifically, she remembered that the "lady from Washington" spent a day and a night at the apartment in 1935 while "Mrs. Cantwell" went to New York for a medical examination. Then she described Priscilla Hiss and her husband, Alger. She was positive that a photograph of Priscilla which was then shown to her was of the "lady from Washington" and she was reasonably sure that the photo of Alger Hiss was the lady's husband. We took Edith Murray to the Chambers farm and there was mutual recognition. But we wanted one more test. During the course of the second trial we took Edith to New York. An agent who had never seen Mr. or Mrs. Hiss accompanied her to the thirteenth floor of the Federal Courthouse. In the crowd outside the courtroom, we had her watch the elevator. When Alger and Priscilla Hiss stepped out of the elevator, Edith Murray grasped the agent's arm.

That's the lady from Washington and her husband, she said.

The second trial of Alger Hiss was, in many ways, a repeat of the first. Typewriter experts testified, with charts and in technical language, that the copied State Department documents and the Hiss correspondence were typed on the same Woodstock.

The typewriter was traced from the Hiss house to the various people who had owned it. Chambers told of his espionage association and his personal friendship with the Hisses. Esther Chambers corroborated it. The Hisses denied all, as the minutiae of the case were presented to the jury. But for reasons which few in the courtroom knew, United States Attorney Thomas F. Murphy, the prosecutor, hit hard at one point in his cross-examination of Hiss.

"Q. Didn't you go to Baltimore with your wife—over to see the Chamberses? A. Never. Never, Mr. Murphy . . .

"Q. Any place in Baltimore to see the Chamberses? A. No, sir.

"Q. At any time? A. Never . . . No time. Never."

And when he was examining Mrs. Hiss:

"Q. Did you see Mrs. Chambers in Baltimore? A. I have never seen her in Baltimore . . .

"Q. And I take it that you did not know she was living (there) under the name of Cantwell, Mrs. Lloyd Cantwell? A. I did not know anything about her.

"Q. All right. So I can say, and drop it, that on your oath before this jury you didn't see her in Baltimore in any shape or form at any address or under any name. A. That is exactly right."

Murphy saved Edith Murray for a rebuttal witness. When she entered the courtroom, a look passed between the Hisses, quick and almost undetected. After the preliminaries, Murphy asked her:

"Q. Did they [the Chamberses] have any visitors? A. They didn't have many visitors, only two visitors that I know of.

"Q. Did these visitors tell you where they lived? A. The lady did. She said she lived in Washington.

"Q. Do you see her here in court? A. Yes, sir. There is the lady right there with the black hat with the thing on its side."

Then, under questioning, she told of the several visits of the Hisses and of the time when Priscilla Hiss had stayed overnight to look after Ellen, the Chambers baby, while Esther Chambers went to New York. "Would you be able to identify her [Mrs. Hiss's] husband?" Murphy asked. "Yes, I couldn't help but remember him," Edith Murray answered. Then she stood and pointed at him.

"Q. What did you call the lady? A. I called her Miss Priscilla."

"That does it," a reporter in the press section said. The "heavy" evidence of typewriters and experts had settled the case, from a legalistic standpoint. But Edith Murray's testimony, simply spoken, was the human clincher. And nothing the defense threw at her could budge Edith Murray. It had, indeed, been one of the finest examples of FBI procedures, as Hoover said. Eleven years after Chambers had first spoken out, Hiss was convicted of perjury for lying about his role in a Communist espionage apparatus and his association with Chambers.

But the sterling work of the FBI in the Hiss case was tarnished by its record in the Coplon case. And what made it the more regrettable from the Bureau's standpoint was that good investigation had been destroyed by what can only be described as sheer bungling. The Bureau was hurt and so was J. Edgar Hoover. He could not plead lack of knowledge, first because it was not true and, secondly, because it would be an admission that he did not have the FBI in iron control.

On the face of it, the FBI's role in the Coplon case had been exemplary. Judith Coplon had gone from her *cum laude* graduation at Barnard College in New York to the post of political analyst in the Justice Department's internal security section. She was an attractive, vivacious girl who worked long hours and won the admiration of her superiors. She had security clearance and handled material dealing with Communist espionage in the United States. The FBI, however, is particularly careful in screening Justice Department personnel, and when it was discovered that she had been seen with a Soviet engineer attached to the United Nations in New York, a red light flashed. Hoover sent a warning to the Justice Department. Judith Coplon was forthwith cut off from access to sensitive information without her knowledge, and the FBI manufactured several "documents" stamped "secret" which were routed to her. At the same time, Hoover ordered a full surveillance.

On March 4, 1949, the FBI learned that Judith was planning a visit to New York. Agents in New York were alerted to keep a close eye on the Soviet engineer, Valentin Gubitchev, while others followed Judith's trail in the city. At 7:23 p.m. Judith and Gubitchev passed each other on uptown Manhattan's 193rd Street and Broadway. Then the two traveled to 42nd Street and Broadway, one by bus, one by subway. The two walked crosstown, several yards apart to Third Avenue, then both dashed aboard the same bus, unaware that the FBI was at their side. At 14th Street, they alighted and walked together toward 15th Street. At this point, the FBI pounced on the couple.

In Judith Coplon's purse, the FBI found a memo on the "secret" documents that had been routed to her at their instigation. They also found several FBI data slips and a typewritten account of her inability to obtain an FBI report on Soviet espionage activities in the United States. In addition was a memorandum on three potential recruits for Soviet espionage. Judith Coplon and Valentin Gubitchev were indicted in New York for conspiracy to commit espionage, and she alone was indicted in Washington for unlawfully removing government documents and for espionage in the employ of a foreign power.

The trial itself was something of a circus. Her lawyer, who had a genius for the malapropism, charged the FBI with "stripping her from pillar to post." Her association with Gubitchev had been a romantic one "because love knows no bounds." The papers in her purse were there because she was writing an allegorical novel. On the stand, Judith Coplon insisted that not only was her love for Gubitchev great but pure—until the government forced her to admit in cross-examination that at the time she was supposedly purely and madly in love with Gubitchev, she was having assignations at hotels, motels, and in the apartment of another man. But though a jury convicted Judith Coplon and Gubitchev, the suspicion had been raised that the FBI had improperly tapped her telephone. The government flatly denied this, but it did not convince the defense.

The first Coplon trial, moreover, had caused the FBI acute embarrassment when the trial judge ordered, and Attorney General Tom C. Clark agreed to place in evidence documents from the FBI's "raw files"—unevaluated reports, rumors, and other material which had not been checked out. These documents uncovered secret informants, exposing informants to possible retaliation. Innocent reputations were besmirched, even though the files had only a tangential relation to the trial. In this, Hoover must be held blameless. In a confidential memorandum to his top aides, Hoover explained that he had been overruled by the Attorney General:

> When the issue arose on the introduction of Bureau investigative reports, I, of course, did not in any way wish to deprive the court or the defense of all the facts bearing upon the issue . . . There were certain reports that could be introduced in evidence without compromising sources of information, other investigations, or embarrassing innocent persons . . . I took a strong stand against making public other reports that would reveal the identities of confidential informants or embarrass innocent persons by the publication of unevaluated complaints and reports. I urged the Attorney General to seek a mistrial or a citation for contempt rather than produce reports with consequent devastating harm to the FBI's responsibility for internal security, as well as the disclosure of as yet uncorroborated information in our files concerning individuals.
>
> The first knowledge I had that the reports had been introduced in evidence occurred after they had been presented in court . . .

But though the FBI had been damaged by the airing of its raw files and the exposure of its methods, the more sophisticated were not critical of the Bureau, and even the *Post,* Washington's most liberal newspaper, came to Hoover's defense. The real harm was of the FBI's making—and therefore of Hoover's, since in a litigation of this sort he rode shotgun all the way. For in pretrial hearings in Judith Coplon's second trial, it became known that during the first trial, even as the government was assuring the court that there had been no wiretapping, there were FBI agents in court who knew that this was not so, yet they had stood mute. When the point was raised during the pretrial hearings the Justice Department was compelled to admit that wires had been tapped, but that they had led to none of the evidence which was used to convict the Coplon-Gubitchev team. When the trial judge ordered that the recordings be produced, the FBI said that they had been destroyed "as a routine matter." But the timing was too pat—right after the government's denial that such taps existed. Hoover argued, with some justice, that the taps had been authorized by Attorney General Clark, but he could not explain away the Bureau's silence when the matter was argued.

To make matters even worse, in the appeal of the first conviction, the fact was elicited that Judith Coplon and Valentin Gubitchev had been arrested without a warrant. Hoover and the FBI argued that there was reasonable cause for arresting the pair, that essential evidence might have been lost had the agents trailing them not acted as they had. But the Court of Appeals, though conceding that Judith Coplon's "guilt was plain," reversed the conviction. Judith Coplon was released, and because evidence in any new trial would, in the legal term, be tainted, that was the end of the story. She married one of her lawyers and lives quietly in Brooklyn. But Hoover and the FBI had been badly hurt. For in the aftermath of the trials, few considered the guilt or innocence of Judith Coplon. They remembered only that the FBI had stepped on its own tail in the apprehension of two espionage agents who might have led them to many more.

16.

Hoover, Truman, and White—
A Tale of Red Herrings

IN 1948, AT THE HEIGHT OF THE CONTROVERSY OVER ALGER HISS, President Truman brushed aside the House Committee on Un-American Activities investigation as a "red herring." Both Democrats and Republicans were shocked by this characterization—repeated twice again by Truman. Many Democrats reacted in fear that Truman's statement would seem to place their party on the side of Communists and subversives—a touchy point in an election year. The Republicans were quietly delighted, convinced that Truman had proved what GOP campaigners had been arguing. Those in the know were aware that Truman's reaction was typical. It was not the facts that he was challenging but his personal interpretation of the motives of those dragging them out into the open. In private, Harry S. Truman made his position crystal clear, but it was not one which could be given publicity. For what the President said to intimates was: "Sure, I know Alger Hiss is guilty as hell. But the Republicans are not attacking Hiss—they're attacking me!" And so he had counterattacked.

But the "red herring" remark rankled. The trial and conviction of Hiss seemed to make the Truman onslaught academic, and the Republicans had a new target when Secretary of State Dean G. Acheson told reporters that he would "not turn my back on Alger Hiss." In the 1952 election, the "Communists in government" issue was a major one, with Senator Richard Nixon, the Republican Vice Presidential candidate, pounding away at it while Adlai Stevenson, the Democratic standard bearer, tried to brush it aside with amusing quips.

But there was one piece of unfinished business—one unopened door in the hundreds of thousands of words of testimony before the House Un-American Committee. Among the Soviet agents named by both Whittaker Chambers and Elizabeth Bentley had been former Assistant Secretary of the Treasury Harry Dexter White. While most of those mentioned in the Bentley-Chambers disclosures and summoned before HCUA had refused to answer questions on the grounds of self-incrimination or made qualified admissions, Harry White had categorically denied every charge against him, lashed out at the committee, and read a ringing statement of his position which won him wide acclaim.

Mr. White: I voluntarily asked to come here before this committee, and the committee has been kind to grant my request. I have read in the newspapers charges that have been made against me by a Miss Elizabeth Bentley and a Mr. Whittaker Chambers . . . I should like to state at the start that I am not now and never have been a Communist, nor even close to becoming one . . . The press reported that the witnesses claim that I helped to obtain key posts for persons I knew were engaged in espionage work to help them in that work. That allegation is unqualifiedly false.

There is and can be no basis in fact whatever for such a charge.

The principles in which I believe, and by which I live, make it impossible for me to ever do a disloyal act or anything against the interests of our country, and I have jotted down what my belief is for the committee's information.

My creed is the American creed. I believe in freedom of religion, freedom of speech, freedom of thought, freedom of the press, freedom of criticism, and freedom of movement. I believe in the goal of equality of opportunity, and the right of each individual to follow the calling of his or her own choice, and the right of every individual to an opportunity to develop his or her capacity to the fullest.

I believe in the right and duty of every citizen to work for, to expect, and to obtain an increasing measure of political, economic, and emotional security. I am opposed to discrimination in any form, whether on grounds of race, color, religion, political belief, or economic status ... I believe in a government of law, not men, where law is above any man, and not any man above law. Those are principles that I have been prepared in the past to fight for, and am prepared to defend at any time with my life, if need be ... (Applause.)

Under questioning, White "affirmed"—he refused to use the word admitted—that he had worked with, hired, and closely associated with a long list of people whose records as Communists and members of various Soviet espionage apparatuses had already been laid before the committee. But he contended that he had neither known of nor suspected their Communist proclivities or affiliations. They were "charming" people, experts in their field, dedicated public servants, who had never in any way revealed any Communist sympathies. He did not, and could not, accept any allegations that they were not what he judged them to be.

Harry White stepped down from the stand something of a hero. He had faced down the Red-hunters, challenged a purportedly powerful committee, and confounded his critics. Shortly thereafter, he died—whether of a heart attack or by his own hand the world will never know—and was cremated without an autopsy. The committee was assailed for having brought on the heart attack. But the country was watching the Hiss-Chambers confrontation, and Harry Dexter White was only from time to time spiritually resurrected as an example of the committee's heartlessness and harassment.

But at the time that Whittaker Chambers presented to the

courts the copied State Department documents and the Hiss handwritten memoranda, he also turned over to the FBI several sheets on yellow lined paper in Harry White's handwriting which detailed United States Navy secrets and other highly classified material which would have had no connection with his work at the Treasury. The subsequent publication of Secretary of the Treasury Henry Morgenthau's papers cast additional light on White's activities. He had been responsible, among many other things, for turning over to the Soviets the plates for printing United States occupation money used in Germany—and Russian presses had turned it out by the bushel, at a cost of many millions of dollars to the Treasury, which had to redeem the Soviet counterfeit in American dollars. He had repeatedly intervened in the interests of the Soviet and Chinese Communists, to the detriment of the United States. And he had carefully seeded sensitive American and international agencies with people who, by 1948, were known to be Soviet agents or conscious instruments of the Kremlin.

But White was dead, and though new evidence cropped up in the Morgenthau papers and in such caches of material as the secret files of the Institute of Pacific Relations, only students of subversion gave them any serious scrutiny. The case seemed forever closed. Investigation of communism in government moved on to far more topical areas and people—and Senator Joe McCarthy was on the march. In the 1952 Presidential campaign, however, General Dwight D. Eisenhower had promised a cleanup of the government, and this had rekindled the controversy.

Then, on November 6, 1953, Attorney General Herbert Brownell Jr. delivered a speech before the Executives Club in Chicago in which he cited the White case as an instance of laxity on the part of the Truman Administration, and of "the unwillingness of the non-Communists in responsible positions to face the facts and a persistent delusion that communism in the Government of the United States was only a red herring." To this he added: "The manner in which the established facts concerning White's disloyalty were disregarded is typical of the blindness which afflicted the former Administration on this matter." President Truman, he reported, had appointed White, then Assistant Secretary of the Treasury, to the post of United States Executive Director of the International Monetary Fund, though he had received two reports from Hoover on White's "spying activities."

The outcry against Brownell took two forms: (1) Truman was being accused of disloyalty, and (2) a dead man was being smeared by an Attorney General of the United States. The latter form of attack subsided when former Truman aides tacitly admitted that White had, in fact, been a Soviet agent. In a series of well-planted leaks, those who had worked with Truman said that he had heeded Hoover's warnings. White, the aides said, had been kept in the government so as not to warn him that he was under suspicion. As the *New York Times* put it, the "reason" given was "that if (White) had been dismissed, the five-alarm bell would have sounded and all the Communists in the spy ring would either have lain low or slid down the pole." Former Truman aides also told of a "meeting" attended by Hoover, Attorney General Tom Clark, Secretary of the Treasury Fred Vinson and the President at which it was agreed to transfer White to the International Monetary Fund so that the FBI could keep a closer watch on him. There were, of course, counter-stories from the Justice Department that this was not so.

Twice the Senate Internal Security Subcommittee asked Hoover to appear before it in order to make the record clear. Twice he refused. But after the third request, when the controversy continued to boil, Hoover merely answered that the decision was up to Brownell. The Attorney General, of course, called Hoover and told him that it would be "proper" for him to testify. As Hoover said years later, "I agreed to testify because the story that was being told reflected on me and on the FBI. They said at the time that I testified because I was angry because President Truman did not appoint me to head the Central Intelligence Agency when it was formed. But everyone in the

Truman Administration knew that I didn't want to head CIA and that I wanted to stay with the Bureau." But before Hoover, accompanied by Brownell, made his appearance, Harry S. Truman took to television to make his case before the public in a fiercely emphatic address. In his broadcast, he made four major points:

As best I can now determine, I first learned of the accusations against White early in February 1946 . . .

Let me read what Mr. Brownell said: "Harry Dexter White was known to be a Communist spy by the very people who appointed him to the most sensitive and important position he ever held in government service." His charge is false . . . He lied to the American people . . .

With [White's] duties thus restricted [by his transfer to the International Monetary Fund] . . . his position would be less important and much less sensitive—if it were sensitive at all—than the position then held by him as Assistant Secretary of the Treasury . . .

The course I took protected the public interest and security and . . . permitted the intensive FBI investigation then in progress [of White and other Communist spies in the government] to go forward. No other course could have served both these purposes.

Brownell took the stand first, before a packed and tense hearing room. He outlined his reasons for making the Chicago speech and then he got to basics:

White entered upon his duties and assumed the office of Executive Director for the United States in the International Monetary Fund on May 1, 1946 . . . On December 4, 1945, the FBI transmitted to Brigadier General Harry Vaughan, military aide to the President, a report on the general subject of Soviet espionage in the United States . . . Harry Dexter White and the espionage ring of which he was a part were among those referred to in this report . . . Copies of this report were sent to a number of Cabinet officers and high officials in the Truman Administration, including the Attorney General . . . But in addition to that fact, I have here a letter from J. Edgar Hoover to General Vaughan a month before that, dated November 8, 1945.

As you know, General Vaughan has testified before this committee that by arrangement with Mr. Truman, when the FBI had information which it deemed important for the President to know about, it sent that information to him—to Vaughan. Vaughan testified that he knew any such report which came to him was to be delivered to the President. The letter I hold in my hand is marked "Top Secret." I have declassified it and will make it public because it does not reveal any security information which would now be damaging . . . If this letter did not come to Mr. Truman's attention, then it would be a very serious dereliction of duty on the part of those who handled it.

The November 8 letter, signed by J. Edgar Hoover was addressed to General Vaughan. It listed a baker's dozen of "persons employed by the Government of the United States who have been furnishing data and information to persons outside the Federal Government, who are in turn transmitting this information to espionage agents of the Soviet Government," and assured the President that the FBI was continuing "vigorous investigation" of these activities. Harry Dexter White's name was second on the list. But despite the November 8 letter and a December 4 report, Brownell testified, it was a "blunt fact" that on January 23, 1946, President Truman announced the nomination of Harry Dexter White to the United States directorship of the International Monetary Fund. The chronology undercut completely Truman's contention that he had not heard of the White case until February 1946.

"But the matter does not end there," Brownell continued. "Because of [the appointment of White], the FBI compiled a special report devoted exclusively to Harry Dexter White and his espionage activities and delivered it, together with a covering letter, by special messenger on February 4, 1946, to General Vaughan for the attention of the President." Another copy was sent to Secretary of State James F. Byrnes, who was so agitated by it that he sent it on to Truman with a covering letter stating that he considered the report "of such importance that I think you should read [it]." Though the report remains classified, the letter from Hoover to Vaughan read as follows:

DEAR GENERAL VAUGHAN: As of interest to the President and you, I am attaching a detailed memorandum hereto concerning Harry Dexter White, Assistant Secretary of the United States Treasury Department. As you are aware, the name of Harry Dexter White has been sent to

Congress by the President for confirmation of his appointment as 1 of the 2 United States delegates on the International Monetary Fund under the Bretton Woods agreement. In view of this fact, the interest expressed by the President and you in matters of this nature, and the seriousness of the charges against White in the attachment, I have made every effort in preparing this memorandum to cover all possible ramifications. As will be observed, information has come to the attention of this Bureau charging White as being a valuable adjunct to an underground Soviet espionage organization operating in Washington, D. C. Material which came into his possession as a result of his official capacity allegedly was made available through intermediaries to Nathan Gregory Silvermaster, his wife, Helen Witte Silvermaster, and William Ludwig Ullmann. Both Silvermaster and Ullmann are employees of the United States Treasury Department, reportedly directly under the supervision of White.

The information and documents originating in the Treasury Department were either passed on in substance or photographed by Ullmann in a well-equipped laboratory in the basement of the Silvermaster home. Following this step, the material was taken to New York City by courier and made available to Jacob M. Golos, until the time of his death on November 27, 1943. Golos, a known Soviet agent, delivered this material to an individual tentatively identified as Gaik Ovakimian. Ovakimian, you will recall, was arrested some years ago as an unregistered agent of the Soviet Government and subsequently, by special arrangements with the Department of State, was permitted to return to the U. S. S. R.

After the departure of Gaik Ovakimian, Golos delivered his material to an individual who has been tentatively identified——[here a name is deleted for security purposes].

Subsequent to the death of Golos, the courier handling material received from the Silvermasters and Ullmann delivered it through an unidentified individual to Anatole Borisovich Gromov who until December 7, 1945, was assigned as First Secretary of the Soviet Embassy, Washington, D. C., when he returned to the U. S. S. R. Gromov had previously been under suspicion as the successor to Vassili Zubilin, reported head of the NKVD in North America, who returned to Moscow in the late summer of 1944. This whole network has been under intensive investigation since November 1945, and it is the results of these efforts that I am now able to make available to you.

I also feel that it is incumbent upon me at this time to bring to your attention an additional factor which has originated with sources available to this Bureau in Canada. It is reported that the British and Canadian delegates to the International Monetary Fund may possibly nominate and support White for the post of president of the International Bank, or as executive director of the International Monetary

Fund. The conclusion is expressed that assuming this backing is forthcoming and the United States acquiescence, if not concurrence, resulting, White's nomination to this highly important post would be assured. It is further commented by my Canadian source that if White is placed in either of these positions, he would have the power to influence to a great degree deliberations on all international financial arrangements.

This source, which is apparently aware of at least some of the charges incorporated in the attached memorandum against White, commented that the loyalty of White must be assured, particularly in view of the fact that the U. S. S. R. had not ratified the Bretton Woods agreement. Fear was expressed that facts might come to light in the future throwing some sinister accusations at White and thereby jeopardize the successful operation of these important international financial institutions.

I thought you would be particularly interested in the above comments, which originated with sources highly placed in the Canadian Government on the subject at hand.

With expressions of my highest esteem,
Sincerely yours,   J. EDGAR HOOVER.

Then, in great detail, Brownell documented the case against White. Repeatedly, where espionage in the Federal government was detected, the culprit would either be a close associate of Harry White or someone who had gotten his position in the government directly through White. And as Brownell spoke, it became obvious that White had not been merely one in a large espionage ring in the government. He had been at the center of Soviet spy activities and involved in all their ramifications. It was obvious, too, that starting with Elizabeth Bentley's allegations, the Bureau had done a superlative job of substantiating them. Some of it had been achieved through a painstaking search of the records. Once the Bureau had been alerted, it had consulted with the Intelligence services of friendly countries and found disturbing corroboration to what it had been developing in Washington. Since Hoover was not intending to build up a case for court action, wiretaps were widely used, though Brownell did not say so specifically.* Before Brownell con-

*Since many of White's associates in the Soviet espionage ring were in the Treasury, some of these taps were placed in the department. Fred Vinson,

cluded his testimony he had in effect put together a *Who's Who in Soviet Espionage* for the Forties. He had also made his case with such pinpoint precision that even the most partisan supporters of the President in the controversy were shaken and, very reluctantly, convinced. But Brownell, in explaining the Bureau's role, went to the nub of the Truman defense—that White had been appointed as a means of trapping the espionage apparatus—when he stated:

It has now been said that White's promotion to the post of Director of the International Monetary Fund was permitted to go through so that he might better be kept under surveillance, and so the investigation of the other members of the ring might be continued unimpaired. It is suggested that permitting White to continue his espionage opportunities might enable the Truman Administration to entrap not only White, but the whole espionage ring. To accomplish such an end would require infinite and detailed care if the national interest was to be at all protected.

In the first place, arrangements would have to be made to insure absolute control of the subjects and the situation . . . If the national interest were to be protected, measures would have to be designed to prevent classified material with a significant bearing on national security from reaching White and the others. Top responsible officials of the United States government, whose duties brought them in contact with White and other members of the ring, would have to be forewarned. Great care would have to be taken to make certain that these spies did not affect the decisions of our government. The records available to me fail to indicate that any of these minimum precautions were taken. The records available to me fail to show that anything was done which interfered with the continued functioning of the espionage ring of which White was a part.

This, of course, reached the heart of the matter, the point of contention. But the record, as cited by Brownell, showed categorically that the members of the White apparatus—and

who was then Secretary of the Treasury, learned of their existence and called Hoover in high dudgeon. "That son of a bitch Harold Ickes is tapping my phones," he said angrily. Hoover explained that it was not Ickes, Secretary of the Interior and a carry-over from the Roosevelt Administration, who had set up the taps, but the Bureau. He also told Vinson, very guardedly, that it was a matter of the national security. "That's all right, then," Vinson answered.

White himself—had been allowed to move about freely, with no security restraints, affecting government decisions and acting for important government agencies. In fact, there was reason to believe, though Brownell never made the point, that the apparatus had quietly pulled strings to get Harry White out of the Treasury, where he was vulnerable, and into an international agency. But more important, any planning of the kind suggested by Brownell would have had to be coordinated by the FBI. In seeking an answer to the question: "Who is lying, Truman or Brownell?"—never put so bluntly but implicit in the controversy—the testimony of J. Edgar Hoover became crucial.

There was some questioning of Brownell by the committee, but it was Hoover for whom both the senators and those in the hearing room waited. The chairman, Senator William E. Jenner, introduced him briefly. The next witness, he said, "should not be called before congressional committees except where a situation urgently warrants it." "This man" was the custodian of the national security and should not be drawn into political controversies. But there had been "a widely publicized rumor that Harry Dexter White was allowed to stay in office pursuant to an agreement with Mr. J. Edgar Hoover." And so, for the first time since his appointment as Director, with the exception of routine annual appearances before appropriations committees to report on the FBI's work and to state its needs, Hoover took the stand and was sworn. Before testifying, he distributed copies of a prepared statement:

There is more involved here than the charges against one man. This situation has a background of some 35 years of infiltration of an alien way of life into what we have been proud to call our Constitutional Republic. Our American way of life, which has flourished under our Republic and has nurtured the blessings of a democracy, has been brought into conflict with the godless forces of communism. These Red Fascists distort, conceal, misrepresent, and lie to gain their point. Deceit is their very essence. This can never be understood until we face the realization that to a Communist there are no morals except those which further the world revolution directed by Moscow.

The Harry Dexter White and related cases are in point. White was only one person on whom self-confessed Communist espionage agents informed—there were others. In this case, the sources who gave the information were co-conspirators and either became inactive or their identities must for the time being remain undisclosed. Corroboration in each instance was most difficult to secure, because the actual facts were known only to a limited group whose personal interests dictated concealment and who conveniently had the Fifth Amendment as a refuge.

Coverage from an Intelligence standpoint and an all-out open investigation looking toward eventual prosecution, are entirely different things. It must be remembered that the acts occurring in the prewar years occurred while we were at peace. In the pertinent time period, our national climate was one conducive to the so-called united front. Communist-front organizations flourished to the point where it appeared that to belong, in certain circles, was to be stylish.

Even today, the feeling is rife in some quarters that the FBI should not even be investigating the loyalty of Government employees. Over the years, the FBI has been the target of attack from persons both in and out of government because of its investigations of subversive activities. Even Harry Dexter White, when we interviewed him in March 1942, spent more time in denouncing investigations of Government employees than he did in furnishing facts. He observed that if the chairman of one congressional committee "was one-tenth as patriotic as I am, it would be a much better country."

The care, caution, and delicate approach necessary in such FBI investigations makes it difficult to develop full facts, particularly when those in possession of them declined to make full disclosures.

The responsibilities for internal security assigned the FBI in 1939 by presidential directive were directed toward the times of emergency rather than periods of peace. That is the situation today. It is still legal for Communists to exercise the right of assembly, free speech, and free thought.

On November 7, 1945, Miss Elizabeth Bentley advised special agents of the FBI in considerable detail of her own career as an espionage agent. On November 8, 1945, a letter bearing the date was delivered to Brig. Gen. Harry H. Vaughan, wherein it was stated:

The Bureau's information at this time indicates that the following persons were participants in this operation or were utilized by principals in this ring for the purpose of obtaining data in which the Soviet is interested.

The name of Harry Dexter White was the second name mentioned in the list of names furnished. The concluding paragraph of this three-page letter stated:

Investigation of this matter is being pushed vigorously, but I thought that the President and you would be interested in having the foregoing preliminary data immediately.

This communication was sent to General Vaughan in line with instructions conveyed to me by President Truman to call such matters in which he would have an interest to his attention through General Vaughan. I might add that the same practice so far as the FBI is concerned was followed during the administration of the late President Franklin D. Roosevelt. In fact, this same procedure was followed during the administration of former President Herbert Hoover.

Therefore there was nothing unusual or significant about my directing a communication to General Vaughan at that time.

In the meantime, our investigation of White and others mentioned by Miss Bentley and Whittaker Chambers, as well as those individuals on whom we had adverse information from equally reliable sources, continued.

A detailed summary memorandum was then prepared consisting of 71 pages, exclusive of the index, setting forth the highlights of Soviet espionage in the United States. This memorandum, dated November 27, 1945, was delivered to General Vaughan by a special messenger on December 4, 1945. Copies of this memorandum were furnished to the Attorney General and certain other interested heads of Government agencies. This memorandum included information on Harry Dexter White.

When we learned that Harry Dexter White's name had been sent to the Senate for confirmation of his appointment as a United States delegate on the International Monetary Fund, we then consolidated the information in our files, secured from sources whose reliability has been established either by inquiry or long-established observation and evaluation, in a 28-page summary dated February 1, 1946, which was delivered to General Vaughan on February 4, 1946. The two-page cover letter of transmittal opened with this sentence:

As of interest to the President and you, I am attaching a detailed memorandum hereto concerning Harry Dexter White, Assistant Secretary of the United States Treasury Department.

This observation was made in this letter:

As will be observed, information has come to the attention of this Bureau charging White as being a valuable adjunct to an underground Soviet espionage organization operating in Washington, D. C.

From November 8, 1945, until July 24, 1946, seven communications went to the White House bearing on espionage activities, wherein Harry Dexter White's name was specifically mentioned.

During that same period, 2 summaries on Soviet espionage activities went to the Treasury Department and 6 summaries went to the Attorney General on the same subject matter . . .

The FBI, of course, has a duty to evaluate its sources of information. In the 28-page summary concerning White, dated February 1, 1946, delivered to General Vaughan on February 4, 1946, the information contained therein came from a total of 30 sources, the reliability of which had previously been established.

In connection with the sources, I would like to mention one in particular, Miss Elizabeth Bentley. From the very outset, we established that she had been in a position to report the facts relative to Soviet espionage which she had done. We knew she was in contact with a top-ranking Soviet espionage agent, Anatoli Gromov, the first secretary of the Soviet Embassy in Washington, D. C., as late as November 21, 1945, in New York City. At a previous meeting on October 17, 1945, Gromov had given her $2,000 to carry forth her work as an espionage agent.

All information furnished by Miss Bentley, which was susceptible to check, has proven to be correct. She had been subjected to the most searching of cross-examinations; her testimony has been evaluated by juries and reviewed by the courts and has been found to be accurate.

Miss Bentley's account of White's activities was later corroborated by Whittaker Chambers and the documents in White's own handwriting concerning which there can be no dispute, lend credibility to the information previously reported on White. Subsequent to White's death on August 16, 1948, events transpired which produced facts of an uncontradictable nature which clearly established the reliability of the information furnished by the FBI in 1945 and 1946.

It must be remembered that in the period from November 8, 1945, to February 22, 1946, our first concern was to safeguard the Government from infiltration by subversive elements, and in this approach, the objective of pointing attention to security risks must not be confused with prosecutive action. During this period the FBI was concerned with protecting the Government's secrets and preventing such infiltration. In fact, I took a strong stand because of premature disclosures that would result if prosecution were initiated, for the following reasons:

1. The evidence necessary to sustain convictions in indictments for law violation is entirely different from that necessary to establish the existence of security risks in sensitive posts in the Government.

2. Some of the evidence, while of an irrefutable nature, was not admissible in a court of law.

Now to return to Harry Dexter White. In a conversation on February 21, 1946, the Attorney General informed me that he had spoken with the then Secretary of the Treasury, the late Chief Justice Fred Vinson, and the President, about White. The Attorney General stated he felt the President should personally tell White that it would be best for him not to serve. I told the Attorney General I felt it was unwise for White to serve. The Attorney General then stated he would like to confer with Judge Vinson and me on the following day, February 22, 1946.

I had luncheon on February 22, 1946, in the Attorney General's office with Judge Vinson and the Attorney General, at which time there was a lengthy conference. I was told that the problem was what could be done to prevent White from taking his oath of office. Judge Vinson did not want Mr. White to serve as a United States delegate on the International Monetary Fund and, in fact, did not want him to continue as an Assistant Secretary of the Treasury.

On the other hand, Judge Vinson stated that the President could be forced to sign the commission since the Senate had confirmed White's appointment. I advised Judge Vinson and the Attorney General that the character of the evidence was such that it should not be publicly disclosed at that time in view of the confidential sources involved.

It was the opinion of Judge Vinson and the Attorney General, as expressed that day at luncheon, that the Secretary of State, the Secretary of the Treasury, and the Attorney General would arrange to see the President as soon as possible; outline to him exactly what the situation was and they would suggest to the President that there were three alternatives:

One, the President could dismiss White and make no statement; two, the President could send for White and tell him he had changed his mind and that he desired White to resign and not serve; and, three, the President could sign the commission, instruct the Attorney General to continue the investigation vigorously and instruct the Secretary of the Treasury that he, as Governor of the National Advisory Council on International Monetary and Financial Problems and of the International Bank, should not be appointed except with approval of the Governor.

It was realized, of course, that should the President follow the second alternative and White should refuse to resign, the President might then sign the commission and take the same action as considered in the third alternative.

I did not enter into any agreement to shift White from his position in the Treasury Department to the International Monetary Fund. This was not within my purview. I was at the meeting to furnish facts, which I did. There was no agreement, while I was present, between the Attorney General and Judge Vinson, other than that they should see the President with the Secretary of State and suggest the three alternatives mentioned above. I was not present in any discussions with the President concerning this matter.

I was advised on February 26, 1946, by the Attorney General that he had seen the President and that an effort would be made to remove

Harry Dexter White, although the Attorney General expressed doubt that this would work out.

The Attorney General further stated to me on February 26, 1946, that he felt that White would go into the job and then would be surrounded with persons who were especially selected and were not security risks. He further stated that the President was interested in continuing the surveillance. I might add White had been under surveillance as early as November 1945. I stated if that was the desire, we would continue the investigation.

At no time was the FBI a party to an agreement to promote Harry Dexter White and at no time did the FBI give its approval to such an agreement. Such an agreement on the part of the FBI would be inconceivable. If this principle were applied to White, it would, of necessity, have applied to others who had similarly been involved in this particular investigation, who were dismissed from Government service when their subversive activities were discovered . . .

Had it been the intent of the FBI to handle the Harry Dexter White and other related cases solely as an Intelligence operation, the widespread dissemination of information that was furnished to various branches of the Government by the FBI would not have been undertaken.

Under date of February 26, 1946, I advised the Attorney General by telephone and subsequently by memorandum, of the receipt of information from a confidential source reflecting the possibility that Harry Dexter White might have received some notice of either the cancellation or impending cancellation of his appointment as a United States delegate to the International Monetary Fund. That information is absolutely reliable. I did not know whether anything had been said to White or whether any action had been taken to cancel his appointment.

The decision to retain White was made by a higher Government authority. Obviously, if a higher authority elected to shift a man rather than fire him, if he was suspect, then it would go without saying that the FBI would continue our investigation as best we could.

If in fact there was any agreement to move White from the Treasury Department to the International Monetary Fund to aid in the FBI investigation and to surround White with persons who were not security risks, then the agreement would have been broken very early because Mr. Virginius Frank Coe, a close associate of Harry Dexter White, became the Secretary of the International Monetary Fund in June 1946, which position he held until December 3, 1952, when he was dismissed after invoking the Fifth Amendment in an appearance before this same committee here last December. It is particularly significant that he declined to answer questions regarding his relationship with White. Information on Coe had been furnished to the

White House as early as February 25, 1946; to the Attorney General, February 23, 1946, and February 25, 1946, and to the Treasury Department as early as March 4, 1946. He recieved his appointment as indicated in June 1946.

From the foregoing, it is clear that the FBI called to the attention of the appropriate authorities the facts, as alleged by reliable sources, which were substantial in pointing to a security risk, as they occurred. It is equally clear that the FBI did not depart from its traditional position of making no evaluation, and was not a party to any agreement to keep White in public services.

That concludes my statement.

The CHAIRMAN. On behalf of the committee, Mr. Hoover, we want to thank you for appearing here at our request. Because of the attitude that I recently expressed in calling you, we want to confine our hearing to this particular matter. We are appreciative of your coming here and throwing enlightenment on this very important subject.

Mr. HOOVER. Thank you, Mr. Chairman.

The CHAIRMAN. Any questions?

Senator BUTLER. I would like to ask one question. What opportunity did the FBI have after Mr. White's transfer to the Monetary Fund to observe his activities?

Mr. HOOVER. I may say, Senator Butler, that the FBI, as I indicated in my formal statement, had initiated an investigation and surveillance of Mr. White in November 1945. He was appointed in the early part of 1946. We continued our surveillance and investigation of Mr. White through 1946 and at times in 1947 and 1948, but I must point out that while he was a member of the United States Monetary Commission, the premises of that Commission are extraterritorial, and the FBI does not have any right to follow any employee or any person onto the property of that Commission. We are under the same restrictions in regard to the United Nations.

Senator BUTLER. Therefore, his appointment hampered your investigation rather than helped it?

Mr. HOOVER. We were certainly hampered as far as surveillances were concerned.

The CHAIRMAN. Also hampered in regard to Mr. Frank Coe, because as I understand, you reported that he was a security risk; and in spite of that, he was appointed in June 1946, I believed you stated, to the Monetary Fund.

Mr. HOOVER. That is correct, Mr. Chairman. I might say that the same problem is faced today by the FBI in conducting investigations of espionage activities of members who are attached to the delegations of the United Nations . . .

Senator McCLELLAN. . . . As I understand your testimony, there was never any conference with you or any suggestion to you for any arrangements with the FBI that the man be kept in Government service in order to afford the FBI an opportunity for further surveillance?

Mr. HOOVER. That is absolutely correct.

The CHAIRMAN. Are there any further questions?

ROBERT MORRIS, Counsel to the Committee: Yes, Mr. Chairman, I have some questions.

Mr. Hoover, you stated in your statement today that from November 8, 1945, until July 24, 1946, 7 communications went to the White House bearing on espionage activities wherein Harry Dexter White's name was specifically mentioned.

Mr. HOOVER. That is correct . . .

Mr. MORRIS. If you had made a public protest of any kind, you would have been clearly outside of the scope of your authority?

Mr. HOOVER. It would have been most presumptuous to make a public protest. I am merely a subordinate official of the Attorney General. I do not make the policy. I am advised of the policy to be followed. . . .

JAY SOURWINE, Assistant Counsel: I have just one question.

Mr. Hoover, in your prepared statement you may remember at the top of page 8, as the copy was handed out, you said,

In fact, I took a strong stand because of premature disclosures that would result if prosecution were initiated, for the following reasons.

It occurs to me that there is a possible room for misunderstanding there, and I want to ask if this is a correct understanding of what you say. You took a strong stand in favor of ousting subversives from Government without waiting for a trial or for sufficient evidence to convict in court?

Mr. HOOVER. I was opposed, Mr. Sourwine, to the disclosure, either as new items—and there had been a number of leaks that had emanated from the Department of Justice and other agencies of the Government, upon cases in which we were then actively engaged. I also opposed the production in court at that time, or presentation to a grand jury, of some of this material, because of its highly confidential sources. Those sources could not be produced in court because of the nature of them. That is the position I took as to that. I never did at any time, and the records of the Bureau will conclusively sustain this statement, ever recommend to any agency of the Government or ask any agency of the Government to retain in its service any employee to aid the FBI in the conduct of any investigation.

The CHAIRMAN. Any further questions?

If not, we thank you, Mr. Hoover, for appearing, and you are excused.

Mr. HOOVER. Thank you very much, indeed.

Hoover's testimony demolished every point made by Harry Truman and by Democratic leaders. But it also exposed him to charges that he had acted out of political motivation or personal spite. There was also an outcry, for the most part from those who chronically resented the FBI, that he had "compromised" the Bureau and destroyed its impartiality. Those who did not know of the warmness of his relationship with Franklin Roosevelt accused him of harboring secret Republican sympathies. All of this hurt Hoover and the FBI and left running resentments in some political circles.

But Hoover never felt that he had strayed from the strict line of duty or acted in any way other than that of a conscientious civil servant protecting his organization. "Neither I nor the Attorney General implied that President Truman was disloyal or pro-Communist," he said in his defense. "He was blind to the Communist menace and used very bad judgment. But I would never have testified before the Senate had he not drawn me and the FBI into the controversy. By explaining the promotion of Harry Dexter White—and by having others say that he had acted on my advice—he made the FBI look ridiculous and inefficient. Only my appearance could have set the record straight completely. I knew I would be attacked for it, but I could not shirk my responsibility to the Bureau or allow the world to believe that we had been duped."

17.

Hoover, Civil Rights, and Crime

IN THE POSTWAR YEARS, JOHN EDGAR HOOVER AND THE FBI FACED two law enforcement problems which made the pursuit of a Dillinger, a Nazi agent, or a Soviet spy seem like a relaxed and uncomplicated pastime. These problems were (1) a new type of crime wave, and (2) civil rights. The FBI had broken the back of Thirties mobocracy by implacably tracking down the Bonnies and the Clydes, the George Barkers, and the Alvin Karpises. It had made a commendable record in gathering evidence of peonage in the South. It had upset the plans of Soviet and Nazi agents. But the postwar era brought a new kind of crime to American society and another concept of civil rights.

Crime in the thirties had been the property of the criminals. Professionals manned the submachine guns and held up the banks. The areas of criminal activity were clearly defined. The major criminal activity confronted by the FBI which at all fell into the amateur category was car theft. But in the postwar period, crime became pandemic, striking everywhere with recruits from all classes. It became, in part, a national sport, induced by a breakdown in the social restraints which, in a real sense, are the only sure effective inhibitors.

Before the war's end, Hoover had predicted the coming wave which would take crime out of the tenderloin and plant it in the affluent suburbs. "It is well," he said in 1944, "to analyze the conditions that breed crime today, in order that we may prevent it tomorrow. One of the primary causes of the alarming increase in crime among our young people, for example, has been the disintegration of the home as a guiding influence. The tremendous number of parents who have entered the armed services and war industries no longer can exercise sufficient control over their sons and daughters. The mushrooming of industrial cities, where facilities for recreation and wholesome living are inadequate, deprives thousands of children of the benefits of a normal way of life."

The dramatic rise in crime during the first ten years after the war—27 percent over the 1937–39 statistics—and the horrendous figure of one serious crime for every 13.9 seconds which Hoover announced at the end of the postwar decade were bad enough. But for Hoover, whose traditionalist values focused his attention on juvenile crime, the picture was even grimmer. Living with the reports from local police departments, he knew that young people under eighteen accounted for almost 43 percent of the arrests made for major crime, with about half of these under age fifteen. The burglary statistics alone showed that 53 percent of those arrested were under eighteen.

By law, the FBI could not intervene in the enforcement of local laws—the laws that cover most crime in the United States. Congress had steadily expanded the functions of the FBI since the day that Hoover had been sworn in as Acting Director of the Bureau of Investigation. But local crime was a local concern, and Hoover had fought fiercely and consistently against any efforts to make the FBI a national police force. That concern was deep, as those who knew him well at the time have stated. If he would not—and could not without making the FBI a mammoth agency—involve himself in the effort to contain juvenile crime, he still felt that the Bureau's facilities should at least be made available to local authorities.

It was the success of the FBI Academy which convinced him that an instrumentality should be created to aid in the fight on juvenile crime. In 1946, therefore, Hoover created within the Bureau a Juvenile Delinquency Instructors School. Agents were taken off other duties and assigned to make an in-depth study of juvenile delinquency, its causes and its possible cures. The leading authorities in the field were invited to Washington to lecture these agents and to serve as consultants. Agents were then sent out to speak to local police, to pass on new and developing techniques, to offer advice on such routine matters as the setting up of boy's clubs, the enlisting by law enforcement authorities of Parent-Teacher Associations—or the Boy Scouts or church groups. But mostly they stressed the importance of parental interest—a theme which, as affluence and permissiveness seized the nation, he elaborated on with increasing vehemence.

"Criminal behavior is learned behavior," he wrote for the *Syracuse Law Review.* "The child and the adolescent are impressionable, and their active minds develop codes of morality no higher than those to which they are exposed. The environment which the adult community provides its growing children is the most important factor underlying the behavior patterns cultivated by the normal child."

In the years that followed, the permissiveness which he had deplored in the middle Fifties assumed greater proportion. To what Hoover saw as moral laxity in the home was added external factors—sexual promiscuity among teenagers, the rising use of marijuana at all levels and in all ages of the society, the lowered thresholds in the standards of what was pornographic which led eventuality to an anything-goes attitude, and the acceptance as a legal, philosophical, and moral premise of the belief that right or wrong existed only subjectively in the mind.

Unfortunately for Hoover, he expressed his growing concern in terms which had lost their validity to generations nurtured in a vocabulary which rejected the morality of the past with laughter or anger. Had he spoken in the new language of psychology or psychiatry of the practical pitfalls of the new "life style," he might have reached the consciousness of many confused Americans. But he usually spoke in terms which derived from his Sunday School days, thereby opening himself to jibes that he was not "with it"—presumably a devastating criticism. When he wrote an article for *Woman's Home Companion* whose title was "Mothers . . . Our Only Hope," he lost his audience immediately because motherhood was no longer in fashion.

In 1945 he had written an article for the *Rotarian* which unwittingly summed up the case against him—"There Will be a Postwar Crime Waves Unless—It's Blocked By Direct Action Sparked By a Revival of Some Old-Fashioned Virtues." Fourteen years later, he would be telling a House Appropriations subcommittee:

Basically, the present increase in criminal activity reflects a moral deterioration among vast segments of our population. Not only does this moral deterioration exist within the criminal element itself, but it also has corrupted millions of other American citizens who obey the law themselves yet passively tolerate immorality and disrespect for authority within their communities . . . Growing numbers of our citizens have been afflicted by a sickness which I call the "decadence disease." Its symptoms are lethargy, self-indulgence, and the principle of pleasure before duty.

A year later he would tell the same committee that the moral decay which led to crime was reflected in "the willingness of many law-abiding Americans to compromise their ideals if an easy dollar can be made." Nine years after that, when the latest crime figures showed a one-year increase of 17 percent, with a rise in robberies of 29 percent, Hoover testified that "crime has reached such proportions that morality, integrity, law and order, and other cherished principles of this country's great heritage are fighting for their very survival in many communities today."

Hoover did speak out in practical terms, but in so doing he was stepping on the toes of the probation, parole, and rehabilitation bureaucracy. "There are three ways to put a brake on crime," he would say. "The first is prompt apprehension. The second is prompt trials and the elimination of delays such as repeated postponements and plea bargaining. The third should be substantial sentences which match the type of crime committed." In this third point, he stood in opposition to the fashionable views of the penologists that punishment does not deter crime—that, it fact, it encourages it. Hoover's reaction to the outcries of the professional parolers was tough and bitter: rejecting the whims of "those gushing, well-wishing, mawkish sentimentalists."

For this he was compared to the "hanging judges" of the American frontier or accused of wanting a return to seventeenth-century British law under which a pickpocket could be hanged and the guilty could be forgotten in filthy prisons. To this, Hoover had a simple answer. He was not opposed to the principles of parole but to "the maladministration on the part of those in charge of the programs." In 1959, for example, he cited the significant statistic that ninety-three of the FBI's "Ten Most Wanted" fugitives since 1950 had received parole or other forms of clemency. Ten years later, he told a congressional committee that of the first three hundred criminals on the "Ten Most Wanted" list, 234 had received some form of judicial leniency or special favor. "There's a new privileged class in this country," he stressed, "the repeating offender. The victims of crime must be wondering and asking, when they hear all that clamor for the unlimited rights of criminals, whether they have any civil rights as well."

By one of those paradoxes so common in contemporary society, Hoover was at the same time under sharp attack for his demands that justice be swift and rigorous and his failure to come to grips with "organized crime" or the Mafia. Speaking technically, Hoover had rejected the idea that the Mafia was what crime reporters and some congressional committees had insisted it was—a nationwide organization directing and coordinating all criminal activities, all corruption, in the United States. In this, he was right, for crime in America has always followed ethnic lines. If there was an Italian "Mafia" there was also a competitive Jewish "Mafia" and an Irish "Mafia"—to name but three of the groups. As the Negro emerged stronger in the country, there also came to be a black "Mafia."

But Hoover's view did not mean that there was no organized crime in the United States or that the FBI was not concerned. The FBI acted where it could, where it had the facilities or where law permitted it to act. Somewhat plaintively, Hoover would say:

People come to and ask me whether something can't be done to clean up their cities or their towns, to drive out the racketeers and the mobsters. I try to explain that the kind of crime they want to eradicate— call it "organized crime"—doesn't come within the Federal jurisdiction. I tell them, "Go back home and elect honest men, efficient and hard-working men, to public office." And they tell me, "We don't want to get mixed up in politics." What they mean is that some of the people they would like me to get rid of sit on the respectable side of the table though they are still involved with the rackets. They don't want to face up to this, or to take the risks of battle, so they tell the FBI to do it.

Critics of Hoover and the FBI charged repeatedly that they had no interest in organized crime, the Mafia, because any investigation would be long and difficult. What Hoover wanted, such enemies of the FBI and Hoover as Fred Cook and William Turner wrote, was quick and easy crimes which would improve the FBI's arrest-and-conviction record—auto theft, for example. In this charge, there was one small element of truth. Hoover did drive the FBI to solve crimes which added to the Bureau's impressive record of convictions. And he did believe, though he never quite put it that way, that a criminal in the hand was worth two in the bush. He also knew that it was futile to take on the crime which is entangled with legitimate business or local politics until the community—national or otherwise—was ready for it. To do otherwise would snare the FBI in endless wrangles with political machines and the Washington power structure—wrangles which would achieve nothing and damage the Bureau. He would be vindicated in this years later when, in following the leads of congressional corruption, he would be accused on the floor of the Senate of running a Gestapo. And he would remark bitterly then that those who most lambasted him for not taking the lead in these areas would inevitably be the same critics who reproached him for being too active an investigator.

But the major accusation made against Hoover in the Fifties and Sixties was that he had no interest in enforcing the various civil rights statutes, that he deliberately held the FBI back, that he was anti-Negro and anti-Semitic. The last of those charges was laid to rest in 1959 by B'nai B'rith, a Jewish organization whose investigative arm, the Anti-Defamation League, zealously tracks down even the slightest hint of anti-Jewish feeling. In that year, there was a series of bombings of synagogues and Jewish religious schools. This caused considerable concern in a Jewish community which remembered all too well the Hitler era. But a statement by Philip Klutznick, president of the 400,000-member service organization, gave Hoover and the FBI high marks for their "deep concern" and for their assistance in "reducing the threat of continued bigot-inspired violence." And Klutznick added, "The investigative efforts, training assistance, and scientific services" of the Bureau had been of "tremendous value" and B'nai B'rith had "cause to appreciate that in troubled times such as these the nation possesses an effective public servant in Mr. Hoover and the agency he heads."

The anti-Negro charge centered around assertions that there were "not enough" blacks in the FBI. To this, Hoover had a direct and simple answer: "I won't appoint a man to the FBI because his uncle is a powerful senator. And I won't appoint a

Negro just because he's a Negro. There are Negroes now in the FBI and they got their jobs like everyone else—by careful examination of their qualifications, the same examination that any other applicant receives. There has been no case of a Negro who was qualified being turned down. There will never be. But I do not intend at this time or at any time to bring into the FBI any man, regardless of his race or his creed, if he does not measure up to the FBI's standards." The American Civil Liberties Union shouted in outrage at Hoover's attitude, claiming that it demonstrated a deep-seated race prejudice and an undemocratic attitude, but Hoover never budged. To those who cared to find out, he also showed that very few Negroes applied for FBI jobs, a fact that civil liberties groups cited as proof positive that Hoover was racist.

From the beginning of his tenure, however, Hoover had investigated cases of peonage—forced labor—in the South and presented the Justice Department with sufficient evidence to bring about a series of convictions. In 1944, long before the civil rights agitation began, Hoover had directed the FBI to investigate the death of Robert Hall, a thirty-year-old Negro who had been beaten to a pulp by the sheriff and his deputies in Newton, Georgia. Working against the hostility of the community and the local police, the FBI built up a case to show that Hall had been beaten to death in violation of a Federal law which prohibits anyone "acting under the color of law" to deprive any person willfully of his rights, privileges, and immunities under the Constitution of the United States.

The sheriff and two deputies were indicted on evidence provided by the FBI and convicted. The Court of Appeals sustained the conviction. But though the Supreme Court noted that the Hall case was a "shocking and revolting episode in law enforcement," it ordered a new trial on the ground that the jury had been improperly instructed by the trial judge because he had failed to state that the defendants could not be convicted unless they had acted "willfully" to deprive Hall of his constitutional rights. In the second trial, the defendants were acquitted because the government could not, obviously, prove that they had beaten Hall to death in "willful" violation of his civil rights. The crime could be proved, but not what was in the minds of the defendants at the time they committed it.

Hoover was aware, in the mid-Forties, that the problem went deeper than the statutes. Referring to the Hall case, he said: "We can have the Constitution, the best laws in the land, and the most honest reviews by the courts—but unless the law enforcement profession is steeped in the democratic tradition, maintains the highest in ethics, and makes its work a career of honor, civil liberties will continually—and without end—be violated." In the area of constitutional rights, therefore, the FBI was damned if it did, damned if it didn't. As late as 1956, he could tell a House Appropriations subcommittee that in "civil rights cases, the Bureau is in a situation that if it obtains facts which result in prosecution it is unpopular and if it doesn't obtain facts, it is unpopular. Our sole purpose is to do our job objectively."

But being objective did not suit many of those who felt that the FBI had no right to enter into cases that, until then, had been the prerogative of the states. Even when Hoover, reading the reports of his agents on specific cases, held that there was no Federal jurisdiction, he found himself the target of attack. In 1952, for example, Hoover looked into what seemed like a violation of civil rights in Gainesville, Texas, at a correctional school for girls. Studying the reports, he decided—and the Justice Department agreed with him—that the Federal government had no right to intervene. Yet Governor Allan Shivers took off after Hoover for "snooping." In a letter to Shivers, Hoover laid it on the line. "We of the FBI certainly have no apologies to make to anyone for doing our duty in carrying out the instructions of the Attorney General in enforcing the law of the land," he wrote. "Should the day ever come when the Director of the Federal Bureau of Investigation has the discretion of choosing those laws which his service will enforce, then indeed we will have a Gestapo, and I can assure you that I will have no part of it."

When Governor John S. Fine of Pennsylvania argued that FBI investigation of civil rights violations treated the states as "quasi-criminals," Hoover replied that he was merely following the dictates of an act of Congress. And he added very pointedly that "it would appear that if the Governors are opposed to this law, their recourse would be to go to Congress and seek repeal of the law rather than level their attacks upon the FBI."

For FBI agents working in the South, Hoover's attitude caused considerable trouble. They had always worked in close cooperation with local police officials on ordinary criminal matters. But when the Bureau, at Hoover's direction, moved into civil rights matters, these officials took it as a personal affront. They could not understand the logic of the situation, and they believed that Hoover had sold them out to the northern liberals. When Hoover told them, as diplomatically as he could, that law is law, or more bluntly that "I can't be guided by any considerations that what the Bureau does will make us more or less popular in your community," they turned on him with varying degrees of anger.

"For some people, civil rights was politics," Hoover later remarked to a friend. "But for me it was a matter of law. If you look at it that way, our investigation of the Kansas City vote frauds in the Thirties was also politics—and civil rights, too. We went in and proved that there had been a stealing of votes. We examined the ballots and found erasures, fingerprints of those who had no right to be handling those ballots, and indentations which showed that ballots had been marked one on top of the other. We gathered enough evidence to convict more than 250 persons. Our investigation broke the Pendergast machine in Kansas City, but we were simply enforcing the law. In Mobile, Alabama, before the war, we conducted an investigation because we believed that freedom of the press was being abridged by underworld elements. We lost that one when the Court of Appeals reversed the conviction, but we believed that we were upholding the Constitution."

When Hoover was accused of lack of interest on civil rights, he would proudly wave a resolution of a grand jury in Rome, Georgia, in a case in which the FBI had produced the evidence which led to the conviction of five members of the Ku Klux Klan who had flogged six Negroes because they had been "up-pity." "The members of the Federal grand jury," the citation read, "hereby resolve: That the following agents of the [FBI] by their great fidelity and singleness of purpose . . . have gone far beyond the line of duty to aid, assist and protect the citizens of the United States and to further the cause of equity and justice in America."

In 1956, moreover, after the Supreme Court's *Brown* v. *Board of Education* ruling had ordered integration of schools and opened up a wide new area of civil rights enforcement, Hoover made his position—and therefore that of the FBI—known in no uncertain terms, expressing both the lawman's view and an understanding of the South's travail. Realizing that the South was a tinderbox, Hoover said:

This mounting tension has manifested itself in overt acts on the part of individuals, organized resistance in legislative bodies, and the creation of organizations on a widespread basis to resist integration . . . If the bloodshed, which both the proponents and the opponents of integration now discuss, is to be avoided, there needs to be real understanding and public education with regard to the factors contributing to the present situation which can boil over at any moments into acts of extreme violence . . . The law-abiding people of the South neither approve nor condone acts of brutality and the lawless taking of human lives. On the other hand, historic traditions and customs are part of a heritage with which they will not part without a struggle . . . The mounting tension can be met only with understanding and a realization of the motivating forces.

But the strongest assault on Hoover resulted from something over which he had no control—the loyalty-security program embodied in a series of executive orders issued by Harry S. Truman. As a result of these Presidential directives, it fell on the FBI to look into the past and present of all persons in the

Federal employ. In the aftermath of the hot war and the advent of the cold war, the Truman Administration had grudgingly agreed that all those holding Federal jobs should be scrutinized for possible acts or associations with Communists and other subversives. Hoover did not want this chore—and as even a casual reading of the *Congressional Record* will show, he implored the Congress not to assign this onerous and backbreaking task to the Bureau. To handle it, 1,700 agents had to be taken off other assignments. But Hoover was overruled by both the White House and a Congress which decided that the FBI could do the job at far less a cost than the Civil Service Commission or a new agency. In carrying out orders, however, Hoover was pilloried for prying into the personal affairs of the Federal bureaucracy and violating its civil rights. That he was asked to go beyond subversion and into such matters as homosexuality piled fuel on the anti-FBI fire.

Unless derogatory information about a government employee turned up in Civil Service files, or in those of the FBI, the Bureau's role was completely routine. Under Executive Orders issued by President Truman, the name of every new government employee was submitted to the FBI. If nothing was found in the files, the employee's form was stamped "No Disloyal Data FBI Files." At no point would the Bureau "clear" or "charge" anyone. It merely reported. It never mounted a field investigation unless there was evidence in its files of disloyalty or a bad security record, unless the Civil Service Commission specifically asked for one, unless the Bureau received complaints of disloyalty, or unless it came across troublesome information in the course of other investigations.

But this did not prevent those unalterably opposed to anything that might expose Communist subversion to scream mightily that President Truman was a puppet of the FBI, which was conducting a police state operation. Communist, pro-Communist, and left-wing organizations held rallies, collected signatures on petitions, and did everything in their power to stop the loyalty program. Because the loyalty forms, prepared by the Civil Service Commission, asked applicants for government jobs to list any organization to which they belonged, Abram Flaxner, of the pro-Communist United Public Workers of America, shouted that the FBI was pressing "a union-busting drive under the guise of a loyalty investigation." He further stated, in contravention of the facts, that the FBI "now has sole and exclusive authority to render judgment on the loyalty of government employees."

Hoover tried to make his position clear and to explain exactly what it was the Bureau did. But few would listen, and when people of impeachable reputation but fuzzy thinking joined in the outcry against what every government in the world does routinely, Hoover felt the issue was important enough to give the press lengthy interviews. Early in the controversy, he had made one point, but this was ignored or brushed aside:

"A government job is a matter of privilege and not a right," he said. "The late Justice Oliver Wendell Holmes put it very neatly in 1892 when he was a member of the Massachusetts Supreme Court. A New Bedford policeman, discharged for prohibited political activity, had petitioned for reinstatement. In turning down the application, Justice Holmes remarked that 'the petitioner may have a constitutional right to talk politics, but he has no constitutional right to be a policeman!'"

In response to the "witch hunt" accusation, Hoover gave *Newsweek* magazine a list of "Ten 'Don't's" to be kept in mind when dealing with the Communist problem:

Don't label anyone a Communist unless you have the facts.

Don't confuse liberals and progressives with Communists.

Don't take the law into your own hands. If Communists violate the law, report such facts to your law-enforcement agency.

Don't be a party to the violation of the civil rights of anyone. When this is done, you are playing directly into the hands of the Communists.

Don't let up on the fight against real fascists, the KKK, and other dangerous groups.

Don't let Communists in your organization or labor union outwork, outvote, or outnumber you.

Don't be hoodwinked by Communist propaganda that says one thing but means destruction of the American way of life. Expose it with the truth.

Don't give aid and comfort to the Communist cause by joining front organizations, contributing to their campaign chests, or by championing their cause in any way, shape, or form.

Don't let the Communists infiltrate our schools, churches, and molders of public opinion—the press, radio, and screen.

Don't fail to make democracy work with equal opportunity and the fullest enjoyment of every American's right to life, liberty, and the pursuit of happiness.

To the surprise of some of his critics and the chagrin of some of his friends, Hoover forthrightly opposed the outlawing of the Communist Party. "Suppressing and outlawing subversive organizations is not the answer," he said on many occasions. "As a nation, we need have no fears so long as the actions of those residing within our shores are open and above board." But his opposition to the Communist Party went much deeper than his strictures against its secrecy and deviousness. What truly troubled him was that it was an agent of a foreign power with designs on the United States—a foreign power, moreover which denied the existence of God or the validity of the Christian ethic.

But these were times of high passion, when the mention of communism or a simple statement that the government had a right to deprive those who would destroy it a Treasury check upset a vocal and powerful minority. Hoover resorted, out of frustration, to interviews with such reporters as Bert Andrews, Washington bureau chief of the *New York Herald Tribune* and a sardonic critic of the loyalty program, to set the record straight and to relieve his frustration. In an effort to rebut the intellectual and academic community, he spoke to a number of newspapermen, *privatim et seriatim,* explaining his position for publication or for background. But those stories that saw the light of day in print appeared and were forgotten. Sitting in his office, he would present his arguments, his statistics—forceful to the eye and ear, but never certain that he was getting through.

"There is a belief in certain quarters that we are not interested in the rights of those we investigate and only out to prove a case," he would say. "But the best answer to that belief is in the record of the FBI itself. But the 11,812 convictions last year from cases investigated by the FBI last year represented 96.8 percent of all our cases taken into court. If we violated civil rights in criminal cases, our powerful adversaries would have established that in open court. But they haven't, as the record will show. Attorneys General since Homer Cummings have been saying this publicly over the years.

Congress gave us the task of handling investigations under the loyalty program. We exercise every care to establish the innocence of those who are falsely accused, just as we seek the facts in the cases of disloyal employees. We have trained our investigators to spot the individual furnishing information who has an ax to grind, who has some ulterior motive. Whenever an agent has reason to believe that this is the case, he is under my instructions to point this out in his report so that government officials and loyalty hearing boards can take this into consideration.

But we do not make up the list of organizations declared to be subversive by the Attorney General. When we receive information that an organization is subversive, we investigate and turn the facts over to the Attorney General for his determination. We do not recommend, ever. Of course, we investigate members of these subversive organizations, under orders from the President. But the FBI has always held that membership in a subversive organization does not necessarily point to a single conclusion. People are attracted to "front" organizations because of an appealing name or duped as to its real intent. In this case, our agents will look beyond membership alone, to overt acts. Where there is doubt as to whether or not we should investigate, we refer the facts to the Attorney General.

Contrary to what our critics and our enemies say, we do not keep files on all citizens or all government officials. If, under the loyalty order, we are required to investigate a government official, of course we have a file on him. But in all other cases, we keep files only on those individuals and organizations where we are in receipt of a complaint which comes within our jurisdiction. What anyone says, thinks, or does is his business so long as there are no allegations of violation of Federal law. If we receive charges that a Federal employee is a Communist, Fascist, or member of the Ku Klux Klan, we ask for facts, not for opinions or conclusions. If those we interview, in an investigation, have no facts, this is stated in our investigative report.*

Hoover was defensive about one point in these interviews:

I have been frequently accused of having an "obsession" with communism. This is not true. If you study the FBI record, you will see that we have stressed the threat to the national security which is most important at the time. When the Nazis and the Fascists were a real threat, our efforts were directed to investigating them. But the Communists had been a threat ever since I became the Director of the Bureau in 1924. Public opinion on this subject has changed, but the Communists have not. The Communist Party and its underground agents have always regarded infiltration of the government service as a top priority project. Several months ago, high officials of the party were issued instructions that those members in the government and in other important or strategic positions were not to attend party meetings or any kind of gathering that might have a Communist tinge. These party members in government were also given strict orders to destroy their membership cards. At the same time, their names were dropped from party membership rolls and high party officials refrained, as a matter of policy, from having any contact with them.

We in the Bureau have always felt that the Communists in the Federal government were a threat to the national security and to America for five reasons. First, it gives them the chance to engage in espionage. Second, it gives them a chance to influence American policy in ways detrimental to our national interest and to sabotage the policy set down by the government if it hurts the Soviet Union. This, more than actual espionage, was the job of Alger Hiss and Harry Dexter White in the forties. Third, it gives them a forum for the more subtle forms

*In the Fifties there were frequent attacks on Hoover because of what purportedly went into these reports. This kind of criticism was usually based on selective tidbits, taken out of context. For example, there was both hilarity and indignation over news stories that the FBI had tagged a man a Communist because he frequently came to his door naked and because, on occasion, he pulled down the window shades when he had visitors. The report, however, clearly stated that the man did come to his door naked and did wander around the house in the same state of undress with the shades up. The report had taken note of this fact because the shades were pulled down only when a known Soviet agent, under FBI surveillance, would visit. This had aroused FBI suspicions, and a further investigation of the home nudist had disclosed serious Communist connections. A few sentences out of the report, however, were employed to make the FBI seem silly or vicious.

of Communist propaganda. Fourth, it provides an opportunity to re-cruit others in government service and to use innocents for their nefarious purposes. And last, they act as employment agencies in government for other Communists, thereby spreading the infection.

Defending the loyalty investigations and the FBI's role, Hoover would turn to the attitude of government employees' unions. "If we were violating civil rights," he said, "and harassing innocent Federal employees, there would be a real outcry from those unions. If we were using the program as a means of union busting, and that charge has been made, those unions would be screaming to high heaven. But look at the record. James Burns, who is president of the American Federation of Government Employees, says that the loyalty program has been carried out by the Civil Service Commission and the FBI 'in a truly American fashion' and that there is no reason for 'hysteria or the notion that this is a witch hunt.' Luther Stewart, who heads another government workers union, says the same. Abram Flaxner, president of the United Public Workers of America, can shout that the loyalty program is a 'union-busting witchhunt,' but the fact is that the FBI has compiled no lists of union members. We have no interest in that, and too many other things to do that fall under our jurisdiction. Leo George, leader of the AFL National Federation of Post Office Clerks, has stated publicly that none of his members object to naming their union connections in government forms."

In the Washington of the late Forties, Hoover's words were reassuring. Those in the highest positions in government knew what the public failed to notice. For example, the State Department had been flooded by some 30,000 employees from wartime agencies, such as the notoriously lax Office of War Information, which had mounted documented witch hunts against *anti-Communists* who found themselves hounded out of their jobs or pushed into unimportant tasks. A substantial number of these wartime agency people had been hired and kept on the payroll without even a routine Civil Service Commission check. In coping with this influx, the State Department had set up an investigative arm, supervised by a three-man panel which prohibited any exchanges of information or contact with the FBI. It required the resources and the know-how of the Bureau to cope with this situation. A careful search of the record shows that thousands had quit their new State Department posts precipitously when they learned that they would be subject to a name check. Others resigned when they were interviewed by the FBI, knowing that they would be required to repeat their denials and affirmations under oath, thereby inviting the penalties of perjury.

There was growing awareness, as public euphoria over "our great ally," the Soviet Union, was rapidly replaced by a realization that the United States was confronted by the most powerful threat in its history to its internal and external security. All efforts at creating an atmosphere for a long and viable peace were being thwarted by Stalin and the international Communist movement. Czechoslovakia had fallen to the Communists after a period of intrigue and brutal murder. And Hoover's increasingly pointed warnings, in speeches and interviews, could not longer be dismissed as the obsessive ravings of a man bent on creating an American Gestapo or NKVD. But this did not prevent some in the media and the liberal/academic community to continue their assaults on Hoover and the FBI.

To bolster their accusations that Hoover was destroying civil liberties in the United States, they dredged up a wartime issue of *In Fact,* a scurrilous newsletter which purported to give the "lowdown" on the press, edited by George Seldes, a former newspaperman whose writings would make a Jack Anderson look like the soul of veracity, accuracy, and honesty. This issue had been devoted to an "exposé" of Hoover, and it found wide currency in certain circles. *In Fact* stated that the "FBI has sought to frame progressive unionists"—in the Seldes lexicon, "progressive unionists" being those later expelled from the CIO for being overtly pro-Communist—that "a witch hunt against civil liberties" had been instituted by Hoover, that the FBI was "performing anti-labor espionage" gratis, that FBI employees were clocked on their visits to rest rooms, that FBI clerks were fired for joining a government workers' union, that Hoover had obtained "faked" evidence in the deportation proceedings against Harry Bridges, a pro-Communist labor leader, by "bribery and intimidation"—in short, that John Edgar Hoover was a very low fellow indeed. The virulence of these charges and their palpable falsity excluded them from verbatim publication by the media, but they were used as a basis for rumor and innuendo. So bad did this become that Morris Ernst, a civil liberties lawyer, felt constrained to answer them in an article for the *Reader's Digest.*

I still remember my start of surprise when I read in the paper one morning in 1939 that J. Edgar Hoover, Director of the Federal Bureau of Investigation, had asked the United States Attorney General not to endorse a law which would legalize a free use of wiretapping. Why was Mr. Hoover opposing a law which would make his own work so much easier? His own words . . . gave me the answer: "I do not wish to be the head of an organization of potential blackmailers."

I had been hearing criticisms that the FBI was made up of 'witch hunters' hounding loyal citizens out of their jobs on the flimsiest sort of rumor; that they tapped telephone wires indiscriminately, learning everybody's private business . . . I wrote articles in which I asked readers to send me any evidence that the FBI had violated a person's constitutional rights . . . All the evidence indicates that the FBI as a matter of unvarying policy had played fair with criminals and suspects . . .

It is natural that loyalty investigations should give us qualms. We shudder to authorize wiretapping and other forms of spying. But they seem necessary to us if we are to preserve our freedom. They have been forced upon us by the [Communist] underground . . . Until Congress is wise enough to pass laws which force open operation of all mass movements, we shall have to protect ourselves against secretly organized attacks . . . The requirement to disclose essential facts is no invasion of privacy . . . Even without such laws, the FBI has handled delicate problems well . . . And although I was the lawyer for certain acquitted suspects, I must admit that Mr. Hoover had a justification in picking up my clients; there was cause for suspicion and no injustice was done.

One of the greatest liberals said in 1941: "I do not believe wiretapping should be used to prevent domestic crimes, with possibly one exception—kidnapping and extortion in the Federal sense. There is, however, one field in which, given the conditions in the world today, wiretapping is very much in the national interest . . . I have no compunction in saying that wiretapping should be used against those persons . . . who today are engaged in espionage and sabotage against the United States." This statement was made by President Franklin D. Roosevelt . . .

The loyalty investigation program has created a misconception about the FBI's function . . . It gathers the facts about a Federal employee and turns over its findings to the head of the [Federal] department . . . And that is all it does, or can do, except that it frequently is able to save a suspect in his job when rumor is doing its best to get him fired . . .

A real smear campaign has been carried on against Hoover's work. Those who feared the Bureau, as I once did, will be glad to know [that] it has a magnificent record of respect for individual freedom. It invites documented complaints against its agents. It has zealously tried to prevent itself from violating the democratic process. Among liberals I am by no means alone in this opinion. A while ago Roger Baldwin, formerly director of the American Civil Liberties Union, wrote to J. Edgar Hoover: "It seems to me that your Bureau has accomplished an exceedingly difficult job with rare judicial sense." For me, that sums up the record.

18.

Investigations and McCarthy

ON MARCH 26, 1947, JOHN EDGAR HOOVER APPEARED BEFORE THE House Committee on Un-American Activities to make one of his regular reports on subversive activities in the United States. For the committee, it was an opportunity to bask in reflected glory. For Hoover, it was an essential part of his work. He appeared regularly before the House Appropriations subcommittee, chaired by Representative John Rooney of New York, a tiger who sheathed his claws lovingly when dealing with a man for whom he had tremendous respect and personal affection. Rooney, who could and often did rip State Department appropriations requests to pieces, was impressed and gratified by the efficiency of the FBI, by the way that Hoover husbanded the funds allotted to the Bureau, and by the FBI's unheard of (in government) practice of turning back to Congress any unused money.

Most of the meat of Hoover testimony before the Rooney subcommittee, however, was heard behind locked doors where he could let down his hair. What he said was sometimes engrossing, sometimes shocking, and always informative—but such was the discipline maintained by Rooney that little of what he told the members leaked out. Appearances before HCUA, however, were Hoover's way of communicating directly to the country, of scoring points against those in the Federal Establishment who thwarted the FBI's work, and of placing on the public records matters which ordinarily would have been lost in the mazes of Executive Department secrecy and bureaucratic obtuseness.

At this 1947 appearance, Hoover disclosed that on March 7, 1942, he had transmitted to the Federal Security Agency a 57-page report noting that one of its employees, Doxey Wilkerson, had been and could still be a Communist. The Federal Security Agency had not responded to the Hoover report, though Wilkerson was quietly transferred to another government agency. On June 19, 1943, Hoover told the Committee, Wilkerson resigned from the government to become a member of the Communist Party's National Committee—a post which, under the party's bylaws, he could not assume unless he had been a member in good standing of the CPUSA for at least four years.

This was not the first time, nor would it be the last that Hoover used a congressional forum to make known the reluctance or refusal of the Executive Branch to root out Communists from the Federal employ. For this, he was roundly criticized by those who quoted his oft-repeated statement that the FBI was simply the investigative arm of the Justice Department, that no policy decisions were or could be made by the Bureau, and that its files were inviolate. It was Hoover's contention that Congress had authorized him to do more than merely collect criminal and subversive data for the exclusive pleasure of the Attorney General, that he was empowered to furnish information on request or at his volition to Federal officials outside the Justice Department, and that there were nothing either legally wrong or morally repugnant about informing the Congress of his varying travails in urging that the law be obeyed.*

Whatever may have been the reactions of those who believed that sweeping unpleasant facts under the Executive carpet was the better part of valor, Hoover—though he jealously insisted on the inviolability of FBI *files*—quietly supplied investigating senators and representatives with FBI *reports* on individuals within the government or orally apprised them of serious situations in which laxity or bureaucratic stubbornness endangered the national security. For the most part, Hoover did not turn over a document, or a précis of one, to Congressional committees or individual legislators except at times of crisis. It was not until Representative Nixon had nailed Hiss to a number of perjuries, significant but tangential to the question of Hiss's activities as a Soviet agent, that Hoover supplied the House Committee on Un-American Activities with material to sustain its suspicions.

The subject of FBI contacts with the Hill, and the transfer of information that followed therefrom, did not become a matter of controversy until Senator Joseph R. McCarthy spearheaded the campaign against Communists in government. Hoover had always favored congressional investigation of Communist activities. It was his strong belief that these investigations served an important educational function, informing the public in a way which was barred to him. In this, ironically, he reflected the views of Woodrow Wilson who, as a Princeton professor, had argued in his writings that this educational function of congressional committees often served the people better than

*In this, oddly enough, he was sustained by Telford Taylor, counsel for various Federal agencies and Senate committees, who later crusaded against congressional investigations and the security program. "Mr. Hoover . . . or other officials of high and discretionary authority in the field of security may, for good reasons and with propriety, make confidential [national security] information available to a Congressional committee."

the strictly legislative role of marking up bills. Hoover therefore welcomed McCarthy's efforts.

From the time on February 9, 1950, that McCarthy had made his Wheeling, West Virginia, onslaught against Federal carelessness—or worse—in allowing Communists to hold government jobs, Hoover had been increasingly friendly. The nature of that friendship can best be explained by a remark to President Eisenhower of Senator Charles Potter, an implacable foe of McCarthy on the Senate floor and in the committee room. "Personally, I am rather fond of Joe McCarthy outside the Senate," Potter said. "Some of my happiest hours are spent having a few drinks with him when we aren't talking business." The McCarthy charm was pervasive—and for a man like Hoover, circumscribed by official duties and official propriety, McCarthy's irreverent manner was a tonic.

There is no doubt that Hoover spent many hours with Joe McCarthy talking "business"—lecturing him on Communist strategy and tactics, giving him leads and insights into the Communist apparatus in the United States, and pointing him in the direction of suspect individuals. It is also undoubtedly a fact that though Hoover never gave McCarthy access to FBI files, he did allow him to see reports written to various high-ranking government officials on Communist infiltration. (It need not be added that McCarthy received FBI reports from other and top-level sources in the Executive branch of the government, as well as from Intelligence agencies.)

But it is also a fact, which close friends of both men can document, that Hoover responded to McCarthy because he saw a similar pattern in the attacks leveled against himself and the Wisconsin senator. But beyond that, there was a very real kind of friendship between the two men. They enjoyed each other's company, went to baseball and football games, and spent relaxed evenings of chitchat together. Hoover's social life had been a limited one, much of it confined to his daily contacts with Clyde Tolson, who radiated little warmth, and the addition of McCarthy to that small circle was a welcome one.

But there was always a tacit understanding that should Hoover's friendship with McCarthy come in conflict with Hoover's loyalty to the FBI, the FBI would come first. As tacitly, McCarthy acknowledged that should their friendship ever be an embarrassment to Hoover, its outward manifestations would cease. McCarthy was not so tacit in making this aspect of his relationship clear to intimates, but they respected his confidence. When McCarthy found himself at sword's point with the Eisenhower Administration, and particularly with Attorney General Herbert Brownell, Hoover's direct superior, he cut off open contact with Hoover and limited himself to highly guarded associations with highly trusted Hoover aides. Both McCarthy and Hoover regretted but accepted the need for this course.

At a time when the McCarthy controversy was raging, however, Hoover risked unpleasant political consequences by openly stating his position on McCarthy:

McCarthy is a former Marine. He was an amateur boxer. He's Irish. Combine those, and you're going to have a vigorous individual who is not going to be pushed around.

I'm not passing on the technique of McCarthy's committee or other Senate committees. That's the Senator's responsibility. But the investigative committees do a valuable job. They have subpoena rights without which some vital investigations could not be accomplished . . .

I never knew Senator McCarthy until he came to the Senate. I've come to know him well, officially and personally. I view him as a friend and believe he so views me.*

---

*The Hoover-McCarthy friendship was picked up by the press and done to a crisp of exaggeration, however. William W. Turner, the former FBI agent, would write in the early seventies: "The closeness of the two men was demonstrated by deed as well as word. When McCarthy's chief investigator, J. B. Matthews, injected an anti-Protestant theme into the witch hunt by charging that the clergy were [sic] tinged with treason—a charge not too unlike the one Hoover himself made in the frenzy of 1940—the resulting outcry was such that it became politically inexpedient for even McCarthy to retain Matthews. So McCarthy fired him, then let it be known that he was conferring with Hoover on the selection of a successor. When the choice was made, it turned out to be one of Hoover's top aides." This, of course, is sheer fabrication. No "top" FBI "aide" ever worked for McCarthy.

In point of fact, on three occasions, when McCarthy found himself pushed to the wall, Hoover's official response—if the FBI was in any way involved—was so narrowly truthful that it amounted to a repudiation, though a knowledgeable scrutiny of Hoover's words based on sufficient background of the matter in question sometimes offered justification of what McCarthy had said.

The first such occasion came on June 6, 1950, when Joe McCarthy delivered a speech on the Senate floor which shook both the country and his opposition. The FBI, McCarthy asserted, had prepared a "chart" for the State Department which showed that as of May 15, 1946, there were "twenty Communist agents," "thirteen Communists," "fourteen Communist sympathizers," and "seventy-seven suspects" in the department. Actually the "chart" had come from a report prepared by Sam Klaus, a State Department security officer, for his superiors, and appended to it was a tabulation as of August 1, 1946. It showed that despite the Hoover warning, there were still "eleven agents," "ten Communists," "eleven sympathizers," and "seventy-four suspects" still on the State Department payroll.

The McCarthy speech had hammered away at two points. The first, that seventy-five days after Hoover had submitted his "chart" to the State Department, the "eleven Communist agents" were still happily ensconced in their jobs. The second was a question. How many of these agents, party members, and sympathizers continued to work unencumbered in the department? But the substance of these charges did not preoccupy the Senate. In the debate, the point at issue became the source of McCarthy's information. The question was thrown at Hoover and he answered that the FBI had prepared no "chart" for the State Department. In this, he was telling the literal truth. This led to accusations that McCarthy had lied to the Senate. But to keep himself and the FBI out of the battle, Hoover failed to say that the chart, however and by whom it had been prepared, was based on reports which he had sent to both the State Department and President Truman—the same reports later cited by Attorney General Brownell in his appearance before the Senate Internal Security subcommittee in 1953. McCarthy did not resent Hoover's sin of omission, and Hoover felt no qualms. He had been asked a question about a "chart" and had answered it.

The second instance in which Hoover retired behind literal truth, to the detriment of broader comprehension, occurred during the investigation by the Tydings committee into McCarthy's original charges. In the course of that investigation, as Senator Millard Tydings carried the ball for a Democratic Administration which wanted no part of a thorough inquiry, McCarthy stated that he would be thoroughly vindicated by an objective examination of the State Department's secret personnel and loyalty files. The Senate thereupon directed Tydings to "subpoena and examine the complete loyalty and employment files of the Department of State"—a move which challenged Executive privilege. Truman refused to surrender the files and Tydings said he would issue no subpoena because he was "a gentleman, not a sheriff." Under pressure, however, Truman finally agreed to let members of the committee see the files, stipulating that they could merely read them in a White House room but take no notes. They were, moreover, to have no assistance from the FBI in this quick perusal.

At this point, McCarthy again took to the floor of the Senate, insisting that the files had been "raped," "skeletonized," and "tampered with" to eliminate "all derogatory FBI material." Tydings countered by producing a letter from Deputy Attorney General Peyton Ford, who stated that McCarthy was a liar and that the FBI had inspected the State Department loyalty files and found them to be intact. "The material turned over to the State Department by the FBI is still in the files," said Ford. At this point, Hoover was willing to face Truman Administration recrimination. In answer to a formal letter from Senator McCarthy, he answered that the FBI "has made no such examination and therefore is in no position to make any statement concerning the completeness or imcompleteness of the State Department files."

Further substantiating McCarthy's assertion that the files had been stripped, Senator Henry Cabot Lodge, a member of the Tydings committee, would later complain that in his examination of the State Department records he had found that "in some of the most important cases, the report of the FBI full field investigation was not included." McCarthy followed this up with affidavits from four State Department employees stating that they had personal knowledge of the "rape" and that they had seen material from the files tossed into wastepaper baskets for eventual destruction. The State Department countered that the wastepaper baskets were "temporary receptacles" in which material had been stored prepatory to its transfer to the security division.

Three weeks after the committee had completed its "examination" of the files, the FBI was called in to make its own check. Not surprisingly, it found them "intact." In his letter to Chairman Tydings, Hoover merely stated a conclusion without adding what he knew to be the pertinent fact—that they had been enriched between the time that the senators glancingly examined them and the time of the FBI inspection some twenty-one days later. In effect, he had bowed to the dialectics of the situation by giving what amounted to "yes" and "no" answers in order not to see the FBI pulled into an acrimonious controversy. Privately, Hoover made his explanations to McCarthy, and they were accepted without rancor.

The third instance occurred during the so-called Army-McCarthy hearings, a dispute in which neither side covered itself with glory. The genesis of that confrontation is long and complex—and strictly not germane to this account. There were personal issues, political issues, security issues at stake, and at the time and under the circumstances no one could have possibly untangled the skein. President Eisenhower was under persistent pressure from the Eastern Establishment, which argued that if McCarthy were not destroyed, he would destroy the

Republican Party. The press campaign against "McCarthyism" was in steady crescendo. The Democrats, even those who sympathized with McCarthy, saw a major political issue which would allow them to regain control of the Senate and the House in the upcoming national elections. And those around Eisenhower fed the humiliation he had felt in 1952 when, in spite of his resentment over a 60,000-word speech McCarthy had delivered before the Senate excoriating General George C. Marshall, Ike's mentor and friend, he had nevertheless endorsed him. It was not the knowledge that he had jettisoned a friend that rankled in Eisenhower, but the fact that political expediency had impelled him to it.

At issue in the Army-McCarthy clash was the question of Communist espionage and infiltration of the Fort Monmouth Signal Center. The validity of McCarthy's charges was widely challenged by the Democrats and the press—though they were later confirmed in almost every instance by the Senate Permanent Investigating subcommittee in a report written by Robert F. Kennedy after the Democrats had regained control of the Congress. (It is ironic that when McCarthy stood on the firmest ground, it turned to quicksand under his feet.)

For Hoover, the Army-McCarthy hearings were a period of trauma. His own files showed that Fort Monmouth had been a locus of Communist activity. The Rosenbergs had begun their espionage activities there and a dangerous Communist cell operated with impunity in its privileged sanctuary. Generals had privately informed him of what was going on. Time and again, his agents had followed espionage leads to the Fort Monmouth gates. But there was a strict separation of jurisdiction, and Hoover could only give quiet and confidential warnings to Counter-Intelligence. He was further frustrated by the awareness that Attorney General Brownell represented the Eastern Republican Establishment in the Eisenhower Administration and would be a dangerous man to by-pass. In his heart, he could wish McCarthy success, but the only possible public posture he could see for himself was strict neutrality.

The Army-McCarthy hearings were launched when, with Eisenhower's blessing, a select committee of the Senate was impaneled to consider McCarthy's charges of laxness in security and the Army's countercharges of impropriety on the part of McCarthy and his staff. They were launched after a futile effort on the part of Vice President Nixon to mediate—an effort which put him in the crossfire of McCarthy adherents and Army supporters—and rapidly became what Nixon said they would be, a "can of worms." Day after day, McCarthy and the Administration clawed at each other, while the Democratic opposition made the most of it. When Secretary of the Army Robert Stevens took the stand to defend the military's security policies, McCarthy produced a two-and-one-half page letter dated January 26, 1951, from J. Edgar Hoover to Major General Alexander Bolling, Army G-2 at the time it was written. It listed thirty-four people at Fort Monmouth about whom the FBI had derogatory information of varying seriousness.

It was a telling blow, for it demonstrated the correctness of the McCarthy thesis. With the letter, he was able to show that the Army had done nothing about the Hoover warning and had, in fact, promoted one of the officers singled out by the FBI. The debate, however, centered not on whether the thirty-four individuals were subversive or on their continued retention at Fort Monmouth. Instead, the authenticity of the letter was challenged by Stevens and by Joseph Welch, the Army's counsel. McCarthy contended that it was a copy of the original, and that it was delivered to him by a young officer in G-2 who vouched for the faithfulness of the text. But he would not disclose the officer's name. The Army implied that it was a forgery, and that it had come from the FBI.

This put Hoover in the middle, and a formal inquiry was made of him: Was the two-and-one-half page letter introduced in evidence a true copy of any communication he might have made to General Bolling and/or G-2? Hoover's answer was narrowly true, but misleading: The letter was not one he had sent General Bolling. This left McCarthy in the position of having based part of his case on a fraudulent document. It took Stevens off the hook and gave Welch an opportunity for putting on a show of righteous indignation. When McCarthy was subsequently able to prove that the document in question was an abridged version of a fifteen-page letter Hoover had written to Bolling, with all sensitive material removed, the damage had been done. That Stevens had hardly acted in good faith in his denials—or that the Army had ignored Hoover's warning—was forgotten. The public remembered only that McCarthy had been caught in a "forgery."

In extenuation, it was said at the time that Hoover did not want to plunge the FBI into the maelstrom of the hearings, and McCarthy never reproached him. Both men were pragmatists and knew that anything beyond the partial truth of Hoover's answer would have turned powerful forces in the Senate and the Administration against him. He had not lightly ducked the opportunity to set the record straight, but as he said privately then, "The FBI comes first." He did not say, as he might have, that McCarthy had taken a calculated risk and lost.

19.

Actions and Reactions in a Changing World

FROM THE START OF HIS TENURE AS DIRECTOR OF THE BUREAU OF Investigation, John Edgar Hoover had always measured success by his ability to do his job and by the nature of his relations with Presidents and Attorneys General. Under Calvin Coolidge, there had been few problems. The major thrust of his work had been to clean up the Bureau, strengthen it administratively, and develop its potential. Under Herbert Hoover, he was still a relatively obscure government official of second or third echelon rank. The President approved of him and, like all men who had contact with him, Edgar Hoover admired and thrived in the relationship. Though the two men were poles apart, Franklin D. Roosevelt and J. Edgar enjoyed each other—the country squire and the Puritan bureaucrat taking pleasure in their antithetical qualities. Roosevelt knew that he could trust the FBI director and Hoover was aware that the President would throw him to the wolves only if political survival demanded it. The FBI, moreover, grew in status and responsibility under Roosevelt, and Hoover was repeatedly given a free hand because it was FDR's method to pose fiefdom against fiefdom.

Under Harry S. Truman, it was another matter. Here were two men of intense and jealous loyalties, and bound to their principles. Hoover could get along with an easygoing politician like Attorney General Tom Clark because he understood his strengths and his weaknesses. But he was never fully at ease with Truman because he could never quite square the HST of the copybook virtues and the intense patriotism with the man who still stood unflinchingly behind men of dubious political virtue or parroted the slogans of his ultraliberal underlings. There was very little that Hoover would not have done in the defense of the FBI, but this was because he believed that the Bureau was in alliance against Beelzebub. Had he been President, he would have fired out of hand everyone of the Truman cronies who was caught with his hand in the cookie jar. But he had his measure of Truman and felt a sense of security.

With Dwight David Eisenhower and Attorney General Herbert Brownell, he lived—politically and administratively speaking—from hand to mouth. Brownell was a brilliant man and a tough one—and this posed no problems for Hoover. But he was a politician of a sophistication that left Hoover uneasy. And President Eisenhower defeated the FBI chief by his combination of superb guile and baffling innocence. Knowing more about the men who governed the country than any other citizen or bureaucrat, Hoover was repeatedly taken aback by Eisenhower's casual cruelties, by his knowledge of the means of politics and his ignorance of its ends. He was never sure that the Eisenhower smile was the precedent of thumbs up or thumbs down. More to the point, he was even less sure of what Eisenhower and Brownell wanted of him.

He acknowledged his debt to Brownell when he was allowed

to appear before the Senate Internal Security subcommittee and clear the FBI of complicity in the Harry Dexter White case. But he was lost when Eisenhower both defended and censured Truman, leaving it up to the electorate to decide whether he stood forthrightly behind the FBI and the Attorney General or deplored the White revelations.

In his long years of tenure, he had learned how to do a President's bidding without soiling his hands or compromising the Bureau. But with Eisenhower, Hoover never knew whether he would receive praise or blame for doing what he was asked to do. And he resented having his superiors use the prestige of the FBI—a prestige which he had labored long and lovingly to enhance—to make points with the press and the nation. His resentment and bewilderment were most pronounced when the FBI was dragged into the case of Anna Rosenberg, adviser to Presidents and a power in New York's financial alleys.

In 1953, Anna Rosenberg had been dragged into the limelight when Ralph de Sola, a former Communist, stated with considerable care that he had met Anna Rosenberg in the Thirties at a party function and that she had been introduced to him as "one of ours." Ralph de Sola, who had long since had his fill of appearances before Congressional committees and had vowed that it would be never again, had been booby-trapped into telling his story by a former newspaperman and a Senate investigator who had sworn that they were simply interested in the information and that they would protect the source. The pair had broken their promises and dumped a de Sola affidavit into the laps of a number of senators who had insisted that it be translated into sworn testimony. De Sola was pilloried, and in the controversy that followed, the Wall Street Establishment demanded Ralph de Sola's head. Eisenhower, who was easily susceptible to the calls of the financial community, stormed and fumed and convinced himself that it was all an anti-Semitic plot. But how to get Anna Rosenberg off the hook when de Sola stood firmly by his guarded testimony?

The only solution was to find some evidence to prove that it was all a case of mistaken identity, and this assignment was passed on to a reluctant Hoover. The Bureau, therefore, was told to find the "other" Anna Rosenberg, who would have to be a woman of roughly the same age who had once been or still was a member of the Communist Party. Hoover was not happy about the unpleasant chore that had been handed to him by the White House, but he set the wheels in motion and the FBI— "theirs not to reason why, theirs but to do or die"—began its search. In due time, an announcement was made that the Bureau had turned up the "other" Anna Rosenberg, but she was never produced to confront de Sola or to speak her piece before the inquisitors of the Senate Armed Forces Committee. The FBI was much praised for its investigative achievement, but Hoover derived no pleasure from these kudos. He could tell himself, and a few close friends, that he had not set policy, had not evaluated what his agents had found. But he knew that the Bureau had been used.

Hoover's real troubles began, however, when John F. Kennedy was elected President and made his brother Bobby, inexperienced in the law, the Attorney General of the United States.* For the first time in his career, Hoover was forced to deal with an Administration that was overtly hostile, that wanted him out, and that saw the FBI as an instrument for political vengeance and/or aggrandizement. Temperamentally, there could be no rapport between Bobby Kennedy and Edgar Hoover. And on a working basis, it was clear from the start that Robert Kennedy had decided to cut Hoover down to size, to make him an arm of the Democratic Party rather than a nonpolitical director of an investigative agency.

Until the Kennedy Administration, Hoover's relations with Presidents and Attorneys General were reasonably private, hidden behind his own reticence and the desire of his superiors not to court public disapproval by openly airing differences. It was not that Hoover had become too powerful to handle, for there

*See Chapter 20 for an account of the Kennedy-Hoover relations.

were attacks on him in plenty. But with the passage of the years, he had become a kind of elder statesman of law enforcement. He had allies in the Senate and House. And his image to the American people remained one of undeviating integrity, bulldog tenacity, courage, and high technical efficiency. He had, moreover, become a kind of spokesmen for millions of Americans who watched the changing *mores* of the country and the unruliness of its youth with sinking hearts, looking to Hoover for confirmation of beliefs that were being rejected as "square" or "irrelevant" and for a restatement of what they felt should be done to return the United States to calmer and clearer days. In the dozen or so years before his death, Hoover was out of step with the intellectuals, with the incoming generations, and with the media—but the middle American was his, and it was to him that Hoover spoke.

In 1959, with the cry for "permissiveness" and "understanding" at full pitch, Hoover courted the anger of penologists, psychologists, and university faculties by issuing a message to all law enforcement officials, in the FBI *Bulletin,* which rang with an old rhetoric:

Are we to stand idly by while fierce young hoodlums—too often and too long harbored under the glossy misnomer of juvenile delinquents —roam our streets and desecrate our cities? . . . Gang-style ferocity— once the evil domain of hardened criminals—now centers chiefly in cliques of teen-age brigands . . . Recent happenings in juvenile crime shatter the illusion that soft-hearted mollycoddling is the answer to this problem . . .

In Louisiana, two teenage gangsters were given life sentences . . . for murdering a man who caught them looting his home. A thirteen-year-old partner, the trigger man in the killing, was sentenced to confinement until age twenty-one. The extensive criminal record of this trio, totaling more than two dozen previous charges, included aggravated burglary, theft, assault and holdup. Not isolated instances, outrages such as these are reported day to day in newspaper headlines across the country . . .

In the past four years, while population in the 10-to-17 age group has gone up approximately 10 percent, arrests of individuals in these same age brackets have increased at twice that rate. [Two years later, Hoover would report that "youthful offenders account for one-half of the burglary and larceny arrests in this country . . . And their rate of participation in more serious crimes—assault, robbery, rape, murder —is steadily rising."] . . . No longer can we tolerate the "tender years" alibi for youthful lawbreaking. This is certainly no time for police to be shackled by illogical restraints based on an unreasoning sympathy for these young thugs . . . Local police and citizens have the right to know the identities of the potential threats to public order within their communities . . .

Certainly a reasonable leniency for children committing first offenses and minor violations is a proper consideration. However, the present major problem is no longer one of bad children but of young criminals. Law enforcement cannot be administered solely according to the yardstick of age. Justice must be meted out to each individual criminal in such measure and such manner as the welfare and protection of society demand.

Early in January 1960, Hoover took a report on the 17th National Convention of the Communist Party USA as a vehicle for expressing his views on another topic which had grown increasingly unpopular with the media and the Establishment— communism. He did so in a manner which hardly veiled his criticism of President Eisenhower, who had invited Nikita Khrushchev, the Soviet Union's top boss, to visit the United States, He described the Communist convention as a "sinister conclave" which, after four days, "adjourned in jubilation. And well they might feel in high spirits—because the Communist Party U.S.A. emerged from this convention more powerful, more unified, and even more of a menace to our Republic." The party convention had been closed to the press, a hermetically sealed meeting which excluded all outsiders with the exception of the FBI agents who had infiltrated the higher reaches of the Communist movement. From them, Hoover had full, almost stenographic transcripts of what went on behind locked doors—and his point–by–point account of the proceedings was placed in the *Congressional Record.* But no one could miss the import of his rhetorical question: "Why is the party so optimistic for the future and the Communists almost gleeful in speaking of Communist possibilities in the days ahead?"

The answer, said Hoover, was "that the recent visit of

Premier Khrushchev has done much to create an atmosphere favorable to communism among Americans . . . In one convention discussion, for example, it was stated that as a result of the Khrushchev visit the American people have open minds towards socialism. Hence the party must learn how to get socialism across to the people and break down misconceptions about the Soviet Union . . . To party leaders, Khrushchev's presence in this country has eased the way for party activities."

The positions taken by Hoover on juvenile crime and communism won him few friends. Congress awarded him a gold medal, but in 1962, when he celebrated his thirty-eighth year as director of the FBI, the message from President Kennedy was hardly one of unrestrained enthusiasm. "I did not want May 10 to pass without expressing my congratulations on your 38th anniversary as director of the Federal Bureau of Investigation," Kennedy wrote. "Yours is one of the most unusual and distinguished records in the history of government service"— which Hoover considered warm words on a cold platter. To forestall a cake-cutting ceremony in his honor, planned and announced by Bobby Kennedy, Hoover made it known that he was spending the day at his desk following his usual daily routine.

The general displeasure felt by the Kennedys manifested itself not long afterward when, in July, a spate of stories appeared in the press that he would be sixty-eight on the following New Year's Day and therefore subject to mandatory retirement. The same stories, inspired by "sources" in the White House and the Justice Department, named as Hoover's possible successor one of Bobby's close associates and a member of the department's secret and ruthless "Get Hoffa" squad, Walter Sheridan. Such a replacement, as official and unofficial Washington was aware, would have reduced the FBI's status to what it had been in the early 1920s.

Hoover was not particularly ruffled by these "leaks," although he complained to friends that it made his job of administering the Bureau more difficult and weakened his muscle with other law enforcement agencies. Almost complacently, he issued his year-end report to the Attorney General in February 1962, detailing the achievements of the FBI. A press release issued by the Bureau told his story to the nation and, presumably, to the Kennedy Administration:

Mr. Hoover disclosed that final tabulations for [1961] will show more than 12,400 convictions in FBI cases compared with 12,021 in 1960; the apprehension of nearly 10,700 FBI fugitives compared with 9,739 last year; and fines, savings and recoveries totaling approximately $150 million—an amount far exceeding the funds spent to operate the FBI in 1961 . . .

Calling attention to major crime problems confronting the FBI, Mr. Hoover stated that a record total of more than 800 violations of the Federal bank robbery and incidental crimes statute have been reported to the FBI this year. Another all-time high was established with the location of nearly 19,000 stolen cars . . .

Other FBI cases singled out for special mention (included) the investigation of attempts to control certain areas of professional boxing by an underworld syndicate . . . The notorious "Frankie" Carbo, "Blinky" Palermo, Joseph Sica, Louis Tom Dragna, and Truman Gibson, Jr., were convicted on Federal extortion and antiracketeering charges . . .

Warning that the United States remains the primary target for Soviet-bloc intelligence operations, Mr. Hoover stated that during the past year two men were convicted on espionage charges—Dr. Robert Sobel, now facing imprisonment for life, and Irvin Scarbeck, who has been sentenced to a term of 30 years. . . . In addition, following FBI investigation, the departure or exclusion of four official representatives of Communist-bloc countries was effected because of activity beyond the scope of their official duties.

The FBI Director described the Communist Party, U.S.A., as "an inseparable arm of the international conspiracy against God and freedom which is directed from Moscow." The Communists in this country are completely subservient to the dictates of their Soviet masters, he said . . .

The FBI Laboratory, which receives specimens of evidence from authorities in all 50 states, conducted more than 230,000 examinations during the past year . . . The FBI's Identification Division. . . . received an average of 23,000 fingerprint cards each working day throughout 1961. As the year ended, its files contained 161,800,000 sets of fingerprints representing an estimated 76,400,000 people . . .

This catalogue of achievements, couched in a form and in language which had become traditional for the FBI, did not spare Hoover from attack from another source. W.H. "Ping" Ferry, vice president of the Fund for the Republic, assailed Hoover for his "sententious poppycock" and for creating "a mischief-making tapestry of legend and illusion" about Soviet espionage and the strength of the world Communist movement. Then Ferry, who was under attack for pro-Communist leanings, argued that Hoover was the "mandarin of anti-Communism in the United States" and "our official spy-swatter." Hoover responded by forwarding to several friendly members of Congress the public record of Ferry's associations, statements, and activities—most of them of a fine Red hue. There were, of course, cries that Hoover was using the FBI files in a personal vendetta, but the FBI could answer—while Hoover remained silent—that there was nothing in the material used against Ferry which could not be found by a reasonably competent researcher in the Library of Congress.

The passage of time and the growing pressure within the Kennedy Administration for his removal drove Hoover in those days of the early 1960s to seek to impress his philosophy of life on what he considered a floundering country. "As I ponder the problems we find ourselves all but swamped by today," he wrote in the *Christian Science Monitor,* "I cannot help thinking that the rules which prevailed in my youth would still work for boys and girls now . . . If I had a son, I believe I could help him most by providing him with these five indispensables: a personal example to follow, an understanding of the importance of restraint and ideals, a sense of discipline, a pride in his heritage, and a challenge to meet. . . ."

But in 1963, the country had moved far beyond the reach of such counsel. The civil rights movement had erupted in the South, thrusting both black and white into demonstrations, marches, sit-ins, violence, counterviolence, bombings, and general disarray. Confrontations were the news of the day, and all sides played politics. Out of the confusion and misery, Hoover and the FBI were expected to restore order and well-being—an utter impossibility for a small organization attempting to deal with an aroused sector of the country. What little chance Hoover might have had of quieting the storm was compromised by Attorney General Kennedy, who insisted on participating in matters which were better left to Federal law enforcement officers and by staging grandiose tableaux to impress the North and win votes for his Presidential brother. The great "confrontation" between Federal forces under Attorney General Kennedy and Governor Ross Barnett of Mississippi, as tapes of their telephone conversations later revealed, was worked out like a ballet right down to such matters as whether the U. S. marshals would have their hands on their holsters or draw their guns when they forced their way into the University of Mississippi dormitory with the subject of the controversy, a black student, James Meredith.

It was Hoover's position that the FBI should not get involved in either the politics or the theatrics of the civil rights movement. He argued that there were Federal statutes to be enforced and that he should enforce them. It was not the FBI's role either to crusade or to evade its responsibilities, Hoover insisted. Simply to play it down the middle was difficult enough, since he was continually accused of doing too much and too little. His task was complicated by the need of FBI agents to have the cooperation of local police in a variety of non-civil rights cases. Southern authorities took the view that any appearance of an FBI agent in a civil rights investigation was a violation of state's rights and a betrayal of old associations.

In January 1963, after a series of bombings in Birmingham, Alabama, Hoover found himself under the usual attacks—that he was doing nothing to solve these terrible crimes or that he was being overzealous. Senator A. Willis Robertson, a Virginia Democrat, forwarded a letter from a constituent which made charges of improper behavior against the FBI, and Hoover used his answer as a vehicle to explain the FBI's position and what it had accomplished.

"My dear Senator," Hoover wrote,

> . . . Both sides in the racial issue have used the FBI's name in recent months to gain support for their respective points of view . . . At the present time, different individuals are citing various totals for the number of bombings which have occurred in Alabama. Some allege the FBI has investigated all of them; others declare we have taken little or no action. Our jurisdiction to investigate these bombings comes from the Civil Rights Act of 1960 . . . but the Department of Justice . . . has instructed that the FBI should not initiate investigations into such cases without special departmental authorization.
>
> The facts of each bombing incident have been presented immediately to the Department and the FBI has been requested to investigate five bombing cases in Alabama, including the one on September 15 in which four children were killed. Due to the nature of the September 15 bombing, the FBI began an immediate investigation and advised the Department of the action being taken . . . If a Federal law within our jurisdiction is violated, FBI agents will conduct a prompt, thorough, and objective investigation. If no Federal law is involved, we will not—and cannot—investigate.
>
> In spite of these facts, we are accused of both exceeding and shirking our duties. Some of these charges stem from a lack of understanding, but many of them come from persons who have a personal interest and distort the truth to suit their own purposes.
>
> Acting within the law, the FBI has recorded a number of accomplishments in the civil rights field. For example, FBI investigations have enabled the Department of Justice to file more than forty suits in five states to end racial discrimination in voting. FBI agents solved the case involving the burning of a Greyhound bus transporting freedom riders through Alabama in 1961. Six persons have been convicted of their part in this crime. An FBI investigation in September 1962, led to the arrest and conviction in State court of four persons for burning a Negro church in Terrell County, Georgia. FBI agents also arrested Byron De La Beckwith, the man charged with the murder of Medgar Evers, the Mississippi leader of the National Association for the Advancement of Colored People . . .

The deepest hurt that J. Edgar Hoover sustained—hurt to himself and a blow to his prestige—was the actively propagated accusation that but for the FBI's delinquency, the assassination of President Kennedy could have been prevented.* He survived this, as he had other attempts at his reputation, battling to present the FBI's position and to show that the Justice Department's obsession over "right-wing extremists" had forced him to neglect the terrorists of the left. (Of course, nothing could have prevented the assassination except for "preventive" arrests of left and right elements in every city that President Kennedy visited—a clear violation of the Constitution which would have caused a storm in the country.)

The arrest of Lee Harvey Oswald for the assassination of Kennedy, and the disclosure of his past as a defector to the Soviet Union and a dedicated Castroite, did little to remove the pressures on Hoover or to lessen the criticism of his anti-Communism. Late in 1963, when the Washington Hebrew Congregation presented Hoover with its Brotherhood Award, Hoover attempted to placate his critics by launching into a fervent attack against "venomous fanatics, whether they are extremists of the left or the right . . . [who] . . . clutter the streets and the mails with their slanderous obscenities, urging impressionable teenagers and unstable adults to acts of hate, terror, and intimidation." But he was to himself and to his rhetoric true when he warned the country was "at war with communism and the sooner every red-blooded American realizes this, the safer we are."

With Lyndon B. Johnson in the White House, the tensions in and around Hoover relaxed. President Johnson made it very clear from the start that he would not impose the mandatory retirement age on Hoover and, on May 8, 1964, issued an Executive Order suspending the requirement "for an indefinite period of time." Again there was an outcry that Hoover had outlived his usefulness, that the FBI was a power unto itself, and that a Gestapo was taking root on American soil, but Hoover brushed it aside by deriding what the *New York Times* ascribed to "a few lonely voices" as the complaints of "do-gooders,

*See Chapter 21.

pseudo-liberals, and out-and-out Communists." In time, as those voices grew in strength, insisting on Hoover's retirement, Johnson would grin, perhaps agree to some of the things being said about Hoover, but sum up his position with typical pithiness. "I'd rather have Edgar in the tent pissing out," he would drawl, "than have him outside the tent pissing in."

It was not concern over an unleashed Edgar Hoover which prompted Johnson's remark. Had Johnson really feared Hoover, he would have fired him or appointed him to a sinecure. But Johnson was a shrewd politician. Though he occasionally expressed annoyance at Hoover, he respected the man and the agency created by him. And he also knew that a Hoover replaced would cause far more problems than a Hoover in office. For one thing, there was the question of a replacement. The FBI files, built up over the years, would be a delayed-action charge with anyone less dedicated to the preservation of their inviolability than Hoover. Dedication, moreover, was not enough. It required muscle on Capitol Hill—and no one in the Johnson entourage could provide it. In addition, Hoover had stood with Johnson in the terrible days and weeks after the assassination of John F. Kennedy—at a time when the Kennedy press and the Attorney General himself were doing everything in their power to humiliate Johnson.

The tie that bound the two men was more than political, however. Hoover and Johnson had known each other since 1934, when J. Edgar had already become "a household word" and Lyndon was a relatively obscure politician. They had been close neighbors since 1945, and it was not unusual for Johnson to drop by Hoover's house for a casual visit. When, on occasion, one of Hoover's dogs strayed, Linda and Luci would search the neighborhood, returning in triumph with the lost pet. As Johnson rose in the Senate hierarchy, becoming one of the most effective and powerful Majority Leader's in modern times, the friendship thrived. This gave Hoover a power base where it was most valuable, and Johnson the best source of information in official Washington.

That friendship had persisted when Johnson became President, and it was no secret within the Administration that he was on the telephone to Hoover on an almost daily basis. It was not information he sought then, although that well never run dry. That strangely arrogant, humble, and complex man who was Lyndon Johnson turned to Hoover for advice, encouragement, and the warmth which a jealous palace guard can seldom give a President of the United States. Hoover, whose public face was becoming one of almost military severity, was relaxed and outgoing with Johnson. But beyond this, he gave the President that undeviating loyalty which Johnson demanded. Hoover even made Cartha DeLoach, another Johnson friend, his *de facto* second-in-command, thereby strengthening the bond and, incidentally, bringing DeLoach's political savvy into the tent.

In 1964, when Hoover was approaching his seventieth birthday and the age of mandatory retirement, Johnson made plain the nature of his friendship in an unusually gracious ceremony in what he called his "backyard"—the White House Rose Garden. There, with Hoover standing at his side, the President offered some old-fashioned sentiments to an old-fashioned man.

All during [my] last trip . . . I kept thinking—what a great nation this is. And I kept thinking that the foundation of our greatness is the ability of our people to solve our problems by reasonable and compassionate means.

There is another reason for America's greatness: the tireless devotion of those men and women who serve the public's welfare.

J. Edgar Hoover is such a man . . . He is a hero to millions of decent citizens, and an anathema to evil men. No other American, now or in our past, has served the cause of justice so faithfully and so well . . .

J. Edgar Hoover has served the government since 1917—he has served *nine* Presidents, and this Sunday, he celebrates his fortieth year as Director of the FBI. Under his guiding hand, the FBI has become the greatest investigation body in history . . .

I am proud and happy to join the rest of the nation in honoring this quiet, humble, and magnificent public servant.

Edgar, the law says that you must retire next January when you reach your seventieth birthday, and I know you wouldn't want to break the law.

But the nation cannot afford to lose you. Therefore, by virtue of and pursuant to the authority vested in the President, I have today signed an Executive Order exempting you from compulsory retirement for an indefinite period of time.

Again, Edgar, congratulations on behalf of a grateful nation.*

But the attacks were mounting. In 1965, The Senate showed a kind of left-handed criticism by enacting a bill which would make the post of FBI director subject to its confirmation—though only on the retirement of Hoover. Americans for Democratic Action, through its leader and spokesman, Joseph Rauh Jr., a civil liberties lawyer whose great sincerity was matched only by his ineptitudes, was pounding the alarm drum, quoting Hoover out of context to prove that he had restrained the FBI from adequate civil rights enforcement. James Wechsler, director of the *New York Post*'s dreary editorial page, was employing his reasoned invective to prove that Hoover was finished—destroyed by the lead feet he had presumably exposed in the investigation of the Kennedy assassination, by his characterizations of Martin Luther King and Bobby Kennedy, and by his admission that he was "one of those states' righters" opposed to the "rather harsh approach by authorities here in Washington" to the civil rights confrontations in the South.** And the editorial pages of influential journals like the *New York Times*, the *Washington Post*, the *Baltimore Sun*, and the *Philadelphia Inquirer* were zeroing in on Hoover and his continued tenure.

The attacks on Hoover, however, descended to a new low

*Johnson had put similar sentiments in writing when he autographed a picture "To J. Edgar Hoover—Than whom there is no greater—From his friend of Thirty years."
**Wechsler was, it should be noted, something of an expert on Hoover. As editor of the *Post*, before his demotion, he had assigned a team of reporters to do a series on Hoover with an eye, among other matters, to "prove" that he was a homosexual. Rumors as to the contents of the series made the rounds of every bar in New York and Washington, but it was never published, thereby keeping the homosexual smear alive and fostering a new rumor—that FBI pressure was responsible for nonpublication.

during the 1964 Presidential campaign, when an aide and close associate of Lyndon Johnson was arrested in a YMCA washroom for what was described as a homosexual act. In a state of emotional collapse, that White House official was admitted to a Washington hospital. White House pressure kept the story out of the newspapers for twenty-four hours, during which time an FBI assistant, learning of the hospitalization but not its cause, sent flowers in Hoover's name. When this was made known in the public prints, there was great glee in Washington. But it was the kind of story that Hoover could never explain. If he had said that he knew nothing of the homosexual charge, he would have admitted that the FBI was not omniscient. If, on the other hand, he claimed knowledge, then he would be convicting himself of friendship with a homosexual.

When coupled to the rumors inspired by the *New York Post* in the fifties, the new whispers hurt the FBI and Hoover. They persisted throughout the Presidential campaign and into 1966. Then they were brought out into the open by Senator Bourke Hickenlooper on the floor of the Senate in January of that year. "About ten days ago," he said, "I received a scurrilous anonymous letter, mailed from Baltimore, alleged to contain a photostatic copy of a letter which was alleged by the writer of the anonymous letter to have been written by J. Edgar Hoover, Director of the Federal Bureau of Investigation, to (the White House official referred to above). The alleged photostatic copy of the letter is so scurrilous and putrid that I do not intend to put it in the Record."

Hickenlooper then told the Senate that he had sent the letter and photostat to Hoover, and read Hoover's answer. That answer was important for what it demonstrated of Communist methods and of their hatred of Hoover.

"The letter you received is one of many anonymous mailings sent to various Senators, Congressmen, and other prominent government officials in the last week," Hoover wrote. "They are part of a concerted Communist smear campaign which was launched a year ago."

The campaign began in January 1965, when several letters of this type were received by individuals who also brought them to my attention. Several more were brought to my attention in April 1965.

Upon examination, the copy of the letter supposedly signed by me was determined to be a crude forgery. Comparison of all the letters disclosed they had all been prepared by the same person or persons. Further comparison with other letters circulated in the past in this and other countries by the Soviet Disinformation Department [a forgery mill to compromise individuals and governments] proved irrefutably that this was a Communist scheme.

You may recall that the nefarious schemes of the Soviet Disinformation Department were exposed in a report prepared by the Central Intelligence Agency last year . . . The study revealed that the Soviet Disinformation Department of the KGB . . . wages a broad-scaled propaganda offensive against U.S. agencies and pointed out that I and the Federal Bureau of Investigation are priority targets for attacks. It also disclosed that the overall objective is to discredit U.S. agencies here and abroad and emphasized that a preferred instrument used by the Soviets in their attacks is the forged document.

Typical of the tactics used in such efforts was the circulation of letters in South America in the summer of 1964. In that case, too, my name had been forged on letters. They were designed to make it appear that the Federal Bureau of Investigation and the Central Intelligence Agency had something to do with the Brazilian revolution of April 1964. The intricacies of that Communist scheme became further apparent when we determined that my signature had been forged to a letter stolen by a Cuban in Havana in 1960.

It was no joking matter for Hoover. But had he been disposed to laugh, he might have noted that the Soviet Disinformation Department was itself a victim of disinformation if it believed that the FBI would work in tandem with CIA on any project, much less a revolution. As to the scurrilous anonymous letter and the alleged photostat of a Hoover letter, they ceased to be circulated once Senator Hickenlooper had put the facts in the *Congressional Record.*

20.

Bobby Kennedy Marches

UNTIL JANUARY 20, 1961, JOHN EDGAR HOOVER COULD MOVE ABOUT in Washington's bureaucratic jungle knowing that in the clinches, he could count on the President and the Attorney General to stand behind him. From time to time, there had been bad moments with Harry S. Truman and a cold shoulder from Dwight Eisenhower. But he had always been treated for what he was—a great law enforcement officer and a personality in his own right. He might lose a battle, but he was never humiliated. And he had come to take for granted, as Washington officialdom did, his very special position in government. But when Bobby Kennedy stepped into the palatial office of the Attorney General in the Justice Department, everything changed. In part this was due to the differences in personality —and the similarities—and in part to Bobby Kennedy's view of his role in the Administration as "prime minister to everything." But most of all, Hoover's troubles with the new Attorney General stemmed from the realization in the "new breed" at Justice that Hoover stood in the way of their plans.

From the very start, Robert Kennedy had made it clear that he considered the FBI a kind of private police for the Administration and Hoover a kind of desk sergeant to carry out orders. Though one of President Kennedy's first official acts had been to reassure Hoover that he would not be fired, he had also let it be known in the echo chamber that is Washington that he did not really want any contact with a man so alien to the cynicisms and idealisms of the New Frontier. To the men who surrounded Kennedy, Hoover was somehow uncouth, a clod who lacked the intellectual perspectives of the Ivy League. Bobby, ironically described by the President as the "second most powerful man" in the United States, was to be Hoover's boss, and there would be no recourse through access to the Presidential ear.

Bobby, who approached all life as if it were a combination of touch football and karate, had decided long before he was sworn in that Hoover would have to go—though he was astute enough politically to know that he could neither make a frontal attack nor fire Hoover outright. The strategy was to make Hoover so angry or so miserable that he would quit. Barring this, he would bend the FBI and Hoover to his will. The atmosphere in the Justice Department, *vis-à-vis* Hoover, was established almost from the first day of Bobby's tenure. Luther Huston, a soft-spoken and perceptive ex-newspaperman who had been Public Information Director for outgoing Attorney General William P. Rogers, saw it at first hand when he said his goodbyes to Hoover.

"I had arranged to see him at a particular time," he has said, "but I had to wait because the new Attorney General was there. He hadn't called or made an appointment. He had just barged in. You don't do that with Mr. Hoover. Then my turn came and

I'll tell you the maddest man I ever talked to was J. Edgar Hoover. He was steaming. If I could have printed what he said, I'd have had a scoop. Apparently Kennedy wanted to set up some kind of supplementary or overlapping group to take over some of the investigative work that the FBI had been doing. My surmise is that Mr. Hoover told Bobby, 'If you're going to do that, I can retire tomorrow. My pension is waiting.' "

Huston's "surmise" was correct. On several occasions, Hoover made that threat and Bobby pulled back. Much as he wanted to get rid of Hoover, the President did not feel that he was ready to take on the Congress and the American public, and he restrained Bobby. But the thirty-five-year-old Attorney General continued to do his best to rub the sixty-six-year-old Director the wrong way. He not only barged into Hoover's office unannounced but summoned him to his office like a clerk— something no other Attorney General had done. He leaked derogatory stories about the FBI and Hoover to an eager Washington press corps, either directly or through the men around him, and created a mythology that lasts to this day—that Hoover had no interest in combatting organized crime or the Mafia, that there were no Negro special agents in the Bureau, that Hoover had no interest in enforcing the civil rights statutes, that the agents assigned to the South were all southerners.

Bobby Kennedy irked Hoover in another and perhaps more basic way. Hoover was the head of the FBI, and any information from the Bureau that went to the Attorney General or any other Justice Department official had to come from him. This was the only way he could maintain discipline in the Bureau —and Bobby tried persistently to by-pass the Director. He would call a Special Agent in Charge or an FBI man working on a case without bothering to speak to Hoover first. This not only undercut Hoover but violated the tradition in the Bureau of a strict chain of command. The Attorney General also ordered the installation of a direct line from his desk to Hoover's, eliminating the secretary who took all of the Director's calls.* Bobby would pick up this phone and bark orders or throw out rapid-fire questions, frequently in the presence of subordinates who gleefully reported these exchanges to others in the department.

There were, of course, deeper causes for the lack of rapport between Hoover and the Kennedy brothers. Bobby considered Hoover stuffy, old-fashioned, corny, and slow. He complained that he could get information more quickly from the wire service tickers in the Justice Department than from the FBI, particularly where that information concerned race riots—which was undoubtedly true since an FBI agent on the scene would be more concerned with investigative matters than in sending a flash to headquarters in Washington. Bobby was, in the exact sense of the word, an activist who had no patience with those who thought long before they acted. When he slammed a book into the stomach of a Justice Department lawyer who was standing by to make a phone call, it was not brutality on Bobby's part, but a congenital inability to understand why anyone should not be in motion.

Hoover, on the other hand, considered Bobby brash, impetuous, bad-mannered, and undisciplined. He believed in setting examples, and when Bobby broke Federal statutes by bringing his dog to work and sending it out to be walked by Justice Department secretaries on government time, Hoover was shocked. He disapproved of the high jinks at Hickory Hill, the Kennedy estate—the drunken parties, the hilarity when guests were tossed fully clothed into the pool. To Hoover, all of this

*William Turner, in his "exposé" of the FBI, recounts how, when Kennedy first picked up the "hot line" between his office and the Director's, it was not Hoover who answered but his secretary Helen Gandy. "When I pick up this phone," Kennedy said brusquely, "there's only one man I want to talk to—get the phone on the Director's desk!" Turner followed this up with another story: "When Robert arrived at his office (after learning of his brother's assassination), he picked up the hot line phone. Hoover was in his office with several aides when it rang . . . and rang . . . and rang. When it stopped ringing, the Director snapped to an aide, 'Now get that phone back on Miss Gandy's desk.' "
Like the story that Hoover never sent condolences to Bobby after John F. Kennedy's death—given wide currency by *Newsweek*—the Turner stories are completely apocryphal.

betokened a lack of moral fiber, and his opinion was confirmed when he learned the details of Bobby's involvement with Marilyn Monroe and the causes of her suicide. As a man of stern Puritan outlook, he was even more shaken by the range and persistence of President Kennedy's exploits in what Hoover called "those sex things."*

There was, as well, a deep political gap between the two men. Hoover not only sounded a call for the older virtues, but he tended toward conservatism in both political and sociological terms. That conservatism was also reflected in his concept of what the Bureau should be, and he bitterly resented the new Attorney General's efforts to intervene in the FBI's hiring practices. More than once, the FBI had been sharply criticized by the liberals and the left for not employing more Negro special agents. Hoover had invariably made the same answer: "We hire according to merit, not race or color." To those who made private inquiry, he would answer that few blacks applied for jobs as FBI agents, and of those, only a handful passed the difficult exams which qualified an applicant for appointment**

Hoover's friends on Capitol Hill were also right of center—Representative John J. Rooney, who ran his House Appropriations subcommittee with an iron hand, the guardian of the public purse, but who boasted that he had never cut a cent from the FBI's budget; Senator Everett M. Dirksen, whose mellifluous periods frequently celebrated Hoover and the Bureau in Senate debate; the southern Democratic bloc and the group of entrenched northern Republicans who deplored the govern-

---

*By a tacit gentleman's agreement, the Washington press corps shies away from mention of the sex lives of Washington officials. The August 1972 issue of *The Washingtonian,* a local slick-paper monthly of some repute, brought much of this out in the open in a article, "Sex, Power, and Politics," which named chapter and verse for John Kennedy as well as a host of others.
**In the sixties, the charge was backhandedly made that the FBI was anti-Semitic because it included very few Jewish agents. The answer to this had to be muted since it opened the door to other imputations of anti-Semitism. But the simple fact was that there were few applications by Jewish lawyers and accountants for the relatively low-paying FBI jobs. In Hoover's last days, moreover, his two top men were Jews, which earned him a smear attack from the *Washington Observer,* a crackpot fringe newsletter.

ment's seemingly inevitable movement left. These were the legislators usually found in Attorney General Kennedy's catalogue of the infamous, avoided or denounced as the occasion warranted. The alliance between Bobby Kennedy and Walter Reuther, the radically oriented president of the United Auto Workers, troubled Hoover, and for good reason as it later developed.

President Kennedy had not been in office for many months before Walter Reuther and his brother Victor, ideologist-in-chief of the UAW, called on the Attorney General to propose that he use the power of the Justice Department to destroy American conservatism, to drive a wedge between the FBI and its millions of supporters, and to attach the label of "extremism" on the Republican Party. It was the kind of plan that the Reuthers would conceive and Bobby accept since it pushed through directly to desired goals, whatever it might do to constitutional guarantees. Bobby therefore asked the Reuthers to put their proposal in writing. They were reluctant to do so, warning that confidential papers prepared for government officials had a way of falling into the "wrong"—or in this case "right"—hands. But on Bobby's insistence that their proposal would be safe with him, the Reuthers agreed.

On December 16, 1961, the Reuthers delivered a twenty-four-page memorandum to Kennedy, entitled "The Radical Right in America Today." And Bobby did not bother to "leak" it. He openly sent copies to all high Kennedy Administration officials and to favored senators and representatives. In time, the Reuther memorandum became known in government circles as the Kennedy memorandum. Its style was a little more sophisticated than Bobby's but its bluntness was not. Its definition of the "radical right" included all those Republicans who supported Senator Barry Goldwater and equated them with extremist kooks.

"Far more is required in the struggle against the radical right than calling attention to present and potential dangers"—dangers which included the declaration by a Midwestern governor of an "anti-Communism week"; the appearance of *Time-Life* executive publisher C.D. Jackson, movie-maker Jack Warner, actors James Stewart and Pat O'Brien, and Representative Walter Judd at an anti-Communist rally; the continued existence of Harding College, a highly regarded conservative institution of learning; the sponsorship of conservative and anti-Communist radio and television programs by various corporations; and the tax-exempt status of a handful of conservative foundations and organizations. Since it was the Reuther/Kennedy contention that the "radical right posed a far greater danger" to the country than the Communist movement, the memorandum called for listing all entities so designated as "subversive"—which would have put *National Review* and *Human Events,* which fell under the Reuther definition since they supported Barry Goldwater, in jeopardy. It was a further contention of the memorandum that the test of subversion was secrecy, which put the Masons in a somewhat difficult position. The Reuthers, with Kennedy's approbation, wanted to place all right-wing groups on the Attorney General's subversive list, although the criterion set by Congress had limited it to organizations which advocated the overthrow of the United States government by force or sought to bring about changes in our system by violence.

All of this troubled Hoover. But what really got to him was a demand that the FBI infiltrate every organization considered "subversive"—which would have included the Republican Party since it was increasingly moving in Barry Goldwater's direction. Hoover was also personally affronted by the Reuther charge that he "exaggerates the domestic Communist problem and thus contributes to the public's frame of mind upon which the radical right feeds." More worrisome to him was the Attorney General's unappealable insistence that FBI agents be pulled off important investigations to carry water for the Kennedy Administration. For the first time in the history of the Republic, government investigators were sent out to pick up adverse comments about the President of the United States made by members of the working press. Newspapermen who sounded off in what had once been the sacrosanct privacy of the National Press Club's members' bar were summoned by key Administration officials and roundly scolded for their temerity. Their anger, however, was directed at Hoover and the FBI, not at Bobby Kennedy who had forced Hoover into a role of tattle-tale.

Shrewdly, Bobby Kennedy used the indignation generated by his surveillance of the press's personal opinions to chip away at Hoover's prestige, and the offended newspapermen became the vehicle for derogatory stories about the FBI. There were persistent leaks that Hoover was on his way out, infuriating him so that he made injudicious remarks about Kennedy, all of which found their way back to the Attorney General. It is, of course, a matter for speculation today, but informed opinion in Washington held that except for the personal intercession of Vice President Lyndon Johnson, Hoover would have been fired or at least cut off at the knees.

Hoover countered by literally obeying Bobby's commands. A prime example of this involved the Kennedy Administration's war with the steel companies over an increase in prices. The Kennedys were furious and turned all the power of the government against United States Steel, which had initiated the price rise after a wage boost dictated by the Steelworkers union, with a large assist from the White House. When several news stories reported alleged remarks at a Bethlehem Steel board meeting to the effect that the steel companies had joined in the price rise under pressure from United States Steel, Bobby thought he had the industry in an antitrust bind. He called Hoover late in the evening and said he wanted the writers of those news stories questioned "immediately." Hoover thereupon did exactly as he was told. FBI agents were routed from their beds and told to quiz the newspapermen.

This was nothing new to the agents. They were frequently given assignments in the small hours of morning. But the press did not take to it in kindly fashion. An Associated Press business reporter, who had written that Bethlehem Steel opposed the price increase but that it had gone along under pressure, was awakened by the FBI at 3 a.m. and told that two agents were on their way to question him. Another business writer was called at 4 a.m. but refused to see the agents. Other newspapermen suffered the same annoyance. There was public and journalistic protest which President Kennedy tried to laugh away by saying that newspapermen woke people up at all hours, and that this was turnabout and poetic justice. Bobby tried to place the blame on Hoover, but he could not get around his use of the word "immediately." There was no doubt that he meant "immediately"—but a friendly Hoover would have softened the order to mean the following morning.

There was another and major cause of friction between Hoover and Bobby Kennedy. The Attorney General wanted the FBI to "infiltrate" the organized crime syndicates. It was Hoover's contention that he could not send his agents into Murder, Inc., the rackets, or the mobs where they would become accessories before and after the fact to serious crimes—robbery, white slavery, murder, embezzlement, extortion, etc. He also argued that to make the attempt would expose the FBI to all the temptations of corruption and big money, returning it to its sorry state under the Wilson and Harding administrations. But Bobby had been sold on the concept of a "Mafia"—a super-holding company for all crime in the United States. Hoover did not accept this Ian Fleming view of crime, though he conceded that there were links between various syndicates, carefully working outside of the FBI's jurisdiction. Most law enforcement officials agreed with him. But Hoover's objections were translated by the Attorney General, and passed on to the press, into a refusal to believe in the existence of organized crime. Hoover, it was said—and this became an article of faith—resisted because it was difficult to cope with organized crime and did not add to the FBI's impressive statistics of arrests and convictions.

The debate came to a crisis when Attorney General Kennedy

learned that Joe Valachi, a small-time hoodlum, had spilled his guts to the FBI and to other Federal authorities. Valachi spoke of a vast organization called Cosa Nostra—"our thing' in Italian —which controlled crime throughout the country. Kennedy wanted to present Valachi to the nation in order to arouse it to action. Hoover reasoned that what Valachi had to say was known to local police authorities. "He can testify before congressional committees or grand juries," Hoover told Kennedy, "but his testimony is not proof. By making his story public, you will only destroy the value of whatever leads he has given us." Publicizing Valachi's story would let the criminals he named take steps to get out from under any possible prosecution. Bobby, of course, triumphed and Valachi was trotted out before the television cameras and the Senate Permanent Investigating subcommittee. He created a sensation, but not a single mobster was arrested or convicted on the basis of what he had to say.

There was another clash between Hoover and Bobby over the Billie Sol Estes case. Estes, who made millions of dollars renting nonexistent grain storage facilities to the Federal government, had very high connections in the Kennedy Administration. But Bobby ignored the investigative reports sent to him by the FBI and only took action when the scandal was splattered all over page one of the nation's newspapers.

But this was only a start. When a witness appeared linking Billie Sol to some kickbacks involving high government officials, his military record somehow made its way to Justice Department reporters, thereby tending to discredit him. At Justice, it was rumored that Hoover had been responsible for disseminating parts of FBI files. Demands by Senator Hugh Scott for an investigation of the leak, which would have delighted Bobby had Hoover been guilty, were refused flatly, and Scott remarked that it had been done "at the instance of some person . . . higher than the FBI in government." The inference was clear.

It is interesting, in view of Bobby Kennedy's later pious outrage at the thought of wiretapping and bugging—the use of electronic devices planted in home, office, or car, to eavesdrop on conversations—that as Attorney General he far exceeded Hoover's requests for very limited powers to employ these investigative techniques. Bobby, in fact, lobbied so strenuously on Capitol Hill for a measure which would have authorized unlimited bugging and wiretapping in internal security cases and other instances of unspecified "serious" crimes, that he was roundly scolded by the *Washington Post* for advocating "police state" methods. Years later, after Bobby had left the Justice Department for the United States Senate, he and Hoover clashed over the use of bugs and wiretaps, with Kennedy denying any knowledge of the practice during his tenure at the Justice Department. It was the hardest public head-on collision between the two men and would have left Hoover badly scarred but for his foresight in getting Bobby to sign certain authorizations and state in writing that he knew of the practice and approved of it.

Precursor of the Hoover-Kennedy clash was the appearance of the Solicitor General of the United States before the Supreme Court in May 1966 to admit that FBI agents had planted an electronic listening device in the hotel suite of Fred B. Black Jr., an associate of Bobby Baker. Baker had been a close associate of Lyndon Johnson in his Senate days, a protégé who had risen to the strategic position of Secretary of the Senate and used his influence to become a millionaire under strange and felonious circumstances. The Baker case had rocked the Administration, and it was widely believed that President Johnson had instructed the Solicitor General to make his admission before the high court in order to throw sand into the legal machinery which was inexorably carrying Baker to prison.

There were some, perhaps more astute, who argued that this was not the case. Baker was overturning no applecarts, and a Johnson move in his behalf was not necessary. But Senator Bobby Kennedy, who had lodged himself as a perpetual thorn in the President's side, was making speeches attacking wiretapping and electronic surveillance. The bug had been planted in Black's room when Bobby was Attorney General. The disclosure, therefore, would impale him on what could only be construed as sharp hypocrisy. (Perhaps coincidentally, the Solicitor General's statement followed other disclosures of FBI bugging in a case involving Las Vegas gamblers and other underworld characters.)

If it was a trap, then Bobby stepped into it obligingly, deploring the Black bugging and assailing the FBI for resorting to such dirty business. He had known nothing about microphone surveillance, he said, nor had Hoover even discussed it with him. On December 5, 1966, Representative H. R. Gross, an Iowa Republican, wrote to Hoover, perhaps at the request of the FBI, noting the spate of news stories about electronic "eavesdropping" and wiretapping without the knowledge or authorization of the Attorney General.

It had been my impression in the past that the FBI engaged in "eavesdropping" and wire tapping only upon authority from the Attorney General. It was my understanding that the FBI has adhered to this policy, and that there exists "full documentation" that the FBI actions were authorized by the Attorney General.

I would appreciate it if you would send me any documentation that authorized the FBI "eavesdropping" that resulted in the overhearing of the conversations of Robert G. [Bobby] Baker, Fred B. Black [and others].

If there is some reason why the documentation itself cannot be sent to me in any of these cases, I would appreciate your assurance that such documentation exists with the name of the Attorney General, Deputy Attorney General, or other Justice Department official who gave the authorization. . . .

Hoover answered with alacrity on December 7:

I welcome the opportunity to answer your letter of December 5, 1966. The questions you raised were most incisive. I have always felt that the Congress, in representing the general public, has every right to know the true facts of any controversy . . . Your impression that the FBI engaged in the usage of wiretaps and microphones only upon the authority of the Attorney General of the United States is absolutely correct. You are also correct when you state that it is your understanding that "full documentation" exists as proof of such authorizations . . .

As examples of authorization covering the period in which you are specifically interested, you will find attached to this letter a communication dated August 17, 1961, signed by former Attorney General Robert F. Kennedy, in which he approved policy for the usage of microphones covering both security and major criminal cases. Mr. Kennedy, during his term of office, exhibited great interest in pursuing such matters and, while in different metropolitan areas, not only listened to the results of microphone surveillances but raised questions relative to obtaining better equipment. He was briefed frequently by an FBI official regarding such matters. FBI usage of such devices, while always handled in a sparing, carefully controlled manner and, as indicated, only with the specific authority of the Attorney General, was obviously increased at Mr. Kennedy's insistence while he was in office.

Attached to Hoover's answer was a memorandum on Justice Department stationery, with the signature, "Robert F. Kennedy" after "Approved." The memorandum stated:

In connection with the use of microphone surveillances it is frequently necessary to lease a special telephone line in order to monitor such a surveillance . . . This activity in no way involves any interception of telephonic communications and is not a telephone tap.

In the New York City area the telephone company has over the years insisted that a letter be furnished to the telephone company on each occasion when a special telephone line is leased by the FBI. It is required that such a lease arrangement be with the approval of the Attorney General. In the past we have restricted the utilization of leased lines in New York City to situations involving telephone taps, all of which have been approved by the Attorney General.

We have not previously used leased lines with microphone surveillances because of certain technical difficulties which existed in New York City. These technical difficulties have, however, now been overcome. If we are permitted to use leased telephone lines as an adjunct to our microphone surveillances, this type of coverage can be materially extended both in security and in major criminal cases. Accordingly, your approval of our utilizing this leased line arrangement is requested. . . .

Also attached to Hoover's answer to Gross was a letter from Attorney General Kennedy's assistant, Herbert J. Miller Jr., to Senator Sam J. Ervin Jr., then voicing concern over accounts of widespread electronic surveillance and wiretapping by the

FBI. Miller informed the Senator that "as of February 8, 1960, the Federal Bureau of Investigation maintained 78 wiretaps . . . as in the case of wiretapping, the technique of electronic listening devices is used on a highly restricted basis. The Federal Bureau of Investigation has 67 of these devices in operation. The majority are in the field of security with a few used to obtain intelligence information with regard to organized crime."

Hoover might have aded, *quod erat demonstrandum.*

But Senator Kennedy was not satisfied. On December 10, he issued a publicity release denying what the documents mutely proved. "Apparently Mr. Hoover has been misinformed," Bobby stated. "He should have consulted Mr. Courtney Evans before issuing his statement. Mr. Evans . . . served as Assistant Director while I was Attorney General. He was appointed by Mr. Hoover as the liaison officer between the FBI and the Attorney General, and in that capacity was present on each occasion when any matter was discussed with any representative of the FBI, including matters referred to in Mr. Hoover's statement. Mr. Evans wrote me this year, and a copy of his letter is attached."

The Evans letter, interestingly, was dated February 17, 1966, long before Hoover and Kennedy had squared off.

"This letter is being sent to you in line with your request and in confirmation of our conversation," Evans, then in private law practice, wrote. "It relates to information furnished to you during your tenure as Attorney General by me as an official of the FBI about the use of telephone taps and microphone surveillances . . .

"On January 10, 1961, while you were Attorney General-designate, a memorandum was delivered to you furnishing a summary on the use of wiretapping by the FBI in serious national security cases. Thereafter, individual requests in these serious national security cases for wiretap authorization were sent to you by the FBI for approval. These were the only wiretap authorizations ever submitted to you.

"Since prior Attorneys General had informed the FBI that the use of microphones, as contrasted to telephone taps, need not be specifically approved by the Attorney General, I did not discuss the use of these devices with you . . . nor do I know of any written material that was sent to you at any time concerning this procedure, or concerning the use, specific location, or other details as to installation of any such devices . . ."

But having set up Courtney Evans as an authority, Bobby set himself up for the counteroffensive he must have known would follow. Within twenty-four hours, Hoover released a statement which labeled as "absolutely inconceivable" that Kennedy or Evans could claim that there had been no discussion or approval of microphone and telephone tap surveillance. The "Approved" August 17 memorandum should have been persuasive enough, but Hoover was aware that Kennedy's Senate office was whispering into newsmen's ears that Bobby had signed it automatically, without reading it, and that there had been no consultation between him and the FBI on the subject. Hoover therefore released two other memoranda, both of them from Courtney Evans to the appropriate FBI official.

The first memorandum, dated July 7, 1961, stated that

. . . in line with the Director's approval, the Attorney General was contacted this morning . . . relative to his observations as to the possibility of utilizing "electronic devices" in organized crime investigations. It was pointed out to the Attorney General that we had taken action with regard to the use of microphone surveillances in these cases . . . The strong objections to the utilization of telephone taps as contrasted to microphone surveillances was stressed. The Attorney General stated he recognized the reasons why telephone taps should be restricted to national-defense-type cases and he was pleased we had been using microphone surveillances where these objections do not apply wherever possible in organized crime matters.

The Attorney General noted that he had approved several technical surveillances in connection with security-type investigations, but that he had not kept any record and didn't really know what he had approved and what surveillances were currently in operation. He said that for his own information he would like to see a list of the technical surveillances now in operation. He added that this could be brought over to him personally and that he would look it over and immediately return it because he realized the importance of having these records maintained under the special security conditions which only the FBI had.

If the Director approves, we will have the list of technical surveillances prepared, delivered personally to the Attorney General and then returned to the Bureau's files.

The second Evans memorandum, dated August 17, referred to the document of the same day which Hoover had released in his letter to Representative Gross. It blew sky high the rumors being spread by Kennedy's office that his signature on the paper had been *pro forma,* without discussion or knowledge of what he had signed. Said Evans:

The Attorney General was contacted on the morning of August 17, 1961, with reference to the situation in New York City concerning the obtaining of leased lines from the telephone company for use in connection with microphone surveillances. This matter was discussed with the Attorney General and he was shown a specimen copy of the proposed letter which would be used. The Attorney General approved the proposed procedure in this regard and personally signed the attached memorandum evidencing such approval.

There was no way for Kennedy to get out from under his denials—or those furnished him by Courtney Evans almost five years after the fact. But he nevertheless made a yeoman attempt to obscure the record. "It may seem 'inconceivable' to Mr. Hoover that I was not aware of the 'bugging' practices of the FBI during my term as Attorney General . . . but the plain fact of the matter is that I did not know," Bobby said in a press release. "On two occasions I listened to what appeared to be recorded conversations with respect to organized crime. On neither occasion was there any indication that these . . . had been obtained by any Federal agency." And then, in a beautiful piece of broken-field running, he added: "Although Mr. Hoover . . . implies that we discussed it, the fact is that he never discussed this highly important matter with me, and no evidence exists supporting his recollection that we did. Indeed, there is no indication that Mr. Hoover ever asked me for authorization for any single bugging device, in Las Vegas, New York, Washington, or anywhere else."

Hoover, of course, had never stated or implied that he had personally discussed microphone surveillances and telephone taps with Bobby Kennedy. His letter to Gross had said that Kennedy was "briefed frequently by an FBI official regarding such matters"—and the Evans memoranda confirmed this. Kennedy's rejoinder was, as a columnist observed at the time, a perfect example of the "where do you live? I moved," ploy. And it worked. The general public remembered the much-publicized denunciations of Hoover and the FBI for unauthorized electronic surveillance, but the documentation in rebuttal was published in abbreviated and fitful fashion. Ironically, though Hoover was in the right and Kennedy in the wrong, the FBI was hurt and Bobby emerged from the encounter relatively unscathed.

21.

Assassinations, Crisis

POLITICAL MURDER CAN BRING POLITICAL CATHARSIS. OR IT CAN CAUSE a jangling of the political nerves which result in frustration, hatred, and after-violence. The assassination of John Fitzgerald Kennedy, thirty-fourth President of the United States, on a Dallas freeway brought out the worst in the American character. Those who had supported him passionately in life, in death enshrined him not so much to create an uplifting image for generations to come but to punish those who had opposed him in life. The literature of his death, with a few noteworthy exceptions, was filled with bitterness and knife thrusts at those who most diligently fought the philosophy and ideology of the man who had squeezed the trigger. Before the world even knew the name of the assassin—or that he was a dedicated Marxist who listened nightly to the hate-filled broadcasts of Fidel Castro's Cuba—Chief Justice of the United States Earl Warren trumpeted that responsibility for the crime belonged to right-wing apostles of hate, and conservatives everywhere wondered what lynch-mob might seize them that night.

Any researcher into the facts of the Kennedy assassination and its postlude is struck by the venom directed against John Edgar Hoover and the FBI for his alleged coldness in the face of tragedy, as well as their alleged failure in not "knowing" that Lee Harvey Oswald, the assassin, was a potential President-killer. This was the problem of the writers of the Warren Commission report on the assassination of President Kennedy. To stress heavily that the FBI had erred in not reporting to the Secret Service that a would-be defector to the Soviet Union, still in touch with Soviet authorities and violently burning against enemies of Castro's Cuba—whether liberals like Kennedy or ultrarightists like General Edwin Walker—was loose in Dallas, would underscore the fact that murder is always an option open to Communists. But to admit that the FBI, in not offering Oswald to the Secret Service for preventive restraint, was following the dictates of the situation would have deprived them of a necessary scapegoat.

Viewed objectively, the fact is that no President and no public figures can be guarded from assassination if the assassin is ready to put his life on the line in order to accomplish his terrible purpose. J. Edgar Hoover made this point persuasively in a memorandum written after the assassination which even the Warren Commission found of merit.

"The degree of security that can be afforded the President of the United States is dependent to a considerable extent upon the degree of contact with the general public desired by the President," Hoover wrote. "Absolute security is neither practical nor possible. An approach to complete security would require the President to operate in a sort of vacuum, isolated from the general public and behind impregnable barriers. His travel would be secret; his public appearances would be behind bulletproof glass. A more practical approach necessitates compromise. Any travel, any contact with the general public, involves a calculated risk on the part of the President and the men responsible for his protection."

In the case of President Kennedy's Dallas journey, the precautions taken were keyed to a media view of that city as "seething" with right-wing hate. Adlai Stevenson, then Ambassador to the United Nations, had been assaulted by a crowd shouting "Down with the U.N." The national press had been filled with stories that Dallas was the right-wing hate and violence capital of Texas and therefore of the United States. All the preparations, therefore, had been geared to a possible attempt on the President's life at the hands of right-wing extremists. The FBI had over the years dutifully turned over to the Secret Service, which is entrusted with full responsibility for guarding the President, such names as it had in its files of potential killers on the far right as they came into its ken. The Secret Service, in preparing for the President's visit to Dallas, concerned itself with an attempt from the same source. Both FBI and Secret Service had, therefore, been locked in by the Administration attitude, stated openly in the Reuther memorandum to Bobby Kennedy, that the real threat to America came from the right and not the left.

Prior to the assassination, the FBI had questioned Lee Harvey Oswald on several occasions. Like the Office of Naval Intelligence and CIA, it had begun a file on Oswald when his efforts to renounce his American citizenship and defect to the Soviet Union in Moscow had been reported in the press. In these interviews, it had learned of him that he was a "Marxist," that he had worked with the Castro-financed Fair Play for Cuba Committee, that he was a liar about the date and place of his marriage to the Russian girl he had brought back from Moscow, and that he had been in touch with Soviet officials in Washington and Mexico City. There was nothing in the FBI files to indicate that he was a Soviet or a Castro agent—nothing about his manner to mark him as a potential Presidential assassin.

The *post mortem* analyses and Monday morning quarterbacking that followed the Kennedy assassination troubled Hoover deeply. The mood of the country would not have tolerated any attack on the source of much of the anti-FBI carping —mostly because it came from the Kennedy family and its adherents and retainers. He could wring some wry humor from the dark tales of conspiracy which made the rounds of Washington's watering spots and found their way into the left-wing press. One such tale, fostered by former FBI agent William Turner, argued solemnly that Hoover, who by law and policy had forwarded to the Secret Service the names of all possible potential Presidential assassins, had withheld the name of Oswald out of a sense of "rivalry" with the Secret Service.

But what wounded him deeply was the kind of snide story which immediately sprang up. He had no particular love for the Kennedys. They had done their best to humiliate him—and that humiliation was double since much of it came from someone whom he undoubtedly would have thought of as a "whippersnapper"—the word later used about Bobby by Lyndon Johnson. But Hoover, whatever his personal feelings, shared with other Americans the sense of shock at a President assassinated. And martinet though he seemed he still could feel for the Kennedys in their time of grief. To make matters worse, as he later confided, it fell to him to break the news to Bobby, lunching that day at Hickory Hill. Hoover had been at his office on the fifth floor of the Justice Department building when the bulletin, torn off the UPI ticker, was handed to him. He picked up the direct phone to the Attorney General's office. Angie Novello, Kennedy's personal secretary answered the call.

"This is Edgar Hoover," he said, his voice almost shrill. "Have you heard the news?"

"Yes, Mr. Hoover, but I just can't break it to him," she answered.

"I'll call him," Hoover said.

Through White House extension 163, he got poolside at the Kennedy house. Ethel Kennedy answered the phone. The

White House operator said, "The Director is calling," and Ethel put him off with "The Attorney General is at lunch." "This is very urgent," the operator said. Ethel held out the phone to Bobby. "It's Hoover," she said. Bobby took the phone and said his hello. "I have very bad news for you," Hoover said, in a voice that Bobby would later describe as "toneless," "The President has been shot."

"Is it serious?" Bobby asked.

"I think so," Hoover said. "I am trying to get details. I'll call you back when I find out more." Bobby put down the phone and moved back to the luncheon table. "The President's been shot," he cried out, and threw a hand over his face.

Like most of official Washington, Hoover was immediately on the phone, trying to get Dallas. So heavy was the strain on telephone facilities that lines were going dead all over the city. When he did get through, there was little he could find out: An FBI agent who had attempted to enter the Parkland hospital where Kennedy was in surgery had been thrown out bodily by semi-hysterical local police who did not recognize him. Finally, Hoover was told that John F. Kennedy was dead. He immediately called Hickory Hill. Bobby was standing by the pool and answered the phone. The Attorney General's description of what followed was given wide currency in official Washington, and eventually was memorialized in William Manchester's *The Death of a President.*

This is how Manchester told it:

"The President's dead," [Hoover] said snappily and hung up.
He expressed no compassion, did not seem to be upset. His voice, as the Attorney General recalled afterward, was "not quite as excited as if he were reporting the fact that he had found a Communist on the faculty of Howard University." Ordinarily garrulous, he had suddenly turned curt with his superior. It would be charitable to attribute the swift change to the stresses of the afternoon. Yet although Bob Kennedy continued in the Cabinet for over nine months, Hoover, whose office was on the same floor, never walked over to offer his condolences. One of his assistants wrote Kennedy a moving letter, and

the agents in the FBI's crime squad sent him a message of sympathy, but their Director . . . remained sphinxlike.

Manchester was merely following the Kennedy script, just as he totally misrepresented Jacqueline Kennedy's actions at the time of the shooting. But even before the account saw print in his book, it was being broadcast widely around Washington. Hoover was many things, but he was not a cynic, and the stories embittered him. His own account, never offered for publication, was somewhat different. To begin with, he shared that state of shock which seized most of the nation. He did not want to be the bearer of the terrible tidings and would have gladly passed the responsibility to one of the White House staff or an assistant director. But he felt that the duty was his, whatever antagonisms existed between himself and the Attorney General. He was not a man given to outward shows of excitement, and he realized that the only way to comport himself under the circumstances was to be as brief and as unemotional as possible. Having expressed his condolences, any further display would have pleased neither himself nor the Attorney General. And Bobby, who was not the kind of man to forget an injury easily, a month later presented Hoover with a Christmas gift— a pair of cufflinks engraved with the Justice Department seal.

But Hoover was caught up in a maelstrom of his own. He had assumed that the assassination of a President was under Federal jurisdiction. He learned quickly, as his agents tried to take over in Dallas, that writing a threatening letter to a President was illegal under Federal statute, but killing him was not. Hoover wanted Lee Harvey Oswald in Federal custody, fearful that he would be lynched. But a search of the law found no loophole for the FBI. That night, at 7:25, Hoover received his first call from the new President. Lyndon Johnson wanted a complete and thorough FBI report on the crime. Hoover hung up and then called the Bureau, assigning a 31-man team to Dallas. The team's orders were to leave immediately. Hoover had other problems. The Dallas police were taking to television to make public every detail of the ironclad case against Oswald. In a fury, Hoover called the Dallas police chief and warned him that there were to be no further disclosures of the evidence being dug up by the FBI and by local authorities. If there were, the Warren Court would have grounds for reversing any conviction. Nicholas Katzenbach, Bobby's deputy, had stepped in as an unofficial Acting Attorney General, and he was attempting to put pressure on Johnson to take the investigation out of Hoover's hands and to set up a board of inquiry.

The night after the assassination, Hoover went to bed certain that the Dallas police were transferring Oswald from the maximum-security cell in their jail to another and secret jail before daylight. At 3 a.m. the following morning, the FBI office in Dallas discovered that the prisoner had not been moved and warned that his life was in jeopardy. But the Dallas police would not budge from a schedule in mid-morning so as to "go along with the press." The murder of Oswald by Jack Ruby, a tavern keeper, "on television" at 11:21 a.m., two days after Kennedy's death, settled a cloud of speculation over the assassination which has not been dispelled to this day—and created new problems for the FBI, new investigations to mount. In one way, however, it gave Hoover and the FBI the jurisdictional opening they needed. The murder of Oswald had, by law, deprived him of his civil rights, and the Bureau could move in.

Then, as plans for the Kennedy funeral reached him, Hoover was handed another problem. Jacqueline Kennedy had decided that she would march behind the caisson bearing her husband's body from the White House to St. Matthew's Cathedral. Accompanying her would be the leaders of the world—Charles de Gaulle of France, Haile Selassie of Ethiopia, Eamon de Valera of Eire, Anastas Mikoyan of the Soviet Union, and the highest officials of the United States, to name but a few. If the assassination were part of a conspiracy—and the murder of Ruby at that time seemed to point in that direction—a gunman's bullet, aimed at the slow-moving procession, could cause an international incident and panic in the country. Hoover advised against it, but the Kennedy family had been given full charge of the funeral ceremony and Mrs. Kennedy would not be budged. With Jackie determined, the foreign dignitaries could not accept the protection of bullet-proof limousines, though Mikoyan was not yet recovered from serious surgery.

The Canadian Royal Mounted Police and the Central Intelligence Agency also expressed their strong concern, but it was Hoover who bore the brunt of the Kennedy family's anger at what they considered his interference. Sargent Shriver, who was acting as a kind of major-domo for his in-laws, exploded when Hoover's warning was repeated to him. "That's ridiculous," he said angrily. "We're all concerned. You don't have to be the Director of the FBI to know that it's going to be dangerous. Even the White House doorman knows that. It's a ploy, so that if anybody gets shot the Director can say, 'I told you so.' It would be a different story if he'd turned up hard proof that some gangster had taken an apartment on Connecticut Avenue, or that an NKVD agent was roaming Washington. Then I'd have to do a double-take. But this is just a self-serving device." Confronted by this attitude, Hoover could only assign every agent available to line the streets and hope for the best.

But everywhere about him there was Kennedy hostility, as there was around President Johnson, whose thoughtfulness and patience knew no bounds in those trying days. The FBI was at work on every scrap of evidence, following every possible lead—fifty agents working night and day with Hoover supervising every aspect. But the Kennedy attitude, expressed at every opportunity to a Washington press corps unashamedly partisan, was that Hoover was somehow responsible for John F. Kennedy's death—Lyndon Johnson shared that implied accusation—and not interested in doing anything more than a routine job.

The appointment by President Johnson of a commission to investigate the circumstances of John Kennedy's death and to evaluate the FBI report prepared for the White House brought no joy to Hoover. For one thing, it reflected on the reliability of the Bureau's inquiry. For another, the commission was headed by Chief Justice Earl Warren, who had neither affection nor respect for Hoover or the FBI. And though any student of the Washington scene could have predicted that the luminaries on the Warren Commission would have little to do with its real work, it was also obvious that the Chief Justice would have a major role in selecting the staff that would hold the hearings and put together the final report. That report, however, though it was hailed as a "slap" at the FBI and Hoover, had but one mild criticism—that Hoover and the Secret Service had too "narrow" an interpretation of what their relations should be and how they traded information. There was implied disapproval because the FBI had not given the Secret Service Oswald's name as a potential assassin, but the report conceded that under the rules then obtaining, the Bureau had acted properly. And the substantial quotation and paraphrase from the FBI's own investigative report indicated that the Bureau's contacts with Oswald gave not the slightest hint of homicidal tendencies or anything but the evasiveness usual among suspected subversives. It also contradicted Bobby's charge, spread by what came to be known in Washington as the Kennedy "underground," that the FBI had done a hurried, superficial, and self-serving job.

One more sharp and destructive controversy whose seeds were planted in the Kennedy years howled about Hoover's head in 1969. It was set off by the disclosure during the appeal of Cassius Clay—or Muhammed Ali—the heavyweight boxing champion, for reversal of a draft evasion conviction. At the insistence of the defense, an FBI agent took the stand in a Houston, Texas, court and testified that on the number of occasions, he had listened in on Clay's telephone conversations. But, he added, there was no tap on the fighter's phone. Clay had called other people whose phones were tapped and who were under electronic surveillance. Under questioning, the agent further disclosed that the people Clay had called were Elijah

Muhammed, leader of the explosive Black Muslims, and Dr. Martin Luther King, who headed the black civil rights movement.

The bugging and wiretapping of Elijah Muhammed was easily understandable. His organization was prone to violence and revolutionary threats, and the man who founded it had been shot dead by some of his own followers. But the tap on King set tempers a-boil in the civil rights movement and the Liberal Establishment. Carl T. Rowan, a former Kennedy official who had returned to journalism and wrote a syndicated column for the *Washington Star,* immediately fired from the hip with a column that rang all the charges against Hoover and the FBI. Characterizing the FBI's interest in King as "illegal" and a "peril" to the nation, Rowan stated categorically: "The whole truth is that Dr. King's phones were tapped, his hotel rooms bugged, and he was personally shadowed right up to the time he was slain in Memphis on April 4, 1968." Where Rowan could have learned of this, when even former Attorney General Ramsey Clark insisted that while in office he had known nothing of any surveillance of Martin Luther King and asserted angrily that considering him to be a security threat was "outrageous," is a question for researchers in journalistic method.

But Rowan added to this by writing: "Could Clark possibly have been unaware that FBI officials were going before Congressional committees and partly justifying larger appropriations by . . . feeding anti-King ammunition to Southerners who despised the civil rights leader—all by way of revealing 'tidbits' picked up through the wiretaps and bugging? Was Clark unaware that certain FBI officials were roaming the country leaking to newspaper editors poisonous stories and what the buggings had allegedly revealed? . . . Were Hoover a more thoughtful man, or as concerned about the preservation of democracy and liberty, he would have resigned long ago . . ."

The Rowan outburst was answered by a typically unpleasant letter from the FBI's associate director, Clyde A. Tolson, in which he decried the "malicious" and "scurrilous" column, asked that the facts be given "equal publicity," and disclosed that "the wire tap on Martin Luther King, Jr., was specifically approved in advance in writing by the late Attorney General of the United States, Mr. Robert F. Kennedy. This device was strictly in the field of internal security and, therefore, was within the provisions laid down by the then President of the United States." This left Rowan out on a limb, but it only told part of the story.

In fact, the FBI's interest in Martin Luther King dated back to a period when he was a relatively obscure Georgia preacher and had not yet attained national and international fame as a civil rights activist and head of the Southern Christian Leadership Conference. Years before, King had attended a meeting of Communist functionaries at the Highlander Folk School in Tennessee and was photographed with them. That had been the start of a King file at FBI headquarters. As King rose in the movement, reports began to pass across Hoover's desk from agents keeping tabs on the Communist Party that King was in frequent and sometimes close contact with high-ranking Communists. When it became clear that King's associations with one important underground Communist leader had passed the stage of coincidence, it was suggested to King by a Justice Department official at Bobby Kennedy's suggestion that prudence and good public relations would dictate a cessation of the relationship.

King agreed, but new reports linked him with another important underground Communist official. Since Robert Kennedy had staked a claim on King's career, a routine FBI report was sent to the Attorney General—a kind of "for your information" memorandum. Bobby had called in Courtney Evans, liaison man between Justice and the FBI, to suggest some course of action which would protect the Kennedy Administration should there be damaging disclosures of an alliance between King's movement and the Communists. According to a memorandum from Evans to Hoover, now in FBI files, Kennedy had initiated talk of a possible telephone tap on King's line. The

Attorney General showed real concern over the possibility of Communist infiltration of the race issue in the United States in general and the Southern Christian Leadership Conference (SDLC) specifically. During this conversation, Evans reported, the Attorney General had asked about the feasibility of installing electronic devices which would eavesdrop on King's conversations.

The FBI's response had been that microphone surveillance of Martin Luther King would be difficult because he traveled so extensively. The question was also raised as to the advisability of such a course of action because of unfavorable political repercussions should it be discovered. On October 7, 1963, after Kennedy had pressed for some surveillance of King, Hoover informed him via formal memorandum that it would be possible to tap two of King's phones—one at SCLC headquarters in Atlanta, Georgia, the other at an address in New York. That memorandum bears the approval signature of "Robert F. Kennedy" and the date "10-10-63" in Bobby's handwriting.

As a result of this surveillance, the FBI had its first independent proof that King was secretly in touch with a high-ranking Communist. Again there was a quiet warning from the Justice Department to King that he was jeopardizing the civil rights movement, and King agreed again to stop these contacts. Hoover, however, found it profoundly worrisome that King still maintained the contacts but through intermediaries. The Puritan streak in him responded with shock when surveillance reports also showed that King was engaged in other activities which, though not subversive, were questionable—to be blunt, the nature and extent of King's extramarital philanderings. Where "those sexual things" were concerned, Hoover had no charity.

In mid-November of 1964, after the landslide victory of Lyndon Johnson, Hoover granted a request, much to everyone's surprise, from Sarah McClendon, a correspondent for Texas newspapers whose gadfly questions had irritated more than one President, for a meeting over coffee with a group of Washington newswomen. For close to three hours, Hoover held open forum. He struck at the Warren Commission for its "classic example of Monday-morning quarterbacking," made it known that he was now sending the Secret Service "thousands of names of beatniks and kooks and crackpots" in line with the Commission's recommendations, but commiserated with the Service because it was "hopelessly undermanned and ill-equipped to do the job it is supposed to do."

Still free-wheeling, he answered charges that he was not attending to business on the civil rights front or sending enough agents to Mississippi. His men there were helpless, he said, because the state was "filled with water mocassins, rattle-snakes, and red-necked sheriffs, and they are all in the same category as far as I am concerned"—an answer to handbills circulated in some parts of the south that he was in league with "Jewish-nigger" conspirators. And then, as his irritation became self-propelled, he lashed out at Martin Luther King, then in the Bahamas preparing his Nobel Prize acceptance speech.

"I remember the notorious Martin Luther King making a speech in the South some months ago where he advised the Negroes not to report any violations to our Albany, Georgia, agents because they were all southerners," said Hoover. On checking, he had discovered that of the five agents in that racially distressed city, one was from New York, one from Indiana, one from Massachusetts, one from Minnesota, and one from Georgia. Then he really let fly with a sentence about King that made headlines all over the country: "He is the most notorious liar in the country."

The reaction was immediate. A group of the major civil rights leaders, visiting President Johnson, demanded action against Hoover but got what they later described as a "noncommittal" answer. King fired off a telegram to Hoover in which he said, "I was appalled and surprised at your reported statement maligning my integrity. What motivated such an irresponsible accusation is a mystery to me. I have sincerely questioned the effectiveness of the FBI in racial incidents, particularly where bombings and brutalities against Negroes are at issue. But I have never attributed this merely to the presence of southerners in the FBI."* And, in a statement released to the press, he suggested that Hoover was no longer rational, that he had "apparently faltered under the awesome burdens, complexities, and responsibilities of his office."

Commented *Time:* "J. Edgar Hoover has many old foes, has made a legion of new ones recently; undoubtedly there will be vastly increased pressures on the White House from now on to boot the old fellow out of his job."

There was a reason, however, behind Hoover's intemperate remark about Mississippi sheriffs and his slash at Martin Luther King. For many weeks, hundreds of FBI agents had been combing the state searching for Michael Schwerner, Andrew Goodman, and James Chaney—three young civil rights workers from the North who had disappeared in Mississippi, leaving behind only their burned car. He had sent his best men to press the search and to open a field office in Jackson with a regularly assigned staff of fifty—in addition to the agents already there, working on the disappearance of the three young men and carrying a load of some twelve hundred other cases. He was working closely with President Johnson, who was on the phone to him as often as four times a day. At Johnson's suggestion, Hoover had traveled to Mississippi for the opening of the new field office, in order to impress on the state the seriousness of the FBI's intentions.

But for all of this, he was being criticized for being a publicity seeker, and his agents, preponderantly nonsoutherners—the Jackson SAC was Roy K. Moore of Oregon, one of the Bureau's most brilliant agents—were being accused by King and by comedian Dick Gregory of being part of the Southern Establishment and covering up for the Ku Klux Klan and the White Knights. Angering him even more was that while the Presi-

---

*Hoover backed his allegation concerning King's attack on southerners in the FBI by producing a clipping from the Chicago *Defender,* a Negro newspaper, quoting the civil rights leader.

dent, his agents, and he were doing their utmost, Attorney General Kennedy, who was the source of most of the anti-FBI rumors, was planning a vacation in Europe. Hoover, in fact, had given direct orders to every agent in Mississippi to "identify and interview every Klansman in the state" and to send a teletyped progress report to him "at the close of each day."

In Jackson, at a press conference, Hoover had laid down the FBI line in no uncertain terms. "This may be a prolonged effort but it will be continued until it is solved—until we find the bodies of those three men who have disappeared and the persons who may be responsible for their disappearance." On the basis of the response given by local law enforcement authorities, Hoover strongly suspected that some of them had taken part in the murder. He knew what his men were up against— threatening telephone calls to their homes, water mocassins slipped into their cars, the open and growing hostility of the local law. If he had spoken unwisely to the newswomen, he had nevertheless been telling the truth. And there was one part of the interview which very few had bothered to quote: that Hoover had tried unsuccessfully to reach King and explain what was being done.

It is ironic that a week before the FBI broke the case—arresting twenty-one men, including several law enforcement officers—Charles Evers, the NAACP leader in Mississippi, told the press, "I think it is time for the President to remove this man without waiting for his retirement. Hoover is a self-admitted states-righter. He is also a racist and a segregationist." But Hoover had the final word. After the Mississippi case had been solved, he met with King in the FBI's Washington office for seventy minutes. At the time of the arrest, King had issued a statement commending "the Federal Bureau of Investigation for the work they have done in uncovering the perpetrators of this dastardly act. It renews again [sic] my faith in democracy."

Neither Hoover nor King ever publicly disclosed what they said to each other at FBI headquarters. King told reporters that the meeting let to "a much clearer understanding on both sides," though he still had reservations about the FBI's motivation. There are reports from those who should know but may not that King began the discussion aggressively but quieted down completely when Hoover showed him transcripts of the telephone and microphone surveillances, a record of political and moral error.

When the men parted, neither could know that in not too long a time—a few years—the FBI would be working as diligently to apprehend the assassin of Martin Luther King, shot to death in a Memphis motel—or that Hoover would be as successful in helping track down King's assailant, James Earl Ray, as he had been in finding the bodies of the three young civil rights workers and putting their murderers behind bars. And of all the ironies in Hoover's life, perhaps the most ironic was that his announcement of Ray's capture should have coincided with the assassination of Robert Kennedy.

22.

The Stormy Final Years—I

IN AUGUST 1970 THE GALLUP POLL REPORTED A SHARP DROP IN THE number of respondents who held a "highly favorable" opinion of the Federal Bureau of Investigation. It was the kind of drop which any politician would have accepted with equanimity—from 84 percent to 71 percent—but it indicated a slippage that did not go undetected by the Bureau's critics. The poll also reported that 70 percent of those polled felt that John Edgar Hoover was doing an "excellent" to "good" job. But again, the *mene mene tekel* was there: 51 percent believed that he should retire. Though on May 10, 1972—the forty-seventh anniversary of Hoover's directorship—seventy-six representatives and senators took to the floor to eulogize him, filling twenty-seven pages of the *Congressional Record,* critical noises were being heard in the Congress from voices which had once joined in the acclaim.

Had the Director, once untouched except at the hands of the liberal-left, fallen down on the job? Had he succumbed to the crochets and infirmities of age? Had his once-deft public relations sense deserted him? Had the FBI itself relaxed into bureaucratic sloppiness? Had Hoover changed? Or was it a political gangup, as Hoover—approaching his seventy-sixth year —insisted?

To a degree it was all of these things—and none of them. Internally, the Bureau was very much what it had always been. Hoover still ran it with an iron hand, imposing his ideas and his methods on the growing force of agents under him. Morale was high, and the FBI carried out its assigned tasks no better and no worse than before. The collapse came about in the Bureau's external relations, in the face it presented to the world. And this had come about through a series of changes in the FBI's top personnel, as the men who had stood between Hoover and outside hostility left his employ.

For years, Louis B. Nichols had been the FBI's second-in-command and administrative right-hand man. The title was Clyde Tolson's, but he had been Hoover's security-blanket and flunky more than an operating assistant. Nichols, a strong man in his own right, had acted as "front" for the FBI when there was trouble on the Hill. If there were raw feelings, Nichols would soothe them; if there were problems, he would find a solution. If Hoover made a bad decision, Nichols was at once sufficiently a diplomat and a pragmatist to persuade him to change it. He had sufficient status in and out of the Bureau to have a kind of independence, never even hinted at with Hoover, to argue a point. His effectiveness derived from Hoover's knowledge and confidence that Nichols was unshakably loyal to him and to the FBI. There were also strong personal ties— Hoover was the godfather of Nichols's son.

When there were attacks on the FBI, Nichols never counterattacked frontally. A friendly newspaperman was quietly informed that if he wanted the facts, they would be available to him. He was, moreover, highly respected by the press. If a newspaperman asked him a question, he would answer it fully or candidly refuse on the grounds of security. He never danced away from the question or give a misleading answer. He never descended like a ton of bricks on those in the media whose reporting or commentary irritated Hoover or the Bureau. And his standard for judging the trustworthiness of those who approached him for information was not ideological but based on careful observation of the man.*

This does not mean that Hoover surrendered any of his authority to Nichols or to anyone else. He still set policy and exercised supervision over important investigations. He dealt directly with Presidents and Attorneys General. But with Nichols running the day-to-day affairs and keeping a ceaseless vigil on the FBI's image, the Bureau did not get into disorderly controversies. The irascible letters that Hoover wrote with greater and greater frequency in later years did not exacerbate officials, editors, and the public. Nichols was, as Jeremiah O'Leary, the *Washington Star*'s man on the FBI beat, said, a "take-charge guy."

Those who followed Nichols carried on, though to a lesser degree, in the same tradition. Alan Belmont, Robert Wick, and Cartha D. (Deke) DeLoach—to name but three—continued to work under the Nichols system. They were unfailingly cooperative with the press and, DeLoach in particular, had excellent contacts on Capitol Hill. They saw their job as one of not only interceding for the Bureau with the world but also of interced-

*In the mid-Fifties, when I was an editor on *Newsweek,* I asked Nichols for help on a take-out I was doing on the Communist party. For several hours I sat in his office while he went through a thick folder from which he gave me facts, background, and other information. Now and then, he would glance at a page and say, "No, I can't give you this." During the interview, he was called from his office for about fifteen minutes. He left the folder lying on his desk where I could have easily gone through it had I been ready to violate his trust. Needless to say, I didn't.

ing for the world with Hoover. And they succeeded with few exceptions in deflecting the lightning that forked out at Edgar Hoover as well as in muffling the thunder that might have echoed from his office.

But in 1970, DeLoach had resigned from the Bureau to go into private business—as his predecessors had done. He was followed by William J. Sullivan—a man with an excellent FBI record and a fine administrator, but lacking the diplomacy and the realism that had marked those who held the post before him. Sullivan's aim was to get the job done, with no thought that the political climate on Capitol Hill had changed, that law enforcement was taking a back seat to "understanding," that the criminal and the subversive were deemed the victims of society, and not vice versa. As one FBI official said about Sullivan:

He was an expert on communism, subversion, espionage, and the radical movement. He wasn't the man to handle the job he was given. The Director needed someone to backstop him with the White House, the press, Congress, the Attorney General and the Justice Department. He wasn't interested in the public relations angle, in keeping the Director out of the newspapers and out of trouble. Strangely enough, where they locked horns, the Director was taking the "civil rights" position and Sullivan was gung-ho for action. Everybody was jumping on the Bureau for taking the law into its hands. The Director was sensitive about this and he put a partial "hold" on the use of wiretaps and microphone surveillances. He also put his foot down on what we call "surreptitious entry" and the "bag job"—that's where agents enter a house or office and go through papers, effects, and so on—even in national security cases.

Sullivan, who's a very good man, couldn't take it and he made a couple of speeches in which he took positions which the Director knew, though the press didn't, ran counter to FBI policy. He said, "Forget the Communist Party and let's get after the spies"—and, believe me, we've got them!—and the Director got mad. You've got to see it his way. The State Department was on his back because it felt that tough action against Soviet agents would jeopardize sensitive negotiations. Attorney General Mitchell didn't want reporters banging on his door. It got to the point where Sullivan and the Director were barely talking to each other. They communicated by memo, and that's no way to run the Bureau. Then the White House switched its line and began calling for what Sullivan had pushed for to begin with—and this made the Director even more jittery. He felt that Sullivan was undercutting him, and he fired him.

Ironically, the press came to Sullivan's defense and there were unsubstantiated rumors that Hoover had locked Sullivan out of his office, that he had been fired because he wanted to "modernize" the FBI. Hoover, whose position should have pleased the liberal-left, was hurt. There was another spate of editorials demanding his forced resignation, and Hoover, who was now handling the small details of Bureau public relations, made matters worse by firing off intemperate letters to newspapers and individuals who criticized him, whether with justification or otherwise. The rhetoric of the Hoover blasts fed insinuations of megalomania. Sometimes Hoover failed to check his facts, leaving him exposed and vulnerable, in letters which challenged the truth of what had been written.

Hoover's controversy with the *National Observer,* a national weekly published by Dow Jones, is a case in point. The newspaper had, in its April 12, 1971, issue memorialized Hoover in a take-out headed "The Life and Times of a 76-Year-Old Cop." It was what is called a "balanced" piece, combining commendation with deprecation, mostly the gossip about Hoover that had occupied Washington cocktail parties for many years. It was not particularly friendly but it was hardly malicious. What errors of fact it contained were par for the course. But what infuriated Hoover was an allegation that his health was so precarious that he needed daily vitamin shots and an undoubtedly apochryphal story that during "a recent 24-hour stint at work, pursuing a hot case, Mr. Hoover was seen holding onto the corridor wall for support. After a moment of apparent faintness he regained his strength." The statement that at seventy-six he could put in a twenty-four hour day should have mollified Hoover, but the suggestion that he really couldn't take it nullified the compliment.

Had a Lou Nichols or a Deke DeLoach been there, the article

would have been ignored. Or a low-key letter might have gone out setting the record straight. Hoover, however—in a technique he may have learned from Lyndon Johnson—went right to the top, to William F. Kerby, president of Dow Jones, with a vitriolic protest. His letter characterized the article as "scurrilous" and as "replete with comments that are not only distorted, but are designed to undermine public confidence in me and the dedicated men and women who serve the American public so honestly, energetically, and selflessly in the ranks of the FBI" —"a slanted, unfair, and sensationalized treatment of this Bureau."

Dow Jones Publications, through its executive editor, immediately asked Hoover for a bill of particulars. FBI researchers could have picked holes in a number of anecdotes presented by the *National Observer*. But instead, Hoover dictated a ten-page answer designed to show the irresponsibility of the reporter who had written the story. Noting that most of the critical comments in the piece were attributed to anonymous sources, a common enough practice in Washington reporting, Hoover then attributed, if only by juxtaposition, a specific passage to this kind of faceless accusation. But the writer had very carefully stated in the article that the source of this anecdote was former Attorney General Francis Biddle. Hoover might have taken exception to what Biddle had written, but he could not fault the *National Observer* reporter for quoting Biddle's words. Henry Gemmill, the editor of the *National Observer,* with sound debater's instincts, seized on this, reproducing in the published exchange of correspondence the page from Biddle's book which recounted the anecdote Hoover had said was false. The rest of his answer was not so persuasive, but that one gross slip was enough to discredit Hoover and make him look foolish.

Newspaper files are full of letters from Hoover denying and assailing other stories about him. In many cases, such as one taking exception to one of the gossip columnist Jack Anderson's typical flights of fancy, Hoover was absolutely correct, but his rhetorical overkill destroyed his point. Hoover later handled Anderson far more effectively when, in a speech to the Society of Former Special Agents of the FBI, he remarked:

There are some who maintain that the only reason I am staying on as Director of the FBI is to be present at the dedication [of the new FBI Building]—a structure which congressional interference has turned into one of the slowest and most expensive buildings to rise in Washington. This is absolute nonsense. At the rate the building is going up, none of us will be around by the time it is completed. This, of course, is the fervent wish of some of my more virulent critics. One of them —his name escapes me for the moment—has apparently fallen off his merry-go-round once too often.

Last spring he spent considerable time sifting through my garbage. I'm not complaining, mind you. In fact, my only reason for mentioning it is that I understand he is becoming increasingly confused between the trash he examines and the trash he writes. Remarkably consistent in his disregard for the truth, my personal garbage sorter recently alleged that I had censured and transferred an FBI agent because he was not properly attired at the time he killed an armed hijacker holding a stewardess hostage at the Kennedy Airport in New York. [Anderson had reported that the FBI marksman had been disciplined because he was not wearing a jacket when drawing a bead on the hijacker—a story that only Anderson could print seriously.] You may be sure that no such censure has ever included anything like the commendation and the $500 check that this cool-headed young man received for averting what could have been a real tragedy. Under the circumstances, is it any wonder that there are some who question the accuracy, no less the integrity and motives of some so-called news scavengers?

The publication of drivel, while admittedly a right, is not the best way of discharging the precious responsibilities of a free press. Criticism, of course, is essential in our democratic society—but criticism, to be valid, must be based on knowledge and a desire to correct deficiencies . . . Criticism without basis is demoralizing and serves the interests of those subversives and criminals who seek to serve themselves and not democracy. . . .*

*Some of Anderson's sniping at Hoover consisted of such earth-shaking disclosures as the fact that Hoover prepared a daily menu for his housekeeper, written on an office memo pad; that he sometimes took Gelusil for stomach acidity and Cepacol for a sore throat; that his garbage contained empty soft-drink bottles; that he drank Jack Daniels Black Label and brushed his teeth with Ultra-Brite; that he wrote letters to the elderly widow of his physician and close friend, ending them "Affectionately" or "With Love"; that a Hoover

Some of the criticism was inconsequential, but Hoover felt that he was called upon to answer it. For example, in 1969, a Trans-World Airlines plane was hijacked by one Raffaele Mini-chiello. When the plane landed in New York en route to Rome, the FBI tried to board it. The pilot, Donald J. Cook, for reasons of his own and the crew's safety, refused to allow this. In Rome, he told reporters, "The FBI plan was damned near a prescription for getting the entire crew killed and the plane destroyed. The FBI just thought they were playing Wyatt Earp and wanted to engage in a shoot-out with a *supposed* criminal and bring him to justice." (Emphasis added.)

Instead of letting the public arrive at its own conclusions, Hoover felt impelled to write a letter to Charles C. Tillinghast, the TWA president, to inform him of Cook's "difficulties in the Air Force" when he was in the service. What those difficulties were, Tillinghast would not disclose, but by making public the existence of Hoover's letter, he gave Senator George McGovern the opportunity to make a charge, based on refutable hearsay, that the Director had refused to allow air marshals on TWA planes. Hoover's letter became part of a new image of "vindictiveness."

The floodgates had been opened, and any charge against Hoover or the FBI found credence in the public prints. Even when the FBI acted properly, there were those who carped, and Hoover's anger was great when the *Washington Post* published a story on page one headed, "FBI Bungles a Hijacking." The facts were simple enough. A hijacker had commandeered a small twin-engine plane dragging his wife along in a kidnap attempt. When the plane landed in Jacksonville bound for the Bahamas, the FBI—on Hoover's instructions—refused to let it be refueled. There was some danger to the pilot, but Hoover held that allowing hijackers to have their way simply encour-

nephew went into debt to pay for the hire of a nurse for his mother; and that Hoover had spent several vacations in La Jolla as the guest of an oil millionaire. In the area of myth, Anderson wrote that Hoover had transferred an agent because his sideburns were too long.

aged others to go out and do likewise. In the shooting that followed the FBI's attempt to capture the hijacker, he killed the pilot, his own wife, and himself.

Days later, the *Post* ran its story. It was based on what the paper romantically called "a hitherto secret transcript of the last transmissions between the pilot and authorities"—a tape routinely made by the Federal Aeronautics Administration and turned over to the *Post* reporter for reasons undisclosed. The transcript offered a verbatim text for what had already been published. But the *Post* story included a brief paragraph, high up, stating as fact that after the tragic shooting someone in the control tower, presumably an FBI man, had quipped, "You can't win 'em all." The last line of the story lamely stated that this remark was not on the FAA tape but reported by anonymous "sources." No proof of this was ever offered, but it was enough to make waves for Hoover.

Trouble comes in bunches, but for Hoover in the last years of his stewardship, it came in a torrent. There was, to begin with, the case of Jack Shaw, one of a group of FBI agents sent to John Jay College of Criminal Justice in New York for special training. While there, he had heard Dr. Abraham Blumberg, one of his professors, deliver a lecture sharply and inaccurately critical of the FBI and J. Edgar Hoover. Three months later, for no apparent reason, Shaw wrote a long letter to Blumberg in which he took issue with the manner in which Hoover ran the FBI, the way he maintained discipline, and how he reacted to bad publicity. He concluded his letter by asking Blumberg that it be kept in "complete confidence" because, "in the Bureau's eyes, however academically intended, my statements would constitute a *prima facie* case of heresy." But having offered his caveat, Shaw inexplicably turned it over to the FBI typing pool which, as he well knew, would bring it to the attention of his superiors. This was precisely what happened, with scraps of the letter fished out of wastepaper baskets ending up on Hoover's desk. Shaw clearly had violated a long-standing FBI rule that if there were any complaints, they should be handled internally, and Hoover sent Shaw a telegram censuring his "atrocious judgment" and transferring him to the Butte, Montana, field office. Shaw refused to accept the transfer, arguing that he did not like the post and that it was an FBI "Siberia"—and he resigned. Hoover accepted the resignation "with prejudice." Shaw thereupon took his case to the newspapers and the courts, contending that he had been victimized by a "capricious and vindictive act of personal retribution." In the press, Shaw was offered instant martyrdom, and Hoover, though dealing with an insubordinate agent, removed the prejudicial comment from Shaw's record and paid him $1,300 in back pay.

The major embarrassment to Hoover came not from the suit that Shaw had filed but from the intervention of Senator McGovern. Taking to the Senate floor on February, 1, 1971, McGovern called to the attention of his colleagues an "appalling situation." At the same time, he introduced into the *Congressional Record* a news account of the Shaw case and the full text of the offending letter. That this text existed raised some interesting questions, for Shaw had fervently assured his FBI superiors that he had destroyed it and therefore could not produce it to sustain his insistence that it was basically a defense of the Bureau. This should have raised other questions about Shaw's good faith. Further compromising Shaw was his admission in this "academic" document that much of his criticism was based on gossip rather than first-hand observation. And though it made some defense against charges that Hoover was a Nazi, it struck hard at the Director. At one point for example, it said:

Tradition has its place, but in the Bureau, apparently this means dragging out the skeletal remains of John Dillinger, "Baby Face" Nelson and "Machine Gun" Kelly at every law enforcement luncheon, and today when there is justifiable concern over international espionage who is really impressed with the FBI's capture of bumbling Nazi saboteurs landing a U-boat [*sic*] during World War II? We are not simply rooted in tradition. We're stuck in it up to our eye-balls. And it all revolves around one key figure, viz., the life and exploits of J. Edgar

Hoover. . . . The Bureau offends the sensitive critic by the way in which it projects its image—with the deft subtlety of a sledge-hammer.

But what was most objectionable in the letter, written to a professor who had repeated in class some of the more outlandish accusations against the FBI, was Shaw's account of how a man advanced within what he described as a "paramilitary system." The method? "Well, there are lots of ways. Requesting a 'personal interview' with Mr. Hoover is probably the most frequently used avenue to advancement," Shaw had written. "Within the allotted few minutes of time, apparently countless Bureau executives today were able to impress 'the man' with their latent leadership capabilities . . .

"I cannot draw on personal experience in this area, but from 'reliable sources' I am led to believe that the personal interview with Mr. Hoover runs as follows: 1) Preliminary greeting and handshake 2) the agent expressing his desire for promotional consideration . . . 3) a brief 'sounding out' and shop-talk about current cases of national interest 4) posing for the official full-profile, colored photograph and 5) farewell handshake. Within this brief period (reportedly timed by stop-watch buffs between 3 and 5 minutes) the Director passes on the merits of the candidate and jots his cryptic analysis on a memo attached to the government personnel file. There are no statistics on how many of the current Bureau hierarchy were catapulted onto the promotional ladder by the formula described above. Speculation is that a considerable number were . . . I would even argue that a mental incompetent (provided only that he wore a dark suit and were otherwise well-groomed) could play an impressive role for so brief a span."

There were other and equally snide references to the Bureau Shaw was presumably defending, which would have warranted his separation and certainly exposed his "atrocious judgment," but they were lost to McGovern. He returned to the fray, holding that Hoover was in "contempt" of the Congress because he had refused to give Senator Edward M. Kennedy further explanations on the grounds that the Shaw case was being litigated and that he therefore would be violating the instructions of the Attorney General if he discussed it. McGovern then brandished a newspaper clipping, a letter to the newspaper which had published the first story on the Shaw case, and told the Senate that whereas Hoover refused to answer questions because of the litigation, he felt free to comment to the press. Because of this "contemptuous action," McGovern called for an investigation of Hoover. Senator Roman Hruska set the record straight by informing the Senate that Hoover's explanation to the press had been written prior to the filing of the Shaw suit, whereas his reply to Kennedy followed it—something McGovern had not considered. "A false issue," said McGovern. And he introduced an anonymous letter "from ten present agents of the FBI" attacking Hoover. When twenty-one officials and agents responded with signed letters to McGovern, he saw it as a plot. Amusingly, in deploring their answers, he got at least one name wrong—that of Hoover's top assistant to whom he referred as "a Mr. Thomas Sullivan." (The name was William.)

Even Vice President Spiro Agnew got into the controversy. McGovern, Agnew quoted, had said that "there is no doubt in my mind that virtually every political figure, every student activist, every leader for peace and social justice, is under the surveillance of the FBI." And Agnew replied:

Even if the FBI were to use as few as four agents per 24-hour day* to keep these political figures under surveillance . . . it would tie up 2,140 agents just to keep an eye on the members of Congress. Since the FBI has a total of only 8,365 agents throughout the entire nation—and the great majority of these operate outside Washington—the agency would be hard-pressed indeed to keep the members of Congress under surveillance. And this doesn't even begin to consider other political figures or Senator McGovern's generous additions of "every student activist, every leader for peace and social justice." Heaven only knows how many of those there are."

*Agnew underestimated the number. Full surveillance would require six.

• 349 •

But the Shaw case was a minor irritant when compared to the troubles which followed the theft of 1,200 documents from the FBI field office in Media, Pennsylvania. That an FBI office had been broken into and all its records stolen was humiliating enough. But among those documents were investigative reports which referred to informants by name. Those informants had been painstakingly recruited, and their usefulness was now ended. But when the newspapers and interested parties began to receive Xerox copies of these documents, forwarded to them by the "Citizens' Commission to Investigate the FBI," a shadowy group which claimed credit for the robbery but never stopped to take a bow, Hoover and the FBI became targets for much condemnation and even more ridicule. A careful choice of documents from which an even more careful selection of quotes was published put the routine work of the Bureau in observing and recording subversive activities in a ridiculous or vicious light.

Much was made of the fact that a telephone operator at Swarthmore College had allowed an FBI agent to see the long-distance telephone records of a philosophy professor—presumably a horrendous invasion of privacy. But the Bureau's reason for its interest in the professor was never mentioned—namely that he was under suspicion of having harbored several fugitives from justice. There was much hilarity because a letter from the leader of a Boy Scout troop, seeking help from the Soviet Embassy in connection with a projected trip to the Soviet Union, was found in the Media papers. There was more hilarity because one of the documents referred to the investigation of a traveler to East Germany who had visited a number of Communist camps. When it was discovered that the subject was fourteen years old, the FBI had dropped the case. Here again, one pertinent fact was omitted: The FBI had taken up the investigation at the request of United States military authorities in Bonn, Germany.

The easy accusation of "racism" was thrown at Hoover and the FBI because of certain documents ordering agents to re-

cruit informants in the ghettos. But the FBI directive specifically stated that the purpose of this recruitment program was
to give the Bureau possible advance warning of riots and other
outbursts, at a time when the nation's ghettos were tinder-dry
and law enforcement agencies were expecting, and frequently
got, serious disturbances in which lives were endangered and
property destroyed.

The greatest outcry, however, was provoked because among
the Media papers was an investigative report on Jacqueline
Reuss, daughter of Representative Henry Reuss, a Wisconsin
Democrat. The FBI's interest in Miss Reuss was understandable; she was active in Students for a Democratic Society, the
extreme radical group which served as seed bed for much of
the campus violence of the late sixties. That interest, moreover,
was not unique. CIA and the police departments of Philadelphia and Milwaukee were also maintaining files on the congressman's daughter.

The least of the crimes attributed to the FBI in this case was
"invasion of privacy," the most serious, that it was a flanking
attack on the Congress, with implications that if Miss Reuss
had been, say, a plumber's daughter, the FBI's interest would
not have been so heinous. Few bothered to determine precisely
what the FBI had in its Jacqueline Reuss file or where her
privacy had been invaded. This, however, is what the Media
field office had on Miss Reuss—none of it potential blackmail
material:

MEMORANDUM
TO   DIRECTOR, FBI
FROM   SAC, PHILADELPHIA (100–51799)
SUBJECT   JACQUELINE REUSS
            INFORMATION CONCERNING—
            SECURITY MATTER

Re Bureau airtels to Alexandria, Et Al, 10/30/70 and 11/12/70.
  MARJORIE WEBB, Secretary to the Registrar, Swarthmore College,
Swarthmore, Pa., an established source who requests that her identity
be protected, on 11/17/70 advised the files of that office indicate that

• 351 •

one JACQUELINE REUSS was born 10/15/49 at Paris, France, and is an American citizen. She listed her residence as 470 North Street, Southwest, Washington, D.C., 20024. She listed her father as HENRY S. REUSS and her mother as MARGARET MAGRATH REUSS, same address as mentioned above. The records indicate that she graduated in June 1967 from Sidwell Friends School, Washington, D.C., and started at Swarthmore College as a freshman in September 1967. The records indicated that she attended the Aiv-Marseilles, Avignon, France. The following two semesters she attended the Paris—X in Nanterre, France. She subsequently returned to Swarthmore College in September 1970 where she is presently attending school. Her major is French and has many courses in the liberal arts field. Her residence while attending Swarthmore College is listed as 905 South 47th Street, Philadelphia. It was noted that in June 1969 she requested a transcript of her credits be sent to the University of Wisconsin.

For the rest, the Media papers simply dealt with FBI business. One memo reported on a Rochester, New York, police department program to enlist the Boy Scouts in the war on crime. Another detailed how FBI offices were linked to the National Crime Information Center so as to be able to trace any firearm, car, person, etc. Memos outlined procedures for handling Army deserters, fugitives, etc. A very precise directive told special agents exactly what authorization they needed for the use of telephone taps. This spelled out the provisions of the Omnibus Crime Control Act of 1968. There were reports on demonstrations and demonstrators, on investigations, etc. Transcripts of telephone taps on the Black Panthers were part of the Media papers. There were instructions on how to cope with rioters and a long catalogue of various incidents.

The Reuss case, however, revived the old stories of an FBI secret dragnet and of the "inhibiting" effect of FBI dossiers. It was an old story, given wide currency by such writers as Tom Wicker of the *New York Times* and Victor Navasky. In 1969, Navasky had written dramatically that "a leaked file, a damaging rumor can, of course, ruin a career. When an Attorney General leaves office, his private files go with him, his official ones go to the archives; but the FBI files—drenched in 'raw, unevaluated data'—remain. And so the Director—with the FBI files as his private library—is de facto caretaker to the nation's reputations." Wicker had carried this theme a little further, in a damned-if-you-do-damned-if-you-don't formulation:

"When the Bureau broke up a homosexual ring," he wrote, "they [*sic*] found that one of the victims was a member of Congress from an eastern state. Wealthy and a father, he had paid blackmail to keep concealed a homosexual episode with a member of the ring. The FBI has carefully kept his secret; it did not, for instance, call him as a witness; it has let him know that he has nothing to worry about—which guarantees, of course, that he is one of the best "friends" the Bureau has on Capitol Hill."

Hoover's answer to this was that the "member of Congress" was not called, like others caught in the toils of the blackmail ring, because his testimony was not necessary. "In any case, the decision was not the Bureau's to make," Hoover said, "but the Attorney General's. We did not and do not make the names of such people public. But had we done so, the press would have been the first to condemn us, just as it condemns us now for remaining silent." But the Media disclosures and the Reuss case had barely begun to ease their way out of the headlines before Hoover was struck again—and again.

His position was by now completely defensive. There were daily news stories that President Nixon was looking for ways to force him out of the Bureau, that the Administration was deeply concerned over his declining powers and the Bureau's sagging morale—two articles of faith among his critics. It was rumored that the President was thinking of kicking him upstairs or of finding him a sinecure with an imposing title. Hoover was aware that the Bureau was not functioning as efficiently as it once had. But he ascribed this not to his policies or to administrative hardening of the arteries but to the rising hue and cry against him. Though his relations with Attorney General John Mitchell were excellent, his direct line to the White House was no longer dependable. Hoover therefore sought to strengthen his ties with Congress. This was a conscious policy and had been one ever since President Nixon had turned over full control of the Bureau to Attorney General Mitchell. But it blew up in Hoover's face late in 1970 when he was testifying in closed session before the Senate subcommittee on Deficiencies and Supplemental Appropriations. Had Louis Nichols still been assistant director, Hoover would never have allowed himself to enter the dangerous preserves of unresolved cases. But Hoover was not only seeking an additional $14 million to increase the number of agents in the FBI, he was also demonstrating to the assembled senators his candor with them. As a veteran of the Washington wars, he should have known that what he said would find its way, either openly or by leak, into the public prints. But in trying to show the magnitude of the FBI's problems, he went further than prudence should have dictated.

Hoover's November 27, 1970, testimony, issued to the press by the subcommittee on the day it was given, was for the most part unexceptionable. Hoover reported to the senators that "some six hundred additional agents will be assigned to racketeer infiltration of legitimate business, with more to be required in the future." He reported further that "as of November 16, 1970, the FBI operated twenty-one telephone surveillances based on authority contained in nine court orders." Nine other telephone taps were awaiting installation based on four court orders. Requests for thirty-five other other telephone surveillances and one microphone surveillance awaited clearance from the Assistant Attorney General of the Justice Department's criminal division. Based on information obtained from the surveillances, more than two hundred arrests had been made during the past eleven months, including three top leaders of the Cosa Nostra.

"We conservatively estimate we will require an additional four hundred agents to handle the initial investigative work acruing under the bombing aspects of the Organized Crime Control Act of 1970, as well as to handle the mounting work being required in connection with other campus violence, aircraft hijackings, and New Left and black extremists," Hoover said, then noted that in the 1969–70 academic year, some 1,800 student demonstrations had taken place, with over 7,500 arrests, 464 injuries (two thirds to police), eight deaths, 247 arsons, and 313 sit-ins or building seizures. ROTC facilities had been targeted 282 times. Property damage was more than $9.5 million. And, he pointed out, just the probe of the killing of four Kent State (Ohio) students had cost the Bureau $274,100, with the 302 agents assigned to the case putting in 6,316 hours of overtime.

And then Hoover slipped. He told the senators:

Willingness to employ any type of terrorist tactics is becoming increasingly apparent among extremist elements. One example has recently come to light involving an incipient plot on the part of an anarchist group on the East Coast, the so-called "East Coast Conspiracy to Save Lives." This is a militant group self-described as being composed of Catholic priests and nuns, teachers, students and former students who have manifested opposition to the war in Vietnam by acts of violence against government agencies and private corporations engaged in work relating to U.S. participation in the Vietnam conflict.

The principal leaders of this group are Philip and Daniel Berrigan, Catholic priests who are currently incarcerated in the Federal Correctional Institution at Danbury, Connecticut, for their participation in the destruction of Selective Service records in Baltimore, Maryland, in 1968.

This group plans to blow up underground electrical conduits and steam pipes serving the Washington, D.C., area in order to disrupt Federal Government operations. The plotters are also concocting a scheme to kidnap a highly placed government official. The name of a White House staff member has been mentioned as a possible victim. If successful, the plotters would demand an end to United States bombing operations in Southeast Asia with the release of all political prisoners as ransom. Intensive investigation is being conducted concerning this matter.

When Hoover's testimony appeared in the newspapers, it caused a sensation. Anti-Vietnam violence had been great, but here was a revolutionary plot to attack the Federal government frontally and to commit perhaps the most hated crime of all, short of murder and rape—kidnapping. On the one hand, there was consternation and fear. But even friends of the FBI were startled that Hoover should have disclosed—even at a closed Senate committee meeting—details of so serious a case while it was still in the investigative stage. Without knowing any more than what Hoover had testified—with the one additional fact that the White House staffer slated for kidnapping was Henry Kissinger, perhaps the closest adviser to President Nixon—the inevitable protestations of innocence for those named filled the air. William J. Kunstler, a flamboyant and expensive defender of radicals ensnared by the law, shouted that it was a "far-fetched spy story" designed to increase the FBI's appropriation. "If Mr. Hoover had the evidence he claims to have," Kunstler said, "then it would be his sworn duty to see that the Berrigans and their alleged co-conspirators are prosecuted for serious crimes."

Representative William R. Anderson, a Tennessee Democrat, wrote Hoover defending the Berrigans as having "followed a course of total non-violence toward their fellow human beings" —a slight exaggeration—and adding: "If there is any substance to your allegations against the Berrigans, Mr. Hoover, I respectfully submit that it is your duty to arraign them before a Federal grand jury to seek an indictment. If, on the other hand, there is no substance, or if your remarks were misconstrued, then certainly we would expect an explanation if not an outright retraction."

The East Coast Conspiracy held a press conference at which Hoover was denounced and categorical denials were made that there was any truth, or even a semblance of truth, in Hoover's testimony. The condemnation was such that the FBI was compelled to complete its case hastily, without its usual precision, so that it could be presented to a grand jury. The Berrigans and others were indicted and tried. But though the government was able to show that what Hoover alleged had been contemplated and discussed approvingly, it could not prove to the satisfaction of the jury that the plot had been more than romantic talk. Much of the government's case, moreover, depended on the testimony of an informant with a seedy and compromised past. The government had counted heavily on the cross examination of the defendants, but when they failed to take the stand, the prosecution was left with insufficient evidence to remove reasonable doubt. The jury failed to convict, and the blame fell to Hoover.

In the months that followed, as the "dump Hoover" movement gained adherents in the Congress, the Director became more aloof and more embittered. He continued to make it clear that he would not resign until his health demanded it. But he was becoming a political liability to the Administration and there was a new spate of rumors that his separation was being seriously discussed by the President and his staff. Like much "inside" Washington news, this was based on conjecture rather than fact, but it only served to cause restlessness in FBI ranks, and efforts by some Bureau officials to by-pass the Director and deal directly with the Justice Department's topside.

In April 1971, however, one attack on Hoover backfired badly and won him considerable sympathy—even some quasi-kind words from the *Washington Post,* which, with the New *York Times,* usually led the anti-FBI opposition. Without warning, Representative Hale Boggs of Louisiana, the Majority Leader of the House, took the floor to demand Hoover's resignation.

"When the FBI taps the telephones of members of this body and of members of the Senate . . . when the FBI adopts the tactics of the Soviet Union and Hitler's Gestapo, then it is time —it is way past time—that the present Director thereof no longer be the Director," said Boggs. And he later repeated the accusation that Hoover was tapping House and Senate phones, promising to produce evidence from his own personal experience and from that of other members of Congress.*

*This was an old and recurring accusation. As far back as 1940, when it was aired on the floor of Congress, Hoover made a categorical denial. The basis for the controversy was a paragraph from an article by columnist Raymond Clapper. "The other big complaint here now is that the FBI is tapping phones all over the place, collecting dossiers on politicians and officials, as well as on private citizens, and serving as an Ogpu. Those charges ought to be investi-

The Boggs animosity was understandable. The previous year, he had been the subject of an FBI investigation, made at the request of the Justice Department, into his connections with Victor J. Frenkil, a Baltimore contractor who was pressing a multimillion dollar claim against the government for work he had performed in the construction of a congressional garage. The investigation showed that Frenkil had sought the help of Boggs in the case—and had also remodeled the Majority Leader's own garage at "substantially below cost" according to a Federal grand jury. His onslaught, the *National Observer* commented, "could be dismissed as the emotional reaction of a man who can never forgive the FBI for investigating him."

Having waved his spear, however, Boggs turned reluctant about the "evidence" he had said was his. When critics of the FBI, who had seen in his attack the first real chance of solid evidence in an area which would destroy Hoover's Capitol Hill support, prodded Boggs, he finally came up with as feeble a story as Congress had heard in many years. Suspecting that his phone was tapped, Boggs told his colleagues, "he had called the Chesapeake & Potomac Telephone Company." One of the company's investigators, Boggs said, "determined that a tap had been placed on my private telephone line but it had been removed in advance of the inspection." Boggs never explained how this could be "determined" since tapping today is done by induction coil and leaves no traces. But the Boggs explanation suffered an even worse fate. *National Oberver* reporters checked with C&P. Two investigators, they were informed, had checked the Boggs phone at his request. "They found no tap and no evidence that there had ever been one," the company said. "They so informed Mr. Boggs directly."

But Hale Boggs continued the battle. He named seven lawmakers who "believed" but had no proof that phones were being tapped. He cited the case of Representative John Dowdy of

gated. Sometimes people think they are being spied on when there is nothing following them except a guilty conscience."

Texas, then under indictment and later convicted of having received a $25,000 bribe. One of those implicated had allowed the FBI to place a tap on *his* phone, and three conversations with Dowdy had been recorded. This "consentual" tap had been installed with a court order, though none was needed. An informant with a tiny tape recorder strapped to his back had spoken to Dowdy in his office, like the earlier instance ruled legal by the Supreme Court. The Boggs accusation, therefore, fell apart, though an effort to keep it alive was made by columnist Jack Anderson, who further embarrassed the Majority Leader by writing that Hoover had spread rumors that Boggs was drunk when he made his initial speech. Since that had been the reaction of many Washington newspapermen almost immediately after wire service printers were clattering out the story, the Anderson "revelation" merely damaged Boggs without helping his case.

The significance of the Boggs caper was not in what it had proved about Hoover—which was nothing—but in the alacrity with which the original denunciation was picked up. A few years before, it would have been met by a storm of denunciation. But even the vindication of Hoover, though it brought him some sympathy and some expressions of regret and support, was a watershed in his career. Attorney General Mitchell could respond by calling on the recalcitrant congressman to "recant at once and apologize to a great American." But the *New York Times,* though gently deploring what it almost conceded were irresponsible charges, nevertheless used them in an editorial which discovered "the hard truth" that the FBI needed "not only a new director but also a major reorganization" and cited unnamed "professionals in the law enforcement field" who asserted that "many of the FBI's methods are outdated and its procedures and organization unresponsive to the central problems it should be tackling."

That argument was echoed by more than a few who had in the past championed the Hoover cause with passion. What methods and procedures were unresponsive and outdated did not figure in the debate. For simultaneous with these disparagements were expressions of fear because Hoover had initiated the use of computers to expedite and systematize the correlation of information on criminals and organized crime—the area in which it was charged he was weakest and most stick-in-the-mud. The patter had been set, and for the first time in an official lifetime which had seen him frequently embattled but always secure, it became open season on John Edgar Hoover.

23.

The Stormy Final Years—II

A STUDENT OF POLITICS, SEARCHING THE KITCHEN MIDDENS OF OUR
contemporary history, would probably find that the date at
which the sustained and almost organized onslaught on John
Edgar Hoover began was years before the late Sixties and early
Seventies. The causative factor was the appointment of Ramsey Clark by President Johnson to the sensitive office of Attorney General. Clark, whose philosophy of law enforcement led
a Washington wit to describe him as "a conscientious objector
in the war against crime," took over his office as a full professor
in a school which teaches that the victim is more responsible
than the aggressor, and that the real culprit is society and not
the criminal.*

*He obviously shared Karl Marx's view that "neither a nation nor a woman can
be forgiven for the unguarded hour in which a chance comer has seized the
opportunity for an act of rape."

In 1970 Clark would codify his philosophy in *Crime In America,* a turgid treatise reflecting the thesis that "crime reflects the character of a people . . . Crime reflects more than the character of the pitiful few who commit it. It reflects the character of the entire society . . . If we are to deal meaningfully with crime, what must be seen is the dehumanizing effect on the individual of slums, racism, ignorance and violence . . . of poverty and unemployment and idleness, of generations of malnutrition . . . of sickness and disease . . . of avarice, anxiety, fear, hatred, hopelessness, and injustice." That he should have seen in these "the fountainheads of crime" at a time when the sharpest rise in criminal activity was in the affluent suburbs and among those who had led pampered lives—a fact thoroughly documented in the reports which he must have read as Attorney General—defies logic.

From the very start of his tenure, it was clear that Attorney General Clark was intent on continuing the hidden war against Hoover which had begun under Robert F. Kennedy. He was aware that he could not fire Hoover, but he could destroy him, and in the years that he served, the Justice Department became an instrumentality for achieving that purpose. Hoover had the ear of the President who told him, as he had before when controversy between Attorney General and FBI Director reached an acrimonious pitch, to "stick to your guns." But everything Clark stood for, from his sociological vaporings to his contention that the violence of the period represented legitimate dissent, was anathema to Hoover. Like Bobby Kennedy, moreover, Clark wanted the FBI to lower its employment standards—a degree in law or accounting being among those he considered onerous—so as to open the doors to the "minorities." As he had with Kennedy, Hoover refused flatly to accommodate himself to this aim—and relations between the two men, and between the FBI and the rest of the Justice Department, were at best strained.

That the two men stood diametrically opposed was known to even the most casual newspaper reader, but their differences were first openly aired when they were called to testify before the National Commission on the Causes and Prevention of Violence, appointed by President Johnson to investigate the assassination of Robert F. Kennedy and the violence which was racking the country. At its first working session, in September 1968, both witnesses discussed the rioting that dislocated the Democratic National Convention in Chicago that summer. Said Hoover:

Months before the (convention) was held, authorities were fully aware that it was the target of disruption and violence . . . During the course of the convention, demonstrators . . . called the police "pigs" and shouted obscenities at them, spit at them, and threw bags of excrement and urine and dangerous objects—such as golf balls with protruding nails—at them. Unruly and menacing mobs gathered, intent on . . . disrupting the convention . . . It is a tribute to the authorities that under these chaotic conditions—deliberately created by ruthless, lawless leaders— . . . the city was not disrupted, not one shot was fired by police at the demonstrators, and not one life was lost . . .

Crime and violence are increasing primarily because there is a mass deterioration in the respect shown for the rule of law in our nation and for some who enforce it . . . Heightening the atmosphere of resentment of authority and irresponsibility to others in our society is the all-too-prevalent defiance of duly established laws and rules that is euphemistically termed "civil disobedience." . . . An attitude of permissiveness . . . has actually been fostered by too many educators, sociologists, clergymen, public officials, and parents . . . There exists a softness and tolerance toward those who violate laws on the flimsy pretext of "conscience" or personal judgment of the "justness" of laws.

It was as direct a rebuke of Clark as Hoover could make without actually naming him, and it was so meant. Clark, of course, saw elsewhere the causes of violence: "Skillful psychological build-ups designed to create apprehension" in the public; "police violence in excess of authority. . . . Firm, appropriate action is necessary when the police violate the law . . . It is the duty of leadership and law enforcement to control violence, not cause it, to seek ways of relieving tension, not to look for a fight . . . An educated, informed and energetic young generation we have raised is intolerant of injustice they see all too clearly, a society that celebrates the power of violence and ignores the pity of it." Then, having found the Typhoid Mary responsible for the chaos that was epidemic at the time, he assured the commission that the chances of falling victim to it in the United States was "once in four hundred years."

There was one other point of conflict between Hoover and Clark. It was Clark's responsibility, though he never mentioned it, to supervise the surveillance operations in the United States. Among these were the harum-scarum activities of the Army's counterintelligence which included record-keeping and shadowing of private individuals nowhere remotely concerned with subversive organizations or causes. Clark had been given this assignment by President Johnson and functioned through the Inter-Divisional Intelligence Unit, which he headed and which pooled the information gathered not only by the FBI but by the Secret Service, the Pentagon, etc. Sensitive to congressional and public concern over scatter-gun approaches and the invasion of privacy, Hoover had ordered a hold-down in Bureau surveillance work. He was, moreover, opposed to having those he considered "amateurs" and "bunglers" handling what was essentially an FBI function. And he realized that when the IDIU's depredations became known, as they did when Senator Sam Ervin spread them across the nation's front pages, they would reflect on the Bureau, however much it guarded against the excesses of the other services. In this he was correct, for when the facts were publicly aired, Clark denied any knowledge with the prepared defense of "I don't care what the documents say"—which, as John P. Roche, Johnson's "intellectual in residence" and a professor at Brandeis University, would comment, was "certainly a novel approach to probative evidence" from "a distinguished lawyer." Ramsey's second line of defense was a whispering campaign blaming it all on Hoover, as well as open criticism of the FBI's lack of concern for civil rights.

Hoover's controversial relations with Clark did not end with the election of Richard Nixon and the appointment of a new

Attorney General, however. The bad blood between them continued to simmer, and it came to a boil when Clark's book, *Crime in America,* was published in 1970. Among other disparaging statements in the book was one which repeated the by-now standard line against Hoover: "The FBI has so coveted personal credit that it will sacrifice even effective crime control before it will share the glory of its exploits. This has been a petty and costly characteristic caused by the excessive domination of a single person, J. Edgar Hoover, and his self-centered concern for his reputation and that of the FBI." Clark also dismissed Hoover as too concerned with communism and not enough with the Mafia.

For Hoover, this was the final insult. Calling in Ken Clawson, a *Washington Post* reporter friendly to the FBI, Hoover struck out in what had then become his characteristic manner. Clark, said Hoover, was "like a jellyfish . . . a softie." He admitted to troubles with Robert Kennedy, with whom, he disclosed for the first time, he had not spoken for the last six months of his tenure. "If ever there was a worse Attorney General, it was Ramsey Clark," Hoover exploded. "You never knew which way he was going to flop on an issue. He was worse than Bobby. At least Kennedy stuck by his guns, even when he was wrong."

Clark answered, though not in kind. "For reasons that are unfortunate in my judgment, the FBI became ideological some time back," he told reporters. "This has put a scale over its eyes." He lamented the "terribly wasteful use of resources" by the FBI and Hoover's "intolerance of different viewpoints" and wondered aloud why the FBI was so bad at investigating "unlawful police conduct." For this, he was berated on the floor of Congress by Representative Rooney, who called him a "pusillanimous nincompoop," a "nitwit," and a "young upstart" who could "not be elected dogcatcher in any political jurisdiction in the United States." He was joined by Representative H. R. Gross, who described the former Attorney General as the leader of "ultra-permissivists" who "fawned" over "revolutionists" and "common criminals."

But the last word was Clark's. For even as the adjectives were flying, he had been organizing a conference to be held at Princeton University under the sponsorship of the Woodrow Wilson School to mount a "scholarly" inquiry into Hoover and the FBI. Joining in the call to this conference were Bobby Kennedy's Assistant Attorney General Burke Marshall and others who had crossed swords with Hoover over the years. The list of participants at this "scholarly" inquisition included Fred Cook, author of the previously mentioned antagonistic study of the FBI, who had been fired from the *New York World-Telegram* for manufacturing a story out of the whole cloth; Frank Donner, another professional enemy of the Bureau, whose appearance before a congressional committee had been marked by a repeated use of the Fifth Amendment when asked about Communist connections; Roger Wilkins, author of the rhetorical absurdity, "But how can a man or woman be considered free when he is shot in his bed as he sleeps at 5 a.m. by his local police?"; two law school professors with impressive records of affiliation with pro-Communist causes, and others of similar views. This group, the advance publicity promised, would present a "clear, dispassionate review" of the FBI's sins, and having conducted a fair trial would proceed to give Hoover an even fairer hanging.

Though one Princeton professor said unblushingly that the conference had "no vested interest in reaching a particular result," it performed as expected. Its high point came when one speaker charged the FBI with suborning murder. But so loaded were the dice that the Princeton conference defeated its own purposes. Walter Goodman, writing in the *New Leader* from a liberal position, summed it up thusly: "An exhibition such as the one put on in Princeton is scholarship as understood by Mark Rudd [leader of the Columbia University riots] and Ronald Reagan . . . For scholars to take part in this kind of sport is demeaning of themselves, demoralizing for the university, and a shameful perversion of a high calling."

The attacks on Hoover, however, mounted almost daily. And

they were taking a new form highly disturbing to him. For the second time in President Nixon's term, there was a spate of press reports that the White House wanted the Director out, that he was becoming an embarrassment to the Administration. There were reports of meetings between the President and his top advisers to discuss the "Hoover question." These reports always referred to unnamed Administration sources who unanimously agreed that Hoover was a good man but that he had outlived his usefulness. The question, according to these sources, was how to get rid of Hoover without making political trouble for the Republicans.

If there was any truth to these stories, it could not be determined by any objective research. At most, they reflected the thinking of a few individuals on the White House staff but could not be linked to the President. And though Hoover reiterated in public and private conversation that he had no intention of resigning, nor had it been suggested that he should, the reports of his liquidation persisted—to the point that Nixon felt called upon to scotch them. At a press conference, he said in answer to a reporter's question: "I am not going to discuss the situation with regard to Hoover's tenure in office when the matter has not been raised with me, either by me or by him. I will only say at this time that I believe it would be most unfortunate to allow a man who has given fifty years, over fifty years, of dedicated service to this country to go out under a cloud, maligned unfairly by many critics." He made the same point in another form.

"I haven't discussed Mr. Hoover's retirement with him," he said in answer to a further prod. "He has not brought it up with me. But if I know Mr. Hoover, such unfair and malicious criticism would tend to have exactly the opposite effect, not to hasten his retirement but to have him dig in."

The President's comment was reinforced by one from Ronald L. Ziegler, the White House press secretary, who brushed aside as "political" the criticism of the Bureau's techniques and activities. Ziegler was referring to a speech made several days before by Senator Edmund Muskie. Taking to the Senate floor, Muskie had said:

I have recently read an FBI Intelligence report written by an agent assigned to cover the Earth Day Rally in Washington last year. Among those whose political actions were reported for the benefit of our criminal, military, and security Intelligence agencies was myself. The FBI report mentions no hint of violence, no threat of insurrection, and no foreboding of illegal behavior . . . I understand that this is but one of about forty to sixty FBI reports of Earth Day rallies on April 22, 1970. I know that at least one other member of this body, and probably others, had some of their speeches and participation in Earth Day rallies subject to FBI surveillance. We must find out the scope of this surveillance over environmental groups and gatherings.

The Muskie speech was clearly "political"—and highly inaccurate. The "surveillance" of himself that he complained of consisted of one sentence in a report running to many pages, "Shortly after 8 p.m. Senator Edmund Muskie (D), Maine arrived and gave an antipollution speech." Contrary to Muskie's allegation that the FBI was conducting a surveillance of environmentalists, the record showed that his speech was just about the only one dealing with the ecology. The rest were inflammatory attacks on the government and on the "system." The FBI was there because among those who addressed the meeting was Rennie Davis, one of those convicted for inciting the riots at the Chicago Democratic convention in 1968. As Hoover would point out, "The FBI would have been derelict in its duty had it not been present when that rabblerouser was going to speak." And there was more than a "foreboding of illegal behavior"—Muskie's phrase—in Davis's remarks. He not only called for "tearing down the capitalistic structure" but urged his audience to "go to New Haven on May 1st to stop Bobby Seale's trial"—a reference to the trial of the Black Panther leader for murder. And there was more than an implied threat when he shouted that any "pigs" in the audience should get out while they could. Muskie's statement that the FBI had been present at "forty to sixty" Earth

Day rallies was cut from the whole cloth.

All these points in rebuttal were made by other senators, and Muskie was able to evoke indignation only among those who needed little encouragement.

Hoover could take comfort from citations from groups such as the National District Attorneys Association, and from the clean bill of health given to him by the Senate's outstanding constitutionalist, Senator Ervin, who announced that he had been able to find no illegal acts by the FBI. But floating over his head were injudicious or improper words he had casually uttered, such as some with which he favored *Time* magazine: "You never have to bother about a President being shot by Puerto Ricans or Mexicans. They don't shoot very straight. But if they come at you with a knife, beware"—words for which he tacitly apologized while feebly insisting that they had no racial implications. He was being condemned by the *Washington Post* because FBI agents on leave were working for the House Appropriations subcommittee, which passed on the Bureau's budget as well as those of other agencies and departments of the government. Chairman Rooney would defend the practice by pointing out what the *Post* writer, Walter Pincus, had failed to report—namely that fourteen of those departments and agencies also had men on loan to the subcommittee—but the article's needle, that the practice precluded "serious House review of the FBI," left its scar.

Everything, in fact, seemed to blow up in Hoover's face. It had been one of his rules that those in the FBI's employ should lead exemplary lives. When a young employee, who had spent the night with a girl who also worked at the Bureau—"fully clothed," they said—was fired for improper conduct, Hoover was assailed for his puritanism and for imposing his own moral views on the staff. This was recalled when two girls on the clerical staff were forced to resign. They had violated the Bureau's "no politics" rules by working nights for the National Peace Action Coalition. One of the girls had taken part in the October 1969 Vietnam Moratorium march as well as other demonstrations and when questioned by the Bureau had shown the effects of her indoctrination by describing the trial of the Chicago Seven, based on FBI investigatory work, as a "frame-up." That the girls were forced out of their jobs for giving their time and loyalty to an organization violently antagonistic to the FBI—and under FBI scrutiny—was seen as a violation of their civil rights, with Hoover as the violator.

To top it all, Hoover was named a defendant in a suit filed by two young lawyers, Cynthia Edgar and Sandra Nemser, who had applied for jobs as FBI agents but were refused because they were women and "could not handle combat situations." Perhaps the nature of their suit could have been evaluated by the witticism of their attorney, the ACLU's Philip Hirschkop, who told a press conference called on their behalf that a woman "can tap a phone as well as the next person." Now, in what had become what Representative Rooney called "an anti-FBI sweepstake," Women's Liberation had joined the race.

Turning seventy-seven on New Year's Day, 1972, Hoover let everyone know that his health was excellent, that he still had to fight against putting on weight, and that he was "feeling better than ever before." He was not retiring, he added firmly. "I don't consider my age a valid factor in assessing my ability to continue as Director of the FBI," he told an interviewer, "any more than it was when, at the youthful age of 29, I was appointed to this position. I was criticized then as 'the Boy Scout.' Now I'm called 'that senile old man.' " In celebration of his birthday, he was invited to Key Biscayne by President Nixon, an act which quieted the rumors of his imminent departure but did not still the hostility against him of a growing group of enemies. Perhaps he smiled wryly when an article about him in *Time* used as an epigraph a quotation from a current phonograph record:

NIXON. I wanted to see you to discuss with you the matter of retirement.
HOOVER. Why, that's ridiculous. You're still a young man.

But the final word was not spoken by Nixon, by Hoover, or by the critics who had for so long urged him to go. Another hand, less biased but more powerful, brought to realization the prediction of an old friend, "Edgar will never leave the Bureau until they carry him out."

Postlude: John Edgar Hoover

ON MAY DAY NIGHT, 1972, JOHN EDGAR HOOVER DIED IN HIS SLEEP. His housekeeper, Annie Fields, found him lying alongside his bed at 8:30 the following morning. The medical report gave the cause of death as "hypertensive cardio-vascular disease"—a heart attack. Irv Kupcinet, a compassionate columnist for the *Chicago Sun-Times* who knew the color of death in a personal tragedy of his own, spoke up for many Americans when he quoted an associate of Hoover: "The chief died a little with every blast from his critics." But death has its own dynamism, and those who survived him were far more concerned with the details of his interment than in any examination of what had killed him.

He could have been buried in Arlington National Cemetery where Presidents, generals, and enlisted men lie in democratic repose. As a onetime lieutenant colonel in the Army reserves, it was his right and his privilege. But he had chosen for his final resting place the Congressional Cemetery, a once-historic but now overgrown burial ground in Washington's Southeast, where he could lie next to his parents. There was poetic logic in this choice of this half-forgotten and unfashionable cemetery. It was, perhaps, his last gesture before a world that had rejected his values and substituted pomp for sorrow.

There was pomp enough in the ceremonies that marked his return to earth. He was borne in a drenching rain to the Capitol Rotunda where he lay in state—an honor accorded only to twenty-one American heroes and statesmen before him, and none of them a civil servant of minor degree in the nation's protocol of death—carried up the thirty-five steps to a hall where republican liberties are perpetuated and enshrined. The census-takers of funerals reported that one thousand of his fellow citizens passed him in sorrowful review on every hour that he lay there, his coffin resting on a catafalque built for Abraham Lincoln.

The Chief Justice of the United States, senators, congressmen, members of the Cabinet—the great and near-great of Washington's rarified society—rubbed elbows with weeping FBI clerks who had ignored Hoover's stern strictures against leaving their work, young people, and the "unimportant" of the nation's capital. It had taken an act of Congress to authorize the ceremonies in the Rotunda, but no votes had been lacking— even from those who had brought anger and frustration to Hoover's last days. In this solemn moment, Representative Hale Boggs forgot the bloody rag he had waved on the floor of the House and, in sincerity, declared that he had never criticized Hoover personally but had "said then, as I say now, that no man has served his country with greater love and dedication." There were warm words from Chief Justice Warren Burger, from John Mitchell and Richard Kleindienst, Attorneys General under whom Hoover had served—and even Jack Anderson squeezed out a few tears.

But there were others in whom the milk of human kindness had curdled who saw no reason to honor the ancient adjuration, *de mortuis nil nisi bonum*. Dr. Benjamin Spock informed the press that Hoover's death was "a great relief." Coretta King, widow of the civil rights leader, read the nation a little homily. "We are left with a deplorable and dangerous situation," she said. "The files of the FBI gathered under Mr. Hoover's supervision are replete with lies and are reported to contain sordid material on some of the highest people in government, including Presidents of the United States . . . Black people and the black freedom movement have been particular targets of this dishonorable kind of activity." Abbie Hoffman, the clown prince of revolution, tendered his joyous obscenities. And Alistair Cooke, Britain's misinterpreter of things American, characteristically distorted the Hoover record, solemnly asserting that Hoover was "skinned and deplored by civil libertarians with, at one time, only the late Senator Joseph McCarthy and Walter Winchell to serve as defenders on the flanks."

From the Rotunda, Hoover's body was carried to the National Presbyterian Church in downtown Washington. The FBI had prepared a press kit for the ceremony, "an artifact without which," columnist Richard Wilson noted, "no state funeral in Washington is complete," and it included an open letter Hoover had written to the nation's students in 1970. "You belong to the best educated, most sophisticated, most poised generation in our history," Hoover had said. "You see things wrong in our society which we adults have minimized or overlooked. You are outspoken and frank and hate hypocrisy. That is good too. There's nothing wrong with student dissent or student demands for changes in our society or the display of student unhappiness over aspects of our national policy"—words which led Wilson to conclude that Hoover was "really a much more complicated man than he had ever let anyone know."

But those who mourned in the bleak church were not reading press kits. They were listening to President Nixon's eulogy, to words which marked John Edgar Hoover as "one of the giants" of our times," "a peace officer without peer," whose "long life brimmed over with magnificent achievement." The President spoke for eleven minutes, as a watchful press noted. "His powerful leadership," he said, "helped to keep steel in America's backbone, and the flame of freedom in America's soul." The FBI would be "a living memorial" to its Director because it had been built "totally on principle, not on personality."

"The American people today are tired of disorder, disruption, and disrespect for law," Nixon continued. "America wants to come back to the law as a way of life, and as we do come back to the law, the memory of this great man, who never left the law as a way of life, will be accorded even more honor." And quoting the Psalms, he wrote the epitaph: "Great peace have they which love Thy law." From there, they carried Hoover's mortal remains to the old cemetery by the dirty waters of the Anacostia River. They presented the flag that had draped his coffin to Clyde Tolson who could only say, "Thank you. Thank you very much." The body was consigned to dust and the soul to God.

On the floor of the House, Representative John Rooney, himself beset by the encroachments of mortality, would rise and say his farewell:

Over the years I got to know Director Hoover very well and indeed we became close friends. He was, despite his unrelenting battle against crime and those who would destroy the American way of life, a truly warm, kindly man. He had at times an almost puckish sense of humor coupled with a deep respect for his fellowman . . . John Edgar Hoover's life was the FBI. It will stand as his monument and every American looking at it will know what a loss his death was to our country. Some will also have the cherished memory of a great human being.

But life moves on with an iron whim. In the days that followed, those who survived him were interested in more practical matters. He had left an estate of $551,500, the press duly noted, almost all of it going to Clyde Tolson. Seventy-two and ailing, Hoover's best friend moved immediately into the house overlooking Rock Creek and submitted his resignation from the Bureau in a one-sentence letter. The press also duly noted the other Hoover bequests—several thousands here and there to his housekeeper and to others who had worked for him, jewelry for his namesakes, and nothing to the surviving members of his family. Had Tolson pre-deceased him, the Hoover estate would have gone to the Boys Club of America and to the Damon Runyon Memorial Fund for Cancer Research, set up by Walter Winchell at the Director's suggestion.

Other men, in dying, could hope that they might rest in peace. But John Edgar Hoover had loomed too large in the affairs of America to be allowed this mercy. If he had traduced the Kennedy family in life, the foot soldiers of the Kennedy family were ready to return the favor. Before the funeral meats had chilled, Victor S. Navasky was creating a new mythology. In life, Hoover had been assailed because, presumably, those who worked for him really harbored hatred in their hearts. Now Navasky discovered that the FBI had "the allegiance of his agents." When Hoover was alive, he had been attacked for tapping Martin Luther King's telephone without the permission of Robert F. Kennedy—a demonstrably false charge. In death, however, the story changed. Hoover, according to Navasky, had "blackmailed Robert Kennedy into authorizing" those taps. The Navasky-Kennedy obituary summed up Hoover's career and his service in these words: "Trivia collector, long-distance eavesdropper, obsessive cold-warrior even before there was a Cold War, item planter, document leaker, bureaucratic blackmailer."

There was no better answer to this than the words of Senator James Buckley, writing in the same issue of the *Saturday Review* which carried Navasky's words:

I am convinced that the criticism made of J. Edgar Hoover during recent years tells us more about the intellectual and moral values of the critics and of the current level of public debate in America than it does about Mr. Hoover . . . What will remain and what will continue to shape the FBI for years to come is his vision of public service as one of the highest vocations and, like all vocations, one infused with meaning and purpose only so far as its principles are not confused with those of other callings . . . At a time when many Americans are beset by doubt, by a loss of faith in ourselves and in our basic institutions, J. Edgar Hoover's legacy can well serve as a guide to us all.

John Edgar Hoover did not wear golden shoes. He was sometimes wrong, sometimes right. But he loved America, he believed in America, and he fought for America. For most Americans, that was enough. For those who knew him, that was a beginning.

Index

Fields, Annie, 372
Fine, Gov. John S., 266
Flaxner, Abram, 269, 273
Fleming, Ian, 313
Floyd, Charles "Pretty Boy," 108, 124
Fly, James L., 175, 176, 179
Flynn, William J., 51, 61, 62, 67
Ford, Peyton, 283
Foreign Agents Registration Act, 52
Foreign Economic Administration, 216
Foreign Service, 218
Forrestal, James V., 216
Forrestal Diaries, The, 216
Fort Monmouth Signal Center, 285–287
Foster, William Z., 49, 55, 57, 63
Fotich, Constantine, 191
Fowler, Rep., 45
Frankfurter, Felix, 64
Frenkil, Victor J., 358
Frick, Henry Clay, 60
Fuchs, Klaus Emil, 212–214
Fund for the Republic, 296

G-2 (Army Intelligence), 149, 153, 157, 175, 181, 195, 203, 205–207, 286
"G-Man," 95, 105, 112
Gable, Clark, 122
Gallup Poll, 338
Game of the Foxes, The, 195
Gandy, Helen, 25, 308n.
Garrison, James, 14
Garvan, Francis P., 42, 51
Gayn, Mark, 218
Gemmill, Henry, 343
George V, 195
George, Leo, 273
George Washington University, 42
German-American Bund, 152, 157
Germany, World War I espionage, 45, 46; World War II subversion and espionage, 149, 150, 157, 158, 163, 178, 179n., 181, 182, 185–203
Gibson, Russell, 124
Gibson, Truman, Jr., 295
Gillis, Lester J., 123n.
Gold, Harry, 214, 215
Goldman, Emma, 45, 60, 61
Goldwater, Sen. Barry, 310, 311
Golos, Jacob M., 166, 245
Gompers, Samuel, 50, 55
Goodman, Andrew, 335
Goodman, Walter, 366
Gouzenko, Igor, 213
Greatest Plot in History, The, 207n., 212n.
Green, Eddie, 141
Green, Sen. Theodore, 170
Greene, Jerry, 223
Greenglass, David, 214, 215
Gregory, Dick, 335
Gregory, Thomas W., 48
Gromov, Anatole Borisovich, 245, 251
Gross, Rep. H. R., 316, 317, 320, 321, 365
Gubitchev, Valentin, 235, 237
Gurnea, Myron, 167

Halifax, Lord, 164, 195
Hall, Robert, 264, 265
Hamilton, Polly, 120–122
Harding, Warren Gamaliel, 66–68, 91, 92, 140, 313
Harding College, 311
Harvey's, 27, 28, 31

Hauptmann, Bruno Richard, 95, 98, 99, 140
Hearst, William Randolph, 139
Hearst newspapers, 223
Hickenlooper, Sen. Bourke, 303, 304
Highlander Folk School, 332
Hirschkop, Philip, 370
Hiskey, Clarence, 209–211
Hiskey, Marcia, 210
Hiss, Alger, 7, 12, 31, 114, 151, 156, 221–234, 238–241, 272, 279
Hiss, Donald, 156
Hiss, Priscilla, 227–234
Hitler, Adolf, and Nazi Germany, 151, 154, 197, 221, 222, 263
Hitz, John, 36
Hitz, William, 42
Hoffa, James, 294
Hoffman, Abbie, 374
Hollis, Herman, 123n.
Holmes, Oliver Wendell, 50, 269
Hoover, Annie M. Scheitlin, 36, 37, 41, 42
Hoover, Dickerson, Jr., 37, 41
Hoover, Dickerson, Sr., 36, 37, 41
Hoover, Halstead Peirce, 39
Hoover, Herbert, 70, 71, 99, 250, 288
Hoover, J. Edgar, respect of FBI agents for him, 7, 8, 339; daily routine, 25–30; childhood, 35–41; college years, 41, 42; early days at Justice Department, 42–46, 51–66; early study of radicalism, and actions against, 44–46, 51–66; transfer to Bureau of Investigation, 67–71; direction of the Bureau, 71–91; the crime years, 92–99, 102–145; relations with FDR Administrations, 99–101, 108, 140–142, 159–161, 164, 165, 170, 171; relations with Kennedys, 285, 291, 294–300, 302, 305–330, 332, 333, 336, 337, 348, 349, 362, 363, 365, 366, 376; and JFK assassination, 298–300, 302, 308n., 322–330; Communist smear campaign against, 303, 304; and civil rights, 23, 24, 55, 56, 86, 257, 263–267, 297, 298, 302, 307, 309, 330–337, 341, 350, 351, 362, 374; and organized crime, 24, 262, 307, 313, 314, 354, 365; fight against wartime subversion and espionage, 45, 46, 149–158, 163–220; and against postwar Communist subversion, 221–256, 277–287, 290, 291, 293–296; and new crime wave, 257–262; and wiretapping, 314–321, 330–333, 341, 357–359, 376; and loyalty-security programs, 267–276; criticism of him in later years, 338–371; death and funeral, 371–377
Hoover's FBI, 14
Hopkins, Harry, 23, 160, 162, 163, 204, 205
House Committee on Un-American Activities, 55, 223, 224, 227, 238, 239, 277–279
Howe, Louis McHenry, 99, 100, 108
Hruska, Sen. Roman, 349
Hull, Cordell, 152, 153, 156, 163, 166, 174, 200
Human Events, 311
Hunter, Fred, 132, 133
Huston, Luther, 306, 307

Ickes, Harold, 23, 247n.
Ile de France, 197
Immigration and Naturalization Service, 58, 59, 121, 179
In Brief Authority, 161
Industrial Workers of the World ("Wobblies"), 48, 51, 55
In Fact, 274
Inslerman, Felix, 229
Institute of Pacific Relations, 241
Inter-Divisional Intelligence Unit, 364

Minichiello, Raffaele, 345
Mitchell, John, 341, 353, 354, 359, 373
Mitchell, Kate, 218, 219
Mitchell, Martha, 30n.
Moley, Raymond, 100, 101, 105
Molotov, Vyacheslav, 170
Monroe, Marilyn, 309
Moore, Roy K., 335
Morgenthau, Henry, 140, 141, 157, 172, 182, 222, 241
Morris, Robert, 255
Morrow, Anne, 95
Muhammed, Elijah, 330, 331
Murphy, Frank, 31, 166, 168
Murphy, Raymond, 224
Murphy, Thomas F., 233
Murray, Edith, 229–234
Murray, Ellwood, 229, 232
Muskie, Sen. Edmund, 368, 369
Mussolini, Benito, 154

Nash, Frank, 108, 109
Nation, 14
National Association for the Advancement of Colored People (NAACP), 298, 336
National Bank Act, 91
National Commission on the Causes and Prevention of Violence, 363
National Crime Information Center, 352
National District Attorneys Association, 369
National Federation of Post Office Clerks, 273
National Motor-Vehicle Theft Act, 83, 88, 90
National Observer, 342, 343, 358
National Peace Action Coalition, 369
National Probation Association, 141, 142
National Review, 311
National Security Council, 13
National Stolen Property Act, 105
Nation's Business, 28
Navasky, Victor S., 352, 376
Navy Department, 157, 171, 174
ND98 espionage case, 192, 196–198, 201
Nelson, "Baby Face," 123n., 124, 347
Nelson, Steve, 208–210
Nemser, Sandra, 370
Neutrality Act, 167
New Amsterdam, 197
New Leader, 7, 155, 366
New Orleans Times-Picayune, 68
New Republic, 9, 168
Newsweek, 7, 269, 308n.
New York City Police Department, 142–145
New York Daily Mirror, 145, 147
New York Daily News, 9, 147, 223
New Yorker, 42, 140
New York Herald Tribune, 148, 270
New York Post, 302, 303
New York Times, 51, 73n., 242, 299, 302, 352, 357, 359
New York World, 51
New York World-Telegram, 12, 366
Nichols, Louis B., 8, 27, 178, 339, 340, 342, 354
Nixon, Richard, 29, 31, 52, 225, 239, 279, 286, 353, 354, 356, 357, 364, 370, 371, 374, 375
NKVD, 204, 205, 208, 212, 245, 274, 329
Noisette, Sam, 25
Norris, Sen. George W., 9, 12, 147, 168, 169
Novello, Angie, 325

O'Brien, Pat, 311
O'Farrell, Val, 140
Office of Facts & Figures, 171

Office of Naval Intelligence (ONI), 149, 153, 155, 173, 175, 181, 194, 195, 203, 205, 324
Office of Strategic Services (OSS), 150, 163n., 204, 205, 216, 217
Office of War Information, 273
O'Leary, Jeremiah, 340
Ollestad, Norman, 21, 22
Omnibus Crime Control Act of 1968, 352
Organized crime and the FBI, 24, 262, 295, 307, 313, 314, 354, 365
Organized Crime Control Act of 1970, 354
Osten, Carl Wilhelm von der, 188
Oswald, Lee Harvey, 14, 299, 323–325, 327, 328, 330
Oumansky, Ambassador, 156
Our Times, 61
Ovakimian, Gaik, 245
Overstreet, Harry and Bonaro, 10, 12, 59n.

Palermo, "Blinky," 295
Palmer, A. Mitchell, 50, 51, 56, 62–64
Palmer raids, 56–65, 70, 166, 179
Parker, Mr., 59
Parker, Bonnie, 126, 135–139, 257
Parker, Gov. John M., 68
Patman, Rep. Wright, 106
Peale, Norman Vincent, 30
Pearl Harbor, 171, 173–178, 182, 183, 185, 186, 187n.
Pearson, Drew, 9, 34, 108, 126
Pegler, Westbrook, 9, 126, 147, 148
Perkins, Frances, 157
Persons in Hiding, 103
Philadelphia Inquirer, 302
Playboy, 14
Post, Louis, 63, 64
Post Office Department, 82, 140, 171
Potter, Sen. Charles, 280
Powell, William, 122
Price, Byron, 172
Princeton University conference on FBI, 366
Prohibition, 86, 91–94, 100, 101, 125
Pump Room, 30
Purvis, Melvin, 120–123

Radiation Laboratory (Berkeley), 208
Ramparts, 14
Rauh, Joseph, Jr., 302
Ray, James Earl, 337
Raymond, Philip, 165, 166
Reader's Digest, 23, 30, 275
Reagan, Ronald, 366
Reed, Otto, 108, 109
Reuss, Rep. Henry, 351–353
Reuss, Jacqueline, 351–353
Reuss, Margaret McGrath, 352
Reuther, Victor, 310, 311, 324
Reuther, Walter, 55, 310, 311, 324
Reynolds, Quentin, 30, 144
Richards, T. F., 69
Richetti, Adam, 108, 124
Richey, Larry, 70, 71
Riesel, Victor, 155
Rintelen, Franz von, 45
Ritter, Major Nikolaus, 193
Roberts Commission, 185
Robertson, Sen. A. Willis, 297, 298
Roche, John P., 364
Rogers, Ginger, 30
Rogers, Lela, 30
Rogers, Will, 119
Rogers, William P., 31, 306

• 384 •